The Moral Philosophy of
T . H . GREEN

The Moral Philosophy of
T. H. GREEN

Geoffrey Thomas

CLARENDON PRESS · OXFORD
1987

Oxford University Press, Walton Street, Oxford OX2 6DP
Oxford New York Toronto
Delhi Bombay Calcutta Madras Karachi
Petaling Jaya Singapore Hong Kong Tokyo
Nairobi Dar es Salaam Cape Town
Melbourne Auckland
and associated companies in
Beirut Berlin Ibadan Nicosia

Oxford is a trade mark of Oxford University Press

Published in the United States
by Oxford University Press, New York

British Library Cataloguing in Publication Data
Thomas, Geoffrey
The moral philosophy of T. H. Green.
1. Green, Thomas Hill—Contributions
in ethics.   2. Ethics—History—
19th century.
I. Title
170'.92'4   B1638.E8
ISBN 0-19-824788-5

Library of Congress Cataloging in Publication Data
Data available

Set by Litho Link Limited, Welshpool
Printed in Great Britain
at the University Printing House, Oxford
by David Stanford
Printer to the University

To the memory of my father

PREFACE

In publishing this study I recognize debts of many kinds.

A version of this book was presented as a Ph.D. dissertation to the University of London in 1983. I should like to express my deepest appreciation to Dr Samuel Guttenplan for the help and encouragement given in so many ways during my research and in the preparation of this book. Thanks are also due to my examiners, Lord Quinton and David Lloyd Thomas, for their valuable comments and criticisms. Professor David Hamlyn read and commented most helpfully on a draft of Chapter 3. The faults of exposition which remain are, of course, mine.

I owe thanks for help received from the staff of the Bodleian Library, Oxford, the British Library of Political and Economic Science (London School of Economics), and the University of London Library (Senate House). I wish to place on record my particular debt of gratitude to the staff of two college libraries. Vincent Quinn, Dr Penelope Bulloch, and Alan Tadiello of the Balliol College Library provided practical assistance of great value; and my grateful thanks are due to Stuart Adams and Christopher Burnham of the Interlibrary Loans Service at Birkbeck College, London, for their relentless perseverance in tracing obscure items.

I wish to thank the Master and Fellows of Balliol College, Oxford, for permission to consult and quote from the T. H. Green Papers. The Curators of the Bodleian Library, Oxford, have kindly granted me permission to list the Bodleian's T. H. Green material.

I am grateful to William Liversidge, Honorary Archivist of Abingdon, for help in attributing an item in the T. H. Green Papers to C. Alfred Pryce.

Two visits to Balliol (15–22 April 1980 and 27 March–4 April 1981) were made possible by grants from the Central Research Funds Committee of London University. It is a pleasure to thank the Committee for its help.

Michael Inwood arranged for me to stay at Trinity College,

Oxford, as a Fellow's guest in September 1980 and again in September 1984. This ease of access to the Green Papers in tranquil and beautiful surroundings was an ideal opportunity for research.

In 1980 I had the advantage of discussing Green's philosophy with a fellow postgraduate, Ben Wempe, of the European University Institute (Florence). Our deep differences of interpretation helped to crystallize my own views; and I wish to thank Dr Wempe for this stimulating encounter. Nor is this all. Students of the Green Papers owe a debt to Dr Wempe, who undertook the laborious task of sorting out misidentified items. My own list of the Balliol papers, included in section II of the bibliography, was certainly easier to produce as a result of his work. I am not in a position to speak in detail of Dr Wempe's book, *Beyond Equality: A Study of T. H. Green's Theory of Positive Freedom*, Delft, 1986, which came to my attention only after my own book was substantially complete.

I also wish to record my gratitude to Sat Pal, whose thought-provoking comments in discussions between October 1983 and March 1984 helped me with the difficult topic of Green's religious ideas.

To Howard Mettler, formerly of Bowdoin College, Maine, I am indebted for his constant and acute discussion of philosophical problems, both in written comments and in conversation. More ancient debts are to be acknowledged to Professor Michael Oakeshott and Professor K. B. Smellie, of the London School of Economics, who first aroused my interest in the British Idealists. I am immensely grateful to Dr David Rees, of Jesus College, Oxford, for much information and comment, of which the notes give only a glancing indication. The usual disclaimers apply but David Rees's wide learning and exact scholarship in the history of philosophy make his friendship a prized possession. Dr John Morrall, of the London School of Economics, has given aid and encouragement, philosophical and personal, over many years.

On general points of classical scholarship I have consulted R. J. Abbott, formerly of Exeter University, and wish to thank him for his skilful advice, generously given.

A characteristically wry and unusual personal kindness should be mentioned. My copy of Green's *Prolegomena to Ethics* fragmented during my doctoral research. I am grateful to Richard Robinson, of Oriel College, Oxford, for presenting me with a replacement, even under the discouraging signal: 'You are quite right in thinking that I do not care for T. H. Green. I believe I never learnt anything from him'. This book is clearly my return signal.

I should like to thank David Bridges, Anne Gosnell, Chris Johnson, Deborah Tyler, and Christine Wilton, for instructing me in the use of word processing programs which enabled fast production and painless revision of my text.

Finally I owe more than I can express to my mother, whose sympathy and encouragement provided a domestic environment without which the commitment to research could scarcely have been undertaken.

G. L. T.

Highgate, London
7 April 1987

CONTENTS

PRINCIPAL ABBREVIATIONS

HM, followed by page number, e.g., HM, 103.
> T. H. Green, *Lectures on the Principles of Political Obligation and Other Writings*, ed. Paul Harris and John Morrow, Cambridge, 1986.

Introductions to Hume.
> Green's two introductions, 'General Introduction' and 'Introduction II', to *The Philosophical Works of David Hume*, ed. T. H. Green and T. H. Grose, 4 vols., London, 1874–5. The introductions are reprinted in Works I, 1–371.

MS, followed by MS number and, if available, page number, e.g. MS 10A, 14.
> Green's manuscript papers held at Balliol College, Oxford. The Balliol MSS are largely unpaginated; and in quoting from them I have thought it better (if no page number is available) simply to cite the MS number than to devise a pagination of my own. In quotations from Green's papers I have used diamond brackets, <is>, to supply obvious words of which Green's omission would make for awkward reading. Square brackets indicate alternatives or additions put into the MSS by Green himself. I have expanded some contractions, as where Green's 'Pl' is my 'Plato'; and I have romanized Green's Greek.

NE, followed by book or Bekker page, column, and line reference, e.g. NE III or 1094a22.
> Artistotle, *Nicomachean Ethics*, tr. Sir David Ross, Oxford, 1969.

PE, followed by section reference, e.g. PE, § 9.
> T. H. Green, *Prolegomena to Ethics*, ed. A. C. Bradley, Oxford, 1883.

Platonis de Republica, followed by page number.
> Green's annotations to *Platonis ... Libros de Republica*, ed. G. Stallbaum, Leipzig, 1823. See Bibliography II.

PPO
> Lectures on the Principles of Political Obligation; Green's 1879–80 professorial lecture course on political philosophy. The text of these lectures is printed in Works II, 335–553. An improved text appears in HM, 13–193.

Rep., followed by book or Stephanus page reference, e.g. Rep. IV or 500C.
> Plato, *Republic*, tr. F. M. Cornford, Oxford, 1941.

T, followed by page or section number, e.g. T 415 or T I.3.9.
D. Hume, *A Treatise of Human Nature*, ed. L. A. Selby-Bigge; revised text and notes by P. H. Nidditch, Oxford, 1978.

Works, followed by volume and page number, e.g. Works III, 519.
The Works of Thomas Hill Green, ed. R. L. Nettleship, 3 vols., London, 1885–8.

Double numbers in brackets refer to chapters and sections of the present book, e.g. (4.7) refers to Chapter 4, Section 7.

Volume numbers for *Mind* in the bibliography relate to the Old Series for 1876–91 and to the New Series from 1892 onwards.

I have in general included short references in the text, e.g. (Works II, 309). Longer references which would cut the flow of the text I have transferred to the footnotes, which also contain comments and collateral information.

INTRODUCTION

T. H. GREEN has a secure place in the history of ideas; my concerns are philosophical. This book rests on four claims: that Green is principally a philosopher, that he is an independent thinker, that his ethical theory and moral psychology yield a coherent body of moral philosophy, that his moral philosophy raises important problems neglected in contemporary discussions. These are large claims. Here I simply explain them; the arguments are developed in the main body of the book.

On the first claim, Green's philosophical stature is subject to a double disregard. His work falls under the heading of nineteenth-century British Idealism. To contemporary philosophy in the Anglo-American tradition this says everything against him. As an idealist Green forfeits even the disreputable charm of an errant ancestor. It has to be said: nineteenth-century British Idealism is a byword for metaphysical grandiosity, slackness of argument, and linguistic obscurity. On the current reckoning, hardly changed since Russell's diatribe of 1914, it is a serrature of 'stupid and trivial confusions',[1] which slits the thread of British philosophical development.

But opposition by preconception is not the only problem with which Green's commentator is assailed. On the other side, there is a subversive style of interpretation, easily recognizable in the secondary literature, which sees a total prefiguration of Green's philosophy in his personal concerns—religious, political, and moral. To cite Green's philosophical arguments, on this style of interpretation, is to evoke the image of a wall of philosophy elaborated for the protection of pre-philosophical interests. This image is far from unplausible; falsity is its only defect. Clearly, however, the claim that Green is principally a philosopher has to be made good against the counter-claims that he is too loose a thinker to be a philosopher by present standards and that his 'philosophy' is merely the protective colouration assumed by other concerns.

[1] B. Russell, *Our Knowledge of the External World*, London, 1914, 49.

Even when Green is recognized as principally a philosopher, difficulties remain. This brings in my second claim. Finding the right label for Green is a tricky business. The term 'Hegelian' has been applied for so long that it is probably inseparable. But this label is difficult to reconcile with the more varied Green of my acquaintance. One aim of this book is to displace the interpretation of Green's philosophy from that monolithic Hegelian base, and to reveal the complexity of its antecedents. The truth is this: in philosophy Green made up his own mind. He took from particular thinkers only what he saw reason to agree with. To locate accurately the boundaries of Green's philosophical agreements and to trace his intellectual debts is no easy matter. So runs the kind of sonorous generality to which notional assent is readily given. What is needed is not notional assent but real recognition, a recognition which is withheld when, just a case in point, Green is numbered among 'the British Hegelians'.

If Green is a Hegelian then the central ideas and arguments of Hegel's philosophy are equally central to the philosophy of Green. However if we call Green a Hegelian the awkward fact cannot be glossed that Green rejects or omits much that is central to Hegel, further that many of Green's own important ideas and arguments are either unconnected with Hegel or antagonistic to his philosophy. All that remains, and what cannot possibly be denied, is the fact of philosophical influence: and Hegel's influence joins that of Plato, Aristotle, Kant, Rousseau as one element in a composite picture. Nor can it be said that the common exaggeration of the Hegelian element in Green, while it offends scholarly discrimination, is otherwise harmless. Consequences ramify. On the one hand Hegelians look to Green for an elaboration or restatement of Hegel's philosophy, only to be disappointed—as Geoffrey Mure deplored the unHegelian residue in the thought of the entire school of nineteenth-century British Idealism.[2] On the other hand many who are antipathetic to Hegel are estranged from Green, having prejudged the character of his philosophy.

Something must next be said about my third claim. As I worked through the secondary literature I realized that what Green's commentators have most in common is a tendency to

---

[2] G. R. G. Mure, *An Introduction to Hegel*, Oxford, 1940, ch. 12.

see his philosophy as confused. This tendency is sharpest in the two most considerable philosophers to have written on Green— Henry Sidgwick and H. A. Prichard. Sidgwick's Green is crudely muddled. Prichard's Green ensnares himself in paradoxes. 'You can approach the truth', Prichard told his students, 'only through the ruins of what is false',[3] and Green's philosophy evidently shortens the route. Prichard's problem is that he peels text from context; Sidgwick's problem is a disagreement so radical that he cannot take Green seriously. Not all commentators repeat these approaches. For my own part I do not claim to have found the sole key to Green's philosophy. In tracing the intricate pattern of that philosophy, however, I claim to find a coherent structure, a definite system of ideas and arguments. I have my own quarrels with Green. But I see in Green's philosophy a defence of freewill, a model of deliberation, a theory of character, an account of moral objectivity, which hang together as a system. Many of the difficulties which commentators have found in Green's philosophy arise when the full system is misunderstood or neglected. So, for example, the question is pressed how a philosopher can be clear about moral rights and yet believe that rights depend on 'recognition'. A favourite crux, but commentators are more often right to think Green wrong than to think him confused.

A system of ideas and arguments is one thing. A moral philosophy possessing contemporary relevance is quite another. The history of philosophy is of no philosophical value, whatever its historical interest, unless it throws light on present problems. That assumption may be contested; I have no hesitation in making it. Then how does the recovery of Green's ethical theory and moral psychology help contemporary ethics? This introduces my fourth claim. Briefly, the Anglo-American tradition takes the concept of action as central to ethics. Persons are agents on a highly narrow construction of 'agency' for which the agent's problem is to decide what he should do in the way of exerting an impact on the external world. Morality and its requirements stand over against the agent. Why should he act morally? Why should he be concerned how his actions affect others? For the mainstream of contemporary ethics the whole of moral objectivity

---

[3] Thomas Higham (Fellow of Trinity College, Oxford, 1914–58, Emeritus Fellow 1958–75): personal communication.

is determined by these questions. Green's moral philosophy has a different orientation. It centres on persons and is neither an act-ethics nor an agent-ethics of any standard contemporary type. For Green, practical reason addresses the question, what kind of person should I be? This question is primary; it carries no presumption of morality. But Green's theory of the human good attempts to interlock morality with the answer to it. This seems to me to allow a more comprehensive view of agents as persons than is available in the mainstream of contemporary ethics. It is also, I believe, the most fruitful approach to the objectivity of morals.

These then are my four claims. The plan is this: the first two claims are set out in detail in Chapter 1, the rest of the book develops claims three and four. A last word before we begin.

Any reflective commentator faces two worries. Will his work replace a reading of the original writings and, given the original writings, is a commentary necessary? No commentary on a philosopher's work should take the place of an original reading. Yet the risk of usurpation is slight when a philosopher is widely disregarded. Even the titles of Green's neglected works are forgotten by all but historians. In the present state of philosophy, commentary offers the best hope that Green will ever be read widely again. More than this, I have aimed throughout to indicate precisely the texts on which my interpretation rests. There are extensive quotations, which allow in fact a closer first look at Green's moral philosophy than the printed sources currently offer. The present commentary is based on research into unpublished material, the T. H. Green Papers held at Balliol College, Oxford. But why should students of moral philosophy, coming to Green's thought for the first time, not plunge straightway into his major work, *Prolegomena to Ethics*? The quick answer is, because Green is a difficult writer. The difficulty is not that he uses a technical vocabulary of the kind which confronts us in Kant or Hegel. It lies in two points.

It lies first in the self-absorbed character of Green's thought. From early in his philosophical career Green was clear on what he rejected, chiefly the empiricist account of mind and reality. On the positive side he believed that a theory of self-consciousness held the key to the final solution of the problems of philosophy. But in the event *Prolegomena to Ethics* is nothing like a set of firm, vigorous deductions from a single comprehensive theory, a smooth universe of ideas ruled by a philosopher. Green formed his positive views slowly, in detail, and with great caution. In much of his writing he is thinking with pen in hand, a method of exposition which certainly mars the incisiveness of his presentation. The difficulty lies secondly in the unrevised state of *Prolegomena to Ethics* and in the circumstances of its origin. The book was written in a deepening shadow of illness in which Green was anxious to elaborate his ideas in some permanent form. In content the book exactly embodies his most developed thought, but the form of exposition is distinctly bad. The main points of the arguments are enveloped, sometimes concealed, in the detours and windings of the discussion. Green was not a skilled literary craftsman, and here the reader's convenience takes second place to Green's need to finish. He never lightens a hard topic. No service would be done by any commentator who failed to stress the inaccessibility of Green's philosophy.

I greatly hope, however, that the reader, when he or she[4] has finished my commentary, will turn directly to Green's writings—patiently, to test what I have said.

---

[4] I shall usually write simply 'he' or 'his', using the words generically to refer to both sexes: this is merely to avoid the constant repetition of 'he or she', 'his or her'.

T. H. Green: Life and Philosophy

1.1 INTRODUCTION

GREEN'S name is rarely cited in current philosophical discussions; and few even among historians of philosophy would claim an exact acquaintance with his work. One reason for the present chapter is, then, simply to retrace Green's life and personality, and the problems, emphases, and preconceptions by which his philosophy is informed. Another reason is less obvious: it is to argue the case for a review of Green's philosophy on a strictly philosophical level. Commentators have not always observed a due distinction between Green's personal concerns and his preoccupations as a philosopher. Because Green had (scarcely orthodox) religious faith, because he thought deeply about religion and held a personal ideal of conscientious citizenship, his philosophical arguments have often been seen as all too plainly built up to serve as the substrata of those personal concerns. But that view obscures Green's proper philosophical stature; the best dissolvent for it is careful history. Even when a line is correctly drawn between Green's personal and his philosophical concerns, however, his philosophy is distorted when it is seen as dominated exclusively by a single set of ideas, with Green depicted as the devoted partisan of Kant or Hegel. That distortion is frequent, particularly in the Hegelianization of Green. Accordingly one aim of this chapter, and the final reason for an excursion into history, is to break the hold of such interpretations and to exhibit the diverse sources of Green's philosophy.

1.2 EARLY LIFE: BIRKIN, RUGBY, AND OXFORD

Thomas Hill Green, the fourth child and second son of the Reverend Valentine Green, was born in Birkin, Yorkshire, on 7

April 1836. Green's mother died when he was 1 year old; and his early education was conducted entirely by his father. At the age of 14 Green entered Rugby School. Lately reformed by Thomas Arnold, the school was very much a source of intellectual and moral earnestness. Among his fellow pupils was the later Cambridge philosopher, Henry Sidgwick. Nettleship, whose *Memoir* remains the chief source of biographical information,[1] records that Green was a shy, awkward, and, in the opinion of his headmaster, E. M. Goulburn, 'constitutionally indolent' schoolboy.[2] This indolence was serious enough to cause surprise to a self-confident Sidgwick when in 1855 Green defeated him in a Latin competition.

Green's shyness and awkwardness persisted far beyond his schooldays. For a series of lectures in Edinburgh in 1866 (Works III, 277–364), he stayed with the Latinist, W. Y. Sellar. Mrs Sellar records the following incident in her memoirs:

... his instinct was rather to shun society; so it was unfortunate that there was an evening party while he was with us—still more unfortunate that the ladies' cloaks were taken off in his room, to which he could not, therefore, retire for refuge. Towards the end of the evening, seeing him looking rather dejected, my husband, to cheer him, said, 'Only two cloaks now, Green, in your room.' 'Till there are *none*,' was the sombre reply, 'it is all the same to me.'[3]

Green was fairly miserable as a schoolboy. This set a pattern of institutional dissatisfaction. His criticisms of Rugby were followed by criticism of Oxford; perhaps he missed his early freedom of education at Birkin. Green was a non-institutional man whose life was spent almost wholly in the institutional life of

---

[1] Richard Lewis Nettleship (1846–93). Nettleship was Green's pupil and later his colleague at Balliol. He edited Green's Works in 3 vols., published between 1885 and 1888. The *Memoir* appears in vol. III.
On biographical sources, separate mention should be made of M. A. Ward's *Robert Elsmere*, London, 1888, in which Green appears as Professor Henry Grey. Although the fact of this representation is endorsed by several writers, its accuracy usually passes without critical comment. My own view is that it tends to set a false impression that questions of religion were Green's fundamental philosophical preoccupation. It neglects the distinction between personal concern and philosophical preoccupation on which the present ch. is based. (Ward's characterization of Green is satirized with gentle acerbity in 'The Decay of Lying', *The Works of Oscar Wilde*, ed. J. Gilbert, London, 1963, 829. Wilde was at Oxford from 1874 to 1878.)
[2] NETTLESHIP, *Memoir*, xiii.
[3] E. M. Sellar, *Recollections and Impressions*, London, 1907, 205.

school and university. His dislike of Goulburn was intense. 'Goulburn is the most unsatisfactory personage I ever came across', he wrote home in 1852. 'He is surly, unfair, hasty, and obstinate ... Besides this he teaches nothing.'[4] Goulburn thought Green not only indolent but unimaginative. 'His mind lacks the imaginative faculty to a grievous degree, but it has the compensating excellence of clearness.'[5] His teachers did not divine a crucial brilliance, but in general he was recognized as an able boy who was content to be mediocre unless a subject keenly interested him, when he would work it through independently. On these terms he fully expected success. His vexation at receiving second place in an English essay competition was clear. What was wrong with his essay? '... all the masters who looked it over liked mine best, but they gave it [sc. the prize] to another fellow because his showed more labour, i.e. came out of thirteen books instead of his own head.' This, Green concluded, 'does not seem to me quite fair'.[6]

Green entered Balliol College, Oxford, in October 1855. He already regarded the university with a certain disrespect: 'the functionaries from the Heads to the servants being wholly given to quiet dishonesty, and the undergraduates to sensual idleness'. The basis of this impressionistic sketch was a visit to Oxford in May or June 1855, a visit on which Green doubted his own complete immunity to the temptations of university life. 'My chief one would be', he wrote to his Rugby friend, David Hanbury, 'those most luxurious canoes, in which one can paddle for hours under the most delicious shade, without the least exertion.'[7] Green's announcement that a Balliol fellowship 'is my great hope at Oxford'[8] is one which preceded the summer visit of 1855; it needs to be offset by his hazy uncertainty, once he reached university, about what in particular to do with his life.

Green's student career was marked by the peculiarity of First, Second and Third Classes. Although his education at Rugby had been mainly classical, he took only a Second in Classical

---

[4] Nettleship, 'Notes for T. H. Green's Memoir', see Bibliography II, T. H. Green Papers: Balliol College, Oxford. Hereafter referred to as 'Notes'.

[5] Nettleship, 'Notes'.

[6] Nettleship, 'Notes'.

[7] Nettleship, *Memoir*, xvi.

[8] Nettleship, ibid.

Moderations in 1857. John Addington Symonds ascribed this result to idleness. 'He was sleepy and idle <in> his first terms at Oxford, and only pulled himself together after Mods and Jowett saying to him: "If you do not get your First, Green, I shall have a great deal to answer for." '[9] Benjamin Jowett, Green's tutor at Balliol, was a dedicated, compelling teacher who felt a personal responsibility for developing his abler pupils; and in 1859 Green duly obtained his First in Greats (a combination of philosophy and ancient history). He subsequently, on six months' reading, gained a Third in Law and Modern History. The First in Greats, the real basis of his academic career, was not regarded as quite certain by his coach, C. S. Parker. 'I feared', Parker wrote to Nettleship in September 1888, 'that he might write too little, and not be always lucid. I therefore teased him much to bring me longer answers less condensed, not short hard sayings needing an interpreter.' Parker continues:

That such anxieties were not quite superfluous the examination proved. After thirty years one may disclose what passed. When my three colleagues first compared notes as to who were clearly in the 1st class, having several pupil candidates, I sat silent. I found my other pupils were all right, but Green, though all agreed his work in quality seemed excellent, from lack of quantity remained as yet an unsolved problem. Soon, however, on further study of his papers, each examiner for himself perceived their merit, admired the multum in parvo of his well-packed answers, and placed him without doubt in the first class.[10]

Green was drawn into philosophy almost in spite of himself. His first academic appointment was not as a philosopher but, in 1860, as Lecturer in Ancient and Modern History at Balliol to cover the absence of W. L. Newman. Although he was elected to a Balliol Fellowship in the same year and in 1862 was awarded the Chancellor's Prize for an essay on 'The Value and Influence of Works of Fiction', he was at this stage still undecided even on an academic career. None the less a certain disquietude, a need to interrogate his own experience, to find a point of anchorage for a coherent view of human thought and activity, made philosophy inescapable.

What distracted Green initially from an academic career?

⁹ J. A. Symonds, Recollections, 7 Oct. 1882, see Bibliography II.
¹⁰ C. S. Parker, Recollections, 26 Sept. 1888, Bibliography II.

Certainly not the Anglican priesthood. Here he resisted family pressure and the influence of Jowett. As early as January 1861 he wrote to his father advising him to enlist a curate, 'as I don't think I am ever likely to take orders'.[11] In June 1863, 'becoming a Dissenting preacher'[12] was marked as a possibility. But Green took no practical steps. Journalism (he declined in 1863 the editorship of *The Times of India*) and a post in the Education Office were among other possibilities he considered. The journalistic option is strange. A good journalist has nimbleness of mind, witching lightness of style. Green was a patiently laborious thinker and always remained a painstaking writer much given to qualification. A career in the Education Office would have made better sense; and in fact Green accepted in 1865 the post of assistant commissioner in the Schools Inquiry Commission. This was the hinge of decision.

Already an academic bias intervened. The Commission had been appointed in 1864 under the chairmanship of Lord Taunton. Its aim was to review the state of education in endowed schools, work already done for elementary schools by the Newcastle Commission and for the public schools by the Clarendon Commission. Green valued the task but disliked its abrasions. His main responsibility was to inspect the independent schools of Warwickshire and Staffordshire and to make a special study of King Edward's School, Birmingham. Inspection was a wide notion, for Green was required not only to ascertain the standard and content of education in nearly a hundred schools but to sound the opinions of parents on the kind of education which they wanted for their children. Inevitably he encountered pre-determined attitudes. There was resentment at intrusion, a resentment which brought Green the novel experience of being slated in the press: '. . . the other day for the first time in my life I was made the subject of a leading article in a local paper, the drift of which was the unsatisfactory nature of private enquiries'.[13] There was suspicion of political extremism and religious unorthodoxy. Green was irritated to learn that other commissioners held him to be 'an extreme man, an ultra-radical in politics, an ultra-liberal in religious

[11] Nettleship, 'Notes'.
[12] Nettleship, 'Notes'; *Memoir*, xxxv, has 'dissenting' for 'Dissenting'.
[13] Nettleship, *Memoir*, xlvi.

opinion'.[14] Added to which, as an outsider, even with co-operation he had the greatest difficulty in discovering what was happening in the schools he visited. A month in the field was long enough for him to conclude that 'I have no real taste for "practical life." I shall go back to Oxford work, let us hope, with more contentment from having tried other work and found it wanting.'[15]

This experience was part of Green's self-discovery as an academic. A new dimension of distaste for 'practical life' emerged when the Commission's recommendations failed to receive the political endorsement for which he had hoped. The Commissioner's central proposal was that endowed education should be organized in three tiers. The first tier of schools would provide a classical education reinforced by mathematics, natural science, and modern languages; the second tier would concentrate on narrowly commercial subjects; the third tier would supply a merely general education. Local authorities were to fix the tier to which each school would belong; standards were to be enforced by regular inspection and examination. In the event the Endowed Schools Act of 1869, passed by Gladstone's government, aimed chiefly to ensure that endowments were better administered. The government failed to take the Commission's wider view of the endowed schools' educational future.

But this was not the whole depth of the matter from Green's side. Education entered the political process in the 1860s because the contrast of British with French and German educational standards was marked. Britain's European rivals did much better in elementary, secondary, and technical education. Witness Matthew Arnold's unfavourable comparisons between British and continental schools. This was not Green's angle of interest. Green viewed the vortex of public education from the apex of Oxford. The universities were his controlling focus in a plan for a national scheme of education in which the three-tiered gradation of secondary schools would open a university education to anybody capable of benefiting from it. Green's vision had two elements. Mid-century reforms at Oxford had expanded opportunities in higher education for the less

[14] Nettleship, *Memoir*, xlv.
[15] Nettleship, *Memoir*, xlvi.

privileged through scholarships and exhibitions. The reform of secondary schools was an inseparable counterpart to university reform in enabling poorer children to use the new opportunities. The existence of a £100 scholarship was of small help to the son of an artisan if his secondary education fell short of scholarship standard. In the second part of Green's vision the universities, with a widened social basis of recruitment, would transform society. Green gives only a glancing indication of how this would occur but he definitely looked to 'a reconstitution of society through that of education' (Works III, 387). The Endowed Schools Act of 1869 fell like a shadow over this vision. But the vision was never shared, much less betrayed, by the Liberal politicians who overturned Green's hopes. The full grounds of his dissatisfaction are set out with sombre animosity in 'The Grading of Secondary Schools' (ibid. 387–412). Green's experience of 'the very limited range in which practical politicians move' (ibid. 388) confirmed his inclination to academic life, where ideas could develop freely.

But what ideas did Green have? What were his personal concerns, and how did they relate to his preoccupations as a philosopher? His three chief concerns were religion, politics, and ethics.

1.3 RELIGION

There was a religious motivation to Green's thought, although only a slight religious content to his philosophy. The keys to Green's attitude to religion are faith and the rejection of 'dogma' in the sense of creed and doctrines.

For Green the central core of religion is faith; faith is the fundamental religious experience.[16] The main sources for Green's understanding of faith are his early 'Essay on Christian Dogma', read to the Old Mortality Society in 1858, and his 1878 lay sermon explicitly entitled 'Faith'. There is one significant difference between the two treatments of what faith

[16] Sat Pal comments: 'By "religion" you mean "Christianity"—one specific, God-based religion. There are other possibilities.' None the less Christianity was certainly the dominant form in which religion presented itself to Green. This is all that my equation of religion with Christianity comes down to.

positively is, but negatively Green's view remained unchanged. Faith is not assent to a system of religious beliefs. The language of the earlier treatment is that faith is a matter of 'intuition' and 'experience'; latterly faith is a 'conviction' issuing in a disposition.

I shall take first the 1878 account, which is more developed and easier to follow. Faith, then, is a conviction issuing in a disposition. The conviction involves a kind of imaginative projection. From our own finite powers of cognition we project a perfect intelligence. From our experience of value we suppose a being which exemplifies perfectly the moral ideal which our ethical thinking and moral conduct only limitedly embody. This is well-worn territory. But the point to realize is that in all this account Green never goes outside the psychology of the religious believer. He does not refer to this account as presenting a formally valid inference by which the existence of God can be logically deduced; he is expressing the psychology of faith.

Green offers a parallel to the operation of faith in the conviction which an artist may have, or which others may have about him (Works III, 269): the conviction, say, that a writer could produce a great novel. The novel is suggested by his work, and greatness is already imperfectly present in what he has published so far. A kind of artistic faith fills the gap between present achievement and future possibility. To the religious sceptic the limitation of this parallel is, of course, that although Green identifies an aesthetic phenomenon which is well-founded, since artistic judgements of the sort he describes are often exactly right, the corresponding gap between the present idea and the present reality of a perfect being is far less certain. But then, the point again to realize is that Green is trying to throw light on religious psychology. He is suggesting an interpretative parallel, not aiming to vindicate a formal analogy.

For Green, faith is a datum. He refers to it as 'a primary formative principle, which cannot be deduced from anything else' (Works III, 263). Though underivative it is not unanalysable: as we have noted, faith is a conviction which issues in a disposition. As conviction, faith relies on 'an element of identity between us and a perfect being, who is in full realisation what we are only in principle and possibility' (Works III, 268).

This conviction 'moves us to seek to become as he is; to become like him, . . . to have the fruition of his Godhead' (ibid.). Such language reflects, I believe, Green's religious sense of the reality of God. I have no doubt that he experienced faith; and I no longer believe, as I did when this book began life as a thesis, that such conversational dicta as 'I believe that when I die I shall see God' embody a mere *façon de parler*. Green's language changed, but an essential continuity holds between his earlier and later treatments of faith. In the 'Essay on Christian Dogma' Green speaks of 'intuition', 'immediate consciousness', 'present experience'. None of these implies complete knowledge. Faith is simply viewed as primary, underivative, self-authenticating. In this way we meet just the same characterization of faith as we examined above. A difference of emphasis between the earlier and later treatments is that in the 'Essay on Christian Dogma' Green examines specifically Christian faith ('the christian consciousness'). The later treatment, as we have seen, attaches faith to more general notions of cognitive and moral perfection. So much for continuity and difference. The philosophical surprises are all to come.

In his developed philosophy Green comes nearest to an invocation of God in his notion of an 'eternal consciousness'. So far from being primary and underivative, the first cry of faith, this notion has every appearance of being the last word of philosophy. It is introduced at the end of a long, complex, post-Kantian argument in epistemology; and its role is to block a slide into subjective idealism. As such it is widely removed from the first stimulus to faith, the simple idea of a perfect being in whom our finite knowledge is complete. The distance separating faith and philosophy lengthens if we consider the second stimulus to faith, that of the moral ideal.

In philosophical ethics essentially two relations are possible between morality and religion: compatibility and derivation. Green certainly does not regard morality as incompatible with religion—as J. S. Mill mounted a moral attack on religion, construing Christian doctrines of the atonement, eternal punishment, and so on as morally offensive. For one thing Green takes a non-doctrinal view of religion. He also acknowledges (PE § 209) the historical role of Christianity in expanding what Peter Singer in our own day has called 'the circle of ethics', the range of living beings whose moral status we recognize. As for derivation, in Green's ethics the claims of morality are explained and defended solely in terms of a connection between the moral good and the human good, the unconditional or 'true good', mediated by a particular account of 'self-satisfaction'. The derivation of morality from religion would involve claims such as the following: that God legislates the moral law (what is right being right because it is willed by God); that he upholds the moral law by reward and punishment; that conscience is the voice of God. Such claims are nowhere visible in Green's ethics. Nor is free will, the basis of moral responsibility, asserted on religious grounds. Green defends free will strictly philosophically. His main argument against determinism, that if the mind were simply a causally generated succession of states it could not be aware of itself as a succession, is a purely philosophical claim. Whatever its final cogency, it involves no reliance on religious considerations. Therefore David Parodi is correct in representing Green as an exponent of *une morale exclusivement laïque et rationnelle.*[17]

After all this, anybody who still supposes that Green's religious ideas passed by a smooth and unbroken transition into his philosophy should tackle Green's expressed views on immortality. On the one hand, Nettleship's notebook preserves remarks such as the one I have already quoted, 'I believe that when I die I shall see God.' On the other, Symonds records Green's view that 'the Philosopher cannot be expected to know more for certain than the rest of men about such things as immortality.'[18] Could there be a clearer separation between the fact of religious faith and the possibility of philosophical knowledge?

To take now the second key to Green's attitude to religion. Green was antipathetic to Christian dogma, i.e. to the formulation of creeds and doctines. This is the most unorthodox area of his religions thought. He rejected any view of Christianity as a set of doctrines, and of Christian belief as 'an acceptance of certain propositions as true upon trust' (Works III, 258). Specifically, Christianity is not for Green a matter

---

[17] D. Parodi, 'L'Idealisme de T. H. Green', *Revue de Metaphysique et de Morale*, 4 (1896), 798.
[18] J. A. Symonds, Recollections.

of subscribing, for example, to the doctrine of the Trinity, or of believing that such miraculous events as the Incarnation and Resurrection took place in history. It is a matter, rather, of the 'intuition', 'present experience', or 'immediate consciousness' to which we referred above. There is a sense of 'faith' in which faith is precisely the 'acceptance of certain propositions as true on trust', but Green regards this sense as secondary and inauthentic. It is primary faith, the 'immediate consciousness' of God, which in a man such as St Paul, with a particular, historically conditioned way of understanding the universe in which he lived, produces a belief in the Incarnation and Resurrection. In dogma this belief becomes depersonalized and formulaic. To make dogma criterial of faith is exactly to reverse cause and effect in religious experience. Faith, 'immediate consciousness', is the primary religious experience of which dogma is the second-order expression. The integral connection of religious belief with historical climates of thought, a familiar point now but an arresting novelty to English religious thought in the mid-nineteenth century, was a major theme of F. C. Baur's *Geschichte der christlichen Kirche*, a work of which Green began the translation.

Green's ideas on dogma derived from two main sources, apart from independent reflection: the writings of F. D. Maurice and those of Jowett.

His repudiation of dogma is, then, at least one area in which Green was influenced by F. D. Maurice (1805–72), though admittedly the generally elusive nature of Maurice's ideas makes their impact on Green hard to delineate with precision.[19] Maurice held, in a famous epigram, that 'Christ came to establish a Kindgom, not to proclaim a set of opinions.'[20] The historical revelation of God in Christ was a fact, for Maurice. But the divine Logos in Christ had always been present in men. The presence of God is disclosed in the peremptory demands of conscience, in the moral emotions, and in the urge of human agents (in the Tennysonian phrase) to 'rise on stepping-stones of their dead selves to higher things'. This immediate awareness

[19] My interpretation of Maurice has been guided mainly by I. T. Ramsey, *On Being Sure in Religion*, London, 1963, and V. F. Storr, *The Development of English Theology in the 19th Century*, London, 1913.
[20] J. F. D. Maurice, *The Kingdom of Christ*, iii, London, 1842, 387.

of God in religious experience must, Maurice contended, take precedence over any attempt to fixate that experience in theological dogma.

Allied to Maurice's influence we must include that of Jowett —the Jowett of 'On Atonement and Satisfaction' (1855) and 'On the Interpretation of Scripture' (1860). Jowett had become acquainted with the wealth of German biblical scholarship. That scholarship supplied his main ideas. The essays deplore the tendency of the Church to solidify scripture into a set of rigid doctrines from 'a priori notions about its nature and origin' and without 'attention to the character of its authors, and the prevailing state of civilization and knowledge, [or] allowance for peculiarities of style and language, and modes of thought and figures of speech'.[21] If we combine the views of Maurice and Jowett we have essentially the position of Green's 'Essay on Christian Dogma'.

Finally in this rapid survey of Green's religious ideas, and still on the question of faith and dogma, we need to secure a loose end from above. The point is this. The leading characteristic of mid-nineteenth-century religious liberalism in England was its relaxation of the anglican creeds. So the suggestion, to Green's embarrassment as an assistant Schools Inquiry commissioner, that he was a religious liberal, even 'an ultra-liberal in religious opinion', does not appear to be extremely wide of the mark. But he indignantly repudiated this suggestion. I believe the explanation to be that Green regarded himself as un-radical in his ideas because, in his own view, he was recovering the correct order of religious experience. He was simply drawing the fundamental religious experience of faith into a fuller light, pulling it clear from the doctrinal overlay of traditional Christianity. Since his task was one of recovery and not of innovation, he was perplexed by the reaction of Christians who saw his ideas as a deviation from authentic Christianity.

Whatever the justice of the matter the following points are clear. Green's religion is pared down to an 'immediate consciousness' of God. He investigates the logical character of religious experience; faith is fundamental, creeds and doctrines

---

[21] B. Jowett, *Theological Essays*, ed. L. Campbell, London, 1906, 209; *The Interpretation of Scripture and Other Essays*, ed. L. Stephen, London, 1906, 55, 73.

are derivate. He produces a philosophy of religion, not a religious philosophy. His general philosophy approaches religion no closer than to recognize an 'eternal consciousness' on grounds of epistemology. Green was a philosopher who was also a religious man. We can acknowledge that he had the religious experience of faith, deny that his philosophy is meant to prove God's existence or to provide a religious view of the nature of morality. This discrimination cuts across a common strand in the interpretation of Green. It is certainly to be recommended.

1.4 POLITICS

James (later Lord) Bryce, an Old Mortality friend from the 1850s, said of Green that 'Politics were in a certain sense the strongest of his interests.'[22] The discussion of politics certainly absorbed much of Green's time as an undergraduate. A. V. Dicey, another member of Old Mortality, an essay and discussion society founded at Oxford in 1856, wondered retrospectively how such discussions had left time for any academic work to be done.[23] It was to politics that Green's imagination responded most receptively; the political was a fundamental category through which he saw the world. His letters and conversation, from his schooldays onwards, were permeated with politics. Writing to his sister from Rugby in

---

[22] J. Bryce, *Studies in Contemporary Biography*, London, 1903, 97. Problems of politics were at the centre of the thought of both Bryce (1838–1922) and Green, though the range of Bryce's interests was exceptionally wide. Both were active Liberals; and Bryce's practical politics extended to government office under Gladstone and Campbell-Bannerman. Green's view of politics was morally judgemental. He was a great disapprover. While Bryce took up particular moral issues in politics, as in his espousal of the Armenian cause, his work, unlike that of Green, is a landmark in the history of political science. As examples, consider Bryce's distinction in *Studies in History and* *Jurisprudence*, Oxford, 1901, between rigid and flexible constitutions; and his approach to comparative politics in *The American Commonwealth*, London, 1888, which looks past formal governmental institutions to the social setting of politics: the role of political parties, interest groups, the social fabric, the influence of the frontier. This work in the development of political science has no counterpart in Green's moral teleology of politics. And in general Bryce's preference for the plainly and severely matter of fact contrasts with Green's speculative bent. For information on Bryce I am much indebted to Leslie Wolf-Phillips of the London School of Economics.

[23] A. V. Dicey, Recollections, 17 Sept. 1882, Bibliography II.

1852 he ironically disdains his reputution in the debating society, whose members 'think me a dreadful Radical, nay a Red Republican'.[24]

Green's 'dreadful Radicalism' never quite disappeared. There was, as Noël O'Sullivan has observed, a streak of wildness in him.[25] In later years 'the English Revolution' was not for him, as it had been for Burke, the controlled political exercise of expelling James II, but the social upheaval of the Commonwealth. Green never freed himself from the spell of the Commonwealth and from the vision of drastic social reconstruction which inspired men such as Sir Henry Vane. In the closing sentences of Green's lectures on the English Commonwealth (Works III, 364) we catch briefly the authentic voice of revolution.

In a relentless, sweeping searchlight, Green's correspondence picks out the main political events of thirty years. He followed political events closely, taking firmly, for example, the Northern side in the American Civil War—that 'great struggle between wilfulness and social right' (Works III, 117). References abound to political events, to the Indian Mutiny, Italian unification, the Schleswig–Holstein Question, the Zulu and Afghan Wars, the German Bund, the Reform Bills of the 1860s. So the list extends. Personalities did not elude critical notice. If John Bright was his political hero, Green regarded Jefferson Davis, Louis Napoleon, Robert Lowe, Palmerston, and Disraeli with the horror felt by later liberal generation for a Franco or Duvalier. The Prince Consort was an object of mild distrust.

Green was closely involved in practical politics and civic activity. He was notable in the social history of Oxford as the first Fellow to be elected to the Town Council by the ratepayers rather than by the university. He adopted a Liberal position on parliamentary reform and spoke on an Oxford Reform League platform for the 1867 Reform Bill. Though in favour of the extension of the franchise he was opposed to proportional representation, at least in the form of the single transferable vote system devised by Thomas Hare, informing Bernard Bosanquet that 'I rather despise all those schemes for detaching people from their locality.'[26] His view towards the exclusion of women was unclear.[27] But he kept to his political commitments, such as they were. So fully was he prepared to resist Disraeli's return to power in 1880 that, in failing health, he set back the completion of his major work, *Prolegomena to Ethics*, to support the Liberal election campaign.

Among social rather than political issues, temperance was also a cause. Green was strictly teetotal. Such abstinence was rare in the university of Green's day, not to press modern comparisons. In his anti-drink attitude he may have been influenced by the incurable alcoholism of one of his brothers. But to ascribe Green's attitude to drink solely to this personal circumstance is too simple a view. It leaves out of the reckoning a major social factor, the history of drink in England. The picture popularly drawn of the nineteenth-century temperance movement presents the temperance reformers as cheerless abstainers who failed to distinguish the use of alcohol from its abuse. But the regulation of alcohol has proceeded far beyond anything which nineteenth-century England knew; and it is not easy at this distance of time to see things in the proportions which they then assumed. Not until 1872, outside London, was there a minimum age limit for the sale of spirits. Even the Licensing Act of 1874 did not prohibit the serving of beer in public houses to children under 16. Adult and child drunkenness was endemic in agricultural and industrial areas alike. This social context is the main key to Green's advocacy of the temperance cause.

For Green intemperance was part of the pattern of nineteenth-century capitalism with its long hours, low wages, and poor conditions. He could not accept the *laissez-faire* policy which, in his view, had produced this state of society. But the link between social conditions and the improvement of working-class drinking habits proved to be less simple than Green at first realized. His initial idea was that better conditions, such as increased holidays and a shorter working day, would automatically cut the incidence of drink abuse. He later recognized that the link between social conditions and drink

[26] B. Bosanquet, *Science and Philosophy*, London, 1927, 266. Cf. T. Hare, *Treatise on the Election of Representatives*, London, 1859.

[27] See e.g. Works II, 537, 539; PE § 267. Cf. R. Barker, 'Citizens and People', *Politics*, 1981, 32.

abuse was too complex to be eradicated in this way since, given the entrenched nature of the drink problem, increased leisure merely created fresh opportunities for abuse. His solution was the scheme known as 'local option' by which local authorities were to be authorized to prohibit the sale of drink. He preferred this plan to an unconditional prohibition by central government, since he believed first that prohibition would be ineffectual unless firmly rooted in local commitment, and secondly that 'the elite of the working class' would supply the basis of that commitment.

The controversy over the regulation of drink that was the occasion in 1873 of public criticism by Green of the Chancellor of the Exchequer, Sir William Harcourt. Green understood Harcourt to oppose tighter controls on the sale of drink to adults as an interference with personal liberty. In a headlong assault Green addressed an open letter to Harcourt in *The Oxford Chronicle* (4 January 1873) and followed this with a personal letter in which, appealing to shared ideas on education, he firmly pressed the question: 'How can it be held right to interfere with a man's freedom by directly compelling him to send his child to school, and yet wrong to interfere with it by indirectly preventing him from drinking himself and his family to rags?'

The full text of Green's letter, dated 31 December [1872], is as follows:

Sir, Remembering Mr. Harcourt's conduct in the House of Commons upon the Licensing Bill, which seemed to admit of more than one explanation, and upon which I was anxious to put the best, I looked with special interest to that part of his Monday's speech (as reported at length in the Times) which dealt with the Licensing question in general. The impression it has made on me—as, I should suppose, on many of my fellow citizens—will not soon be forgotten. It would be tedious to answer in detail his eloquent commonplace about the liberty of the subject, and the impossibility of making men moral by Act of Parliament. We know all about that already. Such language may catch the cheers of the publicans and their friends, but can have no effect on those who know the difference between that liberty of the subject which is compatible with the real freedom of others, and that which merely means freedom to make oneself a social nuisance; between the possibility of making men moral by Act of Parliament and that of removing positive social obstacles to their morality—except to assure them that a politician who uses it can be no fit representative for them. Mr. Harcourt, of course, has deliberately and honestly made up his mind to the course he shall take, but so likewise have some of his constituents. Not merely 'Temperence men,' but all who reckon themselves 'Constructive Liberals' must see that the breach between him and them is as wide as that which separates them from the Conservatives. Four years ago, when the question of the Irish Church put all others into the shade, it was possible to ignore it, but we should be greater fools than Mr. Harcourt takes us for if we ignored it at a time when questions of organic social reform are more and more demanding the attention of Parliament.

It is needless to say that this is not meant as a threat. I have too much respect for Mr. Harcourt to suppose that he is amenable to threats, nor am I entitled to assume that those for whom I speak are numerous enough to make the withdrawal of their support at an election outweigh the enthusiasm of the drink-shops. But I do speak for some, and those are the men who knew their own minds. It is well that everything should be above board, and that Mr. Harcourt should know betimes that a politician who bids for the votes of the publicans cannot have ours.

Green was used to commercial interests screening behind the specious mask of a defence of personal freedom. Harcourt's honourable defence caused Green great unease, hence the vehemence of his reaction.[28]

This brings us to the end of the data that I wanted to consider on Green's politics; and I shall argue that, as we found in religion so in politics, there is a discontinuity between personal concern and philosophical preoccupation. Compare, for example, Green's straight moral denunciation of the American South with his finer discrimination of the philosophical problems of political obligation on this issue (Works II, 420; HM, 83). Or note how, in his political sparring with Harcourt, Green relies on a fairly straightforward concept of freedom: a person's freedom is the area in which he can act as he wants without interference from others. Parents have certain rights to restrict the freedom of children, but they do not have the right and should not have the freedom to act against a child's interest by depriving it of education; Green merely extends this claim to

---

[28] It should be added that no enmity resulted from this exchange. Personal relations remained cordial; and Green enthusiastically supported Harcourt in the April 1880 Oxford parliamentary election.

restrict a man's freedom to drink. In his political philosophy he begins to look rather at the social preconditions of rational self-determination or self-fulfilment. He stresses how a person's interests can be harmed, his freedom of action impaired, because his conditions of life do not enable him even to conceive of certain possibilities of action. From this angle, to be free means to enjoy the social pre-conditions of rational self-determination or self-fulfilment. Green also strongly underlines how, at a certain level of inequality between the members of a society, legal freedoms can be vacuous. We are dealing with much less straightforward concepts of freedom.

There appear to be at least two other discontinuities between personal concern and philosophical preoccupation. First comes the simple point that if politics was Green's strongest personal interest, along the lines we have examined, it certainly did not command his main activity as a philosopher. His two longest philosophical works were a critique of Hume's empiricism and an attempt to set out his own moral philosophy: the 'Introductions to Hume' and *Prolegomena to Ethics*. Secondly, in his philosophical work Green had slight sense of the autonomy of politics. The role of politics is instrumental. Once the unconditional or 'true' good has been found, which it is one burden of Green's moral philosophy to disclose, the political task is to create the conditions for its realization. (The limits of politics are quickly met.) In this moral teleology of politics the notion that politics might not be seen as the promotion of a social ideal, or that social ideals might be irreconcilably discrepant, is not one which deeply informs Green's political philosophy. Yet outside philosophy, in his correspondence and conversation, he had a sharp enough sense of political conflict through his practical commitments. As for religion so for politics: a clear route into philosophy becomes a less distinct track once inside.

1.5 ETHICS

Green has been widely regarded as a moral teacher, a moral persuader. Certainly he was a man of strong moral views. We have noted his intolerance of drunkenness, his disapproval of the inegalitarianism of the English education system, his view of the moral perversity of the American South. But there is a need again to create a dual image which distinguishes Green's personal concerns from his philosophical preoccupations.

Consider the following notes in which Green sees three questions as central to moral philosophy:

What is moral philosophy? Its object is man as active, as active in what way? Not as an animal, and not in the way of art. As active, then, *freely*, and for the satisfaction of desire. In other words, object of M. Ph. is that which *is to be done*. (This involves freedom and desire.)

This gives it 3 questions to answer, (1) What is free action? (the doctrine of the will)—(2) How does man judge that something is to be done? (Doctrine of the moral judgement/conscience). (3) What is to be done (Theory of duties).   [MS 15, Notes on Moral Philosophy.]

The background to the first question, 'What is free action?', is this. The religious man has immediate experience of God; he does not wait on philosophy to prove that God exists. Just so the moral agent has a sense of what he should do; he does not wait on philosophy to vindicate the coherence of the moral point of view. Green never doubted, as a moral teacher or moral persuader, that some human actions are freely chosen. But philosophy is interrogative, critical, reflective. We find in Green's philosophy nothing like Sir William Hamilton's bland assurance that the 'fact of Liberty may be proved . . . [f]rom the direct consciousness of Liberty'.[29] Green argues that free-will is solidly anchored in the phenomenon of self-consciousness. *Prolegomena to Ethics*, Book I mounts a dense and complex argument to show how, if we analyse self-consciousness, one result of that analysis is a proof that decision-making can involve free choice, that deliberation in a sense relevant to moral responsibility is possible. In general terms, that some human actions are the outcome of free choice. Whether the task of proving that this is so is really discharged by the argument which Green offers, is another matter. But his argument is genuinely

[29] *The Works of Thomas Reid*, ii, ed. Sir William Hamilton, Edinburgh, 1863, 975. Hamilton actually identifies a second way of knowing that we are free, in the consciousness of moral obligation. '*How* . . . moral liberty is possible in man or God, we are utterly unable speculatively to understand. But, practically, the *fact*, that we are free, is given to us in the consciousness of an uncompromising law of duty, in the consciousness of our moral accountability' (ibid.). See further the whole of Hamilton's Note U, 'On the Argument from Prescience Against Liberty', 973–81.

reflective and does not rely on any pre-philosophical 'conscious-ness of Liberty'.

The second and third questions can be taken together. 'How does <a> man judge that something is to be done?' is the problem of moral epistemology. The answer which Green gives in his developed ethics is that the requirements of morality are perceived (not necessarily immediately) as a person's character reacts to the multitude of different features of each particular situation. 'What is to be done' can therefore never be covered by the laying down of rules: by purely general judgements about the morality of suicide, divorce, lying, or killing. Green further holds, to complete the picture, that in favourable conditions of society a person's moral character can be encapsulated in his social role. But we already see that Green's views as a moral teacher or moral persuader are in no wise translated across to a moral philosophy of the rule-laying type.

Concerning character there is a further point which can be alluded to briefly. The exact relation between morality and the human good is a topic which we shall need to consider in Chapter 6. For the present, Green is clear that any account of the moral good is subject to general conditions of the human good: conversely and more precisely that morality cannot be the good for man unless it meets the independently-specified conditions of the human good. He talks of the human good in terms of 'self-satisfaction', 'self-realization', 'an abiding satisfaction of an abiding self'. The 'satisfied' man is not someone who has, from time to time, some joy or pleasure; the 'unsatisfied' man is not someone who has, from time to time, grief or ill-luck. The basic idea is familiar enough from Greek ethics. The Greek philosophers sought the conditions of happiness in a state of the soul, a permanent condition of the agent, Aristotelian *hexis*. So for Green 'self-satisfaction' is a constant or continuous state: essentially only an ethics of character will fulfil the conditions of the human good.

1.6 EVOLUTIONARY THOUGHT

Green had religious, political, and moral concerns before he became a philosopher. I have argued, however, that it is a misconception to suppose that the fundamental role of Green's philosophy is simply to vindicate those pre-philosophical concerns. That point I regard as settled. The next task, now that we have taken a first look at Green's philosophical preoccupations, is to see how they drew him into radical opposition to the native traditions of empiricism and utilitarianism and to the growing impact of evolutionary thought. This has a double interest. In the first place, from Green's reaction to evolutionary theory, utilitarianism, and empiricism, we understand his own philosophy more clearly; and secondly, these lines of nineteenth-century thought pull tightly across and meet, in Green's antagonism, like so many threads in a simple intersection.

Initial resistance to Darwin's theory of evolution, in the interests of religion, rejected the theory as incompatible with the scriptural account of creation. Darwin wrote on the origin of species; the clergy read of the origin of man. The resistance to Darwin was of course but part of a running battle between science and religion, a battle which had earlier produced Francis Buckland's *Reliquiae Diluvianae* (1823), attempting to subvert geological findings concerning the age of the earth, and which at the time we are considering provoked Huxley's assimilation of the Bible to the myths of paganism, 'as dead as Osiris or Zeus'[30] for the scientific inquirer. Evolutionary hypotheses had been examined and rejected by Aristotle and Hegel. The work of Buffon, Erasmus Darwin, Lamarck, Wells, and Matthews had pointed suggestively to an evolutionary theory, but on tenuous evidence. Herbert Spencer had advanced his 'Development Hypothesis' in the *Leader* between 1851 and 1854. But in 1859 in *The Origin of Species* Charles Darwin, resuming his ideas of 1837–8 and enriching them with A. R. Wallace's notion of evolutionary branching, produced a unified theory to account for the change in species over time and for their increasing mutual divergence. Central to the theory was a single main principle, that of natural selection. Rival evolutionary mechanisms were rapidly advanced within the scientific community; and the principle of natural selection remained precarious in Darwin's formulation. But Darwin had argued for the theory of evolution

[30] 1860 review of C. Darwin, *The Origin of Species*: see T. H. Huxley, *Lay Sermons, Addresses, and Reviews*, London, 1870, 304.

with a coherent wealth of facts. Darwinian evolution could not be dismissed as ambitious speculation resting on slender evidence.

In the Conclusion to *The Origin of Species* Darwin offered the reassurance that 'I see no good reason why the views given in this volume should shock the religious feelings of anyone.'[31] Less is involved in this reassurance than meets the eye; it amounts to the claim that nobody should be offended to recognize scientific truth. Darwin shrank from religious controversy. He doubted if there had ever been a Revelation; but when Marx planned to dedicate a revised edition of *Capital* to him, Darwin refused. He wanted no public link with an attack on Christianity.[32] Darwin's sensitivities aside, many religionists felt obliged to resist the theory of evolution in the light of scripture. Inconsistency between the evolutionary theory and the account of creation in the first chapter of Genesis would not, as should now be clear, seriously have worried Green religiously, nor would he have been disturbed by the philosophical impact of that theory on the Argument from Design. If the complex adaptations and co-ordinations of living organisms were withdrawn from the design of an intelligent providence and ascribed to natural causation, Green's philosophy of religion does not aim to prove the existence of God from the designedness of the world.

Green has two main philosophical arguments against the theory of evolution. In 'Logic of the Formal Logicians' the implication of Works II, 182, is that the theory is not ultimately explanatory. It assumes a universe of space, time, and matter of which it does not explain the origin. Human self-consciousness, Green further claims, is in the following sense radically incapable of evolution. In knowledge we experience passing mental states but these are 'held together' in consciousness. This 'self-conscious principle' is either present or not. It is not something which could be present in varying degrees of imperfection and, through complex adaptations, finally emerge full-blown in human knowers. This self-conscious principle is essential to Green's argument for free will (3.6). It also leads to Green's view of an 'eternal consciousness' which explains all

[31] C. Darwin, *The Origin of Species*, ed. W. R. Thompson, London, 1963, 455.
[32] G. de Beer, 'Charles Darwin', *The Listener*, 78 (1967), 147.

existence. The philosophical impact of the theory of evolution vanishes in an idealist construction of experience. The specific point is, of course, that if self-consciousness results from 'an assemblage of conditions' of which the evolutionary descent is as firm as that of any biological phenomenon, the self-consciousness, so far from proving that man is not merely a part of nature, is itself a natural product.

Green showed no interest in Spencer's attempt, e.g., in 'The Social Organism' (1860), to link evolutionary consideration with a political theory of minimal government. The explanation is, I think, that since Green regarded the theory of evolution as philosophically unsound and incomplete, he took the political applications of the theory to lack philosophical credibility as a matter of course. Whether he was right to dismiss Spencer in exactly this way is less clear. For Spencer's analogies between biological and social evolution do not depend logically on the theory of evolution, i.e. on the explanation of evolution (Darwin's or his own), but rather on an evaluation of evolution (cf. 6.7). Spencer identifies certain advanced organisms, and draws implications for the progress of society. I will not pursue the point. It may briefly be added that on a similar supposition of basic philosophical error Green undercut and largely ignored the second basis of Spencer's minimalization of the economic role of government, his interpretation of the theory of natural rights. Green regarded the appeal to natural rights as ethically mistaken, save on a special, uncommon interpretation quite different from Spencer's (c.f. 8.9).

The Aristotelian scholar, Ingram Bywater, responded to Darwin's theory with a light reference to Occam's razor.[33] For Green the issues were more serious.

1.7   UTILITARIANISM

Green encountered utilitarianism in the particular forms which it took in Bentham and J. S. Mill. Those forms of utilitarianism appeared to him to have two main defects as a philosophy of ethics.

In the first place, psychological hedonism (quantitative in

---

[33] H. Hutchison, *The Fortnightly Club*, London, 1922, 76.

Bentham, qualitative in J. S. Mill) was a type of psychological determinism which, for Green, was inconsistent with moral responsibility. This is easily the least important criticism of utilitarianism for a modern reader. For one thing utilitarianism is no longer tied to psychological hedonism (2.10); for another, psychological determinism is currently a distinct second-runner to physical determinism in the challenge to free-will. Finally, on a point of scholarship, it is not the case that Mill's moral psychology is fully hedonist. In *Utilitarianism*, chapter 4, he accepts the possibility of habitual action without reference to pleasure. Green's response to hedonistic psychological determinism is essentially Butler's logical object argument that pleasure supervenes on the satisfaction of desire, but that desire is directed on an object, not on the pleasure which that object is expected to give. If I want to know when King William IV died, it will be pleasant to have my curiosity satisfied; but I do not want to know when King William IV died for the pleasure which satisfying my curiosity will yield. So the argument goes.

Green's second main criticism is that we cannot summate the pleasures of a person's whole life; the idea of summation is invalid because pleasures are serial occurences. Everything reduces to the person's present situation. If I choose a course of action which gives present pleasure, this makes my present situation valuable. If the same course of action produces pain tomorrow, the present situation will have no value then; tomorrow I shall simply be in a new situation, one of 'disvalue'. How far this gives a realistic picture of the capabilities of hedonism is questionable. It is not clear why a person cannot calculate a course of action which produces a life containing more pleasurable experiences than painful ones, and gives tomorrow's painful situation 'value' in that context. But we can see how Green's criticism ties in closely to his specification of the human good, which must provide for the agent's constant or continuous satisfaction. If, as Green supposes, the pleasure of one situation has no value even for the same person in another situation since pleasures are serial occurrences, this understanding of hedonism disqualifies utilitarianism in his own view as a theory of the human good.

Green uses other arguments against utilitarianism. In 2.12 we shall note the start of his argument against utilitarian consequentialism. But the logical object argument and the no-summation argument are his principal lines of attack (6.9).

No one can study Green without being struck by one prevailing feature of his political philosophy—its neglect of the application of utilitarianism to politics. How many commentators, I wonder, could cite a passage in which Green criticizes J. S. Mill's *On Liberty*, James Mill's *Essay on Government*, or Betham's *Principles of Morals and Legislation*? Green does discuss utilitarian political theory, but only briefly, as for instance in his criticism of John Austin's definition of sovereignty (Works II, 399; HM, 66–7) and in his acknowledgement that utilitarianism is right to look to the ends of government rather than to its origin (Works II, 348–9; HM, 24; cp. PE § 213, 356). Green's general neglect is traceable, I think, to the same root which explains his disregard of the political applications of the theory of evolution. He was disinclined to consider the political applications of a theory which he considered to be philosophically false. But certain contrasts with utilitarianism are illuminating; there is an implicit criticism of utilitarian political theory in Green's work.

One point is that in its early formulation utilitarianism sustained an 'atomic' conception of the individual: a view of society as composed of externally related individuals interacting self-interestedly. This view was reinforced by an emphasis on the role of self-interest in classical economics, with which utilitarianism was contingently bound up: the *laissez-faire* insistence that the economic pursuit of self-interest produces the greatest good of the community. A direct, unqualified endorsement of *laissez-faire* cannot be drawn from classical economics, however; and I do not mean to deny this. In the prevention of price-fixing, in the provision of public utilities, in health and safety legislation, the role of the state is to induce a perfect correspondence, within the limits of politics, between the economic pursuit of self-interest and the greatest good of the community: Adam Smith's 'invisible hand' works deftly, but not in a vacuum.[34] We have already seen how Green regarded social conditions as harmfully reducing in some cases

[34] See L. Robbins, *The Theory of Economic Policy in English Classical Political Economy*, 2nd edn. London, 1978; and N. Parker, 'What's So Right about Adam Smith?', *Radical Philosophy*, 30 (1982).

the individual's freedom to conceive certain possibilities of action or to translate such possibilities into effect. So in terms of a climate of ideas Green was opposed to the minimization of the economic role of government with which utilitarianism in its early phase (on quite different grounds from Spencer's dual basis of biological analogy and natural rights) was associated. He worked moreover with a quite different conception of the individual as capable of 'realising' himself only in historically determinate social relationships.

If, however, in the older utilitarianism the individual was taken 'abstractly' and ahistorically, that defect was remedied in the work of J. S. Mill. The burden of Mill's *On Liberty* is that the prevailing social context, far from fostering a proliferation of 'experiments in living', inhibited 'the free development of individuality'.[35] Green must peer askance at Mill because of his utilitarian starting-point, but at first glance this emphasis on the social context of action is a definite link between Green and Mill, as is (a further point) their shared conception of character as a central ethical category. In Mill's ethics the relation of this central role of character to the classical utilitarian emphasis on actions and their consequences is a definite crux. That aside, two major dissonances show up between Green and Mill. The first is that Mill's concept of character remains rooted in psychological determinism; the second is that their angles of interest in the social context of action are markedly divergent. Mill sees in a social atmosphere hostile to the formation of independent thinkers and discriminators the prime threat to character or individuality. This 'tyranny of the majority' is the consideration uppermost in Mill's political philosophy. By contrast, Green is not critically worried about the pressure of social opinion. In his opposition to *laissez-faire* he is worried that a person may be, not inhibited by social intimidation from acting independently, but unable in conditions of social deprivation even to conceive certain possibilities of action.

1.8 EMPIRICISM

Green was a close critic of empiricism across an extensive range of topics, but we can distinguish three chief lines of objection.

[35] *Essential Works of John Stuart Mill*, ed. M. Lerner, New York, 1971, 305.

Green broke radically with the serial view of mind which is traceable from Hume through to J. S. Mill. His central objection to this view is that it encounters a paradox: that if it were true, no such view of the mind would be possible (3.6, 4.9). Take the view as presented by Hume. Reducing the mind to 'distinct perceptions' which are 'distinct existences' (T 636), Hume leaves quite inexplicable in Green's view how, if the mind were such a series, it should possess any idea of the series of which it consists. The need for a non-serial mind or subject-self, to hold together the 'bundle or collection of different perceptions which succeed each other with an inconceivable rapidity, and are in a perpetual flux or movement' (T 252), is one part of Green's case for the existence of free will.

We need to be careful in this matter. A distinction is vital between (i) Hume's empiricism, his emphasis on the foundational role of experience in knowledge, and (ii) his atomism, his understanding of the nature of experience as successive and discrete. Green does not quarrel with empiricism directly in the first sense (cf. 3.11). But certainly he rejects Humean atomism, and this is his first line of objection to empiricism. I may add that my discussion of Hume's ethics in the following chapter does not turn on the paradox of the serial mind; the relevant parts of Hume's moral psychology and ethical theory can be expressed separately from the serial view and do not depend on that view (either its truth or its suggestiveness) for their interest. Then to continue, Green's second line of objection to empiricism relates to Hume's 'partitional' or faculty view of mind, and it applies mainly to the relation of reason to desire. Humean reason is nothing like the rationalist faculty of reason which grounds the intelligibility of the real. Its role is purely and doubly instrumental; it is an instrument of knowledge and it is instrumental to desire. As an instrument of knowledge it is confined (in modern times) to working out logical relationships between concepts and establishing matters of empirical fact. As instrumental to desire it can neither determine the ends of action nor supply the motivation to pursue them. Reason and desire are radically distinct; they are separate faculties of mind which can interact but not interpenetrate. Hume's view of the mind as a 'bundle or collection of different perceptions' reduces the mind on its appetitive side to a succession of discrete desires to which reason is merely instrumental. Reason cannot evaluate desire; and the possibility of a rational structure of desire is simply a contradictory notion on Hume's account. But Green holds that self-consciousness enables as person to distance himself from his own desires, to modify their impact, and to create a structure of desire and hence a state of character. If this structure is based on a conception of personal good, it is so far rational. The partitional view of mind, with its picture of reason as purely instrumental to independent data of desire, is one which Green was bound to deny.

His third line of objection to empiricism is based not on the character of mind but on the relation between mind and the external world. His major dissatisfaction is that empiricism, particularly in its Lockean form, mislocates 'the work of the mind' in experience of the external world. For empiricism the sense give one only atomic experiences. Any construction of those experiences into objects and qualities is a superimposition by the mind. Green finds it logically impossible to make out these atomic experiences which owe nothing to mental superimposition; and from this point he proceeds to attack the idea of an absolute heterogeneity between two fixed and separate terms, mind and the external world. The relevance of this to ethics is that if the analysis of self-consciousness shows that mind is independent of the external world in a way which guarantees free will, a proper analysis of 'the work of the mind' in experience equally shows, in Green's view, that the external world is dependent on mind; and so the physical determinist challenge to free will from classical physics vanishes.

1.9 MID-NINETEENTH-CENTURY OXFORD AND CAMBRIDGE PHILOSOPHY

What was available to Green within the Oxford of his day to enable him to counter these antipathetic lines of thought? Mid-century Oxford was not particularly rich in original work of a high order. As reported by the Oxford University Commission in 1852, J. M. Wilson[36] assigned two main causes for this state of

[36] John Matthias Wilson (1813–81); White's Professor of Moral Philosophy, Oxford, 1846–74.

affairs: first that college tutors were compelled to be generalists, stretched across too broad a spectrum of philosophical subjects; and secondly that Aristotle's *Nicomachean Ethics* exerted a baneful influence as an introductory text in moral philosophy:

The Student who first enters on the study of Moral Philosophy in the *Ethics* of Aristotle, is doubly embarrassed. The thoughts are new to him, and he encounters them for the first time, not only in a foreign tongue, but under very obscure forms of expression, for which it is difficult to find an equivalent in his own language. By degrees he becomes familiar with the technical language of the writer, and takes an interest more or less in the questions at issue between Aristotle and his master. But these questions, it should be remembered have, many of them, little interest for us. The knowledge of them is, in many instances, barren erudition, and if this erudition stand in the way of better and more useful acquirements, it is a serious mischief.[37]

But Oxford philosophy was not at a totally low ebb. Aristotelian scholarship in the hands of such men as H. W. Chandler of Pembroke College was respectably conducted, though Chandler's interests were more bibliographical and philological than philosophical.[38] He was best known for his work of Greek accentuation; and his Inaugural Lecture as Waynflete Professor in 1867, *The Philosophy of Mind a Corrective for Some Errors of the Day*, was a strictly undistinguished performance.[39] Besides *Nicomachean Ethics*, we know from the *Memoirs* of Mark Pattison that the *Politics* and *Rhetoric* of Aristotle were studied, together with the Aristotelian logical treatises. Encouragement of the study of Plato's *Republic* is ascribed to William Sewell of Exeter College.[40] I will return in

---

[37] J. M. Wilson, 'Answers from the Rev. J. M. Wilson', *Report of Her Majesty's Commissioners Appointed to Inquire into The State, Discipline, Statutes and Revenues of the University and Colleges of Oxford*, London, 1852 [1482], xxii. 262.

[38] Henry William Chandler (1828–89).

[39] *The Philosophy of Mind a Corrective for Some Errors of the Day*, London, 1867. The burden of the lecture is that beliefs such as those in the existence of God, the immortality of the soul, and free will, which are challenged by materialist philosophies, can be shown by 'an attentive study of the human mind' (p. 39) to be reasonable inasmuch as (*a*) a belief is reasonable if the human mind is so constituted that we are unable to reject it (p. 27); and (*b*) the beliefs cited fall into just this category (*passim*). The lecture is entirely programmatic and not a single argument is offered for either (*a*) or (*b*). The contrast with Green, who painstakingly argues for every claim, could hardly be greater.

[40] R. M. Ogilvie, *Latin and Greek: A Study of the Influence of the Classics on English Life from 1660 to 1918*, London, 1964, 101.

the next section to consider the importance of Greek philosophy to Green (cf. ch. 3, n. 10).

As ever, Oxford philosophy presented a varied spectacle. A version of Comtian positivism was espoused enthusiastically but without philosophical rigour by Richard Congreve of Wadham College. Within the broadly empiricist tradition Bacon was studied: the *Novum Organum* in the 1855 edition of G. W. Kitchin. (This was the basis of Richard Shute of Christ Church's *A Discourse on Truth*, published in 1877, just outside the period we are immediately considering.) Otherwise empiricism was mainly represented by J. S. Mill. H. L. Mansel, whose views we shall notice directly, had re-edited the 1691 logic of Aldrich, but by all accounts Mill's *A System of Logic* (unaffected by the more exciting reform of logic instituted by Boole and de Morgan, but a considerable improvement on the *Artis Logicae Rudimenta* of Aldrich) dominated Oxford logic. Green's interest was not primarily in logic, though he did lecture critically on Mill (Works II, 195–306).

Mansel, elected to the Waynflete chair in 1855, presents a double aspect.[41] In the first place, he was the main channel through which Sir William Hamilton's influence reached Oxford. Secondly, he espoused an idiosyncratic form of Kantianism in the cause of religion. (The existence of a transcendental God, beyond the veil of sense, could be neither proven nor, more importantly, disproven on Kantian terms. Hence a metaphysical agnosticism was used to support a position in theology.) Hamilton's Natural Realism asserted that the external world has an equal reality to mind and that we are directly acquainted with both, not a position which Green could regard as a fruitful starting-point. (He notices Hamilton in 'The Logic of the Formal Logicians' and at scattered points in the Balliol MSS, e.g. MS 10A, p. 30.) Mansel's religious angle was no more engaging. Since, as I have argued in 1.3, Green did not look to philosophy to prove or disprove the existence of God,

---

[41] Henry Longueville Mansel (1820–71). Mansel edited Hamilton's lectures on metaphysics and logic with John Veitch in 1859–60. He replied to J. S. Mill's *An Examination of Sir William Hamilton's Philosophy*, 1st edn. London, 1865, with *The Philosophy of the Conditioned*, London, 1866, and an article entitled 'Supplementary Remarks on Mr Mill's Criticism of Sir William Hamilton', in *Contemporary Review*, 6 (1867). Argument is the lifeblood of philosophy, and Mansel was at least a highly argumentative man.

this attraction of Mansel's Kantian philosophy was for him withdrawn.

The Cambridge philosophical scene inspired scarcely more interest. I shall examine Green's relationship with Sidgwick, personal and philosophical, in 1.17. Other representatives of Cambridge philosophy, apart from F. D. Maurice (1.3), appear not to have exerted an impact on Green. I refer to William Whewell, John Grote, and Thomas Birks.

It would be matter for remark if Whewell's name failed to occur in Sidgwick's conversations with Green. But I can find no evidence that Green read Whewell or that he would have responded favourably to Whewell's work. Whewell, like Green, regarded utilitarianism as mistaken not merely in detail but *au fond*.[42] But Whewell was an intuitionalist. His moral epistemology involves the notion of intuition, through conscience, of 'Ideas' in mind of God (cf. 7.16).[43]

Little of Grote's work was published in Green's formative years. Grote's criticism of utilitarianism, *An Examination of the Utilitarian Philosophy* (Cambridge, 1870) is a shrewd, point-by-point rejection, unconnected with the kind of overarching theory which we find in Green's ethics.[44]

The *scripta minora* of Thomas Birks may be mentioned, but the thin substance of his Inaugural Lecture as Knightbridge Professor, *The Present Importance of Moral Science* (London, 1872), projecting a view of ethics as 'the lawful spouse of Christian theology' (p. 14) and denouncing the extension of the suffrage as subversive of 'the Christian religion, the Protestant Succession, and the Coronation Oath' (p. 21), would seem hardly calculated to engage Green's sympathetic interest.

1.10 PLATO AND ARISTOTLE

Although Green was required for his college work to lecture on Plato and Aristotle, he had small interest in Greek philosophical problems unless they engaged with his own *problematik*. He did

---

[42] W. Whewell, *Elements of Morality*, 2 vols., London, 1845, 67.

[43] W. Whewell, *On the Philosophy of Discovery*, London and Cambridge, 1860, 359 ff.

[44] On Grote see A. M. Quinton, *Utilitarian Ethics*, London, 1973, 83–7; and J. B. Schneewind, *Sidgwick's Ethics and Victorian Moral Philosophy*, Oxford, 1977.

publish in 1866 a long and distinguished essay on 'The Philosophy of Aristotle'; and J. H. Randall has suggested that lines of thought implicit in that essay (regarding the distinction between thought and feeling) would have served Green more fruitfully than the actual direction which he subsequently took in *Prolegomena to Ethics*.[45] On the concept of character, however, which is central to the ethics of both Aristotle and Green, Green thought that Aristotle emphasized too strongly the fixity of character once formed (5.5). Aristotle, in Green's view, insufficiently appreciated the possibilities of moral reform by one's own resolve. Moreover, Aristotle's model of practical reason, as embodied in his account of the practical syllogism, appeared to Green to be steeped in error (7.12). None the less, Green went through a phase of Aristotelian zeal. He enthusiastically approached Aristotle's *De Anima* in the 1860s, producing an efficient and nearly complete translation. Three themes, or occasional theses, in *De Anima* would have attracted Green's attention: the thought/object identity thesis of *De Anima*, III.7; the idea of rational wish; and the unity of mind and the interpenetration of mental activities. But he was unable to develop these ideas from their Aristotelian base. Nettleship records Green's comment that he 'once thought there was a great deal to be learnt from the *De Anima*, but was disappointed in the end'.[46]

Yet Green worked more easily with Aristotle than with Plato. Aristotle appeared to offer sound ideas which were incapable of proper development from an Aristotelian background. Plato offered fewer sound ideas in Green's view. Thus the 'Analysis of *Republic*', among the MSS at Balliol, intersects a key topic in Green's moral psychology but quite without critical engagement. For although the only extant portion of the MS concerns Book VIII, in which Plato's discussion particularly of the 'democratic man' centres on a person's critical relation to his own desires, Green settles for mere paraphrase. There is no sense that Plato is speaking forcefully to current issues. Green has three major disagreements with Plato. In the first place, he criticizes Plato for collapsing the interpersonal depth out of the

[45] J. H. Randall, 'T. H. Green: The Development of English Thought from J. S. Mill to F. H. Bradley', *Journal of the History of Ideas*, 27 (1966).
[46] Nettleship, 'Notes'.

concept of justice. Secondly, the pure separation of reason and desire in Plato's philosophy of mind set an impassable barrier. (Contrast here not only *De Anima's* idea of rational wish but the account of choice in NE VI.2 as a combination of reason and desire.) Thirdly and relatedly, Green complains that Plato lacks a specific concept of practical reason.

The first two points emerge in Green's 'Notes on Moral Philosophy' (MS 15):

Object of Plato's *Republic*: to vindicate right of state, not as a source of natural compulsion, but of rational obligation.

With this view <Plato> exhibits state as organic body, of such a kind that fulfilment of *ergon* of whole is necessary condition of fulfilment of *ergon* by each member. Fulfilment of *ergon* of whole = justice. Same conception applied to individual:—inconsistency of supposing reason, 'spirit', and desire to be complete in each individual, which is done in account of virtue in individual soul, and elsewhere of treating mass of individuals as mere appetite.

Fallacy (1) of supposing individuals to exist apart at first, and then to form societies from 'mutual need' or other reason. Man as born into family, exists in society to begin with. (2) opposite, that because individual is what he is as social, he is therefore fraction, not integer.

(Justice = harmonious activity of the whole, but as each member only 'virtuous' so far as it fulfils its function in harmony with the rest, each of the other virtues involves justice.

According to proper harmony [organization] of the whole, reason rules, as that in virtue of which alone an organic whole of desires and society is possible.)

Result of the Platonic view <is> that there is only one person—the state. Hence communism. Hence also justice in proper sense, as relation between free persons, vanishes.

The two 'fallacies' relate to Plato's discussion of the minimum city of Rep. II. Green's third disagreement, which concerns Plato's lack of a specific concept of practical reason, unfolds as follows. Reason (*to logistikon*) in the *Republic* has two tasks assigned to it: to control the other parts of the soul (*to thymoeides* and *to epithymetikon*) and to pursue its own proper development towards apprehension of the Form of the Good (Rep. 441C–E, 442B, 533E). But the practical task of control is fulfilled by immediate derivation from the theoretical task of apprehension. When *to logistikon* is fully developed and attains *noesis*, it apprehends the Form of the Good and the other Forms in their dependence on the Form of the Good. This apprehension, in which the philosopher contemplates 'a world of unchanging and harmonious order, where reason governs and nothing can do or suffer wrong', necessarily draws the philosopher to 'reproduce that order in his soul' (500C). So theoretical reason produces automatically a practical result. Green was well aware of this aspect of Plato's account of reason, and was critical of it both in his MS 22 remark that 'With Plato attainment of goodness is identified with formation of a true theory of goodness', and in his paper, 'Popular Philosophy in its Relation to Life', in his reference to Plato's Form of the Good, 'the contemplation of which is the final goal of love, and which, once seen, transforms the actions of men to its likeness' (Works III, 103).

I have stated Green's three major disagreements with Plato. There are two minor points on which to end. First, Plato's philosophy of mind does not merely establish a rigid division between reason and desire. It deeply demarcates mind (or soul) and body; these two parts of which a human being is composed are strongly heterogeneous. For Green by contrast the entire material world, including body, is mind-dependent (3.8). Secondly, a qualification to Green's Aristotelian preference lies in the classification of moral virtues in PE, Book III, where Green follows essentially the fourfold schema of Rep. IV. Green was always impressed by the 'speculative achievement' of Plato and Aristotle.[47] On the whole, however, the judgement of Nettleship, himself strikingly different from Green in this respect, appears to me perfectly correct: 'He was not one of those to whom the products of Greek genius have a unique attraction or interest.'[48]

1.11 VERSIONS OF GREEN

But where does Green stand in relation to the moderns? I explained in 1.9 the unappealingness of Mansel's Kantian philosophy; the separate influence of Kant is another matter. Kant had early made an impact on British philosophy. Expositions and anthologies were available from the 1790s

---

[47] Nettleship, 'Notes'.
[48] Nettleship, *Memoir*, lxxi.

onwards; and Kantian penetration was at least far enough advanced by the 1830s for the question to be significant whether the Hamiltonian Unconditioned derived from a misunderstanding of Kant. The Kantian connection, and indeed the whole question of philosophical antecedents, is a thorny topic in the interpretation of Green. This is in general terms to be expected. The thought of a great philosopher is normally construed, after his death, as a body of doctrine which then defines e.g., Platonism, Aristotelianism, Cartesianism, Kantianism. This construal may be a static frame imposed misleadingly on what was, for the philosopher, a transitional and mobile set of ideas. But the major problem which a great philosopher sets is that of isolating his own views and arguments from later accretions. For a philosopher such as Green, not quite of the first rank, attention tends, by contrast, to focus not on the relation of original to continuation but on that of original to antecedents, on the tracing of intellectual debts.

W. H. Walsh refers freely to Green, Bradley, and Bosanquet as 'the British Hegelians'.[49] Thomas Case, an Oxford philosopher contemporary with Green, regarded him as a Hegelian.[50] The versatile economist F. Y. Edgeworth in his *New and Old Methods of Ethics* (1877) associates Green indelibly with Hegel; every reference to Green involves a Hegelian attribution. Green's criticisms of Locke, Hume, and J. S. Mill are said with pointed irony to put 'the non-Hegelian public' in his debt.[51] Antipathy to the expanding 'empire of Hegel'[52] appears to have been acute with Edgeworth at this time. But though his text was written when Edgeworth was still Green's colleague at Balliol, there is nothing to suggest privileged access to Green's views. Citations of Green are purely through his published work. For James Ward, on the contrary, the Hegelian element in Green was slight or non-existent.[53] Andrew Seth and A. J. Balfour stressed rather the Kantian element, and referred to Green as a 'neo-Kantian'.[54] The Italian commentator C. Goretti

[49] W. H. Walsh, *Hegelian Ethics*, London, 1969, 4.

[50] H. Sturt, *Idola Theatri*, London, 1906, 221.

[51] F. Y. Edgeworth, *New and Old Methods of Ethics, or 'Physical Ethics' and 'Methods of Ethics'*, Oxford and London, 1877, 83–4.

[52] F. Y. Edgeworth, 82.   [53] H. Sturt, *Idola Theatri*, 221.

[54] A. Seth, *Hegelianism and Personality*, 2nd edn. Edinburgh and London, 1893, 24–5; A. J. Balfour, 'Green's Metaphysics of Knowledge', *Mind*, 9 (1884), 74.

emphasized a happy combination ('felice fusione') of the thought of Kant and Fichte.[55] Sidgwick was clear that 'Green is a Kantian'.[56]

It seems to me that the only label one can safely affix to Green's thought is the entirely general label of 'idealist', where (to a first approximation) idealism is a metaphysical theory about the relation of mind to its objects such that ultimate reality is constituted by mind. Green's expressed stand 'On behalf of idealism' (Works I, 522; cf. PE § 37) suggests that, on a certain construction at least, he would not have repudiated this characterization, though labels hardly illuminate. The problem in Green's case is threefold. In the first place, such apparently more precise labels as 'Hegelian' are far from perspicuous. The term 'Hegelian' could be construed so widely as to include Marx or so narrowly as to exclude some of Hegel's own (early) work. Secondly, it appears to me quite wrong to assign decisive priority to any single element in Green. What is striking about Green's intellectual debts is their variety. Green's philosophy is compact of Aristotelian, Kantian, Rousseau-ian and Hegelian elements. No one element is fundamental, and to separate the different elements taxes all analysis. A label such as 'Kantian', 'Hegelian', fastened *en bloc*, conceals the variety. Thirdly, even when one takes a single element, say the Kantian or Hegelian, Green's indebtedness is always a distinctly subtle matter. He does not, for instance, adopt Kant's or Hegel's technical formulas. Except in referring to these other writers Green makes no mention of (say) the 'transcendental unity of apperception' (Kant) or the 'dialectic' (Hegel). Rather he is influenced by perspectives and by broad methods of approach.

1.12 THE PHILOSOPHY OF KANT

What then was the relevance of Kant to Green? Why should there be a Kantian element in his work? The answer chiefly

[55] C. Goretti, 'La metafisica della conoscenza in Thomas H. Green', *Rivista di Filosofia*, 1936, 97. Cf. R. Eisler, *Philosophen-Lexikon*, Berlin, 1912, 213: 'Green, the leading representative of English critical idealism, is influenced by Kant, Fichte and Hegel' (Eng. tr. GLT).

[56] H. Sidgwick, *Lectures on the Ethics of T. H. Green, Mr. Herbert Spencer, and J. Martineau*, London, 1902, 3.

concerns free will, but in a complicated way. Mention has already been made of Green's anxiety over the assimilation of man to nature, over the trend (for which the theory of evolution was partly responsible) towards viewing man as merely a part of nature, so that human actions are to be explained not fundamentally by reference to any freedom of decision which human beings may have but in principle in just the same way as anything else in nature is explained, via the laws of evolution and ultimately by those of classical physics.

Kantian idealism is the strongest repudiation of this entire line of thought. For Kant retorts upon the physical determinist who would apply the scientific study of nature to man, that the causal laws which are 'found' to be operative in nature are themselves products of the spontaneity of the human mind. We inescapably perceive, for instance, in causal categories; but what we thus perceive are phenomena merely, to which our thought and sense are relative. We have no assurance that noumenal reality, i.e. whatever lies behind phenomena, is subject to causal determination; and we have some assurance, through moral experience, that human agency has a noumenal aspect which, exempt from the laws of phenomena, gives an opening to free will.

To show that at least some human actions are the outcome of free choice, in a way for which physical determinism cannot account, is one of Green's key philosophical objectives. This we know. But Green's relation to Kantian idealism is by no means straightforward. The Kantian element in his philosophy is strongest in Book I of *Prolegomena to Ethics*, where he applies a transcendental argument to the fact of knowledge. A transcendental argument is, very roughly, an argument which, for any given concept or feature of our experience, works backwards to the preconditions either of our having that concept or without which our experience could not have that feature. Green argues that without self-consciousness we could not have knowledge even so simple as that of a world where things change; and he thinks that self-consciousness provides the key to free will. But his epistemology stops short of Kant's distinction between phenomena and noumena. Green sees mind as the key not just to free will but to the nature of reality. The distinction between appearance and reality is not one between the world as we experience it in thought and sense, and the world as it is beyond the categories of human knowledge. The only distinction which Green will admit is one between the minds of finite beings (you and I) and the 'eternal consciousness', between finite and perfect mind. Again, Kant's official view is that free will cannot be known. We have the idea of free will: the idea of pure spontaneity, of a power to initiate a series of 'phenomenal' events which is itself an unconditional cause, not the effect of anything else. He does not, however, undertake to prove that we have free will. Free will remains a mere postulate. But Green thinks that by his 'self-conscious principle' free will can be established.

On other ethical topics we find explicit criticisms or ambiguous agreement. Kant marks a reaction to Hume. For Hume reason has no motivational force; morality is grounded in human nature. The 'natural' virtues rest on desires which on Hume's account are a standard feature of the human personality. But Kant radically separates morality and desire; no action motivated by desire has any moral value. In morality reason alone is practical because there can be no moral action which is not determined by the idea of law, and only reason can provide the universalizability test which yields the 'maxims' of moral action. Green's ethics involves the notion of a rational structure of desire, from which the Kantian opposition of reason or morality to desire is excluded.

Both Green and Kant hold that in ethics the human person is primary, but this agreement masks a contrast. Kant takes the succession of a person's actions and asks for each action whether it passes the test of universalizability. Any individual action which passes the test reveals a 'good will'. Green, on the other hand, is essentially interested in the kind of person which a succession of actions discloses; he proposes an ethics of character in which ideally a person's character is informed by a rational structure of desire. This contrast is more important than the not specially insightful criticism which follows from it in Green: that Kant's abstract requirement of universalizability gives no one sufficient guidance on what in particular to do. Again both Kant and Green accept what may be termed the sovereignty of the moral self, the special excellence of moral goodness. But in Kant this is linked to reason as opposed to desire; in Green it is linked to rational structures of desire under a theory of the unconditional human good.

In politics and religion, to consider Green's two other main areas of concern, the influence of Kant's political philosophy can be largely discounted. Kant's political philosophy is neither extensive nor, in the view of most scholars, a particularly distinguished part of his work. One might compare the political philosophies of Kant and Green and discover certain compatibilities, but I cannot see that in his political philosophy Kant significantly supplied Green with arguments or ideas. The political ramifications of Kant's moral philosophy are quite another matter. Here two points are specially important. The first concerns the relation of moral value to free choice. For Kant it is because a decision to act is free and rational that it has moral value. In this sense moral value can be realized no further than we freely choose to create it. This viewpoint is definitely reproduced in Green's idea that the enforcement of morality is a contradictory notion. The second point links Kant with Rousseau. Light is thrown on the relation of ethics to politics in Green by the connection which he made between Kant's kingdom of ends and Rousseau's general will. As Green read that connection he took the idea from Kant of a society of moral agents and the idea from Rousseau of a state which both creates (if necessary) and sustains the conditions for such a society to exist. Historically this reverses the order of ideas; analytically it simply puts a specific interpretation on Rousseau's idea of the state as promoting the collective interest identified by the general will. This relation of ethics to politics supplies, in Green's political philosophy, the ends of government and the grounds of political obligation.

In religion, Kant no more than Green looks to philosophy to prove the existence of God. But Kant's religion 'within the bounds of reason alone' differs fundamentally from Green's philosophy of religion on two points. First: God is ranged, along with noumena, among the unknowables of Kant's philosophy. Green, however, claims the possibility of immediate experience of God in faith. Secondly: Kant's 'rational' religion postulates God as guaranteeing in a future life the final coincidence of virtue and happiness, but Green's ethics aims to show the complete adequacy of virtue to the human good without any reference to redressing the balance of virtue and happiness in a future life.

1.13 GREEN AND HEGEL

The most controversial of Green's debts is to Hegel. It would be a project far beyond the scope of an introductory chapter to unravel the full complexities or to set out the complete range of exegetical views on this topic. Equally, the topic cannot be passed over in silence since some commentators have found in Hegel a reliable key, as they suppose, to Green's philosophy. Hegel is an incubus which the commentator on Green cannot easily throw off.

Even anecdotes conspire tacitly to plant a false impression. Consider the following, which comes from Sidgwick's last visit to Oxford. Sidgwick addressed the Oxford Philosophical Society in May 1900 in one of his periodic attempts at the complete demolition of Green's philosophy. In response to his suggestion of a radical incoherence in Green, we are told by Arthur and Eleanor Sidgwick in their *Memoir*, 'a prominent Hegelian made the inevitable suggestion that such fundamental incoherence merely indicated that the region of the ultimate difficulties of thought had been reached, and inferred that both sides of the contradiction should be sustained'.[57] From a Hegelian move to defend Green's philosophy, it is a short step to assume that a Hegelian philosophy is being defended. Sidgwick answered the prominent but anonymous Hegelian that he—Sidgwick—had never been able 'to make out from the school to which he'—the Hegelian—'evidently belonged how they managed to distinguish the contradictions which they took to be evidence of error from those which they regarded as intimations of higher truth'.[58] A palpable hit, but at whom? Not at Green certainly; for Green nowhere seeks to eliminate the law of non-contradiction. In an isolated passage, probably from the late 1860s or early 1870s, Green does observe: 'Syllogism unequal to complexity of real reasoning, for words can only *express exactly* mere objects of sense. The higher the subject of reasoning, the less logic

---

[57] Arthur and Eleanor Sidgwick, *Henry Sidgwick, A Memoir*, London, 1906, 586.
[58] Arthur and Eleanor Sidgwick, ibid.

applies. Principle of contradiction meaningless when applied to metaphysical ideas' (Platonis de Republica, 127). But this derogation of the principle of (non-)contradiction casts no light on any metaphysical argument which Green actually uses. In fact on full review Sidgwick's Oxford occasion shows how incompletely Hegelian some at least of 'the disciples of Green' regarded their master. For a suggestion was advanced during the discussion that Green's incoherence might be remedied by a development of his thought precisely in the direction of Hegel. Sidgwick's own view of the primarily Kantian character of Green's philosophy, cited in 1.11, is a separate matter. But the anecdote as recounted in the *Memoir* hardly displays close caution in estimating Green's relation to Hegel. The topic is full of unchecked myths.

That Green read Hegel is not in doubt; we can point to a cluster of references of which Works III, 125, 129, 142–3 come easily to hand. But the 'Analysis of Hegel', among the unnumbered MSS at Balliol, needs to be taken separately. Two considerations bear on its significance.

In the first place, it is not an independent interpretation of Hegel but simply a translation, identified in 1982, of paragraphs 1–163 of Hegel's *Philosophical Propaedeutic.*[59] The *Propaedeutic* comprises notes for courses which Hegel gave to schoolboys when he was a headmaster at Nürnberg. More strictly it is a compilation by Rosenkranz from Hegel's rough notes. What is 'analytical' about it, hence the title of the MS, is that the *Propaedeutic* summarizes and resolves Hegel's philosophy into its main elements. The analysis is Hegel's own.

Secondly, a question of genuineness has been raised by Ben Wempe.[60] I have re-examined the manuscript in the light of Dr Wempe's comments, which were brought to my attention by Alan Tadiello. Because there are definite variations in style of handwriting between the 'Analysis of Hegel' and the remainder

---

[59] Alan Tadiello informs me that the identification was made by a member of the 1982 Commemorative Conference on T. H. Green, Balliol College. A copy of K. Rosenkranz's edn. of the *Philosophische Propädeutik*, Berlin, 1840, is among R. L. Nettleship's books at Balliol; this is the copy, possibly once belonging to Green, which I have checked. Green's translation ends with the first clause of para. 163: 'Das denken ist die Thätigkeit des Geistes . . .' ('Thinking is the activity of mind').

[60] B. Wempe, *Beyond Equality: A Study of T. H. Green's Theory of Positive Freedom*, Delft, 1986, 62: 'I do not believe that the manuscript . . . was indeed written by Green.'

of the Green Papers, I am not confident that the manuscript is genuine. But we should be alert to the ambiguities of genuineness. If it is not an autograph draft, it may yet be Green's manuscript in a 'fair copy', prepared for him perhaps because he intended to approach a publisher. Nothing hangs on that conjecture for my interpretation of Green's philosophy; I have always regarded the 'Analysis of Hegel' as a minor document. Spurious or genuine, autograph draft or fair copy, as a mere translation it recedes to the margin of Green's relation to Hegel. The implications of the manuscript's uncertain status may be more disturbing to other commentators.

More broadly, in relation to Hegel, there is on the one hand Green's celebrated remark reported by Sidgwick, 'I looked into Hegel the other day and found it a strange Wirrwarr [i.e. chaos or mess]',[61] and on the other his recommendation to English readers to abandon the study of Locke and Hume, 'the anachronistic systems hitherto prevalent among us', for that of Kant and Hegel (Works I, 371, 373). It has been suggested, too, that by the 1870s Jowett was apprehensive of what he put down as Green's Hegelian influence on the undergraduates of Balliol. Can we sort all this out into a pattern at once coherent and faithful to the facts?

Not all the evidence quite supports what it has been taken to imply, in my view. Consider Jowett's hostility to Green's 'Hegelian' influence. Evidence for this hostility is given by Anthony Quinton:

Jowett's attitude to Hegel itself underwent a dialectical change. By the 1870s, suspicious of the effect of Green's earnest obscurities on the undergraduates of Balliol, he was complaining that 'metaphysics exercise a fatal influence over the mind'. But by 1884 . . . he adopted a more favourable posture. 'Though not a Hegelian', he wrote, 'I think I have gained more from Hegel than from any other philosopher.'[62]

Quinton' *Absolute Idealism*, from which this extract is taken, is the most important philosophical discussion of nineteenth-century British idealism in the last half-century. But if we

---

[61] H. Sidgwick, 'The Philosophy of T. H. Green', *Mind*, 10 (1901), 19.

[62] A. M. Quinton, *Absolute Idealism*, Oxford, 1972, 20. 'Absolute Idealism', a common term for the philosophy of Hegel, founds knowledge and reality on an activity of mind unlimited by anything not constituted by mind itself. Kantian idealism, for instance, falls short of this characterization through its admission of 'things-in-themselves' which are impenetrable to mind and owe nothing to its activity.

accept, reasonably enough, that Jowett's remark was meant to apply to Green, what supports the inference that in Jowett's view Green's 'fatal' metaphysical influence was specifically Hegelian? Jowett's remark requires a particular interpretation before it will support that inference. If Jowett had believed that Green's metaphysics was Hegelian, the validity of that view would still have to be assessed. Even so, the view might clarify the remark: the remark would not confirm that Jowett held the view. Two pieces of evidence suggest, I think, a different locus of disagreement between Green and Jowett.

In a letter to A. C. Bradley, Green was at great pains to stamp on rumours of a rift between Jowett and himself:

I have certainly never sought the reputation of a prophet, and if in a small measure and among a small circle I have gained it, I can only wonder why. There is no other way of teaching within my competence than that of trying to satisfy in others the intellectual wants I find in myself, and as I have begun I must go on. But it is good to be made strongly sensible of the bad side of the effect one is producing, which I take to be a tendency to disregard positive knowledge and to lose the faculty of dealing directly with the ordinary intelligence of men. I find this tendency in myself and can therefore understand that others find it more marked in those who have been much under my influence. It is an effect more difficult to prevent than the obfuscation of that average intellect which I may have sometimes produced by pouring too much metaphysics on it too soon.

The latter evil I hope to avoid for the future: but the former is for the time an almost inseparable incident of any bona fide pursuit of philosophy. The only thing is for every one to resist it as much as he can in his own case by forcing himself to acquire knowledge which has no direct philosophical interest and to discuss ordinary questions in the ordinary way.

If you have gathered any impression (through Nettleship or otherwise) that there is any serious want of agreement between me and the Master as to the way in which I should do my business, please put it aside.[63]

The exact date of this letter is not known, but it certainly belongs to the period of Jowett's prejudice against Green's teaching. The sequence of events leading up to the letter can be pieced together with fair confidence. The letter begins with self-reproach: 'When I talked to you last week I was under a

---

[63] Undated letter to A. C. Bradley, Bibliography II.

temporary depression which it was rather weak of me to exhibit and which has since disappeared.' So there had been a conversation which Bradley had followed with a letter in which he brought into prominence the disagreement between Green and Jowett. To this letter we have just read Green's reply. Whether and by what criteria the 'want of agreement' was 'serious' we shall probably never know. But the lines on which Green approaches the matter suggest that the issue was general one of the intellectual clarity with which students emerged from Green's teaching. That issue was addressed by J. A. Symonds in his letter of 7 October 1882 to Mrs Green:

... I have sometimes wondered whether when his own teaching returned upon him in the inexact phrases of disciples, he was not too tolerant of its ineptitude ... It was this tolerance of metaphysical sciolism (if I may venture to put the matter thus) which caused some misunderstanding latterly between Jowett and Green about the education of young men. I would not willingly be misunderstood upon this point. Green had a more vivid faith in metaphysical study as a mental exercise than Jowett has; and his own absorbing interest in the great questions which the philosopher discusses, made him sympathise with those ardent youths who attacked them passionately. Insofar he was without any question unassailable. My own doubt is whether he was not perhaps too lenient to metaphysical vagueness which used the language and pretended to the method, which he had mastered.[64]

Jowett had a hard, shrewd sense of what a liberal education could offer against ambiguity, obscurity, and false profundity. If he recognized a baneful influence emanating from Green's lectures he is likely to have expressed himself with inimitable point. But the issue was more closely connected with Jowett's mistrust of the educational value of metaphysics than with his discomfort at the (supposedly) Hegelian character of what Green was setting forth. The firsthand evidence which we have examined does not suggest that in Jowett's view Green's influence was specifically Hegelian. We have not, however, quite done with Jowett.

For although, in a reaction against Hegel, Jowett observed that 'It's a good thing to have read Hegel, but now that you've read him, I advise you to forget him again',[65] nevertheless the

---

[64] J. A. Symonds, Recollections.
[65] L. A. Tollemache, *Benjamin Jowett, Master of Balliol*, London, 1895, 70–1.

fact is patent that Jowett was one of the earliest channels by which Hegel was introduced into England and specifically into Oxford.[66] The claim which traces the patient, sympathetic study of Hegel to the amateur Scots philosopher James Hutchison Stirling's *The Secret of Hegel* (1865), a claim to be found in J. H. Muirhead's 1927 article, 'How Hegel Came to England',[67] is easily remedied by consulting Sir Geoffrey Faber's *Jowett: A Portrait with a Background* (1957).

Jowett visited Germany with A. P. Stanley in 1844. The precise object of the visit is not clear, though it had from the start philosophical underpinnings—Jowett packed a copy of Kant's *Critique of Pure Reason* on which, as Stanley lambently remarked, they 'supported their wearied minds by alternate reading, analysing and catechizing'.[68] But for whatever reason Jowett secured various introductions, among others to Erdmann of Halle, a follower of Hegel. The specific effects of Hegel on Jowett and the range of his Hegelian reading are not certain. Jowett found mind-expanding the mere effort of confronting Hegel's scope and depth. In the introduction to his translation of Plato's *Parmenides*, Jowett writes of Hegel as 'the most subtle philosopher of the nineteenth century'.[69] But Jowett was not deep-rootedly philosophical. What is quite plain, however,

---

[66] The first tangible impact of Jowett's 'Hegelian' influence was the paper on 'Hegel's Philosophy of Right' by his ex-pupil, T. C. Sandars, in *Oxford Essays*, Oxford, 1855.

Michael Oakeshott's remark in conversation with the present writer, 'Hegel reached Oxford from Scotland', is worth weighing. Though wrong, I believe, about the serious inception of Hegelian studies it holds a degree of truth for the second wave of Hegelian influx directed by Edward Caird and William Wallace. Wallace, who studied at St Andrews and Oxford, became a Fellow of Merton in 1867 and succeeded Green as White's Professor in 1882. From the mid-1870s his translations of Hegel, which are faithful without being strictly exact, threw open a field for the study of Hegel previously closed to undergraduates. Caird, whose *Hegel* appeared in Blackwood's Philosophical Classics in 1883, returned to Oxford from Glasgow in 1893 to become Master of Balliol. It remains no less true, however, that these 'Scottish Hegelians' absorbed their first Hegelian notions as undergraduates at Balliol in the 1860s. At St Andrews Wallace had been impressed by J. F. Ferrier, but Ferrier's allegiances were Berkeleian rather than Hegelian.

[67] J. H. Muirhead, 'How Hegel Came to England', *Mind*, (1927). In view of the impression of tangled obscurity which Stirling's *The Secret of Hegel* conveys to most readers, Green's reaction is interesting: 'My laudation of Stirling has finally confined itself to an intimation of "respect" in one note. I quite agree with all you can say against him. The worst of it is that at the same time so much can be said for him' (letter to A. C. Bradley, 20 Sept. 1873).

[68] Sir Geoffrey Faber, *Jowett: A Portrait With a Background*, London, 1957, 178.

[69] B. Jowett, *The Dialogues of Plato*, Oxford, 1953, ii. 659.

is that Jowett was the point of fusion between Green and Hegel.

What could Hegel offer to Green, given the three main areas of concern which we have identified? In religion, in Green's sense of the historical relativity of creeds and doctrines, there is an element of Hegelian prepossession. The German biblical scholarship which influenced Green's attitude was itself in part a product of Hegel's idea of the growth of human thought and activity in history. But two further points are more troublesome. The first is Hegel's view of philosophy as 'the truth of Christianity', i.e. of philosophy as conveying the essential spiritual truths of Christianity disengaged from their accidental, contingent, and mythical details. For we must remember that Green holds creeds and doctrines to be inadequate to religious experience; their pared-down translation into philosophy is not necessarily the preservation of something valuable. The second point concerns Green's stress on the immediate experience of God in faith, and the ill-favour with which the notion of immediacy is regarded by Hegel. *Encyclopaedia* I, §§ 66–78 is an attempt to unravel the misconceptions involved in this view of religious experience.

In politics Hegel's conception of the social-historical individual, in other words his denial that for human beings the different forms of social dependence are simply an external necessity to the individual, mere means for him to realize his particular ends, but, rather, embody a many-layered truth that human beings are not self-sufficient, was clearly attractive to Green. It was also a central theme of Greek political thought, and Green would have encountered it first in Plato and Aristotle. Again, Hegel's emphasis on the 'cunning of reason', on the logic of unintended consequences by which actions can contribute to a pattern of social development beyond the foresight, awareness, or control of individual agents, is one which has its influence on Green. But that emphasis is equally to be found in the classical economists; the cunning of reason is only a glove for Adam Smith's 'invisible hand' (cf. 1.7); and classical economics would have informed the stork of concepts of any educated man. So the logic of unintended consequences cannot be chained exclusively to some supposedly Hegelian aspect of Green's thought. There is, moreover, a definite discontinuity between Green and Hegel concerning, as Green saw it, the Hegelian idealization of the state. 'Hegel's account of . . . the state does not seem to correspond to the facts of society as it is, or even as, under the unalterable conditions of human nature, it ever could be', Green writes in an oft-quoted passage (Works II, 314; HM, 233). The problem of how far actual states embody the ideal nature of the state, an embodiment on which political obligation depends, was to exercise later idealists— particularly Bosanquet in *The Philosophical Theory of the State* (1899). Green's indebtedness to Hegel is tenuous at the very point, in political philosophy, at which it has usually been regarded as closest.

In ethics the utility of Hegel to Green was yet more limited. It may well be that the question is serious enough whether there can be such a thing as Hegelian ethics. The root of this question returns to the idea of the ethical primacy of persons. From the moral point of view, the claim runs, persons possess central value, whether for example as children of God and repositories of immortal souls in Christian ethics, or as rational autonomous agents in Kantian ethics. Kant captured this idea of the ethical primacy of persons in his second formulation of the categorical imperative: that we should treat humanity always as an end and never merely as a means. But in Hegelian terms, human beings or persons possess only a distinctly inferior grade of individuality and value. On the Hegelian theory of individuality, value is determined by individuality and human beings are highly imperfect individuals. A far greater degree of individuality belongs to a social system: perfect individuality pertains solely to the Absolute.

I am not certain that this attempt to rule out the possibility of Hegelian ethics quite succeeds. Kant grounds the primacy of persons on the moral value of free, rational choice: but social systems might possess properties which make social choice more rational than that of individual persons. In advance of some far-reaching arguments on the emergent properties of social systems, I do not see how the possibility of Hegelian ethics can be closed. What is certain, however, is that Green differs fundamentally from Hegel on the primacy of persons. For Green, persons possess the highest value of which we have knowledge. The Italian commentator, F. M. Bongioanni, observes that Green's ethics takes its point of departure from the concept of a person ('prende lo spunto dal concetto di persona').[70] I think that we can specify that point of departure more particularly.

In the first place, the concept of a person is a boundary concept for Green. On final review, Green insists, all values are values 'for, of or in a person' (PE, § 184, HM, 256). There is a social basis to personal worth since 'society . . . is the condition of all development of our personality' (PE § 183; HM, 256, cp. Works III, 116–17). This fits well with Hegel's animadversions on 'abstrakten Personlichkeit' (*Philosophy of Right* § 37). But Green still presents an ethical and axiological ultimacy of persons which stands in obtrusive contrast to Hegel. 'Our ultimate standard of worth is an ideal of *personal* worth' (PE § 184; HM, 256). The break with Hegel is decisive.

Secondly, Green's moral psychology is an exploration of personality. True, we do not find in Green the sorts of discussion which we encounter in contemporary philosophy: discussions on the coherence of the idea of a disembodied person, on the logical primitiveness of the concept of a person, on the physical criteria of personal identity. Central to Green's moral psychology, however, is the idea of a person's critical relation to his own desires: of the ability which a self-conscious agent has to distance himself from his desires and create a rational structure of desire—to become, in other words, a certain kind of person. The idea of this critical relation is a point on which Hegel's influence is traceable: from *Encyclopaedia* § 476 to PE, Book II is a valid step in the interpretation of Green. But the Hegelianization of Green's moral psychology is limited by the fact that Hegel has very little to say about this area of individual psychology or 'subjective mind'.[71] What he does say may still be interesting; but the full detail of Green's account of desire, reason, character, motive, and action cannot be read as a straight transcript of Hegel's summary treatment of individual psychology.

Finally, the defence of free will is quite different in Green and

---

[70] F. M. Bongioanni, ' "Prolegomena to Ethics" di T. H. Green', *Rivista di Filosofia*, Rome, 1936, 118.

[71] J. N. Findlay, *Hegel's Philosophy of Mind*, tr. W. Wallace and A. V. Miller, Oxford, 1971, Foreword xvi–xvii; D. N. Robertson, *Toward a Science of Human Nature*, New York, 1982, 117.

Hegel. Hegel's defence centres on the claim that teleological explanations of human action are more comprehensive and coherent than the 'mechanical' explanations of physical determinism. Green's defence, his formulation of the 'self-conscious principle', retorts upon empiricism its serial view of the mind. Still, there is a further point. Green's statement of his 'self-conscious principle' in PE, Book I is followed by a metaphysical argument for the identity of thought and reality. This identity is a familiar Hegelian claim; and Green holds Hegel's treatment of intelligibility as the criterion of reality to be distinctly a strength of his system. But Green's own argument proceeds through an account of the relational nature of reality which is set sharply against Locke's empiricist view of relations. Green may reach a Hegelian conclusion but he does so by a line of argument which is very much his own.

In short, then, in religion, politics, and ethics, I do not deny Hegel's influence on Green; I aim simply to correct the excessive scope claimed for it.

1.14 THE MIDDLE YEARS

I have mentioned Green's uncertainty in the early 1860s whether to continue in academic life. It was, I have suggested, the deep-seated need to counteract adverse doctrines with full theoretical rigour (as opposed to the purely practical effectiveness of such figures as John Bright, or the merely polemical engagement of such writers as Carlyle) which drew Green inexorably into philosophy. Green's professional career in philosophy suffered two reverses in the 1860s. In 1864 he failed to obtain the professorship of Moral Philosophy at St Andrews; and in 1867 he applied for the Waynflete Professorship at Oxford but was defeated by Henry Chandler. He was irked by his failure at St Andrews, and not solely because it checked his professorial ambitions. Green attributed his setback to local manoeuvres which, from Oxford, he was unable to neutralize. Disappointment sat hard. 'I find that in order to give oneself a fair chance, all sorts of private agencies have to be set to work.'[72] Seriously harmful to his chances,

[72] Nettleship, 'Notes'.

Green particularly noted, was the sedulously propagated rumour that 'I carry Comtism and materialism to a degree hitherto unknown at Oxford.'[73] Though the rumour was without a scintilla of justification, Green was vulnerable to this kind of assault through his lack of published work. Between the reverses of 1864 and 1867, however, his career advanced. In 1866, on the death of James Riddell, he was appointed a Tutor at Balliol, and on Jowett's election to the Mastership in 1870 and the retirement of Edwin Palmer, Green undertook, in his own words, the 'whole subordinate management of the college'.[74] His professorial ambitions were realized in 1878 when he succeeded J. R. T. Eaton as White's Professor of Moral Philosophy.

Green married Charlotte Symonds in 1871. Charlotte was the sister of John Addington Symonds, whose friendship with Green dated from the late 1850s when Symonds was an undergraduate at Magdalen. Symonds was zestfully homosexual but he was capable of non-sexual friendships; his relationship with Green was certainly not homosexual. Green received specific advice from this unlikely quarter on the proper approach to Charlotte. Symonds thought that Green might exert himself more winsomely in the small talk of courtship. When Symonds pointed this out, Green 'turned rather rough' and answered: 'I am a *royal* nature!'[75] Green always wanted to be taken on his own terms. Even in courtship he could not present a façade for the sake of gaining favour. But Charlotte accepted him as he was. His courtship prospered; and in the ensuing marriage Green's friends marked a shade of change in his demeanour as if a tension had been removed. The sexual nature of their relationship is enveloped in a shroud of uncertainty which I shall not disturb by conjecture. There were no children. Charlotte was intelligent and supportive rather than a close intellectual companion. Green followed philosophical and political activities while Mrs Green ran the home and conducted good works among the poor. Charlotte's father made a marriage settlement of £10,000 a small fortune in Victorian terms. A man of economical habits, Green bade farewell from the start of his married life to all financial anxieties.

[73] Nettleship, 'Notes'.
[74] Nettleship, *Memoir*, cvii.
[75] J. A. Symonds, Recollections.

His health was sound until the late 1870s, but in 1879 the first symptoms of congenital heart disease began to show. From the autumn of that year he was a prey to attacks of sleeplessness and giddiness. *Prolegomena to Ethics*, which was written mainly in this period, was a race against time. During the winter of 1881–2 his health became worse and for considerable periods he was inactive. His book was nearly finished, however, and he believed that the move to a new house in Oxford might help his recovery. The move was never made. He was taken ill on 15 March 1882 and died on 26 March. When lucid in his final hours he talked politics, referring among other matters to the Irish Land Bill and to Bulgarian affairs. 'At 9 a.m. on Sunday 26th he passed away quietly', Mrs Green writes in her Vita, 'quite unconscious of the morning light which he had asked to see if he lived till then.'[76]

1.15 PERSONAL TRAITS

The biographical material held at Balliol, mainly in the form of letters written to Nettleship or to Mrs Green after her husband's death, brings little of a strikingly personal nature to light. Photographs of Green as a young man show a pallid, handsome face and raven black hair. Later photographs suggest a stolidity which is less pleasing. Essentially a private man, Green had few friends. 'His chief concern', said C. S. Parker, 'was to satisfy his own mind.'[77] This appears to have carried over even into social conversation in later life. 'I have sometimes seen him,' W. L. Newman recalled, 'when something was said which called for reflection, walk to the common room fire from his seat in the circle, and after leaning his head against the mantlepiece for a moment, make some remark which went to the heart of the matter.'[78] Such remarks would have been uttered in the soft, clear, northern accent which he always retained. His normal dress was black and grey. This, thought Newman, 'suited him well and was true to his character. He was drawn to plain people—to people of the middle and lower class rather than of

[76] C. B. Green, Vita, Bibliography II. The death certificate in St Catherine's House, London, lists ulcerated tonsils (10 days) and pyemia (4 days) as the causes of death.

[77] Parker, Recollections.

[78] W. L. Newman, Recollections, 27 Nov. 1882, Bibliography II.

the upper, to the Puritans of the past and the Nonconformists of the present, to Germans, to all that is sober-suited and steady-going.'[79] But perhaps the last word may be given to one of the more interesting biographical items, J. A. Symonds's 1882 letter to Mrs Green.

In the face of Symond's sexual idiosyncrasies and the decline of his literary reputation, which has undergone almost a complete eclipse, one might suppose Symonds is of greater interest than his own writings. But this would be a mistake. As a writer Symonds needs to be worked at: good sense and shrewd perception are embedded to the point of concealment in an elaborate and florid style. Few writers have illuminated subjects as disparate as Antinous as T. H. Green. Nettleship is not to be replaced but supplemented. Symonds's reminiscences stand to Nettleship's *Memoir* as an impressionistic sketch to a careful portrait. Nettleship's closest relations with Green dated from the late 1860s. Those relations were mainly academic and philosophical; and in the *Memoir* he was consciously writing for posterity. The uniform dull dignity of Nettleship's portrait is relieved by Symonds's recollections of a friendship which stretched back to the 1850s and had slight connection with academic life or philosophy.

The Green of Symonds's recollections is epigrammatic, vehement, caustic, mocking; and this is as much his authentic voice as the gravitas of his measured pronouncements. Even friends could be treated with the most sovereign contempt. 'Little Barnes will not get his First—it is almost a pity he should bother about it.'[80] Thus in 1860 did Symonds, who at this time carried the nickname of 'Barnes', overhear his own chances being misassessed. Nettleship does not suppress this side of Green, but he misinterprets it as an aspect of youthful severity which gradually softened. Yet the sharp steel of Green's tongue was as active in 1880 as in 1860. Symonds identifies another trait in Green's inability to turn the sides of his thought quickly in response to criticism and query. Henry Sturt's perception is incomplete when he observes: 'Apart from certain fundamentals Green was a hesitating, irresolute, one might almost say a timorous thinker, the sort of mind that is easily nonplussed by

---

[79] Newman, ibid.
[80] J. A. Symonds, Recollections.

objections from a critical pupil.'[81] Sturt does not recount the anecdote from Thomas Case on which this observation is based.[82] The real point is that Green could not divide his philosophy into small blocks for swift distribution in argument. He would have been equally nonplussed by the enthusiastic questions of a disciple.

1.16 PHILOSOPHICAL WORK

How did Green, occupied as a professional philosopher from the mid-1860s with the three main areas which we have identified, and open to the kinds of influence which we have sketched, engage his enemies?

We have cited Green's 1866 essay on 'The Philosophy of Aristotle'. His next publication, and his first significant polemic against adverse doctrines, was 'Popular Philosophy in its Relation to Life', published in the *North British Review* in March 1868. The 'popular philosophy' at which he takes aim includes the views of a broad variety of philosophers from Hobbes, Bacon, and Locke, through Butler and Burke, to Hume. Hume already figures in this article as Green's principal target. He reserves for Hume the respect which in a later but equally mordacious opposition F. H. Bradley reserved for Russell. Green saw Hume as having brought empiricism a thoroughgoing consistency unmatched by any other thinker. As Green regarded empiricism as philosophically bankrupt, he correspondingly regarded the work of Hume as a *reductio ad absurdum* of empiricism. It is in this context that the famous 'Introductions to Hume', Green's first extended publication, must be read.

Green had abandoned at least four major literary projects: the translation of Baur,[83] translations of Aristotle's *de Anima* and, in association with Edward Caird, of the *Nicomachean Ethics*, also

---

[81] H. Sturt, 258.

[82] Sturt refers to 'the President of Corpus' as his source of information: Thomas Case (1844–1925), elected President of Corpus Christi College, Oxford, in 1904. Case was at Balliol, 1863–7; Green was his Greats tutor.

[83] It is doubtful whether Green's intention was ever to produce a complete translation independently. On the evidence of his 12 Dec. 1869 letter to A. H. Clough (see Bibliography III), Green's idea was to start a translation to which others would contribute. This collaboration failed to materialize.

the translation of Hegel. In 1874–5 he published in conjunction with T. H. Grose the philosophical works of Hume.[84] The division of labour appears to have been that Grose confined himself to textual revision and to the essay, 'History of the Editions', prefaced to the *Essays Moral, Political, and Literary*. Green supplied the philosophical commentary: the two Introductions to the *Treatise of Human Nature*, destructive analyses of great power, are wholly his work.

Green's criticism was widely respected. Mark Pattison might mock that Green's 'Introductions to Hume' are longer than the text which they introduce,[85] but Green enjoyed even in the heyday of idealism from 1880 to 1920 a greater reputation for critical exegesis of Hume's philosophical works than as an original philosopher. Selby-Bigge's scepticism about the full justice of Green's attack on Hume was largely disregarded.[86] Green's critical reputation survived even into the 1930s. Stuart Hampshire records that when he began the study of philosophy at Oxford in 1933, Green's 'Introductions' were generally regarded as a complete refutation of Humean scepticism.[87] So recent a commentator as J. H. Randall refers to Green eulogistically as 'the keenest critical mind to appear in England since Hume', while comparatively devaluing Green's constructive position as 'by far the weaker side of his thought'.[88] The 'Introductions' have two main flaws. They are polemical and engaged, offering not a cautious, meditative commentary on

[84] Thomas Hodge Grose (1845–1906). Grose's contribution was his only publication. 'He would speak modestly of his share in the work. He probably deserved more credit than he claimed; in any case, we have reason to be grateful to him for inducing the publishers to associate him with the late Professor T. H. Green.' E. Walker *et al.*, *Thomas Hodge Grose (In Memoriam)*, privately printed, Oxford, 1906.

The edition of Hume is complete save for 'An Abstract of a Treatise of Human Nature', 1740, and 'A Letter from a Gentleman to his Friend in Edinburgh', 1745.

[85] M. Pattison, 'Philosophy at Oxford', *Mind*, 1 (1876), 94.

[86] Norman Kemp Smith's two early papers on 'The Naturalism of Hume', *Mind*, 14 (1905) were the first serious intellectual challenge to Green's Humean criticism. L. A. Selby-Bigge's reference to Green occurs in his Introduction to the *Enquiries* (see 1st edn. Oxford, 1894, vii): 'Of Professor Green's criticism of Hume it is impossible to speak, here in Oxford, without the greatest respect. Apart from its philosophic importance, it is always serious and legitimate; but it is also impossible not to feel that it would have been quite as important and a good deal shorter, if it had contained fewer of the verbal victories which are so easily won over Hume.'

[87] Cited in *Hume: A Treatise of Human Nature*, ed. E. C. Mossner, Harmondsworth, 1969, 26–7.

[88] J. H. Randall, 'T. H. Green', 217, 218.

Hume but a committed and at times ungenerous rejection of his arguments and ideas; and they are too concerned with the relationship between Hume and his predecessors. Green sees Hume's work, in strict linear descent from Locke and Berkeley, as a systematic development of the distinctive contentions of empiricism to a final point of philosophical paradox and implausibility. This connects, of course, with the above point about 'bankruptcy'. But Hume is not only a systematizer and developer. He is also an originator as he realizes new problems, e.g. in causation and induction, barely glimpsed by his predecessors. This should not need saying, but against Green it does need to be said.[89] In this book I shall deal gentler justice to Green than Green extends to Hume. On one point Green's emphasis was precursive. Directing his thunder with especial vigour against the *Treatise*, he stressed the philosophical importance of the *Treatise* at the expense of the *Enquiries*. Contemporaries such as Edgeworth, seeing the *Enquiries* as less deficient in clarity and arrangement and as containing Hume's second thoughts, considered that this reversed the correct order of philosophical importance.[90] But Green's emphasis has been decisively confirmed by the subsequent trend of Hume studies.

Against empiricism, then, Green wrote his 'Introductions to Hume'. Against utilitarianism and other errors as he saw them in ethics, he laboured in his *magnum opus, Prolegomena to Ethics*. This is based mainly on his carefully prepared professorial lectures from 1878 onwards. It is a text with a chequered history, interrupted in its composition not only by the General Election of 1880 but also by Green's failing health. Knowing that he might soon die and caught in a familiar problem for any philosopher when a crucial first inspiration has to expand out into lines of detailed argument, he summed up his feelings to his eldest sister in August 1879:

I have been getting a little writing done, preparatory to a book on Moral Philosophy, but as soon as I seriously begin it, I find how long it will take to do what I want to do, and how little equal I am to it. Writing now is very different from what it was ten years ago. Then there were

[89] Douglas Muirden has brought home to me afresh the one-sidedness of the 'linear-tradition' view of Hume.

[90] F. Y. Edgeworth, *New and Old Methods of Ethics, or 'Physical Ethics' and 'Methods of Ethics'*, Oxford and London, 1877, 84.

much larger vistas of possibility, and I thought I had hold of a key which I find now will not unlock so much as I fancied it would. But I must make a push now, or I shall leave the world with nothing done.[91]

Green's work had previously been chiefly a matter of the thorough, scholarly, provocative critique of other philosophers. Now he had to express his own vision of the moral life. That the task came hard is further evidence that Green is not a moralist telling us how to live but a moral philosopher telling us how to know how to live. The text did not receive his final revision, however, since he had cleared only §§ 1–100 of the manuscript when he died. This portion of the text had been submitted to *Mind*; it was published in three articles between January and July 1882. The full text was edited by A. C. Bradley, as Green had requested in his will, and published posthumously in 1883. Bradley's editorial role was limited to revising some minor imperfections of form and style and to dividing the text into books and chapters.

Green's political philosophy was formulated chiefly in another professorial lecture course (1879–80) and edited by Nettleship under the title of 'Lectures on the Principles of Political Obligation' in Works II. The text of Nettleship's edition, though careful, is not absolutely dependable; and an improved text has been published by Paul Harris and John Morrow.[92]

A further literary project should be mentioned. Green was the senior member of a group formed in the mid-1870s to translate Hermann Lotze's *Logic* and *Metaphysics*. The translation was completed under Bosanquet's editorship in 1884. We shall probably never know the exact provenance of this project, whether Green initiated it or, more importantly, to what advantages he specially looked from the dissemination of Lotze's ideas. Nettleship suggests that part of Lotze's attraction to Green was his critical distance from Hegel. But this does not go to the bottom of the vital question. In the review of John Caird's *Introduction to the Philosophy of Religion* to which Nettleship points to support this claim, Green's belief is that Hegel's philosophy develops into esoteric and dubious complexities which few people will want to go into and on which

[91] Nettleship, 'Notes'.

[92] *T. H. Green: Lectures on the Principles of Political Obligation and Other Writings*, ed. P. Harris and J. Morrow, Cambridge, 1986.

his essential insight into the identity of thought and reality does not depend. This may have marked a new phase in the public expression of Green's own distance from Hegel. But that distance was no greater than before. Nor is it easy to see why, in order to vindicate this belief, the entire round of Lotze's *Logic* and *Metaphysics* should need to be translated. My own—tentative—view is essentially that of J. T. Merz.[93] Green owed no deep, formative influence to Lotze. He was impressed to discover that Lotze had independently come to the same basic conclusion as himself concerning the relational nature of reality.

The main focus of the present book is Green's ethics and specifically his moral psychology. The material to hand regarding Green's ethics, apart from the texts already cited, is the residue of his Works, published under Nettleship's editorship (1885–8) and containing, besides the 'Introductions' and the *Principles of Political Obligation*, a wide variety of articles and lecture courses. (The complete contents of the Works are listed in the bibliography.) Finally there are the Green Papers held at Balliol. The Balliol MSS include, unsurprisingly, much of the material published in the Works, but also unpublished material on Plato, Aristotle, Kant, and Hegel. None of the unpublished material is of a nature radically to alter the interpretation of Green's philosophy, at least in the areas with which we are chiefly concerned. But its supplementary value is considerable and use will be made of it.

I.17 THE IMPACT OF GREEN'S PHILOSOPHY

Green's philosophy excited far-flung comment. Initial attention was intense. Nearly every major philosopher between 1880 and 1910 made some response to Green. Edward Caird, R. L. Nettleship, Henry Sidgwick, Bernard Bosanquet, among names we have already mentioned, but also H. A. Prichard (who still criticized Green into the 1930s), G. E. Moore, A. E. Taylor, S. Alexander, J. S. Mackenzie, G. F. Stout, all expressed views.[94] Even the reserved Oxford Aristotelian, Ingram Bywater,

---

[93] J. T. Merz, *A History of European Thought in the Nineteenth Century*, iv, 3rd edn. Edinburgh and London, 1914, 218–9.
[94] See Bibliography V.

contrived a neat incision with his pronounced distaste for 'philosophers who say "imply" '.[95] In economic theory, in the time taken for disjointed snippets of philosophy to filter through to the general culture, Alfred Marshall included in the 1895 edition of his *Principles of Economics* a reference to Green's views on the measurement of pleasure and pain.

We earlier encountered a reference to 'the disciples of Green' (1.13). Discipleship is not a precise notion. Mackenzie, Muirhead, and Charles D'Arcy very largely accepted Green's ethical argument and conclusions. One would like to know more about Francis Peters, who translated the *Nicomachean Ethics* sympathetically in the light of Green's moral psychology. W. L. Courtney's critique of J. S. Mill cannot be properly understood save in close connection with Green's ideas.[96] Vaguer lines of influence extend to Henry Scott-Holland and . J. R. Illingworth.

Green's influence was not merely national, though the European interest is not always what it seems. If in such works as A. Grieve's *Das geistige Prinzip in der Philosophie Thomas Hill Greens* (Leipzig, 1896) and G. F. James's *Green und der Utilitarismus* (Halle, 1894) the language is German, the writers are not. They simply travelled to Germany in order to demolish Green more effectively. Alexander Grieve was a Kelso Scot; G. F. James was an American, a Mid-Westerner from Normal, Illinois. German philosophers in the last century tended to regard British idealism somewhat disdainfully as a pale reflection of the idealist tradition of Kant and Hegel; and these students did nothing to disturb that impression. In the United States Green was a prime influence on George Sylvester Morris and on the early Dewey. To Morris, Green leapt like a bright flame against the blackness of British empiricism.[97] Beyond the United States Green's impact was delayed. Italian interest arose mainly in the 1920s and 1930s when the British interest of Bosanquet, R. G. Collingwood, J. A. Smith, and H. J. Paton in Italian idealism awakened in turn the curiosity of Italian philosophers about British idealism. A number of articles marked in 1936 the centenary of Green's birth. French attention

[95] R. R. Marett, *A Jerseyman at Oxford*, Oxford, 1941, 110–11.
[96] W. L. Courtney, *The Metaphysics of John Stuart Mill*, London, 1879.
[97] M. E. Jones, *George Sylvester Morris*, New York, 1968, 7.

to Green, first evidenced in Parodi's 1896 article, enjoyed a florescence in the 1950s and 1960s.

Perhaps the least expected centre of interest in Green is Japan. Here the growth point was Rikizo Nakashima's 1892 lecture, 'On British Kantians', delivered at the University of Tokyo. Publications on Green began in 1895 with Kitaro Nishida's article on 'The Ethics of T. H. Green'. Japanese interest has followed two main directions, religious and political. The religious angle, exhibited in Nishida's attempt to connect Zen Buddhism with Green's ideas on self-realization, appears also in the work of Tsunashina Ryosen. Self-realization is the main notion on which Eijiro Kawai relied in *The System of Thought of T. H. Green* (2 vols., Tokyo, 1930) in which he mounted an idealist critique of capitalism. More recently a spate of articles since the mid-1970s has covered a significant range of Green's political philosophy.[98]

Although the level of British attention to Green has subsided drastically, the *Principles of Political Obligation* has continued to enjoy a mild celebrity. This residual interest involves a degree of artificial severance, for Green's political philosophy supervenes on a view of the moral life from which its whole point derives (1.4 but cf. 8.1). Two postwar books devoted wholly to Green, Ann Cacoullos's (*Thomas Hill Green: Philosopher of Rights* and I. M. Greengarten's *Thomas Hill Green and the Development of Liberal-Democratic Thought*, both concerned with his political philosophy, appeared in 1974 and 1981 respectively. Neither text disregards the connection between politics and ethics in Green, but my own view is that since in crucial matters Green's moral philosophy has only begun to come into focus, both Cacoullos and Greengarten risk an unreliable connection. On an incidental note, Iris Murdoch in her rare excursions into political philosophy is held by the critic G. S. Fraser to have been markedly influenced by Green.[99]

On Green's ethics the only significant contributions since 1940 have been those of C. A. Campbell and H. D. Lewis.[100]

[98] This account of Green studies in Japan derives from S. Yukiyasu and Y. Fujiwara, 'The Impact of T. H. Green's Moral and Political Philosophy on Modern Japan', a typescript of which is held at Balliol College, Oxford. I am grateful to Alan Tadiello for calling my attention to this paper.

[99] G. S. Fraser, *The Modern Writer and His World*, London, 1964, 184–5.

[100] See Bibliography V.

A recent text by P. Gordon and J. White, *Philosophers as Educational Reformers: the Influence of Idealism on British Educational Thought and Practice* (1979), is hard to subsume under a neat category, since although it lucidly expounds in broad detail Green's metaphysics, philosophy of religion, ethics, and political philosophy, it does so not primarily by way of critical assessment but as an exercise in the history of ideas. It is not concerned directly with the validity of Green's philosophical ideas and their relevance to present-day problems but (as the title suggests) with their influence on educational reform.

Green's reputation soared, dipped, and plummeted. But we can say more than this. In the first place, it is possible to mark certain stages within the general decline. The constructive epistemology and metaphysics of PE, Book I attracted severe criticism from the very start. A flurry of polemical attention from A. J. Balfour, H. Calderwood, J. E. Creighton, A. Eastwood, G. T. Ladd, and others, persisted till the turn of the century, then spent itself and ceased almost abruptly. The reception of Green's ethics was slightly distracted by the prior publication of F. H. Bradley's *Ethical Studies* (1876) which, falling within the same idealist tradition of moral philosophy, is written in a far more striking and rhetorical style. But after the criticisms of Moore and Sidgwick at the turn of the century, Green's ethics still attracted serious discussion into the 1920s and 1930s in the writings of Prichard, Carritt, and W. D. Lamont. Green's political philosophy, as we have seen, still receives a degree of attention. Secondly, among the major critics of Green's ethics, our chief concern in this book, at least three types of appraisal are discernible.

In the first place, there is a line of criticism associated with Edward Caird and R. L. Nettleship that Green is coherent but incomplete.[101] Some incompleteness is evident. *Prolegomena to Ethics*, as indicated above, was not finally prepared for publication by Green himself. There are loose ends in the text; topics are scheduled but not in fact taken up. For example, the analysis of the concept of freedom promised in PE § 100 does not materialize, and according to § 156 an exposition of Kant should accompany that of utilitarianism but in the text it does not do so. Certain topics are almost wholly neglected or but

---

[101] Nettleship, *Memoir*; E. Caird, 'Professor Green's Last Work', *Mind*, 8 (1883).

lightly touched upon. Green underlines but has little distinctly explicit to say about the unity of the virtues. The charge of incompleteness is of ambiguous validity, however. For sometimes it holds good only for *Prolegomena to Ethics*. If, for example, the analysis of freedom is a lacuna in PE, the deficiency is supplied by the essay, 'On the Different senses of "Freedom" as Applied to Will and to the Moral Progress of Man', prefixed by Nettleship to PPO, so the material exists elsewhere in Green's total corpus to fill the gap. But the subject of the unity of the virtues is not fully considered anywhere in Green's work, published or unpublished. Aside from this matter of incompleteness, however, Caird and Nettleship claimed, quite correctly I think, to be able to trace firm and consistent main lines of argument in Green's moral philosophy.

Secondly, on the far different approach of Sidgwick and Prichard (from their disparate viewpoints),[102] Green is so radically confused that no coherent doctrine is traceable in his work. For these philosophers, Green's whole philosophy is so riven with ambiguities and inconsistencies as to collapse under scrutiny. Sidgwick's name has occurred more than once already; and this is the proper place to examine the friendship between the two men.

Green's friendship with Sidgwick is one of the curiosities of philosophy. My own view, implicit in my characterization just now of Sidgwick's response to Green, is that Sidgwick exaggerated its intellectual depth. After Rugby the relationship largely lapsed during their undergraduate days at different universities, but was revived by a holiday in Switzerland in 1862. Although Sidgwick refers to a 'real interpenetration of thought on philosophical subjects',[103] it is difficult to trace anything but complete and unavailing antipathy in the developing pattern of their views. In the early 1860s, the phase of what Sidgwick calls his 'crude and confident' utilitarianism, the exchange of views was barren, even acrimonious, on Sidgwick's own admission. In later years Sidgwick recognized Green's informed touch in political matters, but there is no evidence that the philosophical deadlock was lifted. 'If we engaged in discussion on a political

---

[102] See Bibliography V.
[103] All quotations from Sidgwick in this paragraph are taken from his 'Recollections', see Bibliography II.

question, I always felt that the chances were that before long his superior grasp and insight would force me to retreat from the position I had taken up. But I do not remember having any similar feeling as regards philosophical discussions.' Finally, the tone of Sidgwick's published criticisms of Green is untypical of a philosophical friendship. As Bosanquet perceptively remarked, Sidgwick adopted the attitude of a (hostile) reviewer rather than that of a (sympathetic) critic, concentrating narrowly on the text before him without reference to other passages of possible relevance.[104] From the other side, Green nowhere, either in his published work or in the Balliol MSS, takes cognizance of Sidgwick's subtle and elaborate revision of utilitarianism in *Methods of Ethics*. Since Green regarded utilitarianism as quite fundamentally mistaken, for reasons which we have examined (1.7), he must equally have regarded any reconstruction of it, however acutely pursued, as finally wasted labour. His discussion of Sidgwick's views in PE, §§ 364–71 simply applies his general critique of utilitarianism, mainly the anti-hedonist attack, to a text in which nineteenth-century utilitarianism received its greatest, if not absolutely its final, development. There was undoubtedly intellectual respect between Green and Sidgwick, but the case for a 'real interpenetration of thought on philosophical subject' is not proven—at most.

The third approach, which I connect chiefly with G. E. Moore and A. E. Taylor, again from different standpoints, is that coherent lines of argument are traceable in Green but that these are pellucidly wrong. Caird and Nettleship assumed that there was nothing essentially at fault with Green's moral philosophy, only that it was, at least in its statement, regrettably incomplete. But Moore alleged that Green's whole approach, of 'metaphysical ethics' as Moore called it in *Principia Ethica*, was vitiated by the naturalistic fallacy; and Taylor, as we shall see in 3.14, argued that Green's 'metaphysic of knowledge' in PE, Book I was barren for practical ethical purposes in a way which defeated Green's intentions. Taylor's argument is radically uncomprehending. The real relation of metaphysics to ethics in Green's philosophy is not remotely what Taylor supposes it to be; and the naturalistic fallacy, on which Moore's criticism

---

[104] B. Bosanquet, Critical Notice of Sidgwick (1902), *Mind*, 12 (1903), 381–2.

principally relies, has proven to be an insubstantial base from which to attack any philosophical position. If the naturalistic fallacy is not itself fallacious, its application to Green quite fails. The 'naturalistic fallacy' is Moore's term for any attempt to define the language of morals in non-moral terms. 'Good', for example, cannot mean 'such as to satisfy some desire', 'productive of the greatest happiness', 'conducive to the survival of the fittest', because the question remains open whether any of these things are good. Since, for example, 'it satisfies some desire, but is it good?' is an intelligible question, therefore 'good' cannot mean 'such as to satisfy some desire'. Exactly matching that question, the offending passage in Green is taken to be PE, § 171, 'the common characteristic of the good is that it satisfies some desire.'[105] But Green nowhere avows or implies that 'good' means 'such as to satisfy some desire'; he is interested not in the meaning of a word but in the criterion of goodness. He tells us something, penetrating or otherwise, about good things, not about the meaning of a word.

1.18 METHODOLOGY

My own approach comes closest to that of Caird and Nettleship. Any other approach I should find a distinct crux in a modern work on Green. Green's philosophy is now widely unfamiliar. There is no clear value in re-introducing it for the sake of demolition. The force and relevance of Green's contribution are for the rest of the book to show. Here is a matter which each reader will have to decide for himself or herself. But a philosopher as severely out of cognizance as Green had better be left unless we are able to offer sympathetic criticism and to try at least for a constructive result.

To go further, Green's ideas do constitute a system, a net-work of significant coherence and complexity. That bare consideration, however, I should not regard as a decisive reason for attending to his work. An extra requirement is to be imposed, which can I think be met, that this system of ideas suggests insights into the problems with which it is concerned,

---

[105] G. E. Moore, *Principia Ethica*, Cambridge, 1903, 139.

with the further requirement again that these problems connect with our own concerns. This last requirement can never be fulfilled exactly in the case of a historical system, since philosophy, whether or not progressive, none the less 'moves on'. The problems of a nineteenth-century philosopher cannot be the precise problems of the present day. (Marx has more in common with J. S. Mill than either has with a contemporary philosopher.) It argues no disrespect for a philosopher if in recovering his ideas we are sensitive to his actual concerns and more sensitive still to the needs of the present. This is, I should argue, the spirit of Green's own remark that 'each generation requires the questions of philosophy to be put to it in its own language, and, unless they are so put, will not be at pains to understand them' (Works I, 373). If one aim of this chapter has been to deny a too easy transition from Green's personal concerns to his philosophical tasks, one aim of the next will be to show how the contemporary relevance of Green's philosophy differs from its historical surface. In Green's criticism of utilitarianism, for example, the main burden is carried by his anti-hedonist and logical object arguments, but if we dip below the surface of Green's text his views open more interesting perspectives on utilitarianism. The ideas are Green's, the emphasis is mine. I shall claim briefly, at the end of the book, that Green is also instructive on a point of philosophical method with regard to the practical relevance of philosophy (9.3).

A word as to critics and commentaries. References to the secondary literature occur but are not frequent in the text. This is not solely because I have been concerned to build my own interpretation of Green, to make up my own mind about his philosophy and its bearing on current issues. Plainly that consideration has applied, yet fresh and independent interpretation may sometimes be aided by the secondary literature as one defines one's own position in sharp and detailed opposition to an established view. When I had worked through the secondary literature, however, the conclusion was inescapable that on Green's moral philosophy nothing in that literature matched the status of, say, Howard Warrender's work on Hobbes, John Mackie's on Locke, J. P. Plamenatz's or G. A. Cohen's on Marx. Some of the secondary literature has been cited and appraised already. We may extend the appraisal.

W. H. Fairbrother's *The Philosophy of T. H. Green* (1896), which is lucid and broadly reliable, offers a good introduction. It is, however, philosophically unexciting, being in the main a popular epitome—an exposition of Green's views for a general, educated late-nineteenth-century public.

Melvin Richter's *The Politics of Conscience: T. H. Green and his Times* (1964), an excellent study in the sociology of knowledge, scrupulously relates arguments and ideas to their sources in social interests and cultural pressures. No detraction from Richter's achievement lies in the consideration that he avoids a living philosophical confrontation with Green. His book has the full atmosphere of *post-mortem* examination. A somewhat unexpected position in Green interpretation is occupied by Jean Pucelle's *La Nature et l'esprit dans la philosophie de T. H. Green* (1961, 1965); the work of a French historian of philosophy is the most comprehensive commentary on Green. But crucially, Pucelle's text is a work of pure scholarship. He produces no new lines of philosophical interpretation and, offering a conspectus of Green's entire philosophy, he exhibits no overriding concern with the topics in ethics and moral psychology which are the main focus of the present book.

A wide selection of the secondary literature is listed in the bibliography,[106] but I have not felt constrained to mark every point on which I differ from one commentator or another. Maurice Cranston's ascription to Green of the view that freewill involves motiveless action is noticed in this paragraph only. Its significance may be allowed gently to evanesce as the book proceeds.[107] On the whole I have argued back explicitly against particular critics only when, from the wide readership of their works, an incorrect picture of Green is likely to have been transmitted influentially, or when a false interpretation marks a special crux.

1.19   PAST AND PRESENT

The historical preliminaries now completed I shall offer an

---

[106] On the political side my bibliography may usefully be supplemented by P. Harris and J. Morrow.

[107] M. Cranston, *Freedom: A New Analysis*, London, 1954, 171.

account of contemporary ethical theory and moral psychology to which Green's relevance will be explained. But a cautionary word must be entered. 'Contemporary ethical theory and moral psychology' may suggest a monolithic structure where none exists. Sharp differences of aim, assumption, and method divide the discussion of key issues such as the causal explanation of action and the explanatory power of intuitive psychology. At least three main topics may be identified, however; and the concept of action will control the initial discussion.

Ethics and Moral Psychology:
Contemporary Perspectives and Green

2.1 INTRODUCTION

IN this chapter I shall argue that significant continuities hold between Green's philosophy and the characteristic concerns of post-1945 Anglo-American philosophy. These continuities, which centre on ethical theory and moral psychology, involve three main topics: (1) the explanation of action, (2) the rationality of moral action, and (3) the nature of agency. I shall argue that Green offers a cogent alternative to the two standard models of action explanation, here termed the belief–desire theory and the cognitive model; that he sketches a subtle and plausible account of the rationality of moral action; and lastly that his account of agency both (i) discloses a more comprehensive view of the agent than is familiar, a view of the integral agent, and (ii) presents a challenge alike to Kantian and to utilitarian constructions of the traditional schema of motive, action, and consequence. These claims, outlined in the current chapter, will be specified more exactly and substantiated in the chapters which follow. They set out what I regard as the main significance for the present day of Green's philosophy.

More in detail our topics connect, and the argument of this chapter develops, through the concept of action. Central to contemporary ethics is an emphasis on moral thinking as practical. Practical thinking is directed specifically on action; it answers the question, 'what should I do?' One theory of action holds that decision-making that can explain action must cite two fundamental and exclusive factors, cognitive and conative. The cognitive relates, in large terms, to perception or reasoning which establishes matters of fact; it is linked essentially to the notion of truth. Call the cognitive factor 'belief'. The conative factor concerns fulfilment or frustration in view of the facts. Call this factor 'desire'. Then we have the belief–desire theory which insists that, however the agent decides to act, the explanation of his action must refer to two factors, his beliefs and desires. For the cognitive model, by contrast, belief is capable of producing action independently of desire. Theories of action explanation, divided in this way, set a particular angle on the rationality of moral action. For the cognitive model perception or reasoning, the cognitive factor, can both determine the ends of action (suppose these to be moral) and motivate the agent to pursue them. This can be done independently of desire; rationality passes into cognition. On the belief–desire theory any account of either the rationality of certain ends of action (suppose these again to be moral), or the possibility of pursuing them, depends inseparably on the agent's desires.

I shall suggest first that the belief–desire theory and the cognitive model are inadequate to an agent's critical relation to his own desires, a relation which I express in terms of 'self-intervention';[1] secondly that, as currently available, these approaches to action explanation confront the rationality of morals with partial, unsystematic theories of the human good. This is the ground covered by our first two topics, the explanation of action and the rationality of moral action. On the third topic, the nature of agency, I shall argue that the emphasis on action in contemporary moral philosophy, on morality as a matter of what a person should do, tends to restrict the view of cognition and conation, belief and desire, virtually to the point of action. The place of moral action in a structure of desire, or in a conception of oneself as a certain kind of person, is overlooked as the 'person' disappears, absorbed into the figure of the 'agent' on a highly narrow view of agency. If, moreover, we regard persons exclusively as agents, as sources of actions in this narrow way, then the claims of consequentialism are strengthened since actions produce states of affairs, and it appears irrational to prefer a worse to a better state of affairs. One implication of this, though others will appear, is that the agent can be 'controlled' by the consequences of his actions; the autonomy of this practical reason disappears.

Before we proceed, I must clarify some points of terminology.

[1] W. P. Alston, 'Self-Intervention and the Structure of Motivation', *The Self*, ed. T. Mischel, Oxford, 1977.

Various terms will appear in this book: 'person', 'self', 'agent', 'individual', 'human being'. The relevant notions are not precisely co-extensive; the context will generally indicate the senses in which the terms are used. Very roughly, a 'person' has certain beliefs, desires, and dispositions to emotion and behaviour; these comprise his 'self' (cf. 4.9). This self is revisable; as active in self-revision and in other ways the person is an 'agent', and in the narrow sense of 'agency', a source of actions in the external world. As an agent, he is related to other agents in a society; in relation to this society he is an individual. In what he values and in what satisfies him an agent is subject to constraints set by his humanity, by the fact that he is a 'human being'. 'Ethics' and 'moral philosophy' I use interchangeably; ethics divides into moral psychology (the main burden of Chapters 4 and 5) and ethical theory (the work of Chapters 6 and 7).

Then to resume: Green's full significance is not simply that he illuminates our three main topics, but that he draws them together in a coherent pattern of argument. At the centre of that pattern is the idea, referred to above, of an agent's critical relation to his own desires. But initially we must take contemporary moral philosophy as we find it: and we find it derected centrally on the concept of action.

2.2   ETHICS AND ACTION

The basic kind of action with which ethics is concerned is intentional action; and the connection with moral responsibility is that (very roughly) the conditions which defeat intentionality also defeat responsibility. If it was physically or logically impossible for me to do an action, or I lacked opportunity, then no intention of mine could have produced the action and I cannot be blamed for not doing it: I escape responsibility. I equally escape responsibility if I did the action but did not do it knowingly, since one can only act according to one's awareness of a situation: my intention cannot be informed by an awareness I do not have. Again, responsibility is defeated if I did an action but the action did not result from any choice of mine, but occurred by accident: just my action of bumping into you when the train jolts. This is not, of course, even in general terms a complete account of responsibility, since I may be responsible, in the one case, for my physical incapacity and, in the other, for my lack of awareness. But plainly an ethics which emphasizes moral thinking as practical, as speaking to the question, 'what should I do?' will be chiefly occupied with intentional actions because these are the only actions I can decide to do.

Then there are three necessary conditions of moral responsibility for an action:

(1) A was able to do X (or to refrain from doing X).
(2) A did X knowingly.
(3) A could have done otherwise, if he had chosen.

This is the minimal characterization of intentional action with which I shall begin; for shortness in referring to these conditions I shall omit 'or to refrain from doing X' as understood. Let us next look more closely at the concept of morality. If, for example, practical thinking answers the question, 'what should I do?' and an agent thinks that he should act on a certain principle, are there constraints on what can count as a moral principle? Formalists such as R. M. Hare hold that just anything can be a moral principle so long as the agent acts on it in relevant circumstances and allows that anyone else, similarly circumstanced, may so act: any principle satisfying these two conditions of prescriptivity and universalizability counts as a moral principle. Philippa Foot presents an opposing point of view in her insistence on constraints of content: that a moral principle 'must be connected with human good and harm, and ... it is quite impossible to call anything you like good and harm'.[2] This is no avoidable issue. If we are to consider the rationality of moral action, then we need some prior idea, a working concept, of moral action itself.

Considerations of human benefit and harm should not, in my view, be allowed to control the definition of morality. For suppose that, by agreed criteria of benefit and harm, someone acted consistently on a principle which paid no heed to such considerations. We should certainly want to say that such a person acted with integrity if he kept to his principle in face, say,

---

[2] P. R. Foot, 'Moral Beliefs', *Theories of Ethics*, Oxford, 1967, 92.

of physical threats or enticing inducements. But if this is a conceptual possibility, the fact remains that morality has typically been seen as answering the question, 'what should I do?' with a requirement to consider other agents' interests beyond the immediate solicitations of self-interest or inclination. This means no more than it says. It does not weight the scales against a view such as Hume's, which allows moral scope to inclination in the natural virtues, or a view such as Aristotle's, which connects morality with the agent's advantage on a theory of the human good. The point is simply that morality requires more of an agent than the bare inclination to help people when he is in a good mood, and that it is capable of sacrificing self-interest to justice if, for example, you and I are equally hungry and I share the cake evenly instead of secretly eating the whole thing. If we think, Platonically, that justice is the health of the soul and that acting justly cannot be contrary to self-interest, this certainly revises the relation of justice to self-interest: but it does nothing to show that justice is the health of the soul when the rationality of moral action is exactly the point at issue. The working concept of morality with which we shall proceed is one on which morality does admit the possibility of acting contrary both to inclination and to self-interest in the intuitively evident sense of our examples above. I accept the possibility of moral egoism, of the view that quite in general it is morally right for someone to pursue his own interests without consideration of others. But morality has not normally been understood egoistically. The question of the rationality of moral action is, for present purposes, the question of how a rational agent can be given cogent reasons for acting contrary to self-interest or inclination, in the sense of the above examples, in the promotion of other agents' interests. For brevity I shall generally express this simply as the question why he should be concerned how his actions affect others. That substantive question is what vitally matters to Green. It is central to a long tradition of ethical discussion; and it determines the principal lines on which the problem of the rationality of moral action is to be taken here.

To summarize: first, ethics is concerned with intentional action, for which the minimal conditions are that (physically and logically and by opportunity) the agent can do the action, that he does it knowingly, and that he can do otherwise if he chooses. Secondly, the debate on the rationality of moral action centres on the question why a rational agent should be concerned, in his intentional actions, how his actions affect others. This points the way ahead. We cannot decide the rationality of moral action without knowing how action can come about. How an agent should act depends on how he can act, on what is capable of determining his actions. This introduces our first main topic, the theory of action explanation.

2.3   THE BELIEF–DESIRE THEORY (1): THE EXPLANATION OF ACTION

The most familiar model of action explanation, which I here term the belief–desire theory, connects intentional action with the agent's beliefs and desires. This theory, deriving in its modern form from Hume (4.2), is more specifically the theory that intentional action results, and can only result, from the conjunction of antecedent desires and beliefs. 'Why did you slim?' 'I thought (believed) it would reduce the risk of heart strain and I wanted (desired) to reduce that risk.' Explicit statement of either the appropriate belief or the appropriate desire may be omitted in practical discourse, it might be conceded. In this nothing more significant is involved than ellipsis. But other points remain to be clarified.

The first point concerns the relevant notions of belief and desire. More precisely: in one sense of 'belief', belief contrasts with knowledge. But fairly emphatically no such contrast is any part of the point of this theory of action. Nor is 'belief' to be contrasted with 'conjecture', 'suspicion', 'certainty', 'surmise', and so forth across the span of cognitive states. Any mental state counts as a belief if its satisfaction condition is a state of affairs that makes it true or false. On the other side, it might sound odd to say that an agent's action can always be explained by reference to his desires since agents may do intentionally what they have no desire to do. 'I had no desire to go to Italy, but I had to — my career required it.' Moreover, we sometimes explain actions by reference to 'whims', 'velleities', 'cravings', 'yens', and so on, in nuanced contrast to 'desires'; and the term 'desire' itself is capable of a considerable latitude of signification. While points of this kind may be noted marginally, they offer little real embarrassment to the theory. Any mental state counts as a desire if its satisfaction condition is a state of affairs in which it is fulfilled or thwarted. Insensitivity to the niceties of usage, e.g. between 'whim' and 'desire', is therefore unimportant; and the possibility of acting contrary to one's desires, in the limited sense of the Italian example, is easy to accommodate by recourse to the kind of distinction made by Gewirth between 'inclinational' and 'intentional' desires and by Anscombe between the different descriptions under which one may both desire and not desire to do something that one does. The desires on which I shall concentrate are, in Gewirth's teminology, 'inclinational', that is desires which possess an intrinsic appeal prompting to action, rather than 'intentional', that is desires which, embodying some aim, may otherwise be unwelcome.[3] I want to apologize to the bully just to get out of his way (intentional desire); I want to see San Francisco Bay, which everybody agrees is a wonderful sight (inclinational desire).

Two further points about the theory may be handled more quickly. One is the question whether the belief–desire theory offers a causal explanation of action; the other concerns the scientific status and future of the intuitive, everyday psychology from which the notions of belief and desire are drawn. I pass by the causal question because my main criticism of the belief–desire theory is that it fails to capture something essential in a person's relation to his own desires; and nothing in that criticism depends on the question whether the theory is causal. On the issue of the status of intuitive, everyday psychology I simply offer two comments: first that the outcome of the debate is still uncertain, and secondly that the issue cannot be resolved within ethics. What I want to suggest is that a major defect of the belief–desire theory stems from a quite different source, a specific incompleteness which disqualifies it as a general theory of action. Far short of any confrontation with neuroscience and cognitive psychology it is inadequate to the everyday, intuitive phenomena over which it ranges.

I start by distinguishing different kinds of desire. Consider the following examples of desires which a person may have:

(1) Cedric wants to see the Belvedere Apollo.

[3] A. Gewirth, 'The Normative Structure of Action', *Review of Metaphysics*, 25 (1971), 240.

(2) Cedric wants to be respected for his deep ideas.

(3) Cedric wants to be a competitive achiever.

These desires fall clearly into different logical categories. In (1) Cedric wants simply the state of affairs which consists in his seeing the Belvedere Apollo; (2) involves a reference to other people's attitude to Cedric, that they should have a certain image of Cedric as worthy of respect for his deep ideas; (3) involves a reference to Cedric's self-image in regard not to other people's attitude to what Cedric is (namely worthy of respect) but to his own attitude to what he should become (namely a certain kind of person, a competitive achiever).

No such ranging of desires into categories, it might be held, could ground an attack on the belief–desire theory, since criticism of the theory on these lines ignores its ability to recognize logically different kinds of desire. On no construction does the belief–desire theory rely on the operation of desires, say, purely of type (1). This is true; it is nothing to the point. With desire-streams as cohesive as (1) to (3), the theory can handle the working of any one desire or of all desires in combination. The problem for the belief–desire theory comes when logically different desires shift out of alignment. Take then the case in which desires (1)–(3) hold, but in which a fourth desire appears:

(4) Cedric want to lessen his desire to be a competitive achiever.

Suppose that Cedric is already a competitive achiever; he is a person who tends to seek out situations, and to enter them, with a view to competitive success. Cedric knows, let us further suppose, that his company will receive a lucrative new contract next week. Cedric has a record of vigorous success in the project-management of contracts; and if he is in the office next week he will almost certainly be selected as the project-leader to manage the contract. All his old desires will then come into play. So great will be his concern to make a success of the contract that he will want to outvie his colleagues for resources, put pressure on his staff to spend unholy long hours at the office. In all he will exhibit that intense competitiveness about which he has lately come to have second thoughts. Cedric is quite clear that this is just what will happen unless he sets out to prevent it.

What then does he do? He looks for reasons not to be in the office next week. He has long wanted to see the Belvedere Apollo; and he knows that if he mentions to Boris the idea of a Roman holiday then Boris will firmly take up the idea and make life extremely difficult if Cedric later tries to abandon it. Accordingly Cedric phones Boris and suggests a holiday. Next week they fly to Rome.

In this example we are clearly presented with split levels of motivation which, for convenience of labelling, I shall describe in terms of first- and higher-level desires. Cedric has a first-level desire to be a competitive achiever; and this is the desire on which he will automatically act unless by intervention of a second-level desire he 'makes it with himself' not to act. It is this phenomenon of 'self-intervention' which causes the chief problem of the belief–desire theory. Essentially that theory works with a straight conception of strength of desire: where the general strength of a desire is measured by our tendency to act on it, and the strongest desire on any particular occasion is necessarily the one on which we act whether or not it is associated with the greatest emotional disturbance. If Cedric's non-competitive desire to see the Belvedere Apollo is stronger than his competitive desire to run the project for the new contract he will go to Rome; if not, he will be in the office next week.

But this is not how the example reads at all. Cedric's problem in planning for next week is that he recognizes that the 'wrong' desire will be strongest in a situation which will certainly come about unless he positively prevents it. If he does go to the office next week then irrespective of his present second-level desire not to be so competitive, that desire will lose out to his entrenched desire to outrun his competitors. What he does, therefore, is to prevent the situation in which that first-level desire will be strongest. He trades on his relationship with the formidable Boris to make sure that he, Cedric, will be well out of the competitive situation next week. This example is of exceedingly modest complexity; we observe examples of greater intricacy every day. It makes, however, an incompleteness in the belief–desire theory.

The phenomenon of self-intervention is to be clearly distinguished from another phenomenon with which it may be easily conflated. Take our original desire-stream, (1)–(3). In the context of those desires we might concede that any agent has some problem-solving to do, and this not simply in the sense that a desire of any complexity generally involves the construction and execution of a plan to bring about the desired state of affairs. A rational agent, we might say, will plan the satisfaction of his desires so as to satisfy as many of them as possible, but not to sacrifice the satisfaction of a major desire for the fulfilment of one that is relatively trivial, and so on through the rules of decision-theory. This presents a picture of the rational agent as both planner (constructing and executing plans to achieve his desires) and meta-planner (with desires about the efficient satisfaction of his desires). Meta-planning is not self-intervention, for in an important sense it takes the agent's desires as given. Through considerations of meta-planning the achievement of a desire may have to be postponed or denied but its rightful presence is unchallenged: the desire is simply a datum on which meta-planning supervenes. Meta-planning desires are second order but they are not evaluative in the way that Cedric's desire to lessen his desire to be a competitive achiever is evaluative.

The net result is that in discussing Cedric's self-intervention we have not abandoned all citation of belief and desire but we have found a need to import more into the explanation of Cedric's action than the belief–desire theory, with its reckoning of strength of desire and even with its reinforcement by meta-planning, has itself offered.

To a first approximation the theory retains its plausibility as to desires (1)–(3). The next step is to examine its application to ethics.

2.4   THE BELIEF–DESIRE THEORY
(2): THE RATIONALITY OF MORAL ACTION

To see how the belief–desire theory approaches the rationality of moral action, it will be useful to define one position from which the theory decidedly does not start. Suppose that we sought to base the rationality of moral action solely on the Axiom of Truth:

Axiom 1: It is always rational to act on what is known to be true.

This might be expanded ethically into the idea that, as a matter of truth, there are moral properties just as there are perceptual properties of objects. I can see that an action is good just as I can see that a flower is yellow. We may detect a disparity in the case of practical thinking: a flower is yellow but an action, yet to be performed, would be good. And particular accounts of moral properties might cause unease, as G. E. Moore's theory of goodness as a simple, non-natural, intuitable property is beset with familiar difficulties. From the standpoint of the belief–desire theory, however, those difficulties do not touch the vital problem that whatever properties there may be in the world, by whatever means apprehended, nothing has yet been said about how apprehension of the property of moral goodness can, just as such, make any difference to a person's actions. It is not that the belief– desire theory must reject the Axiom of Truth, but that it cannot regard the Axiom as sufficient for the rationality of moral action. Indefinitely many facts are relevant, or (more to the point) irrelevant, to action in view of our desires; and no relevance has yet been explained for those particular facts, supposing there to be such, to which in this context the Axiom of Truth relates, namely moral facts.

2.4.1. *The Moral Philosophy of Hume*

From the side of the belief–desire theory Hume is, historically, the major proponent of the view that the Axiom of Truth is insufficient to ground the rationality of moral action.[4] It perhaps smacks of paradox to consider Hume's views about moral action under the head of seeking, from the side of the belief–desire theory, to vindicate the rationality of moral action. Hume undoubtedly espouses the belief–desire theory; undoubtedly also he rejects the possibility that moral (or any other) action can be determined by reason. We shall examine Hume's account of reason in Chapter 4. His moral philosophy is considered here

---

[4] My debt in this section to S. D. Guttenplan, 'Hume and Contemporary Naturalism', will be obvious. See P. A. French, T. E. Uehling, and H. K. Wettstein, eds., *Midwest Studies in Philosophy*, viii, *Contemporary Perspectives on the History of Philosophy*, Minneapolis, 1983.

because, if his views are right, morality is grounded in human nature in a way which might produce much the same result as if moral action were shown to be rational. If morality were shown, on Hume's lines, to be as much a part of human nature as our propensity to form beliefs, then the appearance which advocates of the rationality of moral action are trying to overcome, that morality goes against the grain of 'natural' motivation in inducing the agent to be concerned how his actions affect others, might be cancelled. How then does Hume ground morality in human nature?

Hume rejects what Butler called 'the selfish theory of human nature'. The springs of action are selfishness and limited generosity (T III.2.2). What limits generosity is sympathy, which depends on degree of propinquity (T.II.1.11, III.2.1). The picture is roughly this: human beings are so constituted that they are disposed to help, e.g. their family and friends. This disposition, which is a standard part of human nature, is a motivating force. People do not, typically, take care of their children in order to act morally (to 'do their duty' as parents). They simply are disposed to act in this way. They are also disposed, within limits, to help others less close than their family and friends: in a Good Samaritan situation I am disposed to help perhaps even a total stranger through 'sympathy' with his sufferings, and am more likely to do so if I witness those sufferings than if I merely hear of them. This is just how human beings are. Then how does morality enter? Again through the constitution of human nature: we are so constituted that if, for example, we see a mother helping her child or a man helping a total stranger, we experience a special kind of pleasure, or sentiment of 'approbation', and we apply the concept of virtue to actions which provoke this pleasure. This non-rigorous, broad-brush picture is Hume's account of the 'natural virtues', of virtues which relate to actions to which there is an inbuilt disposition in human nature.

But for Hume natural virtue is not the whole of virtue. Justice on Hume's account is an artificial virtue since the requirements of justice exceed natural inclination. When, in Hume's example at T 479, somebody who has lent me money asks for its return, I do not have the same kind of inclination, a 'natural passion', to return the money as I have to take care of my children or to help strangers whose sufferings I witness. The rules of justice are products of convention; and if we seek their rationale we find at least three prima-facie puzzling characteristics. Those rules may on occasion conflict with direct self-interest (as in the earlier example of the evenly divided cake), with private benevolence (when my inclination to help family and friends conflicts with impartiality), and even with the public interest (when more people would benefit if I did not return the money). ' . . . a single act of justice, consider'd in itself, may often be contrary to the public good' (T 579). The rationale of justice is that we each have an indirect motive for following rules of justice the observance of which by other people tends to our individual interest in the long term, and the general observance of which tends therefore to the interest of all.

Then how can indirect self-interest explain the agent's regard for justice in the light of selfishness and limited generosity? Hume answers in terms of what we should now call socialization: that 'custom and education' so reinforce indirect self-interest that the rules of justice 'take root' (T 500–1). Broadly, I intend to pay back the money because I have been brought up to take a favourable view of precisely such action; I have a 'sentiment of justice'. What makes this socialization possible is sympathy. Sympathy can be directed, brought under social control as we are trained to view situations 'upon the general survey' (T 499): even when the miser insists on the return of his money from the needy we enter sympathetically first into the miser's uneasiness, then into his satisfaction when the money is returned. At this point two contingent defects of Hume's account of justice show up: its overriding emphasis on property rights and the rigidity of its insistence on the bindingness of the rules of justice. But the real problems lie elsewhere.

In the first place, Hume restricts the sense in which justice is an artificial virtue. The sympathy which we feel when we make 'the general survey' is the same which we feel in the Good Samaritan situation described earlier. What is 'artificial' is that custom and education have induced the tendency to make 'the general survey'. The standpoint is induced; but once that standpoint is adopted, the sentiment of justice is as 'natural' as anything that occurs in the case of the natural virtues (T 619–

20). This is what endows the artificial virtues with a moral status. However, if custom and education are incompletely effectual, as notoriously they are, this question arises: if I am disinclined to make 'the general survey' when it concerns a person whom I greatly dislike, why should I strive to adopt the standpoint of justice? Conditions are easily imaginable in which the indirect self-interest of the general system of justice continues to accrue even if I act unjustly towards this person.

Secondly, in the case of the natural virtues human beings act in certain ways and moral approval follows. Justice, and the artificial virtues generally, feature the nicety that the precise opposite applies: moral approval is induced and action follows. It seems that our regard for justice cannot finally explain the 'custom and education' by which the rules of justice are instilled, because it is custom and education which explain our regard for justice. Or put differently: the natural virtues relate to a human good (e.g. being taken care of as a child) which owes nothing 'genetically' to the moral point of view since moral sentiment here reflects our pre-set tendency to act in certain ways. The artificial virtues, by contrast, relate to a human good which is covertly constituted by the moral point of view itself. We regard the natural virtues as a part of human flourishing since we have the corresponding inbuilt desires, e.g. to take care of our children. The artificial virtues cannot be a part of human flourishing in quite the same way, for the corresponding desires are induced by a process of socialization without which we would not have the idea that justice (to restrict ourselves to the paradigm artificial virtue) is a part of human flourishing. Hume brings out this aspect of justice with his usual vivid touch when he refers to the 'artifice of politicians' (T 500).

Hume's moral philosophy is enclosed in a framework of ideas which I have not fully defined: the idea, for example, that the human good to which even the natural virtues relate is purely contingent and subjective. We actually do value the taking care of children, but we might have valued something unimaginably different; and nothing but the human constitution, no 'objective' scheme of values, would be involved either way. The significance of Hume's moral philosophy does not, I think, depend on the plausibility and interest of such extreme subjectivism. The position is this: Hume sets down an account of the natural virtues on which moral action is, if not 'rational', then at least continuous with the ordinary run of human action. For the natural virtues there is no break with normal motivation. The human agent is concerned how his actions affect others; there is no question of inducing this concern. It is not that we need (or in Hume's view, could) address cogent reasons to an agent why he should act morally. Within the scope of the natural virtues, Hume says, we simply do (typically) act morally: the part of self-interest would be to turn over and ignore the baby's squalls, but the (typical) parent is not inclined actually to do this. For Hume there is absolutely no mystery about moral action within the scope of the natural virtues; we only need an account of what human beings are like.

The problem is, as we have seen, that the natural virtues lack the scope to do the full job of morality. Aside from the limited generosity of partiality to family and friends there is no reliable 'natural' inclination to consider other agents' interests beyond the immediate solicitations of self-interest or inclination. This also is a matter of what human beings are like; and the subjectivity which is provocative in Hume's moral philosophy centres on the artificial virtues. Two points arise. First, only indirect self-interest gives the agent a reason for acting justly if socialization has not inclined him to make 'the general survey'. And indirect self-interest may, in particular cases, be outweighed by the direct of self-interest of acting unjustly. Secondly, Hume has identified a problem in the specification of the human good which morality serves: that in the case of the artificial virtues the conception of this good is laden already with moral notions. To justify the artificial virtues to a rational agent in terms which do not presuppose morality must be a prime point of method for any attempt to ground morality on considerations about human nature.

2.4.2 *The Moral Philosophy of Philippa Foot*

Unlike Hume, Philippa Foot does not explicitly espouse the belief–desire theory. But the theory operates as an assumption in much of her work. Two wider differences separate their ethics, however. The first concerns Hume's subjectivism. Foot holds that morality is internally related to considerations of human benefit and harm. She further holds that there are limits to what can plausibly count as benefit and harm. Incontrovertibly, on her account, pain, disease, suffering, and deformation are elements of human harm. The radical Humean scepticism which says that there is no truth of the matter here, but only contingent human preferences and aversions, is no part of Foot's perspective on morality. The second difference relates to the connection between morality and self-interest. This connection is not absent from Hume's account of morality. We have seen the indirect self-interest which supports the artificial virtues. But sympathy, occurring naturally or through socialization, is the mainstay of morality for Hume. Foot's early work represents, by contrast, an express attempt to justify morality on grounds of self-interest, just as her later work opens a broader view of how the rationality of moral action might be understood.

Then to start, Foot executes a double movement. On the one hand, she extricates moral principles from one type of subjectivism. On Foot's view it is perfectly objective, a cognitive matter, to say that morally one ought not to inflict unnecessary suffering. The correctness of such a belief, in regard to the suffering, is guaranteed by the moral viewpoint's being the kind of viewpoint which it is, namely one internally related to considerations of human benefit and harm. It simply is morally wrong to inflict unnecessary suffering, for example in failing to anaesthetize a patient before surgery in standard conditions. But at this point Foot executes her second movement, which is to suggest that the internal relation says nothing, so far, about the rationality of adopting the moral viewpoint. Nor does it follow, in an admission which supposes a commitment to the belief–desire theory, that having a moral belief *ipso facto* motivates an agent to act. It is on the question of rationality, as suggested above, that Foot's most significant shifts have occurred.

Let us base this part of our discussion on the Axiom of Self-interest:

Axiom 2: It is always rational to act from self-interest.

In her early work, as represented by 'Moral Beliefs', Foot argued that a rational connection holds between self-interest and virtue such that an agent, any agent, has rationally compelling reasons for acquiring the moral virtues. There is an obviousness about this connection for such virtues as that of courage. If courage is (approximately) the ability to pursue projects in face of unpleasant obstacles, then whatever projects an agent has possession of the virtue of courage will aid their accomplishment. A similar case, tightly linked to self-interest, can be made out for the virtues of perseverance, patience, and temperance. Courage and these other virtues are, however, self-regarding: they have no necessary reference to other agents' interests. If, through a particular relationship, your interests matter to me, then those interests may be served by my courage in countering innumerable odds. But I may equally exercise courage, perseverance, patience, and temperance quite insensibly to other agents' interests, either ignoring them or working actively against them. The self-regarding virtues never positively require an agent to act contrary to self-interest. Precisely on this score justice presented sharper difficulties for Foot since it 'seems obvious that a man who acts justly must on occasion be ready to go against his own interests'.[5] Such readiness is central to our discussion, for we have taken moral action to involve concern how one's actions affect others. In terms of self-interest the rational justification of morality begins to look distinctly problematic.

In 'Morality as a System of Hypothetical Imperatives' Foot relaxes the connection between rationality and self-interest. An agent has reasons for acting morally on condition that he has certain desires or interests. These need have no connection with self-interest: an agent may have an interest in 'the common good', as Mrs Foot elsewhere expresses the point, or desires of the kind which arise from 'the identification of one man with another in society', as when one person loves another.[6] At the same time any connection is broken between these desires or interests and rationality. If the agent does not have such desires or interests, there is no irrationality in his failing to possess them. The paper is slightly mistitled. Foot's point is not to press for close parallels between morality and precisely the Kantian hypothetical imperative (a suggested parallelism which has provoked many irrelevancies of detailed comparison), but to

---

[5] P. R. Foot, *Virtues and Vices*, Oxford, 1979, xiii.
[6] P. R. Foot, *Virtues and Vices*, 130–1.

deny that moral requirements are categorical imperatives, i.e. such as automatically have reason-giving force.

To summarize: Foot's original approach was to see how an agent might be rationally justified in acting morally because of the connection between virtue and self-interest. This worked for the self-regarding virtues but failed for the virtue of justice. Her present approach is that, in regard to justice, there is no such thing as a fixed connection between virtue and self-interest holding for simply any rational agent, but at best a variable and contingent connection holding or failing to hold for an agent in the light, not of self-interest, but of certain other-regarding desires and interest which he has. These desires and interests are themselves rationally neutral.

Foot is right to deny a privileged connection between rationality and self-interest. That connection may be cut in four places. First, if I identify with your interests (the kind of occurrence which Foot describes) then it is rational for me to pursue those interests; and this is no quasi- or surrogate rationality. Given my desire to entertain you, it is rational for me to surrender my theatre ticket so that you can see the play. Secondly, take the following brief typology of desires. Desires may be classified as:

(1) Self-regarding when, for example, on Saturday I want to renew my rail pass so that I can get to work on Monday.

(2) Egotistic or selfish when, for example, I am determined to get the last petrol in the garage for a pleasure trip although I know my action will deprive a disabled driver of mobility.

(3) Other-regarding as in the theatre-ticket example above or when, aiming for Costas to succeed in his new job, I want to provide all the conditions at home to enable him to do so.

Notice that when I refer to 'self-interest' I take that term motivationally and non-normatively: to act self-interestedly is to act on certain types of desire, and to act on such desires is still to act self-interestedly even if (by some value-criterion) one would be better off without those desires or their fulfilment. Then what are the relevant types of desire? To cite self-interest is to invoke self-regarding desires, desires of which the satisfaction conditions bear no necessary reference to the interests of other agents, and egotistic desires, desires which mean a pointed disregard of other people's interests. Not merely do self-interested desires not necessarily conflict with morality since in particular cases there may be no relevant interests of other people to consider, but the satisfaction of egotistic desires may easily conflict with the agent's own welfare. What if, in the garage example, I have a heart condition in which I have been expressly warned not to drive? Again, if am a smoker on 60 cigarettes a day who squeezes the family budget to support his habit? In both examples I act self-interestedly—and imprudently. This is the second point at which the connection between rationality and self-interest is cut.

Thirdly, prisoners' dilemma situations pose special hazards to the rationality of self-interest. I refer to the games-theoretic constraints on the inter-personal pursuit of self-interest, where in non-zero sum non-co-operative games the promotion of egotistic desires produces the worst overall result for all parties. I mention this problem because it shows how self-interested action, which is commonly taken to be the paradigm of rational action, itself becomes problematic in the theory of rational choice.

Fourthly and finally, any account of self-interest is sensitively dependent on (a notion of) the self whose identity across time holds together the interests which may be 'self-interestedly' pursued.[7]

I shall concentrate for now on the second point (cf. 2.12). See how the considerations on which it relies might be attacked. If we accept that, in a certain sense, the pursuit of self-interest conflicts with the agent's own welfare in the garage and cigarette examples, the pursuit of self-interest is still rational if we appeal to notions of 'enlightened' or 'informed' self-interest. If I do not have a heart condition, or if I press the family budget to buy health food purely for my own consumption, the rationality of self-interest re-emerges intact. I benefit unproblematically at the expense of other people. So the argument goes: and it may be reinforced. For the corresponding notion on the side of other-regarding desires would be enlightened other-regarding

---

[7] On all these matters Derek Parfit's *Reasons and Persons*, Oxford, 1984, is indispensable reading.

interest, as when I am clear-sighted enough to perceive other agents' real needs and the means of their fulfilment. Given our other-regarding desires we may be enlightened in the manner of our consideration of other agents' interests, but nothing has yet been said about the rationality of considering those interests in the first place.

This is the stage at which to recall Hume's account of the natural virtues. It is open to Hume, and to Foot, to point out that human beings are so constituted that they do consider others' interests. People are simply like that, as they are also self-regarding: Hume recognizes, we remember, selfishness and limited generosity. Then *de facto* social identification is a datum of ethics and one which, by the desires to which it leads, makes moral action rational. I want to help because your interests are important to me, and I see that you are in trouble. I therefore lend a hand. This is moral action; and action, moreover, which is rational in light of my desires. But the problem here is one which equally recalls Hume: that if beyond a point the agent fails to identify with other agents' interests, why should this concern him? We reintroduce the problem of seeing how to connect the other-regarding virtues to an understanding of the human good not laden already with moral conceptions. Foot shows how moral action can be rational, given *de facto* social identification; but one cannot fail to signal the total absence of any theory of the human good to ground and extend *de facto* social identification. In this sense on her account of morality there is nothing to choose between e.g. identification with 'the common good', a narrower range of relationships and commitments to other people, and aesthetic self-cultivation. This is perhaps part of her meaning when she says that she is a 'subjectivist, in the good old fashioned sense'.[8]

2.5 THE BELIEF–DESIRE THEORY (3): SUMMARY

The keywords of our critique of the belief–desire theory are self-intervention and subjectivity. The theory is unable to

[8] Quoted by J. Rée, 'Philippa Foot's Definition of Morality', *Radical Philosophy*, 1 (1972), 29.

accommodate the fact of self-intervention in the explanation of action. It views the agents as a 'job manager' in the achievement of his desires. Here is the stream of an agent's desires; the stream needs to be controlled. The satisfaction of some desires presupposes that of others; certain desires require a disproportionate share of the agent's resources for their satisfaction; other desires need to have their satisfaction delayed so as not to block the achievement of other desires. The belief–desire theory allows the agent, as meta-planner, to chart this kind of critical path through his own desires. It does not, however, measure up to situations in which, through a new self-image, the agent seeks to revise his desire-stream drastically, not simply to 'manage' it but to divert its direction and replace its contents. This evaluation of the desire-stream in terms of self-image which is not itself simply a desire or belief is a possibility on which the theory is silent. Here it clearly fails to capture something essential in the agent's relation to his own desires.

We recognize at once that this failure has implications for ethics. For the belief–desire theory can offer no account of how an agent may practise self-intervention in order to create a structure of desire in which he considers other agents' interests beyond the immediate solicitations of self-interest or inclination. But even if this defect of the theory were removed, the problem of the rationality of moral action would remain. Why should the rational agent undertake any such self-intervention on behalf of morality? Abstracting from Hume's special views about reason, we have seen that the Humean response is to suggest that with respect to the natural virtues we already largely have a moral structure of desire. Only indirect and unreliable self-interest, however, 'rationalizes' the artificial virtues for the individual agent. These virtues turn out, for Hume, to have a 'circular' justification: to be connected to an understanding of the human good which is itself laden with moral conceptions. Philippa Foot, whose views on the rationality of moral action we also examined, leaves the rationality of the other-regarding virtues dependent on *de facto* social identification. That a rational agent should extend this identification beyond the limits within which, for him, it happens to fall is a possibility unsupported by any theory of the human good. Morality seems to be a subjective matter; the rationality of moral action is relative to the agent's social relationships and commitments, which themselves are rationally neutral.

Then we are still looking for a theory of action explanation to accommodate the fact of self-intervention, and for an account of the rationality of moral action to explain why, outside the range of those closely associated with him, the agent should be concerned how his actions affect others. At this point we shall examine the second main theory of action explanation, the cognitive model.

2.6 THE COGNITIVE MODEL
(1): THE EXPLANATION OF ACTION

As with the belief–desire theory I shall give the cognitive model in two parts. The first is an account of the model as a theory of action explanation; the second part explains the theory's relevance to the rationality of moral action. One point which deserves mention is that the cognitive model has traditionally been advanced chiefly in connection with ethics. Kant bears the same ancestral relation to the cognitive model that Hume bears to the belief–desire theory. But while Hume intended his theory to cover the whole field of action explanation, Kant uses the model specifically in relation to moral action. In conditions of non-moral action Kant accepts Hume's view of belief (or reason) as ineffectual for action save in conjunction with desire. Quite whether he consistently had to do so is another matter (see Green, Works II, 139–40). But the cognitive model's special connection with ethics means that I shall look at the history of the model differently from the way we took Hume first and then Foot's more recent contribution to the belief–desire theory. I shall first examine a recent attempt to use the model as a general theory of action. Since this attempt, by Thomas Nagel, leads directly to Nagel's account of the rationality of moral action, I shall take that account before examining Kant's moral philosophy.

Nagel's first concern in *The Possibility of Altruism* is to detach us from the explanatory hold of the belief–desire theory, with its insistence that motivation can be secured only by the combination of antecedent belief and desire.[9] Essential to his argument is the distinction which he draws between motivated and unmotivated desires, a distinction set out in the following terms;

... many desires, like many beliefs, are *arrived at* by decision and after deliberation. They need not simply assail us, though there are certain desires that do, like the appetites and in certain cases the emotions. . . . The desires which simply come to us are unmotivated though they can be explained. Hunger is produced by lack of food but is not motivated thereby. A desire to shop for groceries, after discovering nothing appetizing in the refrigerator, is on the other hand motivated by hunger.[10]

Whether Nagel's example of hunger is presented quite correctly is uncertain. Hunger is caused by lack of food and may be a motive in seeking food, but whether it can be specified independently of desires is doubtful since it seems that if an agent does not desire to eat then, whatever the case, he is not hungry. However that may be, and (as has been pointed out to me) the claim collapses if anorexia is specifiable in terms of hunger without a desire to eat, the point of the distinction between motivated and unmotivated desires is twofold: first to suggest that motivation necessarily involves desire only if we include both motivated and unmotivated desires; and secondly to alter the terms of the debate. The contention is that what defenders of the belief–desire theory must now argue is that presupposed to every motivated desire is another, non-motivated desire. But of course it is no argument for the belief–desire theory simply to assume that this presupposition holds good. A motivated desire can be read off from an intention to do something. If I intend to rearrange the garden then it is *ipso facto* appropriate to ascribe to me a desire to rearrange the garden. But this kind of consequential ascription involves no commitment to an unmotivated desire antecedent to the

[9] I have learned most about Nagel from Stephen Darwall's article, 'Nagel's Argument for Altruism', *Philosophical Studies*, 25 (1974). See further S. Darwall, *Impartial Reason*, Cornell, 1983. On incidental points note M. Reba, 'A Second Look at Nagel's Argument for Altruism', *Philosophical Studies*, 25 (1974); and J. Treblicot, 'Aprudentialism', *American Philosophical Quarterly*, 11 (1974). Though I strike an independent line of main criticism I have certainly been informed by these articles.

[10] T. Nagel, *The Possibility of Altruism*, Princeton, 1978, 29.

motivated desire. So far the issue between the belief–desire theory and the cognitive model prompts the image of a dog chasing its tail: for if it can be charged on behalf of the cognitive model that the belief–desire theory simply assumes the necessity of antecedent desire to motivation, it may equally be replied on behalf of the belief–desire theory that the cognitive model simply assumes the possibility of motivation without antecedent desire. What strengthens Nagel's case is a particular account of how motivation without antecedent desire is possible. It is to Nagel's treatment of prudence, which has been generally regarded as the most successful part of his book, that we must now turn.

The possibility of prudential motivation is secured by Nagel through a strong internalism and an account of timeless reasons for action. Nagel's internalism is the view that to regard something as a reason for action is, other things equal, to be motivated to act on it. Given a view which Nagel says that we have about time, that all times are equally real, an agent can be motivated to promote a state of affairs, independently of any present desire, through an acknowledgement that if there is a reason for a state of affairs to exist at any time there is a reason for action at any earlier time to promote it. Because I realize that I shall have a reason to speak Italian on holiday in six weeks' time, to use Nagel's example, I have a reason now to learn Italian, and I can be motivated to act on that reason independently of any present desire to learn the language.[11] The cost of aprudentialism, on this account, is a form of personal dissociation: that the agent fails to view his present as simply one stage in an extended life which is real at all stages. This double-based argument, invoking internalism and timeless reasons for action, whatever its final cogency, at least shifts the cognitive model away from mere counter-assertion against the belief–desire theory.

Since Nagel's account of altruistic, other-regarding motivation is presented as running in exact parallelism to his account of prudential motivation, I shall follow straight on to that account. The shortcomings of the cognitive model as a theory of action explanation and as grounding an account of the rationality of moral action will then clearly emerge.

2.7   THE COGNITIVE MODEL
(2):   THE RATIONALITY OF MORAL ACTION

The general conception of rationality which informs Nagel's account may be termed the Axiom of Consistency:

Axiom 3: Failure to act from consistent reasons compromises the status of a rational agent.

Nagel's accounts of prudence and of altruism appear exactly to match. Internalism is integral to both accounts. Corresponding to timeless reasons for action are objective reasons. An objective reason for action is one definable by reference to 'a predicate R, such that for all persons p and events A, if R is true of A, then p has prima-facie reason to promote A'.[12] A subjective reason, by contrast, is a reason of which the 'defining predicate R contains a free occurrence of the variable p'.[13] So, for example, indexicals such as that 'A is what I desire', 'A will advance my career', count as subjective reasons. Examples of an objective reason would be 'A will be of benefit to somebody', 'A will be in Prince Andrew's interest.' Though subjective and objective reasons are mutually exclusive and jointly exhaustive, 'there are objective reasons corresponding to all subjective ones'. Nagel's claim is that to recognize an objective reason for acting is automatically to be motivated by it (explanation of action) even if it runs contrary to the immediate solicitations of self-interest or inclination. The cost of lacking such motivation (rationality of moral action) is to succumb to a form of 'personal solipsism'.

The premises on which Nagel bases his claim are twofold. The first is that whatever can be said about a practical situation, a situation relevant to action, must be sayable from a standpoint which is person-neutral. ('Sayable' has here the sense of 'judgeable'. Nagel does not rely on the fact of utterance.) Thus if I say (personal practical judgement) 'I have a reason to do such-and-such', must yield two assertions which have the same content inasmuch as 'Shifts of grammatical person, like shifts of tense, cannot be permitted to alter the sense of what is asserted about the circumstance which is the subject of the statement.'[14]

[12] T. Nagel, 90.
[13] T. Nagel, 90.
[14] T. Nagel, 101.

Nagel's second premiss is that, since personal practical judgements are subject to internalism, first-person practical judgements from the subjective standpoint have motivational content. In this way Nagel's internalism links the explanation of action to rationality of action. 'I explained the sense in which first-person practical judgements possess motivational content; the acceptance of such a judgement is by itself sufficient to *explain* action or desire in accordance with it . . . I have referred to this motivational content as the *acceptance of justification* for doing or wanting something.'[15]

The conclusion follows, for Nagel, that if another person judges that I have a reason to do such-and-such then he must himself be motivated towards my doing it in the way either of help or at least of non-hindrance. Rationally must; for if a person is motivated by his own personal practical judgements then he must in consistency be motivated by impersonal practical judgements on pain of what Nagel calls 'practical solipsism'.[16] The cost of inconsistency is that the agent fails to view himself as simply one person among other people.

How then do matters stand? For a range of prudential action, Nagel has produced an argument to show both that, through a particular conception of time, and how, through a strongly internalist account of reasons for action, an agent's motivation can be explained without reference to antecedent desire. Concerning this picture we can say, not simply that nothing in its description immediately rules it out as incoherent, a consideration which supports the bare possibility of the cognitive model, but that it suggests a way in which the cognitive model may actually serve in the explanation of action. We are offered, in other words, a plausible alternative to the belief–desire theory in the explanation of action. As for the rationality of moral action, in our own terms Nagel has offered an account of how an agent may be led to consider other agents' interests beyond the immediate solicitations of self-interest or inclination, an account moreover which has no need to invoke other-regarding desires of the kind cited by Hume with respect to the natural virtues or by Foot with respect to *de facto* social identification. If the agent simply understands the logic of

15 T. Nagel, 109.
16 T. Nagel, 113–15.

personal practical judgements, he is rationally constrained to act morally.

Even this condensed statement of Nagel's ideas raises issues too large to be fully canvassed here. The detailed steps in his treatment of both prudence and altruism have been questioned, as well as their exact parallelism. Briefly: one point is whether the cost of rejecting altruism really is the practical solipsism of failing to view oneself as simply one person among others, and equally whether the cost of rejecting prudence is that of failing to view the present as simply one stage in an extended life which is real at all stages. Regarding aprudentialism, two considerations relevant to Nagel's characterization are, first and trivially, that to reject the claims of prudence in favour of an aprudentialism which values only the present is an acknowledgement of the reality of future stages of the self if only to discount their value against the present. Secondly, an aprudentialist who thinks about the future may quite consistently take forward-directed action because future prospects cause present unease.

But my main comments address Nagel's account of the rationality of altruism, his own construction of the argument for the rationality of moral action. Two considerations appear to me crucially to limit the application of that account. The first is that there simply is no rational constraint automatically on person X, at the cost of 'practical solipsism', to help or not to hinder person Y's doing an action which X recognizes that Y has an objective reason to do. The following example is all too contemporary and plainly coherent. X is a conservationist one of whose major aims is to save the whale. Y is a fisherman whose chief source of income in a shrinking economy is whaling. It is perfectly possible for X to accept that from an impersonal practical standpoint Y has an objective reason for whaling, if whaling is Y's chief source of income. This sets no rational constraint on X to assist Y towards whaling or even not to hinder his pursuit of whaling. Quite the reverse, since either action would offend against X's ecological values. Such examples are legion.

Let it be at once conceded that this criticism neglects Nagel's express admission that one's recognition of another person's objective reason for doing an action defines only a 'prima-facie' reason to oneself to promote that action. But Nagel's own strictures on 'practical solipsism' equally neglect just my type of example. Those strictures introduce the second consideration, which is that Nagel's 'strong' internalism is on closer examination a distinctly diminished affair. Reduced on one side by clash-of-value cases, the motivational pull of impersonal practical judgements is reduced on the other by cases in which a person really is inconsistent between personal and impersonal practical judgements and does incur the cost of 'practical solipsism'.

Such considerations are perhaps of greater significance here than in the context of Nagel's project with its specific aim of showing the possibility of altruism for a rational agent: of showing how, without citing the kinds of desire invoked by Hume and Foot, such a person can be motivated by an impersonal practical judgement to co-operate in an action which he recognizes that another person has an objective reason to do. My criticisms do not suppress that possibility, but they show the narrow limits within which Nagel operates. For he does not overturn the belief–desire theory *en bloc*. That there are such desires as the 'unmotivated' desires with which that theory works, and that unmotivated desires may feature in explanations of action, are possibilities quite untouched by Nagel's view of how 'motivated' desires may be read off vacuously from a person's intention to act. Moreover, this 'trivialization' of desire reacts back on Nagel's moral psychology: it blocks the exploration of ways in which a person may try to prevent that inconsistency between personal and impersonal practical judgements which incurs the cost of 'practical solipsism'. We have seen a limitation of the belief–desire theory. Crudely speaking what the belief–desire theory cannot accommodate the cognitive model will not accommodate: the fact of self-intervention which, through indifference to desire, the cognitive model excludes from its scope. Just the strength of the 'unmotivated' desires with which the belief–desire theory works, in this case desires which are egotistic or self-regarding, may be the main problem of self-intervention for Nagel's 'practical solipsist' who is trying to revise his own motivation. Nagel does not have to confront the problem faced by such a person, given the aim of his project. In a comprehensive moral psychology, however, the narrowness of that project clearly shows through.

So I suggest. But there is a historical system of ethics, never far from contemporary discussion, for which no such self-intervention could have the least relevance to morality. Moral action is the product, in Kant's ethics, or pure practical reason; and no action motivated by desire possesses, or by the nature of morality could possess, any moral value. It is to this system of ethics that we now turn.

2.7.1 The Moral Philosophy of Kant

Kant's moral philosophy can be set out in terms of the question, what can we require of a rational agent? We cannot require that he achieve a certain result. Moral responsibility is capricious if fixed by consequences; the consequences of an action are incompletely within the agent's control. This is Kant's first claim. Then the morality of an action is determined by the intention with which it is done.[17] But how are we to analyse this motive? Kant advances two points. Of these the first is negative: that we cannot require of a rational agent that he be motivated, that his intention should be directed, by certain desires. Desires are contradictory within the same agent and incompatible within different agents. Even the desires on which Hume bases his account of the natural virtues are inconstant and far from universal. What can be required of the rational agent cannot depend on the chance conjunction of his desires. Since, in the case at least of human beings, the content of any agent's motivation is set by his desires, the only condition we can place on rational agency relates, not to a variable content, but to an invariable form. This is Kant's positive point: that there is a requirement on a rational agent to act only on a policy or 'maxim' which he could at the same time will as a universal law.

---

[17] This is a common source of misunderstanding. Once a proposed action has passed the moral test of universalizability (to be explained shortly), no effort must be spared to make it succeed: 'the straining of every means so far as they are in our control' is no less than morality requires. If in the event the agent's means are inadequate to the intended result, that is a separate matter. 'The laurels of mere willing are dry leaves that never were green'; the sentence is Hegel's, the position is Kant's. See H. J. Paton, *The Moral Law*, London, 1966, 60; and Hegel, *Philosophy of Right*, tr. T. M. Knox, Oxford, 1965, 252.

Whatever the content of his maxim, his action will always satisfy this formal description. But how does Kant ground his claim? Reason is essentially lawlike. A reason for me to believe that s is p is equally a reason for you to believe that s is p on the same evidence. A reason for me to do an action is equally a reason for you to do that action in similar circumstances. In rough terms, if the policy on which I act would produce inconsistent results, in ways which Kant specifies, if everyone acted on that same policy, then in Kant's terminology, the maxim of my action does not comply with the canons of reason. The idea of a policy or maxim is, at the present level, fairly straightforward. Take any desire on which I think of acting, the inclination (say) to lie in order to avoid personal inconvenience. To lie because it is convenient to do so is to adopt, as a principle of behaviour, the policy of lying if this is an easy way out of a problem. Just such a policy is a maxim. I cannot, however, will that the maxim of my action in this case ('lie if this is an easy way out of a problem') should become a universal law, for lying depends for its effectiveness on the rule of truth-telling which it violates. If everyone lied for convenience the practice of truth-telling from which lying derives its point would be undermined and lying itself would cease to be effective. The worldly-wise reply, 'but everyone won't act on that maxim, so I can safely buck the system', exactly misses the point. Kant is appealing to a notion of what is appropriate to rational agency as such. I can equally form my beliefs on idosyncratic canons of reason and may even, *per accidens*, arrive at some truths in this way. But this is cognitive irrationality, and the practical irrationality of lying for convenience is precisely parallel to it. The presiding idea is one of rational dignity, of what befits a rational agent.

The requirement on a rational agent to act only on maxims which he could at the same time will as universal laws is the key to moral action. The 'good will', the motivation of a moral agent, is determined exclusively by such maxims. As action on universalizable maxims is all that we can require of a rational agent, so it suffices for morality. Morality, fulfilment of the moral law, simply is a matter of acting on such maxims; and 'morality' here is not meant to refer to some esoteric Kantian reconstruction of the everyday thing. Kant claims emphatically that the main body of everyday moral judgements and beliefs can be recovered from his account of rational agency. Since an action is moral solely by virtue of its form, through the universalizability of its maxim, moral obligation has some clear characteristics for Kant. It does not present itself, like the precepts of technique or prudence, as conditional, subordinate to some proposed end which one might accept or refuse. Its requirements are absolute.

Thus Kant distinguishes hypothetical imperatives, which are simply instrumental to desire and have no authority except in relation to proposed ends ('if you want this, do that'), from the categorical imperative of duty which commands absolutely. The categorical imperative, to act only on maxims which one can at the same time will as universal laws, is a test to apply to any desire on which one thinks of acting. But the categorical imperative itself is a straight requirement on rational agency, unconditional on any independent desire to apply it. Otherwise put: the categorical imperative of duty, offering no motive to obedience apart from the pure idea of rational agency, can have no external object; it beckons to nothing beyond, to any consideration for example that obedience to it would cause happiness. This is Kant's doctrine of the autonomy of morals.

If, however, 'reason' sets this formal requirement on action, so that the rational agent acts only on maxims which he could at the same time will as universal laws, how does this requirement connect with the explanation of action? How is it possible that in conditions of moral action the mere intellectual apprehension that (to take the negative case) a maxim fails to come under a universal law is sufficient to prevent action in dissociation from any desire? First a point of clarification, then Kant's answer.

Kant's adhesion to the cognitive model might be denied; it might be denied that, in the explanation of moral action, Kant supposes mere intellectual apprehension to be sufficient. Kant does reserve a place for desire in the explanation of moral action. Antecedent desire is excluded from moral motivation, but moral apprehension, the apprehension that a maxim fails to fall under a universal law, is ineffectual without a desire to fulfil the moral law. This is the burden of familiar passages in the *Foundations* and in the *Critique of Practical Reason*.[18] When we

---

[18] H. J. Paton, *The Moral Law*, London, 1966, 120; *Critique of Practical Reason*, tr. L. W. Beck, Indianapolis, 1956, 74–81.

unlock the relationship between moral apprehension and desire, however, any deep resemblance to the belief–desire theory vanishes. For on that theory belief and desire are strongly independent. Not merely is each a necessary condition of action, since to explain action we must cite both a belief and a desire, but neither condition is a necessary or sufficient condition of the other. On this point Kant's explanation of moral action differs crucially from anything possible on the belief–desire theory. Moral apprehension produces moral desire, of which it is a sufficient condition. Moral feeling is 'a consequence of this determining ground'.[19] It is also a necessary condition since moral desire, the desire to fulfil the moral law, is 'produced solely by reason'.[20] If apprehension and desire are equally elements in the explanation of moral action, they are not equal elements. A moral desire of which moral apprehension is both a necessary and a sufficient condition is hardly a *vera causa* which propels Kant across the boundary to the belief–desire theory of action. With this point clarified we may now return to the question of how, in the sense just explained, mere intellectual apprehension can produce or prevent moral action.

Kant's answer is given by his two-world metaphysics which disengages the moral agent from the constraints of antecedent desire. Our actions, *qua* 'phenomenal', are determined by their antecedents in time in an unbroken chain of causation which, in conditions of non-moral action, includes our desires. Or rather this is the way in which the human mind is structured to understand the phenomenal world. So Kant holds; but he also holds that, on the reverse side of the same coin, the phenomenal world with its determinist categories is purely relative to human forms of understanding. Kant presumes upon the relation between moral agency and the noumenal world, a world of which at other times he says more cautiously that we can have no knowledge, to identify moral agency with a noumenal faculty of free causality. When we put ourselves in the state of mind of considering what befits rational agency, we enjoy the free causality of noumenal agents capable of cutting across the chain of phenomenal causation through the mere intellectual

---

[19] L. W. Beck, 75.
[20] L. W. Beck, 79.

apprehension that (to keep to the negative case) the maxim of an action fails to come under a universal law.

The dubieties of the phenomenal/noumenal distinction are familiar to any student of Kant. For some commentators the notion of noumenal reality is incoherent, a line of criticism to be found in Green; for others the account of free causality is logically untenable on Kant's view that knowledge is possible only of phenomena, of events, facts, objects, processes, properties, as structured by the human understanding. We shall return to the phenomenal/noumenal distinction (3.11, 5.6). For the present, the dubieties of that distinction must not be allowed to obscure the real significance of Kant's moral philosophy.

The deep drift of Kant's moral philosophy is to insulate moral agency from the impact of desire. A minor role is assigned to the moral desire which is triggered automatically by moral apprehension, but all other desires are seen as extraneous to morality in this sense: that although morality cannot totally disregard them, since they determine the maxims which one tests for rational consistency, they form no part of the structure of morality. In particular, moral action has no connection with the contingencies of human sociability on which Hume and Foot rely in their account of the other-regarding virtues. Morality is practical reason. *Qua* rational agent I have no other way to act than on maxims which I could at the same time will as universal laws; and to act morally simply is to guide one's actions by such universalizable maxims. Morality is possible for me, regardless of my desires; and it is required of me, simply by virtue of my status as a rational agent. Kant's position here is similar to Nagel's, but Kant goes beyond Nagel. Nagel argues that a sufficient account of the rationality of moral action can be given without invoking other-regarding desires. Kant, by contrast, argues that it is necessary actually to exclude such desires, to reject absolutely any consideration of them from our understanding of morality.

This is, I think, a fair representation of Kant's moral philosophy. I shall try to show that Kant's analysis has two main weaknesses from the viewpoint of the present chapter, the first because it takes an incorrect view of the nature of desire, the second because it depends on an incomplete account of maxims in relation to the human good.

Inseparable from Kant's moral philosophy is a particular notion of desire. To capture this notion I referred above to 'the impact of desire' for just its suggestion of an external cause with which the agent has to contend. Except for the moral desires triggered by moral apprehension, desires are mere data of consciousness—'phenomenal' occurrences which we can understand solely in terms of their antecedents in an unbroken chain of causation. But this notion of desire is subject to review under the head of self-intervention. For the burden of self-intervention is exactly that one can revise the structure of one's desires. One is not presented with mere data of consciousness, but with the possibility of developing certain desires and of curtailing the occurrence of reducing the strength of others. Kant is right to this extent: given his view that desires are impacted on the agent, any morality of desire would be 'heteronomous'. The moral law would not speak with unconditional authority, but conditionally on the chance conjunction of the agent's desires. But this view is not one we need accept.

This then is the first weakness of Kant's moral philosophy, its view of desires as mere data of consciousness; and the implications of this view are ramified. A connection can be drawn, for example, with Kant's stress on the one-by-one assessment of moral actions. Two perspectives are available on the autonomy of morals. We can consider a person's actions one by one and assess their conformity to the moral law. Alternatively we can consider actions as revealing a certain kind of person. From this second point of view the moral problem is not purely that of acting in accordance with the moral law; it is one of acquiring a particular sort of general motivation. The criticism would not be correct that Kant omits this possibility. In *Anthropology*, II.A he distinguishes a sense of 'character' in which a man of character acts invariably on determinate principles which he has decided for himself.[21] Such principles may of course be the universalizable maxims of morality. But Kant does omit one of the readiest ways in which the possibility might be realized, through self-intervention. The connection of ideas is as follows.

---

[21] I. Kant, *Anthropology from a Pragmatic Point of View*, tr. M. J. Gregor, The Hague, 1974, 157.

It is not open to Kant to say that a person might, with any relevance to morality, practise self-intervention to promote his other-regarding desires. But in fact a person might do this on grounds even of self-interest (say, because he believes that morality makes for a quiet life) without offence to the autonomy of morals. Consider a parallel. Someone might become a lawyer because he wants a good income; but once initiated into the profession, although the good income duly follows, he does not have to think of money when he accepts a case. He may follow quite different considerations of novelty, sentimentality, or social justice. Just so a person might set about acquiring the moral virtues because a liar needs a good memory, honesty is good for business, and so on. But once he has acquired the moral virtues no consideration, on each occasion of their exercise, of the reason why he decided to acquire them need control his actions. He may (in the past) have acquired the virtue of justice through self-intervention for the sake of a quiet life, but he (now) returns the money because he owes it. If we assess actions one by one then if a person returns the money purely for the sake of a quiet life on this occasion, Kant is right to appeal to the autonomy of morals. But the self-intervention example just described does not fall to that appeal. It is a possibility which Kant must ignore because of his view of desires as mere data of consciousness impacted on the agent.

The second weakness to consider is Kant's account of the maxims of moral action. The folklore which surrounds this part of his moral philosophy obscures a complex ethical doctrine. It is still a common belief that Kant's philosophy of morals is abstract: that he propounds abstract principles of morality but offers no account of how the agent is to go from such principles to particular actions. How, for example, is the agent to pass from the abstract principle that only those actions are morally permissible which could be made universal laws, to a diversity of particular duties? But Kant does not propose an abstract principle; rather he sets down a formal method. The agent is to act in such a way that he could at the same time will the maxim of his action as a universal law. Kant pictures the agent as already having a particular action in mind; what the agent must do is to test the policy or maxim which this action would embody. This test is the formal test of the maxim's

universalizability. There is no question of the agent's being
confronted, *in vacuo*, with an abstract principle which he strives
to fulfil.

Nor—we really must be clear on what we are to criticize—
does Kant's formal method detach morality from all reference to
the human good. It is not as though Kant were presenting the
categorical imperative as a surd element in human life:
presenting the requirements of morality as binding on us, on
pain of inconsistency, without relation to human well-being.
Kant never says that the good will, our compliance with the
moral law, is the sole good. He says that it is the sole
unconditional good. The good will is always good when it
informs our actions, independently of other factors in the
situation. But those other factors may themselves contribute to
the *summum bonum*, the complete human good. Acting on
universalizable maxims is itself one part of the human good, that
part which is determined by the fact that we are rational beings.
Morality is not instrumental to our rational good; our rational
good consists in acting morally. The human agent, however, is
not simply a rational being whose good is virtue but also a
sensuous being whose good is happiness. Virtue and happiness
combine to form the *summum bonum*, or 'perfection' as Kant also
calls it. Then it is quite in order for the agent to plan his actions
with a view to happiness; but the maxims of those actions must
submit to the moral test of universalizability. Since we cannot
achieve virtue for another person, the ideal Kantian society
would be one in which rational beings acted virtuously with a
view to their own perfection and other people's happiness
through completely harmonious plans of action.

This presentation of Kant's account of the maxims of moral
action separates it from common misunderstandings. I believe
that account to be seriously incomplete, however. The point is
this. Kant grants the maxims of moral action a role in relation to
personal happiness and social harmony, but advances no view of
how they are to fulfil that role. An agent, aiming at personal
happiness, is involved, let us say, in various activities. Any two
activities may subsist independently, reinforce each other, or
conflict. The maxims of those activities can be tested for
universalizability, but the problem remains, for activities which

clear the test, of how the agent is to determine which activities
best make for personal happiness; and the problem is repeated
with respect to social harmony. Kant talks as if the only question
about power, wealth, reputation, and the other values of
'sensuous' man concerned their morally conditional character,
but how to establish a hierarchy of such values and to integrate
different values in the organization of his own life may be the
most important question which a person has to answer.

We can take this point further in pressing the heterogeneity of
the two natures between which Kant's view of the human agent
is divided. Kantian man transects the noumenal and
phenomenal worlds. As a rational agent with free causality his
good is to act on universalizable maxims; as a sensuous agent,
impacted by desires, his good is to achieve happiness. The two
aspects of human agency are never brought into the kind of unity
which would enable Kant to consider the notion of a rational
structure of desire induced by self-intervention. A pure division
separates the cognitive and conative aspects; thus the two
weaknesses of Kant's moral philosophy connect.

2.8   THE COGNITIVE MODEL
(3): SUMMARY

Like the belief–desire theory, the cognitive model presents the
distinction between cognition and conation, belief or desire, as
fundamental and exclusive. Unlike the belief–desire theory it
does not claim to be a complex explanation of all possible action;
but it does claim, in opposition to the belief–desire theory, that a
range of action is capable of explanation purely in terms of the
agent's cognition. Thus Nagel argues that a range of both
prudential and altruistic action can be explained by the agent's
recognition of objective time-neutral or person-neutral reasons
for action; and Kant argues that specifically moral action can
only be explained through the agent's recognition of the
suitability or otherwise of his maxim to serve as a universal law.
Kant's account of how this is possible, his two-world
metaphysics, is no more essential to the cognitive model than
Hume's account of impressions and passions is essential to the

belief–desire theory. Nagel offers a coherent picture of how an agent's motivation can be explained without reference to antecedent desire.

In shifting its focus of attention away from desire, the Nagelian version of the cognitive model neglects the phenomenon of self-intervention. This imposes one limitation on Nagel's moral psychology, since the strength of desires which an agent practises self-intervention to counteract may be just the explanation of 'practical solipsism'. The Kantian version of the model withholds the possibility of self-intervention because Kant sees desires as impacted on the agent. Free causality, by which the human agent transects the phenomenal and noumenal worlds, enables moral action independent of desire. Freedom from desire is possible in conditions of moral action, but freedom of desire, in the sense of a structure of desire determined by self-intervention, lies beyond the scope of Kant's moral psychology.

For Kant an action is morally right when it involves a certain consistency, when its maxim is suitable to serve as a universal law. Morality is a matter of acting on such maxims; and to act otherwise is to violate the conditions of rational agency. Thus the rationality of moral action is inbuilt from the very nature of morality and reason. But Kant is unable to ground the values of 'sensuous' man. The maxims of action fulfil a proper role with respect to the agent's happiness, on Kant's philosophy of morals, but Kant offers slight guidance on the relation of different value structures to happiness. Values reappear in the critique of Nagel's account of the rationality of moral action, since in clash-of-value cases there is no rational constraint to help or not to hinder someone whose scale of values differs from one's own, even if one recognizes that he has an objective reason for action.

We have now considered the two standard models of action explanation. Neither the belief–desire theory nor the cognitive model recognizes the phenomenon of self-intervention; and with regard to the rationality of moral action neither model gives a fully satisfactory account of the relation of morality to the human good. Hume's moral philosophy does not resolve the problem of circularity in explaining our regard for justice. Foot makes the rationality of justice depend on certain other-regarding desires and interests which an agent has, desires and interests which are themselves rationally neutral. Nagel's defence of altruism lacks criteria for addressing conflicts of value. Kant's moral philosophy offers a divided view of the human agent in which the rationality of moral action sets bounds to the pursuit of happiness but stands in no organic relation to it; and in which, moreover, the concept of happiness is bereft of any systematic account of conditions for the kind of comprehensive satisfaction which 'happiness' signifies.

2.9   THE NATURE OF AGENCY
(I):   THE INTEGRAL AGENT

In examining the main alternative models of action explanation we have touched the first two topics announced at starting. Such models offer to explain how beliefs plus desires, or cognition alone, can produce action; and to exhibit those desires or beliefs which would make moral action rational from the agent's viewpoint. I have suggested, familiarly by now, that the models possess a common weakness in their failure to recognize the fact of self-intervention. A yet more basic weakness, I want now to suggest, lies in the overriding importance which they attach to the requirements of action. It is as though there were a pre-defined set of tasks required of an agent from the moral point of view, and a resulting problem to see how the agent might be rationally induced to take the appropriate actions. The effect of this assumption has been to truncate our view of the person to the point of action. In Iris Murdoch's vivid image, 'The agent, thin as a needle, appears in the quick flash of the choosing will.'[22] This is the area of our third main topic, the nature of agency.

A connection may at once be drawn back to the phenomenon of self-intervention and the two models of action explanation. The two models fail to make room for self-intervention, but if we neglect that phenomenon in ethics, then our view of the person is limited to that partial glimpse offered by the two models of action explanation. So the agent is construed as acting, as entertaining Foot's desires and interests, as having the

---

[22] I. Murdoch, *The Sovereignty of Good*, London, 1970, 53.

original subjective reasons from which Nagelian objective reasons are generated, as impacted by desires which determine the Kantian maxims to be tested for rational consistency, but largely *in vacuo*. Slight consideration is given, quite in general in current ethics, to such circumstances as the place of an action in a lifeplan which crystallizes and structures an agent's diverse goals and activities, or to the desires which an agent desires to have. This is not to deny all recognition of this complex background to moral action. The term 'lifeplan' is taken from the writings of John Rawls; the critical relation of an agent to his own desires is observed by Charles Taylor and is marked by his distinction between strong and weak evaluation.[23] Rawls gives only a brief statement of the notion of a lifeplan, however; and Taylor for his part leaves much work to be done.

But if we have marked the fact of self-intervention, what of full phenomenon? To take some measure of that phenomenon in relation to a lifeplan, consider the following example of critical reflection. A person feels, to express the point rather dramatically, that his life is one of meaningless toil. He has a well-paid job but his general attitude is negative, he is petulant, sullen, unresponsive; and so he decides to review his motivation. Life, he thinks, must have something better to offer than this. He first sets out a range of career options: he might make a career as a sculptor, as a market researcher, as a teacher, as a librarian, as an entrepreneur. He then sets about ranking these options. Which career would be best for him, which the least suitable? To carry out this process of ranking he uses criteria; he conducts an analysis of values. In this way he works out certain fundamental value categories: cognitive, aesthetic, social, political, economic, religious. Next he weights these criteria. He decides, from recollection and reflection, that for him the most comprehensive satisfactions are to be gained from aesthetic experience (the creation of elegance, the enjoyment of beauty). Next in line, and in descending order, are cognitive values (satisfying curiosity), social values (getting on with people), political values (exercising power), economic values (acquiring

---

[23] C. Taylor, 'What is Human Agency?', *The Self*, ed. T. Mischel, Oxford: Blackwell, 1977. The phrase 'lifeplan' derives from Josiah Royce; for Rawls's use of the concept see J. Rawls, *A Theory of Justice*, Oxford, 1973, 92 *et passim*.

money), finally religious values (indulging a mild sense of the transcendental). Others might compose a different scale of values, but he puts aesthetic values at the head of the list.

At this point he returns to his career options and assesses each option in terms of his weighted criteria, his scale of values. So market research might score high 'cognitively' as satisfying curiosity but low 'aesthetically'; and the aesthetic criterion is more important. That priority has already been decided. Let us say that he fixes on a career as a sculptor, the option which scores highest by the aesthetic criterion. He is not yet an 'aesthetic man'; the aesthetic is not his central motivational thrust. Perhaps from his upbringing he is strongly inclined to pursue the career which pays best, even though that inclination has reduced him to his present state of dissatisfaction. To produce a different motivational thrust he practises self-intervention through the kind of process we have already noted in 2.3. If he forms a structure of desire which reflects his scale of values, and his scale of values preserves logical constraints, e.g. of transitivity, then it is appropriate to say of such a person that he has a coherent structure of desire.

Even at this level of abstraction we have moved upstream from the data on which moral philosophers typically rely; we begin to see where interests, desires, subjective reasons, and maxims might come from. We also begin to see how such a structure of desire might express itself in moral action. The 'aesthetic man' cannot be indifferent to the future of art; and in acting at personal inconvenience to safeguard this future he also advances the interests of those like-minded to himself. He cannot be indifferent to malicious criticism which would injure the reputation of those artists whose work he values. He cannot be indifferent to forgery, with its false appearance of creativity. These are quick claims; and I do not suggest that this briefly defined example is adequate to the complete requirements of morality. It is intended to rotate our perspective on moral action, to substitute the idea that one might work outwards from structures of desire to the requirements of morality for the more usual idea that we should first set down the requirements of morality and then look for the kind of motivation that would rationally induce an agent to act morally.

2.10 THE NATURE OF AGENCY
(2): ACTION AND CONSEQUENCE

The present phase of our discussion will be dominated by utilitarianism, 'the ethics of consequences'.

Utilitarianism has drawn a blizzard of criticism since its first elaboration by Bentham. It is as controversial as ever, but the controversies have changed. From Bentham to John Stuart Mill, utilitarianism was taken to be a form of hedonism: to involve the assessment of actions exclusively in terms of their consequences for happiness, interpreted as pleasure. It was closely allied to psychological determinism, not merely counselling us to seek happiness but holding that actually we unavoidably do so. That we do not unavoidably seek the general happiness, left scope for ethics. Utilitarianism was also, in this early phase, ethically conservative. Intended as an instrument of social reconstruction it was yet far from reconstructive and critical of traditional moral notions. The notion of 'natural rights' may have appeared to Bentham to be contradictory, 'nonsense upon stilts', but John Stuart Mill argues that utilitarianism can accommodate the notions of duty, right, obligation, virtue, even justice (after a struggle in chapter 5 of *Utilitarianism*). Mill also portrays much of past moral thinking, from the Christian ethics of the Sermon on the Mount to the moral philosophy of Kant, as relying unawares on utilitarian arguments.

In contemporary utilitarianism, by contrast, the element of consequentialism has been singled out as the chief feature of the theory; the elements of hedonism and psychological determinism have been largely discarded. Consequentialism, moreover, has been shown to have some surprising implications for traditional moral notions. In this new phase the theory is seen as openly revisionary. A contemporary utilitarian such as J. J. C. Smart conceives of consequentialism as a matter of 'how it would be most rational to act',[24] in terms purely of the consequences of our actions, with no regard for ethical conservatism. Current reactions, in defence of traditional moral notions, are less than satisfactory. Scanning what has been written on utilitarianism convinces me that the theory is seldom

[24] J. J. C. Smart, 'Extreme and Restricted Utilitarianism', *Theories of Ethics*, ed. P. R. Foot, Oxford, 1967, 182.

critically argued with; usually it is simply opposed by 'checking our intuitions'. But if utilitarianism is a revisionary moral theory it cannot be overturned by stressing, for example, that morality involves the notion of a limit, of constraints on action 'whatever the consequences', or by showing that utilitarianism cannot respect the notion of integrity. In the phase under review utilitarianism does not set out to capture our intuitions but to revise them. That is what 'revisionary' means.

A major part of the challenge of utilitarianism connects directly with our discussion of the integral agent. No extensive investigation of agency is to be found in Nagel or in Foot or in Hume. That is, none of these writers have much to say about the place of an action in a lifeplan or about the desires which an agent desires to have. They do not set out to address these matters. Utilitarianism is different: it does not simply omit to develop a view of the integral agent. Rather it denies the relevance of that view, and of the concept of the integral agent, to ethics. The key point is that utilitarianism employs a particular notion of rationality.

To capture that notion I offer the following model of utilitarian rationality.[25] Assume a decision-maker who is planning what to do over the weekend. Such a person might:

(i)   Fix the criteria to use in making his decision (personal convenience, helpfulness to his wife, non-interference with neighbours);
(ii) Weight the criteria (pleasing his wife is more important than keeping on the right side of the neighbours);
(iii) Score each option (tidying the garden, painting the bedroom, driving out into the country) by each criterion;
(iv) Multiply the scores by the weights, total the scores for each option, and do whatever emerges with the highest score.

This choice might feature as an antecedent desire in the belief–desire theory; and the model can be extended to include decision-making in the interests of more than one person. So an interpersonal decision-maker might:

(i)   Fix the satisfaction of antecedent desires as his criterion;

[25] This model simply uses standard ideas from decision theory; I claim no novelty for it.

(ii)   Weight the satisfaction of particular desires according to their importance to different persons;
(iii) Score each possible social choice according to the number of desires which it would satisfy (the number of different desires so the same person plus the number of occurrences of the same desire among different persons):
(iv)   Multiply the scores by the weights, total the scores for each social option, and choose the option with the highest score.

It is not possible to wrap up the whole of utilitarian rationality in these particular personal and interpersonal models, but the models do fit easily the main features of both historical and contemporary utilitarianism. Thus historical utilitarianism would take pleasure as its criterion and identify the highest scoring social option with the greatest happiness of the greatest number. Consequentialism, historical and contemporary, would require choice in accordance with the highest scoring option. Just as easily we can map on to these models two major criticisms of utilitarian ethics in respect to (a) moral rules and (b) the 'tyranny of consequences'.

For traditional moral notions include the idea of rules in the sense of constraints on action which eliminate certain options from decision-making. The position is this: among the most significant moral rules are those which involve what I shall call dominant descriptions such that when an action falls under a particular description, that description is decisive for ethics: as on Kant's moral philosophy no matter what other intentional descriptions an action may satisfy, once it is seen as violating the categorical imperative to treat other persons as ends and never purely as means, morally there is simply no question of doing it. Such a description, a dominant description in my terminology, is not a mere debit item on a balance-sheet; it closes the account. The consequentialist position is quite different. Any option can be considered in consequentialist decision-making, no possibility is foreclosed. For who can say in advance of particular circumstances what action will realize the highest scoring option? Our models make no attempt to incorporate this idea of rules; and it is easy to see from them how the present criticism of consequentialism arises. (If my focus has fallen on act-utilitarianism, the introduction of rule-utilitarianism makes no essential difference. Whether actions are to be assessed in particular circumstances or reliance is placed on the standard consequences of types of action in types of circumstances, the question 'who can say?' still applies.) The models also inject the risk that an agent can be 'controlled' by the consequences of his action; if his situation is contrived in a certain way it becomes rational for him to seek an outcome which, on his own terms, he would completely reject; the autonomy of his practical reason disappears. This view of the 'tyranny of consequences' is of course another major criticism of utilitarianism; and our models include nothing to prevent it. Their point is to present the essentials of utilitarianism and to show how utilitarianism looks to its opponents.

But what is wrong with utilitarianism? Its requirement to choose the best outcome seems a paradigm of rationality. Not this requirement, however, but the method by which the 'best' outcome is determined, is the problem.

Two considerations appear to me to be crucial. Utilitarianism takes the satisfaction of antecedent desire as its criterion of value. The rational agent who plans his weekend in the above example is quite unlike the 'aesthetic man' of 2.9, although I have deliberately allowed some overlap of terminology: the latter is not planning the satisfaction of his desires, he is trying to arrive at desires which will satisfy. For utilitarianism desires are identified, weighted in accordance with their importance (standardly interpreted as strength, a notion in turn understood in terms of the agent's tendency to act on the desires involved), and included in the consequentialist calculation of the best outcome: that outcome is best which satisfies the greatest number of desires, weighted in terms of their strength. But again we encounter the phenomenon of self-intervention. An agent may have desires which self-intervention is working against; instead of a clear set of desires we observe a strugglingly emergent pattern of desire with which the agent will not want to be fully identified in its current state. The strength of a desire, as we have seen, is no guarantee of its acceptability even to the agent whose desire it is. An agent can have a desire but wish not to have it. So the agent is not necessarily satisfied if his antecedent desires are satisfied in accordance with their present strength.

This argument might be countered on behalf of utilitarianism by an agreement to include in the consequentialist calculation the desire not to be identified with one's pattern of desire in its present state. This inclusion might be of unmanageable practical difficulty interpersonally, but theoretically it is quite possible. Since utilitarianism aims to provide a useable model of practical rationality, the interpersonal difficulty is not unimportant. But a second consideration cuts deeper; it is the idea that utilitarianism is basically incomplete in its view of the relation between agents and the states of affairs which satisfy their desires. States of affairs are typically seen as conditions in the external world which enable the satisfaction of desires. Since on the utilitarian account what matters is the satisfaction of desires, states of affairs are of central importance since they enable, or defeat, that satisfaction. But a different account is possible on which this 'external' relation between desires and their satisfaction is replaced by one in which the formation of a structure of desire, or the becoming of a certain kind of person, is itself the state of affairs which a person desires.

This kind of satisfaction is not one which the consequentialist rationality of social choice can directly address. If you are thirsty I can easily address your desire to drink; I simply provide the right liquid. But if your desire is to have a particular structure of desire, or to be a certain kind of person, perhaps with the extra requirement that this personal state is something which you have worked (a part of your achievement) to bring into being, the interpersonal position is very different. A social option cannot straightforwardly provide, e.g. satisfaction conditions for the formation of structures of desire; that formation is down to the person involved. Rather, the social options switch to conditions for example of education in which a person can conceive certain structures of desire as possible. The essential point to realize is that this consideration about the relation between persons and states of affairs which satisfy their desires turns on no mere mismatch of 'intuitions' with utilitarianism. The satisfaction of desire remains at the centre of the picture, as does the assessment of outcomes in terms of their satisfaction; the desire, that is, to have a particular structure of desire or to be a certain kind of person.

We readily see that the fear that an agent might be 'controlled' by the consequences of his actions, since no option can be foreclosed, is not a point on which we have to give way in face of consequentialist rationality or rely on immediate appeals to intuition to justify. Much of the critical literature on utilitarianism centres on examples in which, in carefully engineered situations, the agent is rationally obliged to seek a 'best' outcome quite contrary to his antecedent desires. If we 'internalize' the satisfaction of desire, as when an agent desires to form a structure of desire, the manipulation of consequences in the external world is correspondingly reduced as a way of 'controlling' him; and the utilitarian stress on states of affairs in the external world which enable the satisfaction of desires no longer automatically determines the 'best' outcome in decision-making.

2.11   THE NATURE OF AGENCY
(3): SUMMARY

Contemporary moral philosophy underlines the concept of action. This has two results: first to reduce personality to agency, so that a person is conceived barely as a source of actions; secondly to reduce actions to causes, so that in utilitarianism, the dominant of rationality, actions are conceived barely as sources of states of affairs in the external world.

To consider the second result first. I have argued against utilitarianism that it cannot align the viewpoints of agent and spectator. 'How it would be rational to act', from the agent's viewpoint, may still produce results which, as states of affairs in the external world, are adverse from the spectator's viewpoint. This is an unresolved discrepancy of consequentialism; and I have suggested that neither an 'ethics of motive' nor an 'ethics of consequences' is fully satisfactory.

Cases in which someone desires to form a particular structure of desire, or to be a certain kind of person, are relevant to the first result of contemporary moral philosophy's emphasis on the concept of action, the contracted view in which persons are regarded solely as agents. Here the main point is that a wider perspective, glimpsed in our rapid reflections on the 'aesthetic man', shows how an approach to the rationality of moral action can work outwards from a person's structure of desire to the requirements of moral action, instead of first specifying the requirements of moral action and then, taking the person barely at the point of action, casting about for reasons to induce him to act morally.

This completes my examination of the three main topics announced in 2.1. I shall now present a view of Green as a philosopher from whom on all three topics, we still have much to learn.

2.12 THE RELEVANCE OF GREEN

In the first place Green offers a particular analysis of belief and desire, the cognitive and conative, in terms of a theory of self-consciousness. We have seen, and emphasized, that both the belief–desire theory and the cognitive model rely on a distinction between belief and desire as exclusive factors. Whether action results from the conjunction of antecedent desires and beliefs, as on the belief–desire theory, or belief can explain action independently of desire, as on the cognitive model, both models of action explanation present the distinction between belief and desire as a pure division between sharply bounded categories. Green's central stress is on a structure of desire which a person can bring about by self-intervention, a structure which amounts to a rational organization of desire to achieve 'self-satisfaction', 'an abiding satisfaction of an abiding self'. The structure of desire thus organized is informed by the person's conception of himself: as he acts so we may explain his action in terms equally of how he sees himself and of what he wants. The pure division of belief and desire, cognitive and conative, gives way to an ambiguous scission that requires a novel theory of action which I term 'multi-perspectival'. So a fresh perspective is opened on the debate concerning action explanation. This aspect of Green's philosophy is developed in Chapter 4 on 'Reason, Desire, and Self-consciousness'.

Green's second point of relevance concerns the rationality of moral action. In Green's ethics it is not action which is central but rather desire from which action results. In terms of that structure Green offers a minimum argument for the rationality of moral action on the basis of *de facto* social identification. He then extends this argument to advance a general case for the acquisition of the moral virtues through a systematic theory of the human good, a theory itself unladen with moral notions. The specification of the human good is that it should provide, in the phrase we have already used, 'an abiding satisfaction of an abiding self', that is that it should fulfil the good of a person as a purposive being extended over time. Green identifies five criteria of the human good and argues that those criteria are satisfied by the moral good possessed by the virtuous agent. This part of Green's philosophy is examined in Chapters 6 and 7 on 'The Transition to Morality'.

Thirdly, in stressing a rational, long-term organization of desire, Green provides an account of how such a structure can be built up through the formation of character and of how character operates through motive in the determination of action. This tripartite coverage, of character, motive, and action, offers a more comprehensive view of the agent than is familiar in current ethics. It is set out in Chapter 5; and the point is not that Green merely offers such a view, but that his account of 'abiding satisfaction' through a rational, long-term organization of desire positively requires it. As motive and action are, as we shall see, internally related on the side of the agent through a theory of character, so action and consequence are internally related through a model of social roles in a coherent structure of human organization. The external relation of action to consequence, central to utilitarianism as a revisionary moral theory, disappears. Social roles are also assigned a place in the formation of character and in the exercise of virtue. Moral rules are not dominant descriptions but have a 'presumptive' relevance to action. This area of Green's philosophy is described in the later sections of Chapter 7.

Green's moral philosophy handles all those aspects of the rationality of self-interest listed in 2.4.2. His account of the rationality of moral action covers the consideration of others' interests. His theory of the human good acts as a filter against those desires which harm, or fail fully to promote, an agent's own interests. That same theory excludes the promotion of egotistic desires of which the pursuit creates prisoners' dilemma

situations. Green's idea of bringing about a certain structure of
desire to achieve 'self-satisfaction' involves no assumption that,
by the nature of things, the self is fixed across time; the point is
to create a continuing self under rational conditions, not to posit
an automatically fixed continuant.

At this point a glance back to Chapter 1 shows how the
contemporary relevance of Green's philosophy differs from its
historical surface. In the critique of utilitarianism, for example,
Green himself puts the accent on his anti-hedonist polemic with
its arguments about the logical object of desire and the
impossibility of a sum of pleasures. But he has, from our
own viewpoint, more interesting arguments against consequentialism, arguments which we can bring into prominence even
though Green himself thought that utilitarianism, in the
nineteenth-century form in which he knew it, was formidably
embarrassed by quite other difficulties.

2.13 ETHICAL FREEDOM

Before we can proceed to these matters, however, we need to
look at a question which for Green is of overriding importance
and which colours his treatment of nearly every topic he discusses. I refer to the question of free will.

3

Metaphysics, Ethics, and Freedom

3.1 INTRODUCTION

At least three senses of 'freedom' appear in Green. The first and central sense for this chapter is that of free will in PE, Book I. The second sense is that of interpersonal freedom, 'a social and political relation of one man to others' (Works II, 309). The third sense is that of free agency: to be a 'free agent' is to be self-determined, to have self-mastery (Works II, 308–9). Free agency will be examined in 5.10, interpersonal freedom briefly in 8.5. What, then, of free will?

Free will is not a focal concern of the present book. My aim is not to confront an issue of which the resolution stands outside the limits of ethics, but rather to give an account of Green's ethical theory and moral psychology. For three reasons, however, the issue of free will cannot be avoided altogether in our discussion of Green. In the first place, the principal text of Green's ethical theory and moral psychology, *Prolegomena to Ethics*, is dominated in Book I by exactly this issue. If we regard the present chapter as only an interlude, it is none the less essential in the interests of historical accuracy to take note of an issue which Green at any rate regarded as of critical importance. But secondly, one argument which is involved in Green's defence of free will, the argument based on his 'self-conscious principle', has ramifications beyond the immediate question how decision-making can involve free choice, how deliberation in any sense relevant to moral responsibility is possible. It underpins a person's ability to structure or order his own desires and to alter his character. To introduce these points is to invoke major themes of Green's moral psychology. Thirdly, to understand the precise importance of the free will issue in PE, Book I is a sure defence against certain errors of interpretation, misprisions which have wholly distorted the relation of Book I to the rest of the *Prolegomena*.

To explain more exactly the plan this chapter follows. First I state the view, taken by Green and not uncommon in our own day, that determinism is incompatible with moral responsibility. I then define two kinds of physical determinism to which Green was opposed: reductive materialism (with its insistence that mental events are identical to causally determined physical events) and one-way physicalism (with its insistence that mental events, though not identical to physical events, are causally determined by them). I shall briefly refer to psychological determinism, on which Green held views but which is excluded from the central thrust of PE, Book I. Two levels of Green's critique of physical determinism are introduced: his free-mind argument, involving a 'self-conscious principle', against one-way physicalism; and his ontological argument, involving a relational account of reality as mind-dependent, against reductive materialism. The free-mind and ontological arguments embody the heart of Green's metaphysics. Both arguments are based on an analysis of knowledge. This analysis brings Green into conflict with empiricism over the character of mind and over the relation of mind to the external world. Also over the relation of mind to the external world it sets him against Kant.

Moving to the end, I assess the cogency of Green's critique of physical determinism. I also suggest that the ethical theory and moral psychology which Green offers do not really depend for their interest on the ambitious metaphysics of PE, Book I. I then underscore one point of tension between Green's moral psychology and metaphysics. Closing, I note two misconceptions to which Green's metaphysics has given rise. One: the view of A. E. Taylor that Green seeks to justify ethical conclusions directly by deduction from metaphysical premises. Two: the view of J. A. Stewart that Green invokes metaphysics to prove the existence of God. Finally I amend the minimal conditions of moral responsibility to reflect Green's views more accurately.

3.2 DETERMINISM, PHYSICALISM, AND FREE WILL

Now to business. In 2.2 we characterized intentional action in terms of three conditions:

(1) A was able to do X.
(2) A did X knowingly.
(3) A could have done otherwise, if he had chosen.

These conditions also define a minimal notion of moral responsibility; and condition (3) defines a minimal notion of free will. If free will is necessary for moral responsibility, how is determinism incompatible with free will? To address this question we need first to make a distinction. Determinism involves causality, but the two principles are not the same. The principle of causality is simply that every event has a cause; the principle of determinism is that what is caused is necessitated. Determinism interprets causality in a particular way: that when one event causes another, the two events are so connected by a general law that events of the first type must be followed by events of the second type. None of this follows just from the principle of causality, which is consistent with the view that, for example, laws of nature are irreducibly statistical. Then a determinist denial of free will can be set out as follows:

Anti-Free Will Argument

(i)   Actions and choices are events.
(ii) All events are caused.
(iii) What is caused is necessitated.
(iv) What is necessitated cannot be otherwise.
(v)   Therefore: either A cannot do or choose otherwise.
(vi) Conclusion: in any given situation A could not have done or chosen otherwise.

Both parts of (3) above are blocked by (vi): determinism is incompatible with free will. This is the claim with which I shall mainly work. That a different claim is possible, that determinism may be compatible with free will through a theory of emergent properties, will be canvassed in 3.12.

If it is important to distinguish between determinism and causality, it is equally important to distinguish between determinism and physicalism (or 'materialism' in the language of the nineteenth century). If events which are caused are also necessitated, nothing has yet been said about the nature of those events. We have not said that all events are physical events, nor that all laws are physical laws. Some kinds of determinism do say

this; and others, while accepting that there are mental events
which are irreducible to physical events, assign unique causal
status to physical events. These kind of determinism pose
perhaps the most serious challenge to free will.

Green felt keenly that through determinist attacks on the
possibility of free will, doubt had been thrown on the notion of
moral responsibility if not for himself then for the 'multitude of
the educated' or at least a proportion of 'reflecting men' (PE, §
1). The attacks with which Green is mainly occupied in PE,
Book I derive from two physicalist sources:

(1) *Reductive materialism*. Nature is wholly physical. Mental
    events are identical to physical events, mental states to
    physical states of the brain or central nervous system.
(2) *One-way physicalism*. There are mental events which are
    non-physical but physical events cause mental events,
    mental events are causally inert and never cause physical
    events.

Neither reductive materialism nor one-way physicalism need
be determinist, though Green himself actually encountered
them in a determinist framework. Green confronts reductive
materialism in roughly the above form in his reference to the
views of 'materialists', who 'think of matter and motion as
real in some way in which nothing else is' (PE, § 25; cf. § 9).
Reductive materialism reads 'physical events' for 'events' in our
schema (i)–(vi) and deduces, on a determinist construction, that
A cannot do or choose otherwise. Green addresses one-way
physicalism in the view that 'the human consciousness, as it is,
can be physically accounted for' (PE, § 7; cf. § 5). One-way
physicalism also deduces, on a determinist construction, that A
cannot do or choose otherwise. Man is a part of physically
determinist nature. Physical events cause mental events, and the
mental event of A's choosing to do X is causally determined by a
physical event, Y, which itself is subject to causal necessity.

Two brief historical comments are in order. The first is that
since Henry Chandler cited in his Inaugural Lecture (1.9) Karl
Vogt's notorious simile that the brain secretes thought as the
liver secretes bile,[1] we know that German one-way physicalism

---

[1] H. W. Chandler, *The Philosophy of Mind a Corrective for Some Errors of the Day*,
London, 1867, 10. See K. Vogt, *Physiologische Briefe für Gebildete aller Stände*, Stuggart,

had reached Oxford by the 1860s; it was known about, and this 'cheap materialism' of Engels's vitriolic broadside is likely to have been part of the background against which Green developed his ideas. Similar views were advanced by British writers, G. H. Lewes, W. B. Carpenter, and H. C. Bastian, on whom Green wrote in unpublished notes cited in the bibliography. Secondly, the historical background includes also a major strand of longer-term thinking on the notion of cause. For Aristotle there were four main types of cause: material, formal, efficient, and final. Very roughly the material cause is that in which change takes place; the formal cause is the essential nature of that in which changes takes place by virtue of which it can change from one state to another. The efficient cause is the instrument of change, the source of motion by which change is precipitated; the final cause is the purpose for which the change is made, the goal to which it is directed. Aristotelian final causality is encased in a theology for which God, the self-knowing mind and unmoved mover, is, by the attraction of his perfection, the ultimate goal of change throughout the universe.[2]

Later, parts of this fourfold classification were cut away. It is a familiar story how, in the scientific revolution of the sixteenth and seventeenth centuries, the possibility of knowing essences in nature became increasingly suspect and with it the notion of formal cause. Both Bacon and Descartes excluded the notion of final cause from physical science. This left material and efficient causes: matter, now recognized in its own right and not simply as the inseparable correlate of form, and motion. Thence the mathematical and mechanical conception of nature which we find in Descartes and Hobbes. Hence Green's reference to the view of 'matter and motion as real in some way in which nothing else is'.

1845–7, 206: quoted in F. Gregory, *Scientific Materialism in Nineteenth Century Germany*, Dordrecht, 1977, 64.

Note the earlier, identical language of P. J. G. Cabanis, *Rapports du physique et du morale de l'homme*, Paris, 1824, i. 124–5: 'For a proper appreciation of the process by which thought comes about, we must recognize the brain as the organ of thought, which it produces . . . just as . . . the liver secretes bile' (Eng. tr. GLT). See Adrian Coates's quotation from Cabanis in *A Sceptical Examination of Contemporary British Philosophy*, London, 1929, 25.

[2] This is a high-level view: the Artistotelian universe is encased in such a theology, therefore final causality is so encased. Clearly, however, within nature final causality is

3.3 PSYCHOLOGICAL DETERMINISM

Physical determinism is not the only type of determinism. Psychological determinism offered itself to Green mainly in the form of hedonism. The Benthamite version of hedonism had placed mankind under the governance of two sovereign masters, pleasure and pain, without close regard for mental–physical correlations. Conceivably Benthamite psychological hedonism could be true on a theory of Cartesian occasionalism. A new feature of psychological hedonism in Green's day routed hedonism directly through one-way physicalism. This was the physicalist version of psychological hedonism to be found, for instance, in Alfred Barratt's *Physical Ethics; or The Science of Action* (1869). On this account psychological hedonism was retained, since we unavoidably pursue pleasure and avoid pain, but a physical correlation was introduced in which such pursuit and avoidance were uniquely determined by physical events and bodily states.[3]

Green's confrontation with psychological determinism, *qua* hedonism, is the least straightforward part of his discussion of free will. In the first place, he takes time out to present a more plausible version, as he supposes, of the hedonist case. It had been a problem for hedonism, Green says, to negotiate two points: 'that the mere survey of actions as tending to produce pleasures in which the contemplator will have no share, is yet a source of pleasure to him; and that, among the pleasures taken into account in that estimate of the tendency of an action which determines the moral sentiment, are such as have no direct connexion with the satisfaction of animal wants' (PE, § 4). Green does not accept that evolutionist ideas, reliance on which is another feature of Barratt's text, actually relive psychological hedonism of its embarrassment on these two counts. But the

---

directly a matter of things performing their functions. The heavenly bodies move in order to be like God, but this is not immediately true of biological entities. I have benefited from discussing these topics with D. W. Hamlyn and David Rees, of whom perhaps neither will agree exactly with what I say.

[3] A. Barratt, *Physical Ethics; or The Science of Action*, London, 1869. A short discussion of Barratt is to be found in M. Gayau, *La Morale anglaise*, Paris, 1885, 190–1. See also B. Bosanquet, *Science and Philosophy*, London, 1927, 157; and F. Y. Edgeworth, *New and Old Methods of Ethics, or "Physical Ethics" and "Methods of Ethics"*, Oxford and London, 1877.

immediate point is that Green is here saddling psychological hedonism with baggage which it does not need to carry. No theory of psychological hedonism is committed, just as such, to any assumption that the pleasures pursued will be directly connected with what Green is pleased to call the satisfaction of 'animal wants'. And the point regarding pleasures in which the agent will have no share has critical importance not for psychological hedonism in general but specifically for hedonist psychological egoism. Secondly, Green has an argument against hedonism, the logical object argument (1.7), which, if it goes through, refutes hedonism and takes psychological hedonism with it.

In PE, Book I Green aims his guns mainly at physical determinism. Psychological determinism is meant to be dealt with effectively by this strategy to the extent that it involves the correlation of mental and physical events in the manner of Barratt. To the extent that it might be held independently of this correlation, in the old Benthamite form, Green is clear that he can dispatch it, so taken, with the logical object argument of PE, Book II. The urgency is to confront physical determinism.

3.4   GREEN'S CRITIQUE OF PHYSICAL DETERMINISM

Green's critique of physical determinism in Book I of *Prolegomena to Ethics* is apt to convey an impression of inspissated complexity which is not confined to a first reading. Presentationally Green does advance a very convoluted defence of free will against physical determinism; and commentators have on the whole followed his own pattern of exposition, tracing an intricate pattern through the reticulations of Green's text. I think, however, that we can do better than that. If we distinguish the pattern of exposition from the pattern of argument, separating Green's own presentation from what is operating at a deeper level, we find an argument which evolves in two paths. There is a pattern of free-mind argument and a pattern of ontological argument.

More specifically Green's arguments are these. He first confronts the one-way physicalist view that man is a part of physically determinist nature such that mental events are causally determined by physical events. He argues that knowledge, and specifically our perceptual awareness of change, supposes a 'self-conscious principle' which defeats the correlation of mental with physical events. The self-conscious principle which is present in perception, and by virtue of which the mind is free from physical determination, is also present, Green argues, in desire; and he draws out an elaborate parallelism between desire and perception. This is in essentials his free-mind argument. The accompanying ontological argument, which also proceeds from an analysis of knowledge, aims to show not simply that mind is independent of nature but, in uncompromisingly idealist fashion, that nature is dependent on mind. Mind cannot be subject to physical determination when physical nature itself is a product of mind. These distinct lines of argument, free-mind and ontological, will dominate the present chapter.

3.5 THE ANALYSIS OF KNOWLEDGE

Both the free-mind argument and the ontological argument suppose knowledge: the first our knowledge of a world where things change, the second our knowledge of a world of objects. Green's arguments emerge directly from his analysis of these forms of knowledge. Two general observations are in place.

First, Green's analysis of knowledge has a 'dialectical' aspect. It is well not to press too closely the Hegelian associations of 'dialectical'. PE, Book I's dialectical character is its assumption of a separation or pure division between the cognitive and the conative. Conclusions drawn from the analysis of knowledge in Book I are later applied to the analysis of desire. But as the argument of the *Prolegomena* advances, not only are both knowledge and desire seen as involving an identical self-conscious principle, but in other respects also the pure division between cognition and conation gives way to a tight mutal embeddedness of the two notions. We shall examine this part of Green's philosophical psychology in some detail in the next chapter.

Secondly, Green's analysis is locked within three limits. Green is not a sceptic. He assumes the fact of knowledge and works back, in the manner of Kant, to the conditions of its possibility. But he mounts no enterprise such as Kant's to construct a complete typology of knowledge: a priori/a posteriori, analytic/synthetic, and crucially the cross-division of synthetic a priori. This is the first limit. The second limit is that Green assumes, again in the manner of Kant, a view of knowers as independent knowing subjects. His discussion in PE, Book I takes no account of knowledge in its social setting. Green does not in general underrate the impact of 'the social medium' (6.6). But he does not need to examine the social setting here: his concern is simply to elicit from the fact of knowledge its implications for free will. The third limit is this. The 'fact' of knowledge is not wholly uncontroversial. Manifestly the status of certain kinds of knowledge is more problematic than that of others. An analysis of knowledge which relied, for example, on claims to know a personal God would raise large problems for negotiation in other areas of philosophy before the epistemological issues could be resolved. Such an analysis would not serve Green's purpose of an immediately available and agreed platform in epistemology between himself and his determinist opponents. For this reason Green is anxious to confine his analysis (save for a brief excursus into mathematical knowledge, PE, § 57) to the field of perception, and within this field to the 'simplest possible' kinds of perceptual claim in which 'the particular things we perceive' are 'this flower, this apple, this dog' (Works I, 412; PE, § 63). From Green's own viewpoint the merit of this emphasis is that, given our knowledge of a world where things change and of a world of objects, not only is perceptual knowledge usually granted to be authentic, but in the visual perception of such things as flowers, apples, and dogs 'the independence of matter' (Works I 410) appears most evident. Green can at least not be criticized for choosing examples which specially help the conclusions he wants to draw.

3.6 THE SELF-CONSCIOUS PRINCIPLE

One-way physicalism claims a correlation of mental and physical events such that mental events are uniquely determined by physical events. Green approaches perception with an account of our awareness of change. Such awareness is held by Green to involve 'a self-conscious principle'. Since the point is untiringly enunciated, we have a wide choice of texts:

(1) But a consciousness of events as a related series—experience in the most elementary form in which it can be the beginning of knowledge—has not any element of identity with, and therefore cannot properly be said to be developed out of, a mere series of related events, of successive modifications of body or soul . . . No one and no number of a series of related events can be the consciousness of the series as related. (PE, § 16.)

(2) But neither can any process of change yield a consciousness of itself, which, in order to be a consciousness of the change, must be equally present to all stages of the change; nor can any consciousness of change, since the whole of it must be present at once, be itself a process of change. (PE, § 18.)

(3) . . . 'nature' is a *process of change*, and . . . the derivation of a *consciousness* of change from such a process is impossible. (PE, § 35.)

One might add PE, §§ 32, 65, and 84, the list is readily extensible. Green's argument is that an awareness of change cannot be correlated with any series of physical events. If we are to examine his argument profitably, however, we need to realize that it contains a fusion of notions where really one should make a clear distinction. Also that it can be presented from two angles, analytical and historical.

From the analytical angle Green can be seen as offering an argument which is independent of the particular philosophical psychology with which it is actually linked in PE, Book I and elsewhere in his writings. The following reconstruction puts us on Green's traces. A perceiver is a system, let us suppose, which responds to a series of inputs by a succession of changes in its own state. We may specify these inputs as 'physically' as we like. The tree falls; there is a stimulus to my eye, impulses are discharged along afferent nerve fibres, a complete physiological pattern unfolds. These are physical events. Sensory experience results, I see the tree fall. I am aware of change; I am aware that the tree has fallen.

Green's argument is that physical events have certain connections with time which fail to hold for mental events such as the awareness of change. Physical events have dates and times, phases and durations. We can always ask how long an event took. But the awareness of change, Green argues, is a non-successive unity. Take the physical even of the tree's falling. This occupied, say, ten seconds. For this event there was a half-way point. But no half-way point is possible for the awareness of change, namely for my awareness that the tree has fallen. This awareness is not made up of phases which occur successively; necessarily it occurs 'all at once'. This I take to be Green's view in the passage quoted above in which he says precisely that 'the whole of it [sc. any awareness of change] must be present at once'. It is also, I think, the substance of his otherwise rather mysterious remarks about the 'neutralisation of time' (PE, § 65) and the explanation of 'everyday perception . . . by a principle that is not in time' (PE, § 66).

The argument bears development. For the awareness of change we can substitute any thought that occurs to me. Any thought has the same kind of non-successive unity; note PE, § 71 on understanding a sentence. Then if Green's argument goes through, the correlation of mental and physical events on which one-way physicalism depends is impossible. Physical events have phases which occur successively; and a sequence of phases is logically not the kind of thing which can correlate with the non-successive unity of a thought. And its weakness or appeal is determined by purely general considerations about events, thoughts, and time.

But I think there is a further notion in the passages we have quoted. Let us suppose that mental events can be correlated with physical events. Physical events are successive, temporally discrete; but my successive views of the tree's falling are 'synthesized' in memory, 'held together' as a series when I am aware that the tree has fallen. If the mind itself were a mere series of separate, independent states induced by (and correlative with) successive, temporally discrete inputs, how could I hold together in memory the successive views of the tree's falling? The very idea of a series would be impossible for a mind which itself were merely serial. This is the point of such remarks as that 'No one and no number of a series of related events can be the consciousness of the series as related.' Green is presenting really a separate notion here.

Switch now to the second, historical angle on Green's argument. Green's philosophy of perception is a reaction to the 'sensationalism' of nineteenth-century empiricism, with which it shares the assumption that the senses give one only 'atomic' experiences. Sensations are discrete, atomic: perception involves the superimposition of relations by the mind. A television analogy may help. Let us suppose that I am watching television and that the view with which I am presented, across say ten seconds, is that of a door opening and of somebody entering a room. One account of what is going on would be to say that the television screen fills up, dot by dot, line by line, down its complete length. When the screen is full, it is replaced and another screen is filled in the same way. After ten seconds I can describe what I have seen. Then the sensationalist account of perception is that sensations are discrete, like the dots of which each screen is composed: and the work of the mind in perception is to build up these discrete sensations into pictures, or perceptions, and to hold successive pictures in memory. That is very roughly the sensationalist account of perception.

But the empiricist model of the mind into which sensationalism fits would not be forgotten. Whether Hume adopts atomism in the sense of punctiform, *minima sensibilia*, of which 'simple impressions' consist, I am uncertain; the ink spot example of T 27 appears to support this interpretation. But he undoubtedly adopts atomism in the sense of discrete, successive perceptions ('impressions and ideas', where ideas are copies or images of impressions in memory and imagination) to which experience reduces. Hume constantly pulls us back to what, in his view, is strictly given in experience, 'distinct perceptions' which are 'distinct existences' (T 636). Take a pin-sharp picture of the given; the result, for Hume, is *A Treatise of Human Nature.* What experience gives are distinct perceptions; what imagination takes are material objects, 'necessary connections' between causally related events, mental and material substance. These are not given in experience but are constructions from the 'transition or passage of the imagination' (T 204) across the given; and the mind itself, the subject-self which might be supposed to hold together 'our several particular perceptions' (T 658) when, for example, we are aware of change, is not safe from this process of reduction. James Mill used the term 'feelings' to cover both impressions and ideas; and the claim became common, in the spirit of T 1.4.6 and the language of James Mill, that experience yields no continuant, 'the mind', but only discrete, successive feelings. To Green this appeared the height of paradox. The claim is to be found in John Stuart Mill; and Henry Sturt's suggestion in *Idola Theatri* is that Green retorts upon Mill his own paradox from *An Examination of Sir William Hamilton's Philosophy*:[4]

If, therefore, we speak of the Mind as a series of feelings, we are obliged to complete the statement by calling it a series of feelings which is aware of itself as past and future: and we are reduced to the alternative of believing that the Mind, or Ego, is something different from any series of feelings, or possibilities of them, or of accepting the paradox, that something which *ex hypothesi* is but a series, can be aware of itself as a series.[5]

Green's principle is not explicitly targeted at Mill's text. This might illustrate what George Croom Robertson called Green's 'method of innuendo' against Mill.[6] But Green assails Mill openly when occasion demands (e.g. PE, § 292). To single Mill out for special criticism would obscure Green's point that here is a paradox which vitiates not simply Mill's philosophy of mind but the general empiricist 'serial' model of the mind.

Just to end the account of sensationalism. As previously said, Green shares with sensationalism the assumption that the senses give one only discrete, atomic experiences, *minima visibilia* in the case of perception. His disagreement is that such experiences must at least have 'this or that order of succession, with this or that degree of intensity' (PE, § 46). Otherwise, the point applies from elsewhere, they would present 'nothing but a blank featureless identity' (PE, § 28); and it will be clear when we examine Green's account of the relational nature of reality

---

[4] H. Sturt, *Idola Theatri*, London, 1906, 221.

[5] J. S. Mill, *An Examination of Sir William Hamilton's Philosophy*, London, 1865, 4th edn. 1872, 212–13.

[6] *Philosophical Remains of George Croom Robertson*, ed. A. Bain and T. Whittaker, London, 1894, 379. Reviewing W. L. Courtney, *The Metaphysics of John Stuart Mill*, Robertson observes that 'The author, who seems implicitly to follow Prof. Green in philosophy, does in fact aspire to substitute plain speech as regards Mill for his leader's method of innuendo.'

that features such as succession and intensity are already mind-dependent. Green will not allow 'unrelated' or 'mere' sensations on which perception involves the superimposition of relations by the mind (PE, § 46).

I want now to return from history to analysis and to take stock of a parallelism which PE introduces between perception and desire, one that has strong implications for the issue of free-will.

3.7 PERCEPTION AND DESIRE

The parallelism is instituted at various points in the text of PE: §§ 85, 91, 118, and 121. § 85 is a key text:

... wants, with the sequent impulses, must be distinguished from the consciousness of wanted objects, and from the effort to give reality to the objects thus present in consciousness as wanted, no less than sensations of sight and hearing have to be distinguished from the consciousness objects to which those sensations are conceived to be related. It has been sufficiently pointed out how the presentation of sensible things, on occasion of sensation, implies the action of a principle which is not, like sensation ... an event or a series of events, but must equally be present to, and distinguish itself from, the several stages of a sensation to which attention is given, as well as the several sensations attended to and referred to a single object. In like manner the transition from mere want to consciousness of a wanted object, from the impulse to satisfy the want to an effort for realisation of the idea of the wanted object, implies the presence of the want to a subject which distinguishes itself from it and is constant throughout successive stages of the want.

First a terminological clarification. In the expression 'the consciousness of wanted objects', Green's meaning is almost fully screened from view. Thus if I am gazing in a shop window at a David Sylvian album which I want to buy, Green's language naturally suggests that my consciousness of the wanted object is my seeing the album at whatever distance it is from me. In fact for Green 'the consciousness of wanted objects' is my recognition that I desire X or Y. Then to return: Green appears to be making two points. The first is this. It is important, he suggests, to mark off momentary urges from the kind of desires which one recognizes oneself as possessing across time ('from childhood I have wanted to see San Francisco bay'). It is equally important to mark off one's recognition of a desire from one's decision to act on that desire. My long-standing desire to see San Francisco bay is, *ex hypothesi*, not one on which I have acted, and I have not yet decided even that I will act on it at some indeterminate time. I accept that under competition from more significant desires it may be indefinitely suspended. For Green, to decide to act on a desire is to adopt it as a motive; and the notions of impulse, desire, and motive are central to his moral psychology. This is our introduction to them.

But Green's second point is more fundamental, and is central to the issue of free will. When I recognize that I desire X or Y, this recognition is just such an atemporal, non-successive unity as my awareness of change. It is incapable, accordingly, of correlation with (or of determination by) physical events. And the desire itself is susceptible to a particular analysis to which the Kantian unity of apperception is the key. There must be a unified consciousness in the case of perception, so also in that of desire. There is a difference between merely having sensation and what makes those sensations the consciousness of an object. For such consciousness there has to be a unifying activity on the part of the subject. The same holds true of desire. I can have impulses in certain directions, but to desire an object there must be a unifying activity on my part. Since such unifying activity is necessary to desire, therefore no physical event or series of physical events could be sufficient for desire unless it were also sufficient for the unifying activity on the part of the subject. But this takes us back to Green's claim, and to his arguments, concerning the atemporal unity of thought which is involved in that unifying activity.

3.8 RELATIONS AND REALITY

Green does not rest content with showing, against one-way physicalism. That mind is independent of nature and that the freedom of mind from physical determination in perception carries over into the practical sphere with respect to desire. He deploys against reductive materialism an ontological argument for the relational nature of reality, ar argument on which nature is dependent on mind. To this we now turn. First a summary, then a point of terminology.

The thrust of Green's argument is that an object is nothing but its qualities; qualities are relational; and relations are constituted by the mind. Therefore nothing can exist independently of mind. The point of terminology is simply that the terms 'quality', 'property', and 'attribute' are used by Green interchangeably. This perhaps violates tradition. In the history of philosophy, 'quality' is contrasted with quantity and relation; beyond this point, divergencies of terminology carry nuances in different traditions. In the Aristotelian tradition properties are contrasted with what does not necessarily belong to the subject, namely accidents. 'Attribute' is the vaguest term. But one speaks, or some speak, of the attributes of God; and whatever is true of God is true necessarily, with no distinction between the necessary and the non-necessary (contingent or accidental). So God's attributes may be taken to define his essential nature. These distinctions are quite blocked out of view in Green. In setting out his argument I shall mainly use the term 'quality'. If this suggests a contrast with 'relation', we shall at least appreciate that nothing quite conventional is going on when we see that Green denies a distinction between qualities and relations.

In Green's ontological argument the example of perception, this time of a world of objects, still carries the main expository weight. I cannot here discuss the reduction of objects to events, the Russellian view of an object as, to a first approximation, what happens in a segment of space-time. If we accept, as I do for present purposes, an ontology of objects, Green makes a distinct claim about the perception of objects: 'all perception is consciousness of relation' (Works I, 411). 'Consciousness of' here means 'acquaintance with'. To see a flower, Green tells us, is to be acquainted with a complex or 'nexus' of qualities: the flower is purple, white, and red. 'Nexus' covers, I believe, two ideas. First, as to individuation, (perceptual) objects are sets of qualities. Qualities are universals and are related to objects as members to sets. If one object has qualities X and Y, and another has qualities Y and Z, Y is a member of both sets; and for there to be two objects one must possess a quality which the other lacks. Secondly, as to identity, an object is a composite of qualities, a whole of parts; if the qualities change, its parts vary, and (along a range of possibilities) the object is no longer in the same state or no longer exists.

Green's current point about perception is that any quality, considered separately from one relation, from the 'nexus' (set or whole), is still relational. 'Attributes mean relations' (Works II, 170). Immediately this looks wrong. Some qualities are relational. Take the example of a flower of which the red petals are wider than the purple stem. The objection to the view that all qualities are relational qualities is that the stem's quality of being purple, for instance, seems to contain no relational element at all. 'Wider than' is relational; 'purple' is not. But Green has an answer to this objection. His view is, I think, that for something to be purple is for it to have a determinate relation to the continuous series of shades and colours of which the spectrum is composed.

To understand this view clearly we have to turn to the 'Introduction to Hume', where it is advanced with reference not to colours but to tastes. On Green's analysis, if I judge 'this is sweet', then it is 'the relation of this [flavour] to other flavours which constitutes the determinate sweetness' (Works I, 35–6). The point is not, I think, that descriptive terms form sets whose members acquire their sense by mutual contrast, so that without a contrast with 'bitter', 'sour', 'cloying', and the rest, terms like 'sweet' would lack meaning or at least their present meaning. Green's point is rather that the fact of contrast is integral to the existence of a quality. To exist a quality must bear a determinate relation to other qualities of a relevant range. To express the point in the later terminology of W. E. Johnson, any quality which an object may have is a 'determinate' or a 'determinable'. But if all qualities are relational how are relations, and hence all qualities of an object, constituted by the mind? At this point we need to look at Green's critique of empiricism.

3.9   THE CRITIQUE OF EMPIRICISM

Empiricism offers an account both of what and of how we know. Green's self-conscious principle, which we have already examined, can be taken as a criticism of the empiricist account of how we know: that we know through a series or succession of mental states of which, Green claims, the empiricist analysis is paradoxical and incoherent. Thus Green objects to the empiricist view of the character of mind. But he also objects to its account of what we know, to its view of the relation between mind and the external world. This is our present topic.

In Locke's view, which is here central to Green's critique, what we know, at least, are 'simple ideas' of sense experience such as colours and shapes. These ideas are simple in the sense that nobody lacking them could arrive at them imaginatively by combining other ideas which his experience had provided; and simple in the further sense that all other ideas, namely 'complex ideas', are produced by compounding and abstracting simple ideas. Simple ideas mediate between the mind and the external world. Just what this means is, of course, a distinct problem in the interpretation of Locke. Locke is clear that we always have ideas when we perceive. It does not follow from this that all we perceive are ideas; and it is not clear that Locke held this second view. Green suggests that Locke's theory of perception slides unawares from one view to the other (Works I, 13). Ideas are one element in Locke's theory, qualities are another.

Locke is confident of one thing about the external world. Objects in the external world have primary qualities: such qualities 'as are utterly inseparable from the body, in what state soever it be', namely, 'solidity, extension, figure, motion or rest, and number' (*Essay* II.8.9 ff.). Of primary qualities, ideas are representational. We can be mistaken about an object's shape, but any object must have a shape; and the same point applies to the rest of the primary qualities. Objects really do have primary qualities; and only primary qualities resemble actual qualities this resemblance fails. Secondary qualities 'in truth are nothing in the objects themselves but powers to produce various sensations in us by their primary qualities—as colours, sounds, tastes, etc.' (ibid.). Again it is unclear just what this means: 'nothing ... but' is plainly ambiguous between 'secondary qualities are nothing in the objects themselves but rather, on the contrary' and 'secondary qualities are nothing in the objects themselves over and above'. Locke is at least saying, however, that the secondary qualities of objects do not resemble our ideas of them.

Green's approach to Locke is to say in effect: let us assume the view, which at any rate Locke does not explicitly repudiate, that all we perceive are ideas. In our knowledge of the external world the role of relational thinking, for Locke, is solely to put ideas, simple or complex, into sequence, combination, or comparison. I might have, for instance, two sense impressions, or 'ideas', one of a patch of yellow, the other of a patch of red. The relational element would enter with the thought that I saw one patch before the other, or that the patch of red was larger than the patch of yellow. All relations are superimposed by the mind. As Locke formulates the point, relation is 'not contained in the real existence of things, but [is] something extraneous and superinduced' (*Essay* II.25.8), 'the workmanship of the mind' (*Essay* III.5.14.). Relational thinking may be explicit (as when we think of Tad as a father) or tacit (as when we think of him as young). But Locke is quite clear that there are 'absolute' or 'positive' terms 'signifying something absolute in the subject' (*Essay* II.25. 1, 3). When one sees the whiteness of a tulip there is no suggestion, on Locke's account, what in one's perceptual experience one 'brings two things together, and as it were, takes a view of them at once', which is the essence of relational thinking. There is only 'the bare consideration', the perception, of the whiteness of the flower (*Essay* II.25.1, 3). But this is just what Green denies: every quality, even the whiteness of this tulip, is relational and all perception involves a consciousness of relation. How is this so?

The collapse of qualities into relations is pressed polemically against Locke:

Simple ideas or sensations we certainly do not 'make for ourselves'. They therefore and the matter supposed to cause them are, according to Locke, real. But relations are neither simple ideas not their material archetypes. They therefore, as Locke explicitly holds, fall under the head of the work of the mind, which is opposed to the real. But if we take him at his word and exclude from what we have considered real all qualities constituted by relation, we find that none are left. Without relation any simple idea would be undistinguished from other simple ideas, undetermined by its surroundings in the cosmos of experience. —(PE, § 20).

Green is here severing fairly artificially from its context a fragment of Locke's theory. In Green's epitome, Locke concedes that relations are 'the work of the mind'. But not only does Locke not hold that all qualities are relational qualities, more importantly the sense in which Green holds all qualities to be relational is quite different from that in which Locke holds some qualities to be relational. On Locke's account a relational quality is such a quality as, in our early example, the petals' being wider than the stem, in contrast to an 'absolute' quality such as the whiteness of the tulip. This sense of 'relational' is not Green's sense of 'relational' in which the fact of contrast (here present in his reference to 'its surroundings in the cosmos of experience'), a determinate relationship to other qualities, is integral to the existence of a quality.

Then Green's view that all qualities are relational, and that all relations are mind-dependent, depends heavily on the expiricist concession that relations are 'the work of the mind'. But, as have seen, really different views appear to meet here in the same words; and this is not critically clear when in passages like the above Green sets an appearance of pressing empricism sorely with the consequences of its own view of relations. One point should be clear, however. If all qualities are relational, and all relations are mind-dependent, then Green need not be disturbed by the reminder that while Locke holds that we always have ideas when we perceive, he perhaps does not hold that all we perceive are ideas. Green's critique can cut through this epistomological enclosure of 'ideas'. For whatever qualities objects have, regardless of the 'simple ideas' of primary and secondary qualities which they produce in human perceivers, these qualities must still be relational and still be mind-dependent. That is what qualities are.

3.10   THE ETERNAL CONSCIOUSNESS

But of what minds are we talking? Any form of idealism short of solipsism must handle a problem set by the limits of human perception: that of the existence of object currently unexperienced by human observers. Is there really no tree in the quad if nobody is in the quad to see it? The example is famous and is used advisedly. Certainly we shall understand Green better if we draw out some relevant contrasts with Berkeley

(Works I, 133–60). For Berkeley the solution to this problem lies in the existence of God. The tree still exists but is not unperceived. It is perceived by God. Now this view of a permanent perceiver is not totally dissimilar from Green's account of an 'eternal consciousness' which creates and sustains the system of relations in which reality consists. But in one crucial respect the eternal consciousness stands to human observers quite differently from Berkeley's God. For Berkeley's God has a causal relation to human observers. All that exist are minds and their ideas; and God causes those ideas in which human knowledge exists. For Green, by contrast, human observers 'participate ' in the eternal consciousness which they are also said partly to 'reproduce'.

The concepts of participation and reproduction are perhaps the most puzzling notions in Green's account of the eternal consciousness. Nobody has ever been satisfied with them. From Sidgwick's predictable onslaught to J. A. Smith's mild remonstration that Green 'left undeveloped, and somewhat obscure or ambiguous, his doctrine of the relation between the Universal Mind and our finite minds',[7] commentators have supposed that this patiently constructed house of cards collapses at the first breath of criticism. Three directions of inquiry should, I think, be blocked. One is suggested by C. C. J. Webb in his view that the problematic relation of the eternal consciousness to individual human knowers is simply an aspect of the generally dubious status of the human individual in British idealism.[8] Equally and relatedly problematic, for Webb, is the relation of the individual to society. And we may grant Webb the examples he forgoes. In certain moods both F. H. Bradley and Bernard Bosanquet see the human individual as an element separated by a kind of false abstraction from the social pattern. About Green the truth, as usual, is rather more complex. His is a 'personal' idealism which cannot be smoothly assimilated to this strand in the social philosophies of Bradley and Bosanquet.

Nor, secondly and relatedly, does direct recourse to the

[7] J. A. Smith, 'The Influence of Hegel on the Philosophy of Great Britain', *Verhandlungen des ersten Hegelkongresses vom 22. bis 25. April 1930 im Haag*, ed. B. Wigersma, Tübingen and Haarlem, 1931, 64.

[8] C. C. J. Webb, *A History of Philosophy*, Oxford, 1949, 196.

philosophy of Hegel supply the clue we need. If Hegel held that all reality is the expression of Absolute Mind, Green might be said to hold equally that all reality is the expression of the eternal consciousness. But Hegel believed that reality develops by a pattern of contradiction in which movements and activities provoke opposition from which fresh movements and activities emerge, only themselves to be opposed in a continuous 'dialectic' of growth. And he believed that the only way of understanding such a system of reality is by a 'dialectic' of knowledge in which one partial truth yields place to its opposite and both are reconciled in a more complete truth, which in turn is negated as the dialectic pulls us remorselessly through progressively higher levels of knowledge. Great exception has been taken to Hegel's logic in mirroring the two dialectics. But the present point is that no such triadic, dialectical relationship is essential to Green's account of the eternal consciousness and human knowledge, or is even to be found in it.

The third false direction of inquiry takes us to Plato's theory of forms. In Plato the forms are timeless entities existing in their own right, discernible by the intellect, of which sensible particulars are imperfect reproductions or imitations (*mimesis*) or in which they participate (*methexis*). Here are exactly the terms used by Green to describe the relationship between the eternal consciousness and finite knowers. We may safely conjecture that Green had read the *Phaedo* and *Parmenides* in which these terms appear. But this is an obvious debt of terminology, not a deeper debt of inspiration.

In Green's view Plato's theory of forms was bound up with a conception of dialectic as a process of progressive abstraction. This view is perhaps truer of the later dialogues than of the *Republic*. In the *Republic* dialectic moves up, through the destruction of hypotheses, to an unhypothetical first principle, the Form of the Good (Rep. VI and VII). Later dialogues, the *Sophist* and *Politicus*, apply a method of division and collection to highly general forms; and in the *Sophist*, interrelations emerge at an extreme level of generality (251D–257D). But in remarks on the *Republic* Green fastens upon generality and abstraction as the crucial weakness of Platonic dialectic and the theory of forms *tout court*: 'Plato's Dialectic vitiated by conception of thought as process of abstraction, which begins with individual thing as a complex of attributes and gradually "makes abstraction" of these till it reaches the "Pure Being" which = pure nothing' (Platonis de Republica, 201).[9]

The correct approach is this. Green 'recognized the constitution of things by intelligible relations' (Works I, 151). His view is that objects in the external world are mind-dependent. But this is not to say that reality is dependent on the human mind, much less on the mind of any individual human knower. 'External' does not need scare quotes. Reality as a system of intelligible relations, of knowable things, is constituted by the activity of the eternal consciousness. An object is nothing but its qualities; and the determinateness of the qualities which sensible particulars instantiate is the work of this consciousness. The system of intelligible relations, of determinate qualities instantiated in sensible particulars, constitutes the realm of the knowable. Against the knowable stand individual human knowers, who not only 'interpret it amiss' in particular false beliefs within the system (Works I, 131; cf. PE, §12) but are also capable of more radical error in false beliefs about the system, e.g. in failing to understand that sensible particulars are mind-dependent. In light of this position Green changes Berkeley's 'esse is percipi' to 'esse is intelligi' (Works I, 149).

How does this clarify the concepts of reproduction and participation? Green's view of the relation of the eternal consciousness to human knowers is twofold. In the first place, the eternal consciousness is 'the complete self-consciousness' (Works I, 131). It creates and sustains the system of relations which constitutes the realm of reality, the realm of the knowable. Human knowers can know in part what the eternal consciousness makes knowable. This distinction between partial and complete knowledge replaces the distinction between appearance and reality generated by the empiricist account of 'ideas' which mediate between the mind and objects in the external world. Secondly, both the eternal consciousness and human knowers are self-conscious. Just as self-consciousness is

---

[9] Green reveals no interest in another aspect of Platonic dialectic, in which it is informed by the notion of conversation, of philosophy as a method of question and answer (e.g. *Protagoras*, 334C–336D). But then, one distinguishes two principal faces of philosophy: Socrates arguing in the market-place and Descartes meditating in the isolation of his room. Green's own practice of philosophy was, in this respect, firmly Cartesian.

presupposed to human knowledge, so it is presupposed to the activity of the eternal consciousness in creating and sustaining the realm of the knowable. The activity of the human mind in self-consciousness replaces the Berkeleian picture of human knowledge as standing in a passive causal relation to God. To express this twofold view Green uses the metaphors of participation and reproduction to describe the relationship between the eternal consciousness and finite knowers. The siginificance of those metaphors is exhausted by that relationship; they should not be allowed to intrude as an independent source of puzzlement in the search for Green's meaning.

3.11 GREEN *CONTRA* KANT

The relational account of reality is Green's attempt to answer reductive materialism, but his account is also applied critically to rival idealisms. To that of Berkeley, as we have seen, but also that of Kant. If qualities are relational, what is unrelated must be quality-less; and what is quality-less cannot exist. (Green must exclude that existence itself is a quality.) This invalidates, from Green's position, Kant's view of the triad of sensation, intuition, and conception. One might take Kant in this way: Kant's view involves the notion of sensation as providing unmanipulated, absolutely unqualitied data of sense which supply the 'matter' of intuition. This 'matter' is synthesized under the a priori forms of space and time to yield a sense of 'this here now'. The understanding (*Verstand*) operates through twelve categories or concepts which, under the four headings of quantity, quality, relation, and modality, are the basic terms in which alone we can think of objects at all. Knowledge requires the interplay of intuitions and concepts. Just how this works on Kant's account is extremely complex in detail. But the broad picture is that the faculty of judgement (*Urteilskraft*) gives knowledge by combining intuitions and concepts through six schematized categories which Kant calls substance, cause, reciprocity, possibility, actuality, and necessity. This leaves everything to be said in the elucidation of Kant, but the significant point for present purposes is that Green lodges his objection at the start of this elaborate chain of ideas. The first link, between sensation and intuition, must be revised since Kant's unqualitied 'matter' of intuition cannot be allowed. The grounds of the revision have implications for the phenomenal/noumenal distinction which is fundamental to Kant's defence of free will.

When we have knowledge of an object, the unqualitied 'matter' of intuition corresponds (in a way which, on this interpretation, Kant never clearly specifies) to the unexperienceable thing-in-itself or noumenon which lies beyond phenomena (*Critique of Pure Reason*, A30). This is the sense of Kant's dictum that the understanding makes nature but out of a material which it does not make. Part of Green's objection to Kant is in terms of internal consistency. If all that we know of noumena is barely that they exist, we cannot have any knowledge of their commerce with the phenomenal world of the kind claimed when it is said that the unqualitied 'matter' of intuition corresponds to the noumenal and is the noumenal's contribution to the understanding's construction of nature. The supposedly non-relational noumenal bears inconsistently the relation of contrast to, differentiation from the phenomenal. But Green's main point is that Kant's unqualitied 'matter' of intuition cannot, *qua* quality-less, exist. There is therefore no such matter for the noumenal to correspond to. This leaves only the understanding to construct nature. Reality is relational and relations are constituted by the mind. Nothing lies beyond relational experience. Green's is an idealism which must in consistency trust in its account of reality 'not to a guess about what is beyond experience, but to analysis of what is within it' (Works I, 449; cf. Hume's 'we cannot go beyond experience', T xvii).

I do not want to enter far into the exposition of Kant; but I do not think one needs to do so in order to raise some doubts about Green's way of taking Kant. Very roughly, sensation supplies the 'matter' of intuition; the spatio-temporal relations between sensations provide the 'form'. All that follows from this is that, whatever qualities sensations may have, they are not spatio-temporal. It does not follow that sensations, before they are synthesized under the forms of space and time, are quite without qualities, and so, on this point at least, I am unpersuaded by Green's critique.

3.12 THE CRITIQUE OF PHYSICAL DETERMINISM: REVIEW

We have now examined Green's defence of free will: his free-mind argument and his ontological argument. The free-mind argument contains, in its 'self-conscious principle', really two separate notions: first the notion that any thought has a non-successive unity, secondly the notion that the idea of a series would be impossible for a mind which itself were merely serial. The free-mind argument aims to rule out the correlation of mental and physical events on which one-way physicalism depends. This argument is accompanied by a wider-ranging ontological argument, set against reductive materialism, which tries to show that nothing can exist independently of mind. It is, Green urges, a 'hysteron proteron' (PE, §9), a radical error, to seek the explanation of mind in physical nature when physical nature itself is a product of mind. This whole pattern of argument, which claims not alone that mind is independent of nature but that nature is dependent on mind, starts, one recalls, from agreed facts—from our knowledge of a world where things change and from our knowledge of a world of objects. What are we to make of it?

That question is, I think to be resolved into three others. First, are the free-mind and ontological arguments self-consistent and jointly coherent? Secondly, are they valid? Thirdly, what is the relationship between these arguments and the ethical theory and moral psychology which they introduce? Specifically: are they compatible with the ethical theory and moral psychology, and does the interest of Green's ethical theory and moral psychology really depend on the validity of these arguments?

On the first question there are no obvious inconsistencies in either the free-mind argument or the ontological argument, at least as they have been presented. Moreover, the two arguments have a certain complementarity. Considered purely in isolation the free-mind argument, with its 'neutralisation of time', introduces a discontinuity between the human mind and the rest of nature. The human mind has a mysterious dimension of atemporality. Mysterious, not because Green fails to argue his case, but because, even if his argument goes through, the human mind appears strikingly as a kind of rift in nature. The ontological argument, with the connection which it draws out between the human mind and the eternal consciousness, ends that discontinuity. Not merely is mind independent of nature, but nature is dependent on mind. Complete continuity is restored in an idealist construction of experience.

But what of the validity of Green's arguments, our second question? The notion of the non-successive unity and atemporality of thought is not a conception unique to Green. The phrase, 'non-successive unity', belongs to Peter Geach, who defends a notion apparently similar to Green's.[10] But B. A. Farrell's critique of this notion as revealing not that thought is mysterious, but that the cortical 'decisions' from which thoughts result fall below the threshold for detecting duration, at least shows that there is a serious problem here involved which requires further consideration.[11]. Green might reply that duration implies a process or series of events which need to be 'held together' as a series if thought is to result. And so we come to his second notion: that the idea of a series would be impossible for a mind which itself were merely serial. I think that there is a sense in which this marks an important point, that there are aspects of mind for which physical determinism cannot provide an account. I shall return to this point shortly. On the relational account of reality, to turn to the ontological argument, I cannot see that Green makes out his case.

Green's argument divides naturally into three parts. He holds first, that an object is nothing but its qualities; secondly, that qualities are relational in the sense that (in the later terminology in which the point may be put) all qualities are determinates of a determinable; thirdly that qualities, and therefore objects (since an object is nothing but its qualities), are mind-dependent because relations are 'the work of the mind'. One point which might be urged is that Green's argument uses 'quality' in two ways: for example to refer to whiteness as a quality and to refer to the whiteness of this flower. But clearly, in terms of this example, his major claim is that whiteness as a quality is mind-dependent, and if the quality is mind-dependent then so (in any

[10] P. T. Geach, *Mental Acts*, London, 1957, 105.
[11] B. A. Farrell, 'Thoughts and Time', *Philosophical Quarterly*, 22 (1972). I owe to Farrell's article the idea of the television example in 3.6.

sense relevant to Green's argument) is the instantiated whiteness of this flower. I think the real weakness of the ontological argument is more basic. The argument relies crucially on the empiricists' concession that relations are, in the phrase quoted, the work of the mind. But Locke, whose *Essay* is mainly involved here, did not hold that all qualities are relational in Green's sense; and Green advances, so far as I can tell, no arguments of his own to show that to be the determinate of a determinable is to be mind-dependent.

On the third question, concerning the relationship between the free-mind and ontological arguments and the ethical theory and moral psychology which they introduce, R. E. Hobart discloses a tension in his well-known 1934 paper, 'Free Will as Involving Determination and Inconceivable Without It'. Hobart refers to Green's view of atemporality and characterizes him as holding that when we decide to act on a desire we identify ourselves with it 'by a "timeless act"'.[12] This is a fair representation; it sets a problem. On Green's view of atemporality, the agent is lifted out of time. Causality and determination work across time. If the agent identifies himself with a desire, decides to adopt it, by a timeless act, this identification cannot be subject to causality and determination. But Green's moral psychology is certainly not indeterminist in the sense of claiming that some events, namely human actions, are uncaused. (At PE, §103 he uses the phrase 'free will' to refer to this kind of indeterminism, Hume's 'liberty of indifference'. This is a stylistic matter only, a matter of historical usage; it affects nothing of substance for the philosophical question of free will, namely whether an agent can choose otherwise than he does.) As a proponent of free will Green sets himself not simply against determinism of the kind represented by reductive materialism and one-way physicalism, but against in-determinism, the ethics of haphazard. Green holds quite explicitly (PE, §§ 97–111) that for any given state of an agent's character, the kinds of desire on which he will act are fixed. Such fixity is precisely one part of having a certain state of character. He does not accept that an agent's character is unrevisable across time, but that is a separate matter. Character

---

[12] R. E. Hobart, 'Free Will As Involving Determinism and Inconceivable Without It', *Mind*, 43 (1934), 2.

is flexible but actions are fixed. If, then, there is this tension or incompatibility between one part of Green's free-mind argument and his moral psychology, the interest of that moral psychology clearly does not depend on the validity of that part of Green's argument. But just what does Green need to support his ethical theory and moral psychology? I suggest that the answer requires nothing like Green's full-blown metaphysics.

The central worry in Green's mind is the rigid determinism of classical physics. Applied to free-will and moral responsibility such determinism posed the sort of challenge which A. S. Eddington vividly presented when he asked: 'What significance is there in my mental struggle to-night whether I should or should not give up smoking, if the laws which govern the matter of the physical universe already pre-ordain for the morrow a configuration of matter consisting of pipe, tobacco, and smoke connected with my lips?'[13] We are no longer dealing of course with classical physics. But even if we were, it is questionable whether we would need the kind of defence of free will which Green offers. The argument goes as follows.

Physics is the basic science of matter, but systems of matter have emergent properties which require patterns of explanation—chemical, biological, psychological, economic, and the rest—distinct from those of physics itself. It is at once a paradox and the simple truth that physics can probe the fundamental nature of reality and not tell us familiar facts. The fact, for example, that a plant undergoes photosynthesis. 'Photosynthesis' is a notion which fits into a pattern of biological explanation of which physics, quite properly, gives no account: physics is not biology. Biological explanations, however, are consistent, comprehensive, and valid. It is clearly not the case that the biological explanation of photosynthesis is a pseudo-explanation of something of which the real explanation lies within physics. Biological properties are emergent properties. Although our account of them must be consistent with physics (a constraint on all explanation), none the less it is not deducible from physics.

Just the same appears to hold for psychological explanations. It makes perfect sense to explain a person's actions in terms of

[13] A. S. Eddington, 'Physics and Philosophy', *Philosophy*, 8 (1933), 41. Quoted in R. E. Hobart, 16.

his beliefs, desires, intentions, and the rest. Capacities to believe, desire, and intend are emergent properties of the physical systems we call human beings. Relative to our interest in explaining ourselves to other people and other people to ourselves in the common transactions of life, psychological explanations set out in terms of those capacities can be consistent, comprehensive, and valid. If, believing a vase to be hideous, I hurl it through the window, this explains the broken glass. The explanation must be consistent with physics but cannot be deduced from physics. Then the suggestion about Green is this.

Take the ideas on which Green strongly insists—that we can decide to act on a desire or to resist it, that we can plan against the future occurrence or strength of a desire, that as we form our character so we act on certain kinds of desire but that character is always revisable over time in the light of our values. Provided that those ideas have a clarifying role, that they are accurate to our experience in ways which explain human action, then an ethical theory and a moral psychology to which they belong need only be concerned not to make any claims which conflict with physics. But physical determinism, or whatever may be true of physical states and events, cannot provide an account of the emergent psychological properties of physical systems. Those properties may here be grouped under the heading of self-consciousness: for example one has a desire, is aware that one has it, and on the basis of that awareness can decide whether to act on it. This awareness marks, I think, the main significance of Green's notion that the idea of a series would be impossible for a mind which itself were merely serial. The point Green really needs is that we not only have desires but are aware of having them; we can become, in the strictly limited sense of this example, objects to ourselves. In fact Green uses just such a locution when he characterisizes a person as a 'self-objectifying consciousness' (PE, § 182), and elsewhere when he says that the 'making of oneself an object to oneself <is> the foundation of all morality' (MS 15).

On an endnote, although I have bound myself here to Green's relational account of reality, on occasion Green's language easily fits the view of a mind–body relationship from which psychological properties could emerge. A. C. Bradley transcribes a passage in which Green observes of the 'animal organism' that 'At times (during sound sleep) it is only organic to life, not to thought: in this state it is *most* perfectly organic to vegetable life. At other times (in disease) it is but imperfectly organic to vegetable life and, in consequence, but imperfectly organic to thought.'[14] And in MS 22 Green concedes, in discussing self-consciousness, that 'No doubt, without definite conditions, this unity of consciousness, as operative in each of us, would not be.' In the fragmentary manuscript on 'Mind and Matter' the point is even allowed, in respect to such physical conditions, that 'the organization' of the animal organism is 'determined by heredity'. For all Green's 'idealism', the eternal consciousness generates to all intents and purposes an external world (the 'outer world' of MS 15) and a physical basis of mind on which self-consciousness depends and from which it emerges.

3.13 METAPHYSICS AND EPISTEMOLOGY

In the introduction to this chaper I referred to Green's free will and ontological arguments as embodying the heart of his metaphysics. I shall examine in the final two sections of this chapter two misconceptions to which Green's metaphysics has given rise. First a word on the notion of metaphysics and on the relation of metaphysics to epistemology.

The term 'metaphysics' has traditionally picked out two things. One, the study of the most fundamental features of reality or the most fundamental categories of thought: such categories as those of identity, individuation, and existence. Green has little to say directly about identity and individuation. Two, the attempt to achieve, by pure reason, a knowledge of the nature of reality which transcends the world as experienced. This second activity is Kant's proscribed investigation of the 'transcendent'. We have seen in the 'beyond experience' quotation of 3.11 Green's attitude to this kind of investigation.

---

[14] A. C. Bradley, 'Passages Copied by ACB from 1872 Logic Notebook of THG's', Bibliography II.

But two questions which metaphysics has always been taken to include are the existential questions: 'what is there?' and 'what is it to exist?'

If metaphysics faces the question, 'what is there?', then Green's analysis of knowledge discloses to his own satisfaction that ultimately there are just three kinds of thing: the eternal consciousness, the finite minds which are reproductions of it, and mind-dependent objects. And 'what is it to exist?' Clearly, to be a mind or to be dependent on a mind. These are short answers to difficult questions which I cannot discuss here. But our account of Green's metaphysics in this chapter does put a thatch of explanation over the baldness of the definition given of metaphysics in 'The Logic of the Formal Logicians':

This question, what the object of knowledge is (or, How is knowledge possible? What are the presuppositions as to our relation to the objective world from which we must start in inquiring what the method is by which we come to scientific knowledge?), is the question of metaphysic.—(Works II, 158.)

The presuppositions of knowledge add up, finally, to the relational nature of reality.

3.14 METAPHYSICAL ETHICS

Green has frequently been regarded, criticized, and dismissed as a proponent of 'metaphysical ethics'. G. E. Moore considers him briefly in *Principia Ethica* in a chapter so entitled; and A. E. Taylor engages in a long polemic against Green in the second chapter of *The Problem of Conduct* (1901) under the heading 'Some Arguments in Favour of a Metaphysical Ethic Considered'. Taylor attributes to Green a view of 'the necessary dependence of ethics upon metaphysics',[15] a view particularized as that of holding ethics to depend 'upon the metaphysical analysis by which the existence of an "eternal self" as the subject of rights and duties is established'.[16] This dependence has the twin corollaries on Taylor's interpretation that (i) 'apart from this metaphysical analysis, no theory of moral obligation is

---

[15] A. E. Taylor, *The Problem of Conduct*, London, 1901, 59.
[16] A. E. Taylor, ibid.

possible' and (ii) 'upon this analysis, without any further basis in psychology, a satisfactory theory of ethics can be erected'.[17]

A. J. B. Widgery in his 'Additional Chapter' to Sidgwick's *History of Ethics* (1931) includes Taylor sympathetically among those who contend that Green's 'metaphysical reasoning is barren for ethical purposes', and he describes Taylor's aim as one of 'freeing ethical theory from the metaphysical presuppositions with which Green associated it'.[18] Nor is it only Green's critics who are interested in the logical relation of his ethics to his metaphysics. Green's early commentator, W. H. Fairbrother, remarks by way of comment rather than blame that 'a great body of thinkers (of whom Plato in the ancient world, Green in modern times, . . . are typical) do, as a fact, base their teaching directly and, as far as possible, deductively upon the results of their metaphysical investigations'.[19]

But what do these metaphors of 'base' and 'dependence' really signify? How might ethics 'depend' on metaphysics in the way of 'deduction' from metaphysical premisses? Let me put an example to this kind of possibility. Suppose a religious metaphysics in which human persons are creations of a perfect God. Suppose further a certain structure of ethics:

(1) Metaphysical premiss: human persons are creations of a perfect God.

(2) Moral principle (derived from metaphysical premiss): human persons ought to be respected.

(3) Moral rule (derived from moral principle): promises ought to be kept.

(4) Moral precept (derived from moral rule): wage agreements ought to be honoured.

(5) Moral judgement (derived from moral precept): the Dime Bank should honour its latest wage agreement with its employees.

I neither endorse nor dismiss this structure; its role is to illustrate a deductive model of ethics. Two points are quickly apparent. In the first place, the metaphysical premiss that

[17] A. E. Taylor, ibid.
[18] A. J. B. Widgery, 'Additional Chapter' in H. Sidgwick, *History of Ethics*, 6th edn. 1931, repr. London, 1967, 284.
[19] F. H. Fairbrother, 'The Relation of Metaphysics to Ethics', *Mind*, 13 (1904), 43.

human persons are creations of a perfect God does not truth-functionally imply the moral principle that human persons ought to be respected. Then we are not dealing with strict logical deduction. Perhaps this is a fault simply of the particular example, but I suggest not. I think that what is normally at work in ethical 'deduction' is a looser but certainly not a vacuous notion. The notion is that one's metaphysical views 'dedicate' one to certain ethical views, that they 'commit' one to those ethical views; that one's ethical views 'follow from' one's metaphysical views by a kind of informal logic, that certain ethical views are 'appropriate' in the light of one's metaphysical views.

But now we encounter the second point: that even on this looser notion of deduction, deduction can fail. In our example, the moral precept that wage agreements ought to be honoured is meant to follow from the moral rule that promises ought to be kept. The derivation can always be barred, however, by an argument to show that what one aims to derive actually conflicts with the moral principle that human persons ought to be respected. This is a permanent possibility. Thus somebody presented with the precept that wage agreements ought to be honoured might respond: 'Can't you see what a distressing and ennervating thing it is to work for wages, to sell one's labour on fixed conditions? It's depersonalizing.' And so the theme of alienation might be introduced and warmly pursued, with the suggestion that wages and wage agreements really conflict with the moral principle of respect for persons. Again I neither endorse nor dismiss this argument. We certainly seem to be in trouble, however, with a deductive model of ethics. In terms of our example I take it that when Widgery holds Green's 'metaphysical reasoning' to be 'barren for ethical purposes' his idea is the following: first that moral principles cannot be strictly deduced from metaphysical premises, secondly that even on a looser notion of deduction we could never safely derive moral precepts and moral judgements from metaphysical premises for the kind of reason indicated by the alienation argument.

To defend Green here one has simply to say that he does not attempt to derive a structure of ethics from metaphysical premises. Green's view is that ethics presupposes free will: if either reductive materialism or one-way physicalism is true, then moral responsibility is impossible and ethics is at an end. In broad terms Green's method is Kantian and 'transcendental'. He works backwards from ethics to metaphysics, from the presuppositions of moral responsibility to the metaphysical guarantee that those presuppositions hold good. In this sense alone, not at all the sense he intends, Taylor is right about the 'dependence of ethics upon metaphysics'.

Green's ethics is enclosed in a framework radically different in kind from the 'deductive' structure of our example above. Green does not attempt anything like the derivation of rules, precepts, and judgements from a principle of morality. He offers an ethics not of principles and rules but of character and of what I shall term 'moral presumptions' (7.17ff.). PE, Book II is largely occupied with exploring the interplay of reason, desire, motive, character, and action. Taylor's view that, on the 'metaphysical analysis' of Book I, 'without any further basis is psychology, a satisfactory theory of ethics can be erected', is plainly unhinged. PE, Book II is the 'basis in psychology' of Green's ethics. On Taylor's other point, I have already covered the topic of the 'eternal self' in discussing Hobart.

3.15 THEOLOGICAL ETHICS

Not only, however, has a falsely 'metaphysical' construction been placed on Green's ethics, but also 'theological' interpretations have found the key to Green's 'Metaphysics of Knowledge' in an argument for the existence of God (J. A. Stewart) or an attempt to rework the doctrine of the Sonship of Man (Henry Sturt).

Sturt's idea[20] had always seemed to me obscure until I realized how the metaphor of 'participation' (3.10) might be taken. If the eternal consciousness differentiates itself as a network of individual human knowers who thus 'participate' in it, then the eternal consciousness might be said to be incarnate in those minds. The main source of the trouble here, and the chief support for theological interpretations, is precisely the eternal consciousness which, as C. C. J. Webb points out, Green

---

[20] H. Sturt, 251.

does on occasion refer to as God.[21] It is well not to emphasize such language of Green's too strongly, however, for certainly one feels here if anywhere the poignancy of Pascal's distinction between the God of Abraham and the God of philosophers. If St Augustine's God was drawn down from heaven by the weight of his love, Green's eternal consciousness might spare itself the descent. (Cf. Works I, 129, 133) The eternal consciousness fulfils a metaphysical role in the theory of knowledge to secure the relational account of reality against the charge of subjective idealism. It is a God invoked to explain the origin of the universe, and to block the conclusion that only human minds exist; it is not a God of mercy. The impression is hard to resist that more is required for the Johannine theme of *filii Dei sumus*.

Yet of course Green does have a richer, more specifically religious notion of God. I conceded in 1.3 that there was a religious motivation to Green's thought; and it must fairly be said that he does refer to God in connection with morality. Thus he talks of God as a model for the ideal moral self: God is 'the ideal self which no one, as a moral agent, is, but which everyone, as such an agent, is however blindly seeking to become' (Works III, 225). But no idea is involved here of a dependence of morality on religion. The origin of morality in Green's view is the kind of interactive support which occurs in the family; and Green believes that the fully expanded moral life, of which this is the start, satisfies certain pre-defined criteria for the human good. Green nowhere suggests, moreover, that in deciding what to do generally or in particular situations we can rely on anything but attention, perception, and reflection.[22] The notion of God as a model of the moral self can safely be jettisoned for any work which it does in Green's ethics.

To consider now J. A. Stewart's interpretation of PE, Book I. Stewart precisely reverses the real relation of epistemology to religion in Green. For Stewart the epistemology of PE, Book I is set up as it is, i.e. with 'the primacy of self-consciousness . . . dwelt upon with such insistence', chiefly in order to support 'the theistic inference' and thus to prepare the ground for the possibility of 'personal relations between man and God' and

[21] C. C. J. Webb, 196.
[22] cf. M. Platts, 'Moral Reality and the End of Desire', *Reference, Truth and Reality*, ed. M. Platts, London, 1980, 76.

'personal immortality'.[23] This is almost wholly incorrect. The direction of the 'inference' is wrong, as the argument of this chapter has shown at length. Moreover, Green does not look to philosophy to prove the existence of God: we have immediate experience of God in faith (1.3). Nor is the reference to faith decisive for personal immortality. Faith for an orthodox Christian is faith in a God who provides for personal immortality: but Green is not an orthodox Christian. In PE he is distinctly reserved on the issue of personal immortality (PE, § 185, 189), and, whatever his personal convictions, is plainly unwilling to take a definite philosophical stand on it.

3.16 CHARACTER AND FREE WILL

In our statement of a minimal notion of moral responsibility (3.2) one condition needs to be amended to reflect the results of the present chapter. This is condition (3): 'A could have done otherwise, if he had chosen.' For we have seen that Green applies a concept of character in a way which makes this condition, as it stands, ambiguous or inaccurate to this moral psychology. Green holds, as we have seen, that for any given state of an agent's character, the kinds of desire on which he will act are fixed. In this sense, on any particular occasion for any given state of character, it is not the case that A could have chosen differently. This is not inconsistent with (3), but it makes (3) less than fully informative. A more adequate version of (3) is (3A):

(3A) A could have done otherwise, if his character and desires had been different.

Green definitely accepts the free formation and revisability of character. An agent is responsible for the present state of his character and can change it. But formation and revisability take time; and there is not 'indeterminate possibility of becoming and doing anything and everything' (PE, § 106) as at any time an agent's character actually is.

We shall examine Green's concept of character in Chapter 5. First we must bring more clearly to light the ideas on reason,

---

[23] J. A. Stewart, 'Ethics', *Encyclopaedia Britannica*, iv, 10th edn. London, 1902, 307.

desire, and self-consciousness which are integral to the concept of character and which dominate Green's complete ethical theory and moral psychology. One way of stacking this chapter with the two following is quite simple. In the present chapter we have confronted the question how decision-making can involve free choice, how deliberation in any sense relevant to moral responsibility is possible. In Chapter 4 we shall explore Green's detailed view of deliberation, his account of what deliberation consists in. In chapter 5 we shall see how deliberation produces action.

4

Reason, Desire,
and Self-consciousness

4.1 INTRODUCTION

Green's view of deliberation is a response to Hume. It is other things besides; it is a critical re-elaboration of Kant and Hegel. It is one part of a general philosophy which, extending across Green's published work and the Balliol manuscripts, covers almost every field of philosophical inquiry. But it is at least a response to Hume. The centre of Green's target is Hume's denial that reason can be practical. Green rejects three views which are involved in that denial or associated with it: (a) Hume's non-motivational view of reason, (b) his separation of reason from desire in a 'partitional' view of mind, and (c) his 'bundle of perceptions' view of the self.

I propose, then, to adopt what may be called the Humean angle on Green. If we follow Green's response to the three Humean views which I have cited we are taken, through the issues which the exploration of that response involves, the intricate weave and lattice of cross-reference between reason, desire, and self-consciousness, to the heart of Green's view of deliberation. Moreover, Green's close critical relation to Hume fits well with the wide attention which Hume's philosophy has received in recent times, and makes the Humean angle specially appropriate. In terms of accessibility Hume is the ideal propaedeutic to Green.

In thus suggesting that Hume provides the right context for setting out Green's view of deliberation, I do not mean that we should make frequent reference to Green's minutely critical, ungenerous, and often inaccurate study in his 'Introductions to Hume'. Nor do I mean that Hume's views need to be couched exactly and solely in terms of his own philosophy of mind, with its battery of 'ideas', 'impressions', 'secondary impressions', and

the rest. There are disagreements of permanent substance
between Green and Hume on practical reason; and on these the
present chapter centres.

My programme is as follows. First I set out Green's
opposition to Hume organizing the exposition around the three
views mentioned, and developing in the process Green's multi-
perspectival model of deliberation. In this model four aspects of
deliberation are analysed as Green examines: (1) the obvious
way in which an agent can employ his beliefs simply to realize his
desires; (2) the interplay between the cognitive and the conative,
as, for example, desires are abandoned in the light of new
beliefs; (3) the critical separation between an agent and his own
desires when he practises self-intervention, for example, to rid
himself of a particular desire; and (4) the formation and revision
of complex structures of desire in the light of a self-conception
or self-image. Having separated Green from Hume and
articulated Green's own view of deliberation, I consider two
problems for Green's multi-perspectival model: his account of
the relationship between theoretical and practical reason, and an
objection drawn from Hobbes and Sidgwick to the fourth aspect
of the model. Finally I draw out some connections and contrasts
between Green's views on reason, desire, and self-
consciousness and those of Hegel.

4.2 HUME: THE NON-MOTIVATIONAL VIEW OF REASON

Hume's non-motivational view of reason and his partitional view
of mind are closely linked: it is because he partitions the mind as
he does that reason is 'impotent' on Hume's philosophical
psychology. But the two views are capable of separate exposition.
The non-motivational view of reason is embodied mainly in
Treatise, II.3.3 and III.1.1. Subordinate remarks occur in
Appendix 1 to the *Enquiries*. I shall concentrate on the *Treatise* as
the main exposition and as philosophically the more trenchant
work.

If reason cannot motivate, what is 'reason'? To take our
general bearings, and without entering into a full linguistic
analysis, we can say that 'reason' and its derivates are commonly
used in two ways: first to refer to a mental faculty (power,

characteristic, etc.), as in the tag that 'man is a rational animal'; secondly to identify an object of knowledge or belief, as when we adduce the 'reasons' for someone's action or the 'reasons' for accepting a theory. Hume's is a faculty view of reason; and his view has two levels. Hume sometimes thinks of reason as the cognitive in general. Whenever, and by whatever means, we form a belief that something exists with certain qualities, and whenever we interrelate existents or qualities (believing, say, that the same existent cannot have contrary qualities simultaneously), we enter the area of reason. This concept of reason may be ascribed to Hume on two grounds: first that he uses 'reason' and 'understanding' interchangeably, as when he discusses the place of reason in ethics in terms solely of what 'the understanding' can yield (T 463), and secondly that, for Hume, the understanding operates purely in the two spheres to which I have referred. It establishes 'matters of fact and existence' and 'relations of ideas'. At times Hume reclassifies these two spheres in the threefold distinction between knowledge, proofs, and probabilities, which again encompasses the area of reason (T 124).

Beneath this wide concept of reason, however, Hume employs a more narrow construction. Here reason is restricted, within the broad area of the cognitive in general, to what is capable of 'assurance' (T 193), by which he means, I think, 'certainty and demonstration' (T 463). So taken, the range of reason expires, and we enter the area of imagination, where beliefs transcend the given (T 193). Thus, and famously, causal beliefs are excluded from the sphere of the rational; regularities, 'constant conjunctions', between types of events breed confident expectations but never disclose 'necessary connexions'. One event never makes another happen; or rather no such connection between events is given in experience. The demonstrative covers mathematical truths (of which algebra and arithmetic alone 'preserve a perfect exactness and certainty', T 71). The certain but non-demonstrative, the set of beliefs which 'fall more properly under the province of intuition than demonstration' (T 70), relates to logical truths, degrees of quality, and similarities (so I interpret 'contrariety', 'degrees in quality', and 'resemblance', ibid.).

If Hume contrasts reason with imagination when he is

interested in 'certainty and demonstration', it is the wider concept of reason which informs his contrast between reason and passion when he insists that reason cannot motivate. I shall say something about his view of the passions in the next section. For now, given this concept of reason, Hume is quite clear that reason has by itself no motivating power, no 'original influence' (T 415). '... reason alone can never produce any action' (T 414); it is 'perfectly inert' (T 458), 'utterly impotent' (T 457).

Hume's idea is plain enough. The cognitive in general will never alone get me to do anything. So for instance I might while away my boredom in the cashier's queue by working out, through calculation my cause and effect, how the local bank might safely be robbed if its closed-circuit television were blanked out. But dreaming up an ingenious scheme does not of itself lead to action; this time the scheme is just to distract my boredom. Again I might accept the following: your car was stolen on Wednesday last, James was out of the country all that week. I deduce that James did not steal your car. That deduction, just by itself, does not lead to action. I might be indifferent to you, to James, to the fate of your car. I might not even offer you a lift.

4.3 HUME'S PARTITIONAL VIEW OF MIND

But if reason cannot motivate, how is action to be accounted for? Since reason is an 'inactive' principle (T 457), what is the active principle from which action results? At this point Hume's partitional view of mind enters the picture. Hume has a sharply sundered view of the mind. On the one side is reason or 'understanding', the cognitive in general. On the other side are desires or the 'passions' or 'affections' in Hume's terminology, the conative in general. There can be interrelation between these two sides of 'human nature'; and emphatically in Hume's philosophical psychology both reason and desire are necessary if action is to occur. This is Hume's version of the belief–desire theory (2.3). 'Human nature' is 'compos'd of two principal parts, which are requisite in all its actions, the affections and understanding' (T 493). However, if reason and desire can interrelate, and both are requisite, to produce action, the motivational pull is all on the side of desire, the 'affections' or 'passions'. It is desires which motivate by setting the ends of action. 'Reason is, and ought only to be the slave of the passions, and can never pretend to any other office than to serve and obey them' (T 415). So everybody quotes. But what is Hume passing through the customs under the heading of 'desire'?

Desires on Hume's account have the following characteristics: (1) they have a felt quality, (2) they are involuntary, and (3) they lead directly to action in accordance with their strength and the recognition of means to fulfil them.[1] The first feature appears to hold for some desires, not for others. It is unimportant for Green's rejection of Hume and I shall not refer to it again. The second and third features suggest an image of desire as an irruptive element in human experience. Desires break upon the agent's consciousness, with varying degrees of strength from the faint to the overwhelming; and the role of reason is simply to ease the flow of this pre-rational stream. An agent can use deductive and inductive inference to achieve the desires which thus impinge upon him. But such as desires are, so no other role is possible for reason in the practical sphere. This is, I think, the explanation of Hume's phrase that reason not merely is but 'ought only to be' instrumental to desire. There is an entire congruence between reason and desire on this understanding of their respective natures. Things could not have been otherwise; there is nothing to regret.

4.4 HUME AND ARISTOTLE

Then reason can neither set the ends of action nor furnish any motive to action. Can we trace a connection here between Hume's view of reason and that of Aristotle, whose practical philosophy has been justly admired in recent times? In *Nicomachean Ethics*, Book VI, Aristotle says that the understanding or intellect moves nothing (NE 1139a36). The possibility of a connection was not lost on Green himself. In Balliol MS 20, 'Aristotle: Ethics. V. VI. VIII', he observes:

The representation of phronesis as educated deinotes, this being

---

[1] D. Milligan, *Reasoning and the Explanation of Actions*, Brighton, 1980, 34–6.

faculty which calculates means to an end which it does not constitute, lends colour to notion that Aristotle held reason, in its practical application, to be 'only slave of passions', in Hume's phrase.

Green repudiates the Hume–Aristotle connection with a counterfactual:

If Aristotle's view were that phronesis merely calculates means to <an> end which it does not give—if its being necessary to virtuous action merely meant that, inasmuch as virtuous action = one which produces greatest pleasure, it cannot take place unless balance between pleasure sought for and pain involved in its attainment is rightly struck—his view would be mainly the same [sc. as Hume's view of reason: GLT].

Green is right, though the problem really starts in NE III. In the practical sphere Aristotle does not confine reason to deliberation about means to an end given independently of reason. Certain Aristotelian passages engender a different impression. Aside from Book VI, to which Green here restricts his attention, at various points in NE III (e.g. 1112b11 ff., 1113b3–4) Aristotle seems to separate wish (*boulesis*) from deliberation (*bouleusis*) and purpose or choice (*prohairesis*), in terms of a distinction between end and means. *Boulesis* sets the end; *bouleusis* and *prohairesis* select the means. It must be borne in mind, however, that for Aristotle happiness, the final good, is a matter of activity and that, as is clear from NE I (1094a1–2 and 1094a22), some activities are chosen for their own sake. Then we can deliberate about, and choose, the components of an imperfectly conceived happiness, and not merely the means to a previously given end.

4.5 THE CONCEPT OF PRACTICAL REASON

Hume's non-motivational view of reason produces, evidently enough, the claim that reason cannot motivate. His partitional view of mind produces the claim that reason cannot set the ends of action. In combining these claims we have Hume's denial that reason can be practical. If reason were practical it could both set the ends of action and furnish the motivation to pursue those ends. In fact, Hume argues, it can do neither. Reason is 'theoretical' reason. It is, in Reginald Jackson's phrase, reason 'by which you know'—the cognitive in general.[2] The concept of practical reason thus excluded, only the practical application of theoretical reason remains. Reason can fulfil only two roles with respect to action. It can lead to action either by the agent's inferring the existence of something which, so inferred to exist, he then wants, or by the agent's calculating cause and effect to secure what he antecedently wants. Hume says (T 459):

> ... reason, in a strict and philosophical sense, can have an influence on our conduct only after two ways: Either when it excites a passion by informing us of the existence of something which is a proper object of it; or when it discovers the connexion of causes and effects, so as to afford us means of exerting any passion.

The first of these two roles may suggest a more active than merely instrumental aspect of reason. Reason mobilizes desire: having inferred the existence of something I then want it. The point could certainly be developed so as to damage Hume's denial that reason can be practical. But the way in which Hume himself understands it is that desire remains as fortuitous as ever and retains its motivation pull. If I am susceptible to desire X, then reason can mobilize desire X: without that susceptibility it cannot. Reason here is not instrumental to an antecedently existing desire, but its leading to action is purely conditional on a specific susceptibility to desire. Minus that susceptibility, reason is 'utterly impotent', 'perfectly inert'.

Among the ways in which Hume is significant, one is in this very denial that action can accommodate anything more than the practical application of theoretical reason. Hume distinguishes, for the first time in modern philosophy, between practical reason and the practical application of theoretical reason. He isolates the two components of the concept of practical reason, the idea that reason can both motivate and set the ends of action, and rejects the concept as useless. Hume sets a sceptical perspective on the concept of practical reason so challenging that every subsequent attempt to vindicate the possibility of practical reason has had to meet his arguments. Commentators who insist that the full practical role of reason even given its confinement to inductive and deductive inference is wider and more complex than Hume acknowledges, miss the obvious. Hume is not trying

---

[2] R. Jackson, 'Practical Reason'. *Philosophy*, 17, (1942), 359.

to present a detailed account of the practical application of theoretical reason in the full subtlety of its ramifications. His main focus is negative, on what reason cannot do. It can neither set the ends of action nor furnish any motive to action. This is the challenge which Green faces.

4.6 HUME'S VIEW OF REASON: GREEN'S CRITIQUE

Green is quite clear that Hume is wrong. Reason can be practical. Let us move their views into alignment by noting first that, in Hume's view, reason, having as we have seen no 'original influence', can neither move the agent to action nor, a point of which we have not taken separate stock, restrain him from action. As Hume has it (T 413, 415):

> Nothing is more usual in philosophy, and even in common life, than to talk of the combat of passion and reason, [and] to give the preference to reason ... But if reason has no original influence, 'tis impossible it can withstand any principle, which has such an efficacy, or ever keep the mind in suspence a moment. Thus it appears, that the principle which opposes our passion, cannot be the same with reason, and is only call'd so in an improper sense. We speak not strictly and philosophically when we talk of the combat of passion and of reason.

Significantly Green expresses in his own terms a similar repudiation of the combat of reason with desire or 'passion'. It is a palpable solecism to talk of 'Desire ... conflicting with Reason' (PE § 129). Sidgwick, whose excursions into Green studies are not unfailingly fortunate, interprets this repudiation along the lines that Green is denying the phenomenon of *akrasia* or weakness of will, that one may act from desire contrary to one's rational judgement.[3]. Green is, on the contrary, fully alive to this phenomenon, as PE, §§ 137 and 179 confirm (cf. 7.12). But even Bosanquet, whose interpretation of Green usually has a certain sureness of touch, fails to identify the real difference between Green and Hume which lies beneath the apparent agreement here. He rightly contradicts Sidgwick's interpretation, but then observes: 'I take it that Green is

---

[3] H. Sidgwick, *The Ethics of T. H. Green, Mr. Herbert Spencer, and J. Martineau*, London, 1902, 23.

speaking in a sense akin to that of Hume', and there follows a quotation from the 'combat of passion and reason' passage cited above.[4]

Hume rejects talk of the combat of reason and passion or desire because, on his own account, reason and desire, the cognitive and the conative, are strongly heterogeneous in such a way that they are not the kinds of thing which could enter into 'combat' in any relevant sense. Briefly, reason establishes what is the case: desire relates to what we should like to be the case. No 'conflict' is possible. If a desire arises through some false inference then, agreed, the inference is false: the desire is not 'unreasonable'. Green's repudiation of any conflict between desire and reason rests on a different footing altogether.

For Green the conflict between desire and reason is impossible not because they are so heterogeneous that they cannot conflict, but because no such absolute separation as Hume writes into his account of reason and desire survives critical analysis. This is a radically different perspective. We interpret the drift of Green's approach in such remarks as the following: 'Thus thought and desire are not to be regarded as separate powers, of which one can be exercised by us without, or in conflict with, the other. They are rather different ways in which the consciousness of self . . . expresses itself' (PE, § 136). Hume maintains that reason cannot set the ends of action or supply motivation because of its heterogeneity from desire. Green maintains on the contrary that no such heterogeneity obtains, and that reason can therefore be practical. Both Hume's view of the impotence of reason and his partitional view of mind are here under attack. But if desire and reason are not sheerly separate, as on the Humean model, can we specify more particularly the relation between them?

Part of what is involved here can be seen by reflection on the view of reason as a mental faculty (4.2). A division opens between those who regard reason as a kind of impersonal force, the 'natural light' of Christian philosophers such as Bossuet, [5] and those who, like Kant, regard it rather as a capacity for structuring experience—on the theoretical side a structure of intelligence which enables us to organize experience into

[4] B. Bosanquet, Critical Notice of Sidgwick, *Mind*, 12, (1903), 383.
[5] J. B. Bossuet, *De la connaissance de Dieu et de soi-même*: ch. 1, § 7, Paris, 1741.

knowledge. Hume sets aside the idea that 'impersonal' reason has a normative function ('to guide our conduct', as Bossuet held). Green's interest is decidedly in 'structural' reason. He goes so far at one point as to suggest that it cannot be significantly held that 'the desires as organized by reason are different from reason as organizing the desires' (MS 20, 'Aristotle's Ethics'). The topic is the most complex in Green's philosophical psychology.

4.7 THE MULTI-PERSPECTIVAL MODEL: ASPECTS (1) AND (2)

The desire–reason relationship in Green is, to borrow Mark Pastin's useful phrase from a different context,[6] multi-perspectival. The desires on which I shall concentrate are, in Gewirth's terminology from 2.3, 'inclinational' rather than 'intentional'. Green's moral psychology can accommodate both kinds of desire, but I shall keep mainly to inclinational desires for ease of exposition. We need to examine four aspects of the desire-reason relationship. The first is the purely external aspect captured by Hume's account of the practical application of theoretical reason. At one level Green quite accepts that reason, the cognitive in general, can at least mobilize desire and serve desire instrumentally in that 'influence on our conduct' which Hume concedes. I shall not make heavy weather of this aspect of the multi-perspectival model. We have seen in outline what Hume takes the practical application of theoretical reason to be; and Green acknowledges this application implicitly in his criticism that the practical scope of reason is so limited when he refers to Hume's licence of 'no other function' than those we have cited (Works I, 348). In this acknowledgement less is involved than meets the eye at first sight. It is to be taken solely

[6] The phrase is from Mark Pastin, 'The Multi-Perspectival Theory of Knowledge', P. A. French, T. E. Uehling, and H. K. Wettstein, eds., *Midwest Studies in Philosophy*, v, *Studies in Epistemology*, Minneapolis, 1980. I certainly do not claim Professor Pastin's authority for my application of his phrase to Green's model of deliberation, a very different context from that in which Pastin uses it. I can only say that I began to think of Green's model differently, and in the way here presented, after I had read Pastin's article.

as a recognition that I can, e.g. in wanting to visit India, calculate possible ways of financing a holiday (thinking of such likely expedients as embarking on a crash savings programme or entering free-holiday competitions). The same recognition conciliates the negative side of Hume's picture. 'I may, e.g., contemplate payment of a debt as a possible event, consider how much money would be required for the purpose, how the creditor would behave when he got his money, and so on, without being affected by any desire to pay' (PE, § 152). This is mere thought in the sense of 'otiose contemplation' (PE, § 150). Green offers, in other words, a bare gesture towards familiar phenomena; for he does not allow that, explored with sufficient depth, this purely external relation is other than an unreal abstraction.

The second aspect is, even so, presented only at the level of what may be termed critical common sense. This is the aspect which stresses 'the mutual involution' of desire and reason (PE, § 135). On the one side, the use of reason (or 'understanding' or 'thought', terms which Green uses interchangeably with 'reason') involves desire. 'In all exercise of the understanding desire is at work. The result of any process of cognition is desired throughout it. No man learns to know anything without desiring to know it' (PE § 134), an observation which, incidentally, slightly jars upon Green's previous concentration in Book I on the simplest forms of perceptual knowledge. (For the present point is more obviously true of the process of learning a language than of seeing that the flower on the table is white.) On the other side, desire involves reason. 'So soon as any desire has become more than an indefinite yearning for we know not what, so soon as it is really desire *for some object of which we are conscious*, it necessarily involves an employment of the understanding upon those conditions of the real world which make the difference, so to speak, between the object as desired and its realisation' (PE, § 134, Green's emphasis).

I assign this second aspect to the level of reflective common sense. Although it casts initial doubt on the pre-reflective idea of reason's purely external relationship to desire, it does so in terms which are plainly accessible to reflective common sense and rely on no special philosophical viewpoint.

4.8 THE MULTI-PERSPECTIVAL MODEL: ASPECT (3)

The third aspect of the desire–reason relationship in Green is that of critical distance. Hume, we recall, defines a picture of desires as leading directly to action in accordance with their strength and the means available to fulfil them. This is the third characteristic of Humean desires listed in 4.2. Reason simply eases the satisfaction of the surd, inexorable flux of desire. But Green stresses the possibility of a particular kind of reflexive relation in which an agent can stand towards his own desires. The exploration of this relationship will carry us through the third and fourth aspects of the multi-perspectival model. In the third aspect Green identifies two facets of the relationship.

In the first place, whatever one's desires one can imagine oneself in possession of a different set of desires. Here Green does not signify the fact that one may be self-deceived about the desires one really has, but that one can always envisage having different desires from those one actually has. This facet is marked in Balliol Ms 10A, 'Other End', 8, when Green refers to the self 'which is perpetually detaching itself' from the desires 'which it adopts as its filling'. Secondly, he holds that for any particular desire one can decide not to fulfil that desire. In other words, there is a distinction for the human agent between desiring X and deciding to get X, the kind of distinction which Green expresses for instance as that between 'the consciousness of wanted objects' and 'the effort to give reality to the objects thus present in consciousness as wanted' (PE, § 85; cf. 3.6). Green is not setting the scene for a Stoic doctrine of *apatheia*. A person's ability to detach himself from his desires has no place, for Green, in any theory of the renunciation of desire. There is slight risk of gaining the wrong impression from PE, but Green's language in the MSS lends itself to misinterpretation, as when for instance the point about 'perpetual detachment' is otherwise put in terms of an 'attitude of perpetual negation'.

On this critical relation of the agent to his own desires, truth and tradition about Green are less than usually at odds. I accept, in spite of earlier strictures on the Hegelianization of Green, the essentially Hegelian origin of this element in Green's moral psychology. It is not Kantian, Aristotelian, or Platonic in any hard sense, and it does appear openly in Hegel's *Philosophy of Mind* (*Encyclopaedia*, § 476).

Any such view as Green's, which seeks to cut a gap between having a desire and deciding to act on it, has an obvious point to negotiate: the point presented in Anscombe's remark that 'the primitive sign of wanting is *trying to get*'.[7] Certainly if there were no connection quite in general between desiring and trying to get, then the concept of desire would be of limited use. Its key role is to explain action. If having a desire never led one to act, the concept of desire would be so far redundant. But we can take this point and still accept Green's view. Green holds that an agent's decision to act on a desire is not entailed by his having that desire. Green survives Anscombe.

Hume can offer a reply, of course: to decide to act on a desire is simply to act on a different and stronger desire. But we should miss what is most characteristic if we assessed Green's view purely in the light of an objection such as this. Consider the following example.

Isabella has a weakness for sugar. She has just poured some tea. There is sugar in the house; she cannot resist using it. She knows perfectly well that, other things equal, she will still succumb to sugar this time next week, though she has heard that sugar is harmful to her health. Such is the regular and re-current strength of her desire for sugar. But she works to reduce the strength of that desire. The following day she buys a pot of Red Bee honey. Her desire for sugar is still dominant: when she makes tea, out comes the sugar. The next day she visits the local library to confirm from books on diet the real harm that sugar is doing to her health. Still she takes sugar with her tea. Later she buys tea of which the flavour is less unpleasant without sugar. And so the process goes on. Eventually she takes Red Bee honey instead of sugar. There is sugar in the house; she resists using it. Here, then, is self-intervention which has worked to reduce the strength of a desire (2.3). This is nothing like Hume's picture of a clean fight between competing desires; the contest has been fixed.

Three remarks are to be made about the example. First it qualifies the involuntary nature of desire, one characteristic of

---

[7] G. E. M. Anscombe, *Intention*, 2nd edn. Oxford, 1963, 68.

Humean desires noted in 4.2. When Isabella desires honey next week, the desire does not simply impinge on her; it is a desire which she has positively induced. Secondly and relatedly the example takes a diachronic view of the agent, a view across time as opposed to the 'freeze-frame' view to which Hume's account of action and desire is best angled. Hume tells us what will happen, given opportunity and the relative strength of desires, at any particular time. Today the desire for sugar prevails; this time next week the dominant desire will be for honey. That a desire will prevail according to strength and opportunity is exactly the characteristic of Humean desires from which our example took its point of departure. In the example, however, a desire leads to action (today the desire for sugar), but the agent can also decide whether, in future, that desire shall lead to action. Hume's notion of strength of desire relies on the idea of involuntary strength. It is plausible for the structure of desires which an agent has at any particular time. As my desires are now, so I act: here is a degree of involuntariness. This suggests my third remark. From 3.12 Green's denial is predictable that an agent has 'an indeterminate possibility of becoming and doing anything and everything' at a particular time of action (PE, § 106). But he insists that, if for present action the agent is 'stuck' with a structure of desire, he can always impart a different structure to his desires by self-intervention across time.

4.9   HUME: THE 'BUNDLE OF PERCEPTIONS' VIEW OF THE SELF

In its fourth aspect the multi-perspectival model takes up and develops the idea of a structure of desire. Here, to serve his future existence and well-being, the agent models an increasingly systematic structure of desire. The aim, in Green's language, is to achieve 'an abiding satisfaction of an abiding self' (PE, § 234). Perhaps we may talk of 'happiness': not that Green uses this term, possibly because of its hedonist associations. One of his favoured general terms is 'perfection' (e.g. PE, § 370). Before considering more closely the details of the fourth aspect of the model, however, we need to say something about Green's treatment of the 'self' whose 'abiding satisfaction' it addresses.

That treatment places Green in contrast to Hume: and here as elsewhere the Humean contrast is keenly avowed by Green himself. But to rush critically at Hume is to race across a terrain of trip wires: it is not enough to cite Works I, 339–41, 'Hume's Account of the Self', and be done.

There are, to begin, ambiguities in the notion of the self. There are, as well, several segments to Hume's total theory of the self; and there is, finally, a superficial plot and subplot in the contrast between Green and Hume.

First, then, theories of the self are subject to an ambiguity. By the 'self' we may refer to the beliefs, desires, and dispositions to emotion and behaviour which a person has at a time or across time, and which he may wish to change (call this the object-self or A-self): we may also refer to the owner of those beliefs, etc., the continuant which, persisting through time, is not to be identified with them but supports or owns (the metaphors vary) now one set of beliefs, desires, and dispositions, now another set (call this the subject-self or B-self). This may be a Cartesian substance or something quite different; I am simply explaining the notion. Hume is plainly aware of both notions: of the first when he adduces those 'incessant revolutions' (T 191) which our beliefs, etc., undergo, and of the second when he engages in his polemic against mental substance (T 1.4.5.).

That polemic forms part of Hume's negative account. His total theory of the self divides into three segments: his positive account, his negative account which exposes false views about the self, and his reservations in the Appendix to the *Treatise* concerning his own positive account. Significantly, that part of Hume's negative account which rejects the idea of mental substance is closely similar to Green's own position.

Hume denies the Cartesian theory, advanced e.g. in the Sixth Meditation, that we have a clear and distinct (and therefore true) idea of the self as a mental or thinking substance. We have no impression or idea of substance, mental or material. There is no B-self (or at least, there is no rational justification for believing in such a self): there is only the A-self, which Hume reduces to a succession of mental acts and events. In rejecting Hume on the A-self, Green will not endorse Descrates on the B-self. He will have no truck with any notion that the self is the 'ghostly entity' of Ryle's late polemic, existing apart from beliefs, desires, and dispositions or, to follow Green's list, feelings, desires, and thoughts.

For Green says: 'the self, as here understood'—i.e. in the presentation of his own view—'is not something apart from feelings, desires and thoughts' (PE, § 101). And in the preceding paragraph he is yet more emphatic:

'Do you mean,' it may be asked, 'to assert the existence of a mysterious abstract entity which you call the self of a man, apart from all his particular feelings, desires, and thoughts—all the experience of his inner life?' To such a question we should reply, to begin with, that of 'entities' we know nothing, except as a dyslogistic term denoting something in which certain English psychological writers seem to suppose that certain other writers believe, but in which, so far as known, no one has stated his own belief. (PE, § 100).

As an argument this is not quite decisive. A commitment to the existence of an abstract entity might be logically implicit in a philosopher's position even though not explicitly avowed and recognized by him. But Green's language here, his insistence that what he is interested in is 'not something apart from feelings, desires and thoughts', confirms his emphasis on the 'particular feelings, desires, and thoughts' which an agent may have.

Green does not talk of substance. But part of what is involved here is, I think, the traditional idea of substance as property- or quality-bearer. Itself quality-less, substance 'supports' qualities; substance is that in which qualities 'inhere'. But if the abstract 'entity' to which feelings, desires, and the rest belong is a substance in this sense, we know from 3.11 that the quality-less cannot exist.

If, however, this rejection of abstract entities, of the nonentity of mental substance, unites Green with Hume, Hume's positive account is less welcome. His reduction of the A-self to a succession of mental acts and events has already been referred to; and it is expressed in many familiar passages. Hume observes of the self: 'When I turn my reflexion on myself, I never can perceive this self without some one or more perceptions; nor can I ever perceive any thing but the perceptions. 'Tis the composition of these, therefore, which forms the self' (T 634). Nor is Hume willing to concede that this might be a mere personal singularity: 'I may venture to affirm of the rest of mankind, that they are nothing but a bundle or collection of different perceptions, which succeed each other with an inconceivable rapidity, and are in a perpetual flux and movement' (T 252).

These claims make up the first part of Hume's positive account of the self, his no-self theory of the self. No A-self persists through time; only discrete, successive 'perceptions', Green's 'feelings, desires, and thoughts', are given in experience. The notion that beliefs, desires, and dispositions persist through time, and compose a continuing self, is due to the 'passage of the imagination' over 'distinct perceptions' (3.6). Hume's own imagination makes this passage easily enough in his theory of character, on which 'our actions have a constant union with our motives, tempers, and circumstances' (T 401; cf. T 411). But that is another story.

A fuller discussion of this activity of the imagination is readily forthcoming. Hume explains in T 1.4.6. how causal relations and resemblances between discrete, successive mental acts and events produce the notion of a continuing self. This positive account is radically rejected by Green. If the mental life were really as atomic as this, Green argues, even the fiction of a continuing self would be impossible to form. Resemblances, for instance, occur between two or more 'perceptions', but what continues between any two perceptions to recognize the resemblance? Nothing, on Hume's account, since the mind is nothing but a succession of discrete perceptions. Then, by a curious logic, something has to persist between perceptions if their resemblance is to be recognized, and this recognition of resemblance creates the illusion that something persists between perceptions.

But there are, of course, two critics of Hume's account of the self: Green, and Hume himself in the Appendix to the *Treatise*. Hume marginally misstates his own difficulty, in my view. He says that he can neither reconcile nor relinquish two principles: '*that all our distinct perceptions are distinct existences,* and *that the mind never perceives any real connexion among distinct existences*' (T 636). The tension which his account reveals, however, is not between these two principles but between the second principle and an apparent matter of fact, that Hume needs more to explain the mental life than his positive account allows. That is, he cannot draw from his positive account of the self, with its rigid emphasis on the sheerly discrete, any answer to the kinds of question Green puts. Hume seems to need a continuant which recognizes resemblances, and observes the 'constant conjunctions' (regularities) in which causal relations consist. Yet that continuant is excluded by his own philosophy of mind; and so Hume candidly admits, 'all my hopes vanish, when I come to explain the principles, that unite our successive perceptions in our thought or consciousness' (T 635–6).

Now, this difficulty which Hume finds in his own theory of the B-self, and which Green so heavily underlines, does not exhaust the present contrast between Green and Hume. It is the surface plot. For it interlocks with the second characteristic of Humean desires, their involuntariness (4.3) and to mention desires is to enter the sphere of the A-self. If on Hume's positive account of the self desires are discrete, successive experiences which we simply undergo, this neglects (and makes incoherent) the manner in which a person's desires may be deliberately organized to a high degree in what I shall call interest systems. This is the subplot, the point substantially at issue in Green's moral psychology.

Green believes that Hume's view of discrete, successive desires not only neglects what I may call this 'organizational' angle; it also grants desires, along with the whole range of mental phenomena, a false independence. In MSS 24 and 20 he presses the point (discussed above) about 'abstract entities' and holds that just as 'the Self, apart from feeling, desire and thought, . . . would be nothing at all', so 'the particular feelings, desires, thoughts . . . are abstractions, except as existing in and for a subject which distinguishes itself from itself; which presents itself to itself as having these feelings, desires, thoughts.' It is not Green's self which is a 'mysterious entity'; it is Humean feelings, desires, and thoughts, 'distinct perceptions', which are merely 'so-called realities of experience' existing 'only logically not really'. I do not propose to carry the terminology of 'A-selves' and 'B-selves' as an extra backpack; I have used it simply to isolate the strands of a tangled issue between Green and Hume. Green insists that we can form, and make systematic changes in, structures of desire. We can scan our desires in this 'self-interventionist' way. Questions about 'abstract entities', Cartesian mental substances, A-selves and B-selves, subject-selves and object-selves, must not be allowed to obscure this plain, basic insistence. But the issue between Green and Hume had to be clarified; for it is easy, in reading Green's texts, to miss the exact collision with Hume. At this point I return to the fourth aspect of the multi-perspectival model.

4.10   THE MULTI-PERSPECTIVAL MODEL: ASPECT (4)

In the third aspect of the multi-perspectival model the agent intervenes to alter a present structure of desire—to reduce the strength of present desires, to introduce new desires. The fourth aspect is one in which an agent focuses not simply on individual desires but on entire systems of desire in relation to his future existence and well-being. The goal is to achieve some kind of personal satisfaction over time; and Green has various ways of referring to this. He talks of 'an abiding satisfaction of an abiding self', 'a satisfaction on the whole', 'a possibility of perfection'.[8] This goal may be sought through an organization of desire in terms of systematic interests, integrated wide-interest systems, 'cases of concentrated purpose' such as the promotion of a parliamentary career or the management of an estate (PE, § 128). In its most developed form deliberation under the fourth aspect of the multi-perspectival model involves the desire to be a particular kind of person.

So David desires to become, say, a journalist. A college graduate, he now wants to enter a school of journalism. He completes the course; he now wants to get a job as a junior reporter on a local newspaper. This obtained, he thinks more closely about his future. An interest system forms. He wants to specialize. The culture and welfare of the Indian community in Britain are his main concern. Access to the more powerful medium of a national newspaper means a swift move to Fleet Street if his career is to prosper. For such a move a good record in his present job seems essential. Here, then, is an arrow direct

---

[8] This language is not without its drawbacks: 'self-satisfied' can, colloquially, be used to describe a person who is overpleased with himself and his achievements. Any such association must of course be cancelled.

to the future along with a present plan. Fixed on the conception of himself as a journalist he is immune from internal conflict, or at least resolute in putting rival conceptions firmly out of mind as they are suggested by friends. 'Enter Politics', says one. 'I was relying on you for that variorum edition of Bolingbroke', says another. Clear about his major aim to make Fleet Street he is quite ready to abandon his instrumental aim of marking up a good local record if, as is unlikely, he can make Fleet Street direct. This will make his behaviour in staying a year with the local paper or abandoning it after a month equally consistent as opportunity presents.

In the meantime plans are set. David wants to acquire as many influential Fleet Street acquaintances as possible and to find out the relative attention paid to ethnic affairs by different national newspapers. He also sets out to learn an Indian language, say Punjabi, as an aid to first-hand reporting in his future job. From this aim positive and negative purposes flow: the intention to enrol for Punjabi evening classes, and to forgo even John Schneider movies which clash with his commitment to study. His interests are thus a part of his single dominant interest system or have to accommodate themselves to it. Within his single dominant interest-system he is conscious of freedom of action. If he prefers Gujurati to Punjabi, then with equal relevance he can switch to that instead. If he believes that Indian philosophy is grossly undervalued, he can emphasize this aspect of Indian culture—or a different aspect if his inclination points another way.

4.11 THE MULTI-PERSPECTIVAL MODEL: REVIEW (I)

The message that Green's model carries can be put in simplest terms. In deliberation Hume subordinates the cognitive to the conative; Green diversely interrelates them. Subordination is one type of interrelation; and Green allows that I can straightforwardly work out ways of satisfying just any desire I happen to have: equally that a desire can be triggered by what I discover to be the case. I want the book because I have seen it. The twin role to which Hume thus confines the practical 'influence' of reason is exhibited under the first aspect of Green's model.

Under the second aspect Green begins to qualify the Humean picture of reason and desire as simply separate. In facing a complex subject matter, for instance, I shall not arrive at accurate knowledge unless my desire to learn propels me across the inevitable hurdles of difficulty and disappointment. This is, no doubt, true. But I do not claim that it is the heart of what is interesting in Green. The separation of reason and desire is further qualified by the third aspect of Green's model. Here my belief about a particular desire, the belief for example that in spite of its present strength this desire is harmful to me, can start a process of self-intervention by which I reduce the strength of that desire. This is far more significant, because contemporary philosophy of mind barely recognizes the phenomenon of self-intervention (2.3). Under the fourth aspect the model shifts its focus. No longer does it centre on the kind of intervention by which an agent alters the strength of a particular desire, prevents its occurrence, or fosters a new desire. Rather, attention now falls on the creation of an increasingly systematic structure of desire. Any agent at any time will have a multiplicity of desires. There is no guarantee that they will make a consistent set; and no likelihood that they will, without self-intervention, fall into the kind of structure which forms the backbone of a lifeplan. At the limit, self-intervention sets going a process of which the end state is that I become a particular kind of person in line with a self-conception.

Two comments need to be made at this point. First, desire is a central concept of any comprehensive model of deliberation, but so far we know very little about Green's account of desire. We know that he rejects three Humean characteristics of desire: that desires (*a*) are necessarily involuntary (*b*) lead directly to action in accordance with their strength and the means available to fulfil them, and (*c*) are discrete, miscellaneous items. We need to have more than this from Green, however. We require a positive analysis of desire. And, second, we need to recall our point of departure. If the dispute between Green and Hume turns on a substantial difference of ideas, that difference is whether reason can be practical. But to date the multi-perspectival model gives us descriptive psychology: it does not show how anything which can usefully be called 'reason' can set the ends of action or furnish the motivation to pursue those ends. If the model tells us how we start, it does not suffice for our destination.

Then two replies. Green's analysis of desire is presented in the next section. On Green's account desire, self-satisfaction, and self-realization are closely bound up; I take them in order. I then open up Green's analysis of reason. Reason and self-consciousness are tightly related, and are therefore taken together. This network of concepts supports Green's independent account of practical reason.

4.12 DESIRE AND SELF-SATISFACTION

Green's own view of desire emerges in PE, Book II, when he remarks that language misreports the real nature of desire. An explorer says, 'I want that buried treasure'; a hungry man says, 'I want some food.' The object of desire readily appears to be some substance or thing—the treasure, supposing it to exist, or the food. Green stresses, quite in line with recent writers like Kenny, that desire relates to some activity or passivity of the agent. 'The food which I said to want, the treasure on which I have set my heart, are already in existence. But, strictly speaking, the objects which in these cases I present to myself as wanted, are the eating of the food, the acquisition of the treasure' (PE, § 86). (There is a recurrent minor polemic in PE against the misleadingness of language. PE, § 23, 54, 58, 107, 118, 127, and 129 are here in point. Although, in PE at least, Green does not pursue F. H. Bradley's line of reproaching language, *qua* instrument of the discursive intellect, as inherently distortive, none the less his suggestion to Nettleship 'that he might approach philosophy from the side of language'[9] is not so innocuous as may at first appear.) On Green's account, in contemporary terms, the logical form of 'I want X' is 'I want to $\emptyset x$' where the free variable '$\emptyset$' is to be replaced, as applicable, by such verbs as 'kiss', 'invoke', 'eat', 'raze', 'adulterate', and 'name'. It will be obvious how this account is to be expanded to include passivities of desire: 'I want to be reassured by you.' For

---

[9] A. C. Bradley, ed., *Philosophical Remains of Richard Lewis Nettleship*, London, 1897, lii.

convenience I shall keep to activities: 'I want to cut some flowers', 'I want to buy a new car.'

On egoism of desire Green holds a view which we shall examine more fully in the next chapter when we set out his concept of motive (5.3). He argues that any adoption of a desire, any decision to act on a particular desire, is governed by a conception of 'personal good'. But this does not mean that the desire on which I decide to act is inherently self-interested. If, for example, I want to buy a new car this might be only because I believe that you need to use one. I so identify with your needs that those needs give me a reason for wanting to buy and trying to get a new car. That I see my personal good as including the relief of your needs does not make my desire to buy a new car self-interested. My personal good involves a reference to your interests for your sake, because of the relationship between us. Self-interested desires of course abound. But the completely general analysis of desire should ignore self-interest. Green is right.

The final point for now is that Green recognizes a distinction between simple- and composite-activity desires. The terminology is mine but the distinction is Green's in the 'concentrated purpose' passage to which we have already referred. In that passage Green says that a desire 'may admit of description by a single phrase' when it 'really involves the satisfaction of many different desires' (PE, § 128). The distinction is easy to explain by examples. A friend assures me that the word 'brouhaha' occurs in the opening paragraph of Henry James's *The Golden Bowl*. I am slightly sceptical of this and decide to check; I want to know if that word occurs. It is just as well that I do check. I shall not trust anything else my friend tells me about Henry James. But the desire to know about the occurrence of a word is satisfied by the one-off activity of reaching for a book and looking inside. If, by contrast, I want to take an intelligent interest in world affairs, that desire is tightly webbed in a net of interlocking desires from which it acquires body and substance. Having that desire means that I shall want to buy an informative daily newspaper, follow the best television journalism, talk to knowledgeable people, and so forth. The desire cannot be satisfied in the one-off manner of the desire to settle my uncertainty about Henry James.

Self-satisfaction requires a structuring of composite-activity desires. Let us add some detail to the example of David, and develop the idea of a wide-interest system. For convenience of phrasing I shall refer to composite-activity desires as composite desires, and to simple-activity desires as simple desires.

One of David's wide-interest systems is his desire to become a particular kind of journalist. This is a composite desire which is embodied in a whole series of simple desires; and it cannot be satisfied except through the fulfilment of those simple desires across time. Wanting to become a journalist on Indian affairs involves wanting to write a good article this week, another article next week, another article next month. A 'wide-interest system' is simply a shorthand reference to such simple desires thus connected; and one interest-system will co-exist with others for the same person. David has another wide-interest system, we may suppose, which centres on his desire to play goalkeeper for his neighbourhood football team, a composite desire which embodies itself in a whole series of simple desires to do with training, weight-watching, and so on.

For David to be a satisfied person, as opposed to his merely having this or that desire satisfied, two conditions are requisite. First, his wide-interest systems (the 'various interests' of PE, § 234) must be integrated. For if those systems conflict, if (say) his enthusiasm for football interferes with his 'concentrated purpose' of becoming a particular kind of journalist, he has a problem. The problem may be diversely resoluble. But as long as the conflict lasts, as long as there is a failure of fit between his wide-interest systems, there is a tension in David's life: his desires do not form an 'organic whole' (*Nicomachean Ethics*, Copy A, 50). He is not, in Green's sense, a 'satisfied' person.

The second condition is that the 'plan of life' (Works II, 525; HM, 170) which David's integrated wide-interest systems constitute should be 'in process of realisation' (PE, § 234). This process is consistent with innumerable failures *en route*. David's lifeplan will not be dissipated if he fails to train well enough for next week's match, though it will be dissipated if his career in amateur football goes like a dream, but no opportunity materializes in the long term to become an Indian affairs journalist. David achieves self-satisfaction, 'an abiding satisfaction of an abiding self', as his composite desires are realized overall, however gradually and with whatever short-term reverses.

Note, incidentally, that the idea of a lifeplan here includes nothing like the empty 'rectangle' with which Bernard Williams associates it.[10] The agent systematizes or distances himself from desires which he already has. This is the growth point of a lifeplan. Nor need the framing of a lifeplan be a once-for-all operation. Such a plan is open permanently to revision, not least through the interplay of different aspects of the multi-perspectival model. The earlier, more instrumental phases of deliberation may reveal shortcomings in the practicability of a lifeplan.

4.13   SELF-REALIZATION

The term 'self-realization' occurs more frequently in Bradley than in Green, though Green does use it (e.g. Works III, 224). Two charges have been brought against the notion of self-realization. In the first place there is the charge that the notion involves the idea of making the self real: but by what agency is the self 'realized', the criticism is urged, if the self is not already real? To invoke any such notion is to enter a maze of absurdity. Secondly, the notion is held to be vacuous. In the sense in which every person has indefinitely many structures of desire which might be realized, the notion is dismissed as giving no guidance on which potentialities, which structures of desire, should be developed. But Green's philosophy must be guarded from too swift an intrusion of the critical spirit. There is nothing absurd or vacuous in Green's notion of self-realization; he might have expressed it differently.

When Green talks of 'self-realization' he has the idea simply in mind of creating the kinds of wide-interest systems to which attention has been drawn above. What we 'realize' in self-realization are increasingly systematic structures of desire in increasingly integrated wide-interest systems. In self-realization we do not create 'the self', *ex nihilo*, but a particular kind of self

---

[10] B. Williams, 'Persons, Character and Morality', *The Identities of persons*, ed. A. O. Rorty, Berkeley, 1977, 209.

from the possibilities which the third and fourth aspects of the multi-perspectival model disclose. Green's reference to a 'conscious contrast between an actual and possible self, and . . . an impulse to make that possible self real' (Works III, 224) should leave no room for doubt or misunderstanding. So much for the first criticism. The second criticism would be significant if Green merely specified the possibility of systematic structures of desire to secure 'an abiding satisfaction of an abiding self'. As we shall see in Chapter 6, however, Green's account of the unconditional good sets boundaries within which self-satisfaction may reliably be sought.

4.14 SELF-CONSCIOUSNESS AND REASON

When Green tells us that self-consciousness and reason are identical, he says what is against our preconceptions. He refers to 'reason, as self-consciousness' (Works I, 305, 353): and holds that 'Reason is the self-objectifying consciousness' (PE, § 203). Taken without interpretation this equation seems so egregriously implausible as barely to be worth considering. It may also appear patently Hegelian. For Hegel precisely holds in the *Phenomenology of Spirit* that 'self-consciousness is reason'[11] But an excursion into Hegel is unnecessary. Having noted this point of contact we can make out Green's position quite clearly on lines already traced. I shall return to Hegel to sketch a larger perspective on self-consciousness in 4.17.

The third and fourth aspects of the multi-perspectival model really present a view of self-consciousness. As we know, self-consciousness is not a matter of acquaintance with a Cartesian mental or thinking substance (4.9). The ability to distance oneself from one's desires in such a way that one is not merely subject to them (as on Hume's account), but can decide which to satisfy, is a function of self-consciousness. This is, moreover, a rational function, that of seeing one's desires as a system, an 'organic whole'. We can obtain further light on the reason–self-

---

[11] *Hegel: The Phenomenology of Mind*, tr. J. B. Baillie, London, 1964, 272; J. Hyppolite, *The Genesis and Structure of Hegel's Phenomenology of Spirit*, tr. S. Cherniak and J. Heckman, Evanston, 1974, 226.

consciousness relationship if we look at a text from Green's 'Notes on Moral Philosophy':

This relation to self—active self-consciousness—gives man conception of this good as a whole. As it is condition of conflict of desires, so of adjustment of this conflict; of subjection of immediate desire to general good of man.

This relation called logos reason (which in Plato and Aristotle appears rather as consciousness of universal than of self, but this comes to the same).

It rules the man, because it constitutes him man—because it is that which will he or will he not, makes his appetitive and sensitive experience a *system* (MS 15, emphasis in Green.)

Parts of this text make points which I shall not develop. Behind the 'will he or will he not' passage is the idea that, in the sense of PE, § 127, desires 'qualify each other'. In deciding to act on a desire there is always some reference to the impact of fulfilling that desire on other desires. The 'consciousness of universal' passage must I think be taken to relate, as far as concerns Aristotle, to the emphasis on a 'general account' of the human good, e.g. at NE 1104a5. What the passage mainly helps us to see, however, is the interrelation of self-consciousness and reason in the third and fourth aspects of the multi-perspectival model. Under those aspects, we recall, the agent critically distances himself from his desires, and forms, or tries to form, a systematic structure of desire to secure 'an abiding satisfaction of an abiding self'. Two points emerge. First, it is a function of self-consciousness (Green's 'active' self-consciousness in the above passage) for an agent to practise this critical detachment and to concern himself about his future existence and well-being; only a self-conscious being could do this. And secondly, it is a function of reason to view our desires as constituting (potentially) a systematic structure. The kind of self-consciousness in projecting a systematic structure of desire is inherently rational through the very idea of a 'system'.

Green tells us more about reason. We noted that for Green one of the main seats of the weakness of Hume's philosophical psychology lies in its thorough separation of reason and desire. (In the moral psychology of the *Republic* the same weakness vitiates Plato, whom Green criticizes for 'supposing reason, "spirit", and desire to be complete in each individual': MS 15, 'Notes on Moral Philosophy'.) Green observes at one point in MS 20, 'Aristotle: Ethics':

Reason, completely developed, on the one hand; appetite on the other, are supposed to be fighting. But really it is only by false abstraction that we speak of reason as complete, till it has perfectly bodied itself in feeling and desire.

Again in MS 10A, 'Other End', 21:

But it does not follow that 'pure Reason' as operative in human world is separate from, or pure of, desires. On the contrary, *reason*, in its human, as opposed to merely *natural*, expression, just = desires as an organic system pervaded by self-consciousness.

These passages carry more freight than we actually need. In speaking of reason as embodying itself 'in feeling and desire' Green is relying on the kinds of metaphysical argument examined in Chapter 3. To see a flower is to see a complex of qualities: a complex is a system, and only reason yields the idea of a system. But a more interesting way of reading the passages is to regard Green as de-mythologizing reason. To reason practically just is, he urges, to do such things as to think about one's desires in certain systematic ways. It is not to call on some independently specifiable agency or faculty, 'reason', to which the task of systematization is assigned. (Against faculties, see PE § 6).

Green acknowledges a distinction between theoretical and practical reason. He distinguishes between ' "reason" in that sense in which we suppose it to be employed in our knowledge of the relation of things and in the process of arriving at general truths', e.g. theoretical reason, and 'reason' in the sense of an agent's ability to present his 'self to himself as the object of his action', i.e. practical reason (Works II, 133–4). Taken in this way, practical reason has a narrower sphere of operation than the general area of what Green calls 'practice'. For the differentia of practice is that it involves 'the apprehension of a world . . . which *should be*' as distinct from 'a world which *is*' (PE, § 85). But, in the simplest terms, we can use reason to change the world in line with our desires, not only to revise the structure of our desires. This appears to mark Green's distinction between practical reason and the practical application of theoretical reason.

It is worth observing that in its fourth aspect the multi-perspectival model heals the cognitive motivational split of 4.2. Reason is a structure of intelligence which enables us to conceive a coherent organization of desire; the desires so organized furnish reasons for actions.

4.15   THE MULTI-PERSPECTIVAL MODEL: REVIEW (2)

Hume denies that reason can be practical: reason can neither set the ends of action nor furnish the motivation to pursue those ends. But reason for Green is not what it seems to Hume; and when the real nature of reason is appreciated, Green argues, the concept of practical reason emerges in a different light.

As self-conscious agents we can critically distance ourselves from our desires and, by self-intervention, create increasingly systematic structures of desire. In 4.12, departing from Green's terminology by keeping firmly to his ideas, we referred to life-plans, composite desires, and wide-interest systems to explain how desires thus structured might yield 'an abiding satisfaction of an abiding self'. The capacity for thinking about our desires as systematic structures is practical reason. Reason thus construed is closely bound up with self-consciousness: only a self-conscious agent could think of his desires across time, and the idea of a system is available only to an agent endowed with reason.

The sense in which reason sets the ends of action is this. Reason 'in the practical sense', critically reviewing the set of an agent's desires *qua* system, is 'the capacity on the part of . . . a subject to conceive a better state of itself as an end to be attained' (PE, § 177). If in Green's terms we call this conception a 'practical idea', we see also how reason can furnish the motivation to pursue a revised structure of desire. A 'practical' idea is precisely one which an agent 'strives and tends to realise' (PE, § 87). In other words, the propensity to strive for its realization is an important dimension of any practical idea. This is Green's version of internalism.

Green's concept of practical reason is distinctive in two ways: first, simply in the fact that the multi-perspectival model is not a direct transcript of any other account of practical reason. We may catch Hegelian echoes (4.13); and when Green summarizes the fourth aspect of the model by saying that it cannot be significantly held that 'the desires as organized by reason are different from reason as organizing the desires', there is an obvious affinity to the Aristotelian 'desiderative reason' or 'ratiocinative desire' of *Nicomachean Ethics*, VI.2. But the model as a whole is no mere reproduction of what is available elsewhere. Secondly, the multi-perspectival model has a modern peculiarity in not being linked immediately to ethics. Certainly Green aims to use the model in an account of the rationality of moral action. He argues for instance that the kind of systematic structure of desire which is basic to the fourth aspect of the model can evolve from the requirements of a social role, and that to fulfil such a role is to act morally. If I am an administrator, my job requires me to treat like cases equally--an operational definition of justice. This curve of argument is not to be climbed quickly; here it merely indicates the moral connections Green wants to make. Such connections are widely removed from the immediacies of Kant and Hume.

Kant takes us straight from reason to ethics. Reason, theoretical or practical, is the faculty of rules. In regard to conduct it is a filter which, imposed on the myriad of an agent's desires, yields universalizable 'maxims' (2.7.1); and to act morally just is to act on such maxims. The link is direct. Hume's dismissal of the concept of practical reason also involves a direct link between reason and ethics, but a negative one. The sting behind Hume's assertion that reason can neither set the ends of action nor furnish the motivation to pursue them is evidently and predominantly ethical. Ethical rationalism, with its view of moral principles as truths of reason, was historically the chief litigant in claims for the practical power of reason. The explicitly ethical polemic of *Treatise* III.1.1 simply reveals what has been the main target all along.

4.16 TWO PROBLEMS

I now consider two objections to the multi-perspectival model. Structures of desire serve a particular value, that of enabling 'an abiding satisfaction of an abiding self' or, to vary the formula, 'a satisfaction on the whole' (PE, § 85). But that satisfaction can itself be evaluated. Leave moral approval out of the question; it does not belong to the present stage of our inquiry. What if systematic structures of desire are of the kind generally thought 'low', 'poor', or 'thin'? Take an example. Steve has two wide-interest systems. The first centres on getting completely intoxicated by 10.30 each day; the second turns on collecting football programmes when he is sober. Each composite desire unfolds into a series of simple desires; and the composite desires are fully compatible. Steve has integrated wide-interest systems. Does he present an ideal image of self-satisfaction? The answer expected is negative; this is the first objection. But this line of criticism ignores Green's theory of the unconditional human good to which reference was made in 4.13. Green argues that there are constraints on what can provide 'an abiding satisfaction of an abiding self'. A person may, Steve does, seek satisfaction where it 'is not to be found' (Works II, 308; HM, 228). We shall look more closely at this argument in Chapter 6. For now the point is decisive that Green does not offer the multi-perspectival model in isolation from a further account of self-satisfaction. The model aims to *introduce* the idea of self-satisfaction, 'the idea of a satisfaction on the whole', not to say the last word about it.

The second objection may be put as follows. Granted that the agent can create increasingly systematic structures of desire, why should he do so? Why should he aim, in Green's language, at 'an abiding satisfaction of an abiding self', for self-satisfaction through integrated wide-interest systems and composite desires? Green constructs one picture of the agent. Hobbes, for instance, constructs quite another.

Hobbes sees the human agent as subject to the impact of a constant stream of desires, that 'perpetual and restless' influx 'that ceaseth only in death'.[12] For 'while we live, we have desires, and desire presupposeth a further end'.[13] 'But for an *utmost* end, in which the ancient philosophers have placed *felicity* . . . there is no such thing in this world, nor way to it, more than

---

[12] T. Hobbes, *Leviathan*, ed. M. J. Oakeshott, Oxford, 1946, 64.
[13] T. Hobbes, *Human Nature*, in D. D. Raphael, ed., *British Moralists* 1650–1800, i. Oxford, 1969, 5.

to Utopia'; 'there can be contentment but in proceeding'.[14] For Hobbes, therefore, at no point in the agent's life is he nearer to happiness or contentment as an end state, or 'felicity' as Hobbes calls it, than at any other. The appropriate image is that of a circuit in which success consists not in reaching a finishing line but simply in being able to continue running.

This is Hobbes's view of 'felicity': and in criticism of Green, Sidgwick's picture of 'the normal condition of human life: desire—fruition—calm, fresh desire—fresh fruition' is no different in essentials. Sidgwick endorses this 'continually renascent satisfaction' as sufficient for happiness.[15]

Two comments are appropriate to Sidgwick. First, Sidgwick's 'continually renascent satisfaction' and Green's 'abiding satisfaction of an abiding self' should not be regarded as separate and antithetical processes. Green's wide-interest systems and composite desires involve simple desires which fit exactly into Sidgwick's pattern of desire, fruition, fresh desire, fresh fruition. So Green is not departing absolutely from anything to which Sidgwick can agree. He is simply going beyond what Sidgwick considers necessary. Secondly, in criticising Green, Sidgwick implicitly invokes the kind of notion on which Green relies. For Sidgwick says in effect that an agent's future existence and well-being can be safely left to 'continually renascent satisfaction'. But to say this is to make just the kind of forward-reference involved in Green's notion of an abiding satisfaction of an abiding self. Sidgwick might reply that Green still has not shown that 'abiding satisfaction' requires composite desires rather than simple desires. If composite desires make up a lifeplan, however, Green's agent has not merely the 'continually renascent satisfaction' of fulfilling his simple desires: he has the additional satisfaction of knowing that in the process of their fulfilment his lifeplan is being realized. Sidgwick cannot plausibly deny that this is an extra consideration. An agent may forgo this additional satisfaction, but why should he do so?

On a side note there is a further objection to be considered, one urged by John Dewey. I believe Dewey's objection fails; but the response to it will be easier to make out when we have

[14] D. D. Raphael, ibid.
[15] H. Sidgwick, 61–2.

outlined Green's theory of the true or unconditional human good. I postpone Dewey to 6.10

With the current two problems handled, I now wish to look further at Green's relation to Hegel. I have claimed (4.15) that Green's multi-perspectival model is not derivative from Hegel. But the philosophy of Hegel hovers over any writer who speaks of 'reason, as self-consciousness'. On investigation some crucial differences open up. I base my exposition on *Philosophy of Right*, §§ 4–6, *Encyclopaedia*, §§ 400–74, and *Phenomenology of Spirit*, Section AA.

4.17   GREEN AND HEGEL ON SELF-CONSCIOUSNESS

In Hegelian terms Kant is ahead of Hume, and Green is ahead of Kant. Kant identifies the level of abstract self-consciousness. 'I am I', as Hegel labels Kant's invisible witness, the 'I think' which accompanies all our representations. Hume cannot reach so far even as this, for lack of an 'impression' to support an 'idea' of the self. The next level of self-consciousness is Hegel's stage of 'appetite' in which the agent is aware of discrete natural objects which he wants. On again to another level, we enter Hegel's stage of recognitive self-consciousness in which the agent is aware not only of objects of appetite in the external world, but of other self-conscious beings. His first response to this awareness is to resent another's status as self-conscious, capable of inconvenient purposes, and to seek accordingly to destroy him. But already one agent's self-consciousness is reinforced by another's; and the next response is the desire not to destroy but to dominate. Here is the view of others as *manipulanda*. This is the phase of self-consciousness to which Hegel's famous discussion of the master–slave relationship belongs. The master merely uses the slave in order to secure various ends for himself. The slave has no autonomous status. On a further level still is the community of self-conscious beings who recognize one another as self-conscious and autonomous.

Hegel presents in this way a series of levels of self-consciousness. As a counterpart is an ascending series of relations in which the agent may stand to his own desires. At the level of appetite one desire simply follows another. Only at the level of mutual recognition between self-conscious and autonomous beings, Hegel in effect argues, is the agent able to systematize his desires in structures of the sort with which the multi-perspectival model is concerned in its later aspects.

This is the merest sketch of Hegel's complex and obscure account of self-consciousness; and plainly it is not strictly a historical development that Hegel has in mind. The point is analytical: that the notion of self-consciousness can be approached at several levels. How far may the Hegelian account be ascribed to Green?

Green knew the relevant parts of Hegel. Nothing in Green's own account of self-consciousness excludes Hegel's account. But three comments are in order. First, Green nowhere commits himself to anything like the explicit Hegelian account of levels of self-consciousness. Secondly, his account of reason and self-consciousness, while it can accommodate the Hegelian theory, does not presuppose or otherwise require it. We were able earlier to explain and defend Green's account without relying on Hegel. That Hegel's theory is a framework in which Green's account might be placed, a framework of which Green was aware, does not show that Green accepted that framework broadly or in detail. Moreover, clarity diminishes as we turn from Green to Hegel. The question which presses anxiously on the reader of Green is to know the use of his account. Its substance is clear, but is this is how we start, where do we end up? I gave a brief indication above. But suggestive as the Hegelian theory may be, and graspable in general terms, its polemical role against Hume and Kant is clearer than its exact substance. Thirdly, the Hegelian framework has extensions which Green emphatically repudiates. Thus the structuring of desires in a lifeplan is secured in Hegel through a social organization of which the value is greater than that of the individuals whose desires it structures. The relevant notion of *Sittlichkeit* is one which finds a diluted reflection in Green (7.6). The ethical and axiological ultimacy of persons in Green's philosophy (1.13) is, however, a point on which Green and Hegel are irreducibly divided.

The closest parallel in Green to Hegel's levels of self-consciousness, and probably a reflection of Hegel's influence, is his view of different levels of practice. Action is seen first as the simple transformation of the external world. In desire we apprehend 'a world ... which *should be*' (PE, § 85) and act accordingly. This kind of action in line with desire defines the first two aspects of the multi-perspectival model. In the third and fourth aspects we observe the agent altering the desires from which he acts; practice turns back upon the agent himself. In a later chapter we shall see a final level of practice in which the state of society is altered so as to widen the variety of lifeplans an agent can conceive and choose to carry out (8.4 ff.;cf. 1.4).

4.18 A STRUCTURE OF ARGUMENT

This chapter has centred on Green's multi-perspectival model of deliberation. We have set out the internal structure of that model by exhibiting it under the four aspects of Humean instrumentality, reflective common sense, critical distance, and the idea of integrated wide-interest systems. Green's model, which interlocks critically with the philosophy of Hume, has been shown to be distinctive and not to be unduly derivative from Aristotle, Kant, or Hegel.

In relation to Green's own philosophy the multi-perspectival model extends in two directions. One is vertical, as the model connects with an account of character and motive to make a comprehensive philosophy of action. (If we extend the connections back to the account of mind, knowledge, and reality given in Chapter 3, we edge towards what Howard Mettler has called 'a whole model of a human being'.[16] This takes us into Chapter 5. The other direction is horizontal, as the model extends through ethics and politics. In Chapter 6 we shall see how Green defines five criteria for the human good, his view of what can provide that 'abiding satisfaction of an abiding self' in the idea of which the multi-perspectival model culminates. Then in Chapter 7 we shall take up Green's view that the requirements of a social role can fulfil those criteria and create the increasingly systematic structures of desire which are basic to the fourth aspect of the model. As a social role fulfils the

---

[16] Howard Mettler, personal communication.

human good, so also it encapsulates a morality. Therefore morality in turn is bound up objectively with the human good. Finally, to expand the point introduced at the end of the last section, the main role of politics, which we shall examine in Chapter 8, is to remove social conditions which prevent an agent from conceiving or creating certain systematic structures of desire, visualizing or fulfilling particular lifeplans, within the constraints of morality: and to enable interpersonally the abiding satisfaction of abiding *selves*. To draw out the connections here described is to trace a definite pattern of thought, a structure of argument.

5

Character, Motive, and Action

5.1 INTRODUCTION

Character fulfils three roles in Green's philosophy: it explains action; it defines free agency; it grounds the moral virtues. The relation of character to the virtues will be examined in Chapter 7 (see in particular 7.18). The first role is likely to encounter a degree of resistance, the second a degree of puzzlement.

Talk of character comes as an unwelcome idiom in contemporary ethical theory and moral psychology. From one point of view character appears to be a dispositional category; and on two common theories of dispositions to cite a disposition is to predict hypothetically or to summarize, but not to explain. On one theory a dispositional statement is simply a future hypothetical. The rubber band is elastic; if pulled it will stretch. Nick is obstinate; if you prove him wrong he will disregard your arguments. On another theory a dispositional statement merely summarizes. Glass is fragile; it tends to break. Mary Lou is bossy; she tends to take charge in any social situation when a decision has to be made. But nothing is explained by citing Nick's obstinacy or Mary Lou's bossiness. So the explanatory role of character is far from straightforward. From another point of view, that of Sartrean existentialism, the concept of character is a pitfall of bad faith: a dodge by which to persuade oneself that certain forms of one's own behaviour are necessary or inevitable. To take seriously the concept of character involves the self-alienation of regarding some part of oneself, namely one's character, as constraining radical freedom. Thus the concept of character is seen as ethically undesirable by the existentialist, as explanatorily vacuous by the dispositionalist.

If Green can break these objections, the role of character in his philosophy may still look puzzling. Three questions are likely. In the first place, if one role of character is to define free agency, why should Green need a concept of character, as defining free agency, if free will is secured by the kind of arguments we considered in Chapter 3? Secondly, if for any given state of an agent's character the kinds of desire on which he will act are fixed (3.12), how is character compatible with free will? Thirdly, how does the multi-perspectival model of deliberation, outlined in Chapter 4, connect with an account of character, when the essence of deliberation is attention but the essence of character is habit and the essence of habit is an unconsidered repetition of patterns of behaviour?

The plan of the present chapter is this. We have our basic problematic: to see how character explains action and defines free agency. First I set out the machinery of Green's theory of character: the concepts of action, motive, and of 'wide' and 'narrow' character. The explanation of action by character is explained in terms of a 'rational point' analysis; and free agency is identified with character on the narrow construction. Having defined Green's theory of character and expounded its working, I then proceed contrastively and set Green's theory against the rival theory of J. S. Mill in *A System of Logic* and *Utilitarianism*. (Separate notice is taken of the implications of Mill's *On Liberty*.) The central difference between Green and Mill is that Mill is interested in character primarily as a source of actions; Green is interested in character primarily as a mode of self-realization. Two more detailed disagreements are explored concerning the relation of motive (*a*) to action and (*b*) to consequence. The main work of the chapter thus completed, I close on two topics: the will, and the existentialist critique of character. On the first I show that although Green uses the language of 'the will', his explanation of action by character involves no objectionable notion of the will as a faculty of volition such as we find, e.g. in Prichard. On the second topic I show how Green can answer Sartre.

5.2 ACTION

One of the principal aims of modern philosophical psychology has been to elucidate the nature of action. Wittgenstein's question, 'What is left over if I subtract the fact that my arm went up from the fact that I raised my arm?'[1] sets the need to distinguish an action from a mere movement. There is no consensus on how that distinction is to be made. One approach is to try to define a set of necessary and sufficient properties for something, anything, to count as an action. Charles Taylor proposes such properties as goal-directedness and in-tentionality.[2] Another approach is that of H. L. A. Hart, who suggests a disjunctive set of non-necessary, non-sufficient criteria which leave the concept of action, in Waismann's phrase, 'open-textured'.[3]

Green's marked divergence from this style of elucidation is that he does not take our pre-analytical ideas about action as given and then ask how they can be organized to clarify the distinction between an action and a mere movement. He is selective from the start, ready to allow that there are actions which are instinctive, accidental, performed during sleep, or done strictly under compulsion (PE, § 96). He has slight interest in the distinction between those actions and mere movements. Instead, he emphasizes motivated actions, where a motive is 'an idea of an end, which a self-conscious subject presents to itself, and which it strives and tends to realise' (PE, § 87). Such actions Green calls 'moral' or 'distinctively human' actions (PE, § 87, 91). These, for him, are the actions with which ethics is concerned. But what is a motive?

5.3 MOTIVE

Green's account of motive is above all an account of desire. Roughly consider certain ways in which a desire might be relevant to action.

(1) We might cite a desire on which someone perhaps acted but on which we do not know whether he actually did act, or we might cite a desire on which, relative to a given criterion, someone would have been justified in acting but on which we do

[1] L. Wittegenstein, *Philosophical Investigations*, I, § 622, tr. G. E. M. Anscombe, Oxford, 1958.

[2] C. Taylor, *The Explanation of Human Behaviour*, London, 1964, *passim*.

[3] H. L. A. Hart, 'Acts of Will and Responsibility', *Punishment and Responsibility*, Oxford, 1970.

not know whether he acted. Such examples yield the 'motives' famous in crime movies and detective fiction. We do not know whether Alfred killed his father, but we do know that he stood to gain financially from his father's death; we know also that Alfred urgently wanted money. He had a motive for killing his father. If we later discover that it was Abel Baker who did the deed, we do not have to withdraw the ascription of motive to Alfred. Alfred did not kill his father, but he had a motive for killing him. Green recognizes this sense of 'motive' when he acknowledges motives as 'outward inducements' (MS 10A, 'Other End', 3): but if 'outward', yet never external to the agent's desires. The prospect of financial gain is not automatically assignable as a motive. If Alfred, having renounced the world, had no desire for money, he had no motive of financial gain for murdering his father.

(2) We might cite a desire on which (we know that) someone plans to act or on which he actually has acted. When Kisha telephoned Vena in the middle of the night, he wanted to disturb her sleep: it was no less than she deserved. In acting on that desire Kisha, in Green's language, adopted it as a 'motive'. A motive is a desire on which we decide to act or (relative to a particular situation such as Kisha's) one on which we have already acted. This is the sense of 'motive' which is central to Green's moral psychology, though he also notices (in order to dismiss) the usage in which a motive is a desire on which we are undecided whether to act (PE, § 103). A motive, then, is a desire (PE, § 91). But Green asserts something more: that to decide to act on a desire is to see the realization of that desire under the aspect of some personal good. This is what he says: 'The motive is every imputable act for which the agent is conscious on reflection that he is answerable, is a desire for personal good in some form or other' (ibid.). This view traces to Aristotle, who lays down the principle that we act only with a view to some good (NE I.1). (In Plato we meet the Socratic view of desire as for the real or imagined good, e.g. *Meno*, 77B–78B. But the present point concerns not desire but action.) Green continues: 'It is superfluous to add, good *to himself*; for anything conceived as good in such a way that the agent acts for the sake of it, must be conceived as *his own* good' (PE, § 92). If the rider, 'to himself', is superfluous, then why does Green even notice it as a

possible addition? E. F. Carritt is right to read here a point against Hobbes, who says that 'of the voluntary acts of every man, the object is some good to himself'.[4] But we need as much care to realize what Green is not saying as to establish what he is really getting at.

Green holds that, in normal human action, to act is to act not by impulsion but for a reason. I am thirsty and want to drink. I decide to satisfy that desire, and to do so now rather than to wait until I have finished something else that I am doing. I shall finish that job better if I break now for a coffee, I argue to myself— perhaps self-deceptively. This kind of decision-making is what Green is getting at in speaking of a motive as a desire for personal good. To act on a particular motive is to act for a reason.

Then what is Green not saying that lends a cutting-edge to his saying this? There are four points. First he is not endorsing what Butler called the 'selfish theory of human nature'. As we saw in 4.12, I may take my personal good to involve a reference to your interests by reason of my involvement with you: there need be nothing selfish in my motivation when I act on a desire to buy a new car for you. Green continues the PE, § 92 passage quoted above: 'It is superfluous to add, good *to himself*; for anything conceived as good in such a way that the agent acts for the sake of it, must be conceived as *his own* good, though he may conceive it as his own good only on account of his interest in others, and in spite of any amount of suffering on his part incidental to its attainment.' An agent may of course act from selfish motives (Works II, 434; HM, 95). But selfishness is a contingent matter, not an ineluctable fact of human nature or a conceptual necessity on Green's account.

Secondly, Green is not claiming that a desire, just any desire, is the product of a conception of personal good: that only on condition that I regard the realization of X is desirable in terms of a conception of personal good can I desire X. Some desires are of this kind, those reflective desires for example which derive from a lifeplan. But desires of 'purely animal origin' (PE, § 86) simply occur. I am thirsty: my desire to drink is not the product

---

[4] E. F. Carritt, *Morals and Politics*, Oxford, 1935, 27, 128; T. Hobbes, *Leviathan*, ed. M. J. Oakeshott, Oxford, 1946, 86.

of any belief that drinking is a desirable form of activity. It is the decision to act on a desire that embodies a conception of personal good.

Thirdly, Green is not claiming that the conception of personal good which a motive embodies has necessarily the full reflective depth of the fourth aspect of the multi-perspectival model. The idea of self-satisfaction, of 'an abiding satisfaction of an abiding self', stands at the limit of a conception of personal good. Short-term and fragmentary ideas may inform the conception of personal good on which on a particular occasion or quite regularly a certain person acts. Fourthly and finally Green is not maintaining that conceptions of personal good are self-authenticating. Any conception of personal good is answerable to the facts; and it is perfectly possible for somebody to have a radically mistaken conception of personal good, for him to direct his actions to 'objects in which, according to the law of his being, satisfaction of himself is not to be found' (Works II, 308; HM, 228). This points to Green's theory of the unconditional human good to which we shall turn in Chapter 6.

On a historical note, Green's account of motive marks a significant departure from Kant. Green aims at a fully unified theory of action to cover all forms of 'distinctively human' action. Kant in contrast produces radically disparate accounts of moral and non-moral motivation. In so far as a person adopts the moral point of view, Kant argues, he is a free agent; and the moral point of view, reflected in the notion of *Sollen* and in the judgement 'I ought', is capable of determining a person to action irrespective of his desires. With respect to all actions not determined by moral judgement, a person is, as Green critically observes of Kant, 'a member of a merely natural world' (Works II, 109) controlled by a psychological mechanism of pleasure and pain. Green insists that, on the contrary, by virtue of the self-conscious principle which enables a person to detach himself critically from his desires and to decide which to satisfy, human motivation is non-natural and free. The distinction between moral and non-moral motivation, so far from separating the moral agent Kantianly from his desires, centres on specific differences between the desires pursued under the common forms of a 'personal good'.

An end point, to emphasize Green's unified theory, is that the desires which are adopted as motives may be either 'inclinational' or 'intentional' in Gewirth's terminology from 4.8: desires, in other words, which appeal intrinsically, or desires which simply embody some aim by reason of the situation one is in. This point will recur directly, as we consider the concept of character.

5.4 CHARACTER

The final element in Green's theory of action explanation is that of character. Character is not temperament or, in a more recent sense than Green recognized, personality: a susceptibility to optimism, say, or to melancholy or depression. Green says of character that it signifies 'the way in which a man seeks self-satisfaction' (Works II, 142). It fixes 'what the kind of personal good', referred to in the last section, 'shall be' (PE, § 95). It is, moreover, the ultimate ethical category, 'that to which moral predicates are ultimately relative' (Works II, 142); and why this is so I must explain in due course (7.11). But the first essential is to establish a basic distinction which dominates Green's treatment of character: that between a wide and a narrow construction. The distinction is not one which Green makes explicitly. Nor is he confused between the two constructions. But we cannot adequately handle his treatment of character without making that distinction ourselves. The distinction is not specially difficult: to a first approximation it can be set out as follows.

Suppose I say that a person has such and such a character. Suppose I also say that someone is a person of character. These ordinary language claims are different. In the first sense just everybody must have a character. For however a person behaves, that behaviour identifies truistically the kind of person he is, his character in the first, wide sense: weak, hesitant, and immature, or strong and imperious, with whatever situational relativity applies. Basically, as one behaves so one is capable of behaving, and this is the character one has. But not everyone is a person of character, in the second, narrow sense, even if we cut away the ethical associations from that phrase. To be a person of character, or to be a character, is to be self-determined. It is (minimally) to have what Bernard Williams has called 'categorical desires':[5] desires with which one identifies, on which one acts, desires which are not immediately up for negotiation if other agents find them disagreeable. A person of character in the second, narrow sense will necessarily have a character in the first, wide sense. Everyone has. But certain kinds of wide character are ruled out for a person of character in the narrow sense. I cannot have categorical desires, as described, and be weak and hesitant in relation to them. Conversely, if I am generally weak and hesitant, I cannot be a person of character in the narrow sense. This is not a hard distinction to make out; it may be hard to make precise.

One point, however, to save disappointment later. It would be of no use, for purposes of disconcerting Green, to argue that here are two concepts of character, about the relationship between which there are puzzling questions. Character, wide or narrow, always signifies 'the way in which a man seeks self-satisfaction'. The narrow construction simply introduces a certain typology of character: here is one type of character, identified minimally by the agent's possession of categorical desires. It is merely one possibility of which the wide construction of character admits. In terms of what has gone before, 'wide' character includes all the inclinational and intentional desires which feature in the explanation of action. 'Narrow' character centres on the kind of systematic structure of desire of which we have traced the outline under the fourth aspect of the multi-perspectival model. The point may be added, however, that a correct analysis of *akrasia*, or weakness of will, depends (for Green) on understanding the interactions of which wide and narrow character are capable (7.12).

The wide construction of character is most in evidence when Green talks of a person's character as simply defined by that person's way of seeking self-satisfaction. As I seek self-satisfaction so you find my character. But this prompts us back to the second theory of dispositions cited in 5.1. For the objection may be made that the wide construction of character merely summarizes how I behave; it explains nothing. To see

⁵ B. Williams, 'Persons, Character and Morality', *The Identities of Persons*, ed. A. O. Rorty, Berkeley, 1977, 207 *et passim*.

what Green means, however, by this wide construction of character we need to remove the summary view from the picture; and this is easy to do.

The summary view confounds frequency or regularity with habit. Character involves habit, and there is even an idiom which allows us to say that I can do something habitually, i.e. with a high degree of frequency, without having the habit of doing it. Suppose I habitually get up early. Of course this is to say that getting up early is something I do with a high degree of frequency. Perhaps, though, I make a totally independent decision each morning, after a survey of the day, the usual result of which is that I get up early. On this condition I do not have a habit of early rising; the only habit shown here is that of daily decision-making of which (contingently) the result is almost invariable. A helpful backdrop to Green's wide construction of character is Aristotle's analysis of habit and Kant's analysis of free action. Aristotle's analysis has two main elements. It is the second element, the second kind of habit recognized by Aristotle, which is most relevant.

5.5 GREEN AND ARISTOTLE ON CHARACTER

Aristotle notes two distinct kinds of habit.[6] In the first place, and not our major concern, habit (*hexis*) indicates any acquired capacity. If I have learnt German this is an acquired capacity of which we can say two things: it is a possession (I have a knowledge of German), and it is a capacity which I retain even when I am not using it. I read no German last week; I may read some tomorrow. Such *hexis* is a disposition (*diathesis*) which automatically produces action (*energeia*) unless prevented by circumstances or choice. Put German in front of me tomorrow and I shall read it, but not if I have lost my glasses and not if I decide to do something else. Secondly, habit indicates something not simply acquired but contracted, like a second nature (*De mem.*, 452a28). When an agent continues or repeats a particular kind of action the relation between agent and action changes; the condition of the agent is modified. A habit is a

---

[6] Aristotle, *Metaphysics*, Δ20, 1022b4–10; 22, 1022b19–29; *De Memoria*, 452a28.

disposition to do a particular kind of action induced in an agent by the continued or repeated doing of that very action itself. The action is one to which the agent becomes accustomed, a condition in relation to which Aristotle talks of *ethos*. Thus repetition features in the formation of habit; and repetition, or the tendency to repeat, is the essence of habit once formed. The formation of habit relies on an element of plasticity in human agency (however often a stone falls, it never contracts the habit of falling); and Aristotle powerfully analyses the role of education, social custom, and law in the moral habituation of the young.

But he does not satisfy Green. There is a similarity between Green's view of the ethical ultimacy of character and Aristotle's view of the *phronimos* or practically wise man and ideal agent whose *hexeis*, dispositions, afford the criteria of *arete*. In a broad perspective Green is in line with both Plato and Aristotle in seeing such terms of assessment as 'courageous', 'just', 'temperate', as applicable primarily to persons rather than to actions. The Aristotelian connection loosens, however, when we consider the revision of character, the alteration of habit. It is easy to think that Aristotle makes the agent more passive than he really does in relation to the process of habituation brought to bear on him by education, social custom, and law; the agent's choice or purpose (*prohairesis*) is his own response. Aristotle's opinion at NE, 1114b is, however, that only the beginnings of *hexis* are under the agent's control. Beyond that point the obduracy of *hexis* may be insurmountable. While Green wants to argue for the relative fixity of habits, of character traits, he is unwilling to accept that for the normal agent a habit, however deeply ingrained, cannot be altered under the third aspect of the multi-perspectival model of deliberation.

For any such view as Green's, how important is the point that the heroin addict has ceased to be free in the sense of being able to deliberate, to make decisions and carry them out? Very important, but the point is one which Green plainly recognizes. I referred to the 'normal' agent; and Green accepts that the mind has a material base which, in particular cases, may be sufficient to defeat the kind of decision-making on which his model depends. He concedes, for instance, that 'disease may derationalize a man, in <the> sense of rendering the animal system no longer organic to the rational ego' (Aristotle B, 39). The material base of mind in Green's philosophy is as firm as any physicalist could wish; the dependence of nature, which includes our bodies, on the eternal consciousness does nothing to liberate the proper functioning of the human mind from, e.g. states of the brain. (And there is no reason why Green cannot allow the impact of evolution on that material base.) In a crude image, but I know of none better: the mind is like a set of scales which in equipoise is accurate and self-regulating in the measurement of weights. Derange its physical mechanism, and its self-regulation has gone. Alter the physical basis of mind, and the kind of decision-making on which Green's model depends goes too: perhaps it will take with it some of the mythology about Green's idealism (cf. 3.12).

5.6   GREEN AND KANT ON CHARACTER

If Green's disagreement with Aristotle centres on the revisability of character, his disagreement with Kant centres on the freedom of action which character allows an agent in particular situations.

The criticism is not unfamiliar that Kant's ethics lacks any adequate notion of character. Bernard Williams explicitly criticizes Kant on this score.[7] Certainly the good will, which has some claim to be Kant's ultimate ethical category since it is that in which alone moral value ultimately resides, seems hard to equate with character. As C. C. J. Webb observes: 'although the capacity for exercising (the good will) constitutes the essence of our personality, yet (it) abstracts altogether from the features that distinguish one person from another, and belongs in common to all rational beings'.[8] Kant has the concept of character. In his *Anthropology* he addresses the concept with his customary penetration.[9] The question is how character mediates between ethics and action.

[7] B. Williams, 215.
[8] C. C. J. Webb, *God and Personality*, London, 1920, 120.
[9] I. Kant, *Anthropology from a Pragmatic Point of View*, tr. M. J. Gregor, The Hague, 1974.

John Stuart Mill thought the notion of character an integral element in Kant's ethics. On the issue of free will Mill reports in his *Examination of Hamilton* that:

According to Kant, in his Metaphysics of Ethics, . . . capability of prediction is quite compatible with the freedom of the will. This seems, at first sight, to be an admission of everything which the rational supporters of the opposite theory could desire. But Kant avoids this consequence, by changing . . . the *venue* of free-will, from our actions generally, to the formation of our character. It is in that, he thinks, we are free, and he is almost willing to admit that while our character is what it is, our actions are necessitated by it.[10]

The *locus* for this Kantian view is the 'Analytic of Pure Practical Reason' in the *Critique of Practical Reason*. Green expounds Kant to the same effect:

It may be allowed, that if it were possible for us to have an insight into a man's character [Denkengsart], as exhibited in his inner no less than outer action, so thorough that every slightest impulse should be known to us as well as all outward circumstances acting on him, we could predict his future conduct as certainly as <the> occurrence of an eclipse; and for all that it may be maintained that he is free. (MS 10A, 37.)

When I suggest that Green disagrees with Kant I must also point out that I do not think Green identifies the disagreement quite precisely. Consider Green's further exposition of Kant:

Every psychical event is to the man what his character [he himself] makes it. But is not this character simply the result of previous psychical events? No: (Kant would say): each of these events has been determined—has been made what it is—by presence to it of 'transcendental' self.

Is not this what Aristotle means, when he says we are *synaitioi ton hexeon*? Not quite.[11] According to Aristotle we are only synaitioi, as having control over the first step in formation of hexis. According to Kant, it is hopeless mistake to try to find free causality at beginning of series of empirical determination.

Same mistake as making creation a *first event*. The unconditioned is nowhere to be found in the series of the conditioned, which is endless.

---

[10] J. S. Mill, *An Examination of Sir William Hamilton's Philosophy*, 4th edn. London, 1872, 517.

[11] The Aristotelian reference is to NE, 1114b23: 'responsible for our states of character'.

Of empirical series of events related to individual's life there is no beginning in time any more than of world. They in fact *are* the world. 'But how can I have given their moral character—their relation to me as moral being—to events that happened before I was born?'

(To this Kant does not seem to give any clear answer. It can only be answered on supposition that the self, in virtue of which alone I am a moral agent, is the eternal self.)

The imputability to me of guilt of actions, which form part of an empirical series stretching endlessly backwards, only explicable on consideration that the same self-consciousness, through which alone antecedents of these acts have a moral relation to me, constitutes power of so modifying them as that they shall be compatible with good will.—(MS 10A, 37–9.)

Green's debate with Kant is conducted as if both were dealing with the same problem in ethics over the explanation of action, but I do not think this is so. Green holds that character, 'the way in which a man seeks self-satisfaction', is not physically determined. I cannot see that Kant has to agree with Green on this. We can put some detail on Kant's ethical attitude to character if we look at another Kantian term, *Gessinning*. Just as every moral action for Kant is grounded in a maxim, so maxims themselves are grounded in the subjective disposition, *Gessinning* or character, of the agent. Kant need not hold that character, here the maxims with which an agent enters a situation relevant to moral action, is anything other than a 'phenomenon' capable of regular causal explanation in terms of prior events and conditions. This must, on Kant's own account, be true of what he calls the agent's 'empirical' character to which subjective disposition belongs. What Kant does hold is that, with whatever 'empirical' character one enters a situation relevant to moral action, the mere intellectual apprehension that a maxim fails to come under a universal law is sufficient to prevent action. That is what we saw in 2.7.1. If such freedom of moral action belongs to the Kantian agent in his 'noumenal' character, then noumenal character has nothing to do with the character of Green's agent and his desire-dependent search for 'self-satisfaction'.

Kant's moral agent is free, despite the 'phenomenal' determination of his empirical character and of the actions produced or brought about by it, through the 'critical' viewpoint that reconciles the phenomenal and the noumenal. The sort of reconciliation involved can be set out quite informally. To use a non-Kantian metaphor: phenomenal events form a pattern, like a rug. We can stretch the rug in different ways, and the pattern changes. But whatever happens, the rug has so many strands, of such colours, criss-crossing at so many points. Those strands represent the phenomenal. Their interrelations are never broken: in terms of them we can describe the rug and make all kinds of predictions about it. The noumenal is the pull which stretches the rug to make a different pattern on the underside.

This is not argument by example but exposition by metaphor. It claims to be nothing more, but Kant's own explanations are figurative and obscure. When Kant grants the predictability of action from empirical character he is simply conceding that the pattern of phenomenal events, the system of appearances, is never broken; the noumenal pattern equally retains its integrity. How far this reconciliation is really intelligible is of course a sharp puzzle of Kantian commentary. What should be quite clear is Kant's distance from Green. Green's idealism means a rejection of the phenomenal/noumenal distinction (3.11). Kant betrays no sense of the revisability of desire which is inset in the third and fourth aspects of Green's multi-perspectival model of deliberation. It is not, for Kant, that the agent can express himself freely through desire. Rather, in moral action the agent can act independently of desire.

Because Kant maintains that empirical character can determine action, and action still be free, Green reads this as very much his own view. But the similarity is quite deceptive. Green's agent is free to form and to revise his own character by self-intervention in his desires. Kant's agent, by contrast, is free *from* his own character by noumenal freedom in moral action. Green allows nothing like Kant's freedom to act, point-blank, irrespective of character, through mere intellectual apprehension. This aspect of Green's moral psychology has been sufficiently insisted on (3.12). His agreement with Kant, against Aristotle, is in holding that the freedom relevant to moral responsibility is a permanent feature of (normal) human agency. Kant believes that this freedom is permanently present noumenally; Green believes that it is permanently present through the possibility of self-intervention. Neither can accept that it might be fleetingly present, then disappear after the first stage of habituation.

5.7 CHARACTER: THE WIDE CONSTRUCTION

The upshot of this discussion is to re-emphasize that character, on the wide construction, is not a mere summary concept. If a person is regularly willing to forgo his rights in order to avoid unpleasant confrontations—he has that kind of intentional desire when faced by the first insensitive bully to come along— then one may correctly start to talk here of a habit which controls his actions. The more often he forgoes his rights, the more difficult it becomes for him to assert them. Inclinational desires are no different in this respect; the more often Isabella gratifies her desire for sugar (4.8), the harder it is for her to resist taking sugar. This, for Green, is no casual banality. The examples may vary and are not his own, but the point matters that 'A man's possibilities of doing and becoming at any moment of his life are as thoroughly conditioned as those of an animal or a plant; but the conditions are different' (PE, § 106). The conditions are set by habit, the internal base which grounds a person's tendencies to action. That base also undermines the idea that to cite character is merely to unwind a string of hypothetical predictions. And human habits are distinguished from animal habits by the possibility of self-intervention.

Habits arise in various ways: I may imitate the actions of another person in order to please or annoy him, I may be induced by drill, conditioning, or self-interest to repeat a certain type of action. In habitual action the first action conditions the second, the second the third, in such manner that actions of a particular type become easier to do (their execution requires less attention, their non-performance becomes more difficult) the more often that type of action is done. Repetition produces habit; habit produces repetition. In a psychologically exact account we should need to specify such conditions as the distraction of intervening events which can defeat or impair habit formation as thus described. But we see here the standard conditions for the formation of habits. Certainly Green has nothing more precise to offer.

A mere condition, a habit, is never sufficient to produce action. The condition needs to be completed by an occasion, by 'circumstances' in Green's language. The essence of habitual action is that in (what we recognize as) the same circumstances we act in the same way. This point is, however, easy to mistake. There is a tendency to suppose that habitual action is something like Xavier's always wearing his red tie when he wears a blue suit because this is a dress combination instilled by his parents. But to act in the 'same' way can involve the 'sameness' of analogy. In exactly similar circumstances I may act in merely analogous ways, in analogous circumstances I may act in exactly similar ways: habitual action is not reducible purely to acting in exactly similar ways in exactly similar circumstances. The concept of analogy opens a seldom examined link between character and imagination.

Consider, just to glance at that link, the habit of a man who typically administers a crushing rebuke when he supposes that he is being treated with less than due respect. In Green's language this desire to rebuke is, in relevant circumstances, his motive to action, and that action embodies his understanding of a personal good. Such a habit is nothing at all of the red-tie sort. On the one hand, the agent must interpet disrespect in a broad variety of situations: the waiter shows disrespect in serving new arrivals before him; the street urchin shows disrespect in shouting to him to kick back a stray football; the shop assistant shows disrespect . . ., and so forth, as protean disrespect haunts an obviously sensitive life. On the other hand the kind of rebuke that crushes must vary with the situations in which disrespect is shown. A Wildean epigram may humiliate the waiter; the street urchin will be impervious, like as not, to such artificial silliness. There is a play of imagination in this kind of case which is quite missing from the example of Xavier's red tie. I shall return to the idea of analogic responsiveness in 7.19; its main interest comes later in our discussion in a quite different context. For analogic responsiveness is typically displayed when a person has been trained or initiated in the requirements of an intelligent 'practice' rather than simply drilled or conditioned to behave in certain repetitive ways of the red-tie sort.

It is important to realize that the habits in which an agent's character consists, on the wide construction of character, may be of any degree of disorganization or weakness. Green is certainly not presenting a view of the normal human agent as, at any given time, tightly and smoothly habit-bound across the whole spectrum of action. His narrow construction of character centres, by contrast, on strength and organization of habit. A habit has, moreover, no isolated significance. I can indicate the typical manner in which a habit displays itself in a particular person: Tom's habit of liberality is typically displayed in handing money on the slightest request to entire strangers. I can indicate the relative strength of Tom's liberality; he is far more liberal than Cornelius, who displays similar behaviour only if he is really flush with cash. But the significance of Tom's habit cannot be isolated from 'the way in which he seeks self-satisfaction'. If most of Tom's habits centre on a form of life in which money is largely unimportant (Tom is, say, a novelist who seldom has much money and whose daily needs are met by an indulgent patron), then liberality is a feature of his character but it is practically irrelevant. If he has a family to keep and a small, irregular income to live on, his liberality might disorientate every plan he makes and spread like a stain across the hopes of his wife and children. Liberality would then be a major feature of his character, one that properly predominates in our description of the kind of person he is.

A habit comes into play in particular circumstances. In so far as recent theory of action has employed the notion of circumstances it has been, as in Melden's work,[12] to emphasize social context as definitory of action, so that it is my raising my arm in a car at a road junction which characterizes my action as one of signalling. This is not Green's approach. An example which he frequently uses will give us the first materials on which to work. The example is that of Esau in Genesis who, reduced to great hunger, sold his birthright for food. Green specifies and enumerates Esau's circumstances:

One 'circumstance' no doubt is his hunger. ... Of the other circumstances bearing on Esau's action, or of the most important among them, it could not be admitted that they are merely physical at all, even in their origin or antecedents as distinct from their bearing on his act. We may perhaps classify them roughly under three heads—the

[12] A. I. Melden, 'Action', *Essays in Philosophical Psychology*, ed. D. Gustafson, London, 1964.

state of his health, the outward manner of his life (including his family arrangements and the mode in which he maintains himself and his family), and the standard of social expectation on the part of those whom he recognises as his equals. All these have their weight in affecting the result which his character yields under the pressure of animal want.—(PE, § 97.)

There is, if we sift this through, an ambiguity about the notion of circumstances by which Green is certainly not confused but about which he is not explicit. The kinds of circumstances which Green is chiefly concerned to analyse are those subjectively present to the agent—action results from Esau's character taken in conjunction with his hunger (which he feels), the standard of social expectation (which he apprehends), and so on. This I shall term an internal view of circumstances: to talk of circumstances in this sense is just another way of saying how an agent understands his situation. But there is of course an alternative, or supplementary, external conception of circumstances. On that conception the circumstances of action may be completely unknown to the agent—Belinda, walking down the country lane, may be in great danger quite unawares. The external view of circumstances appears in Green's acknowledgement that 'circumstances may prevent' an action from having its intended effects (PE, § 146). On the internal view there is nothing to deny, on Green's account, that an agent's understanding of his situation may include the recognition of a character trait. If I know that I have a tendency to panic under stress, this tendency is an extremely pertinent 'circumstance' if I am offered a high-pressured job. Another point is that Green realizes that such circumstances of action as 'the standard of social expectation' themselves reflect the interaction of character and circumstances by past agents.

The more detailed explanation of action by character is to be considered in 5.9 after we have clarified the 'narrow' construction of character.

5.8   CHARACTER: THE NARROW CONSTRUCTION

On Green's narrow construction a person's character encompasses not merely how he will habitually act in certain situations but how he feels committed to acting. Perhaps improbably a quotation from Nietzsche may help. When Nietzsche says, 'If one has character, one has also one's typical experience that recurs again and again',[13] this is true enough on Green's wide construction of character. But such an experience may be only something like the realization, 'I'm letting him impose on me again', which has nothing to do with character more narrowly construed. Allowing somebody to impose on me is certainly not something to which I feel I have any commitment. Having character on the narrow construction, having what Green calls a 'strong character', means that 'it is the man's habit to set clearly before himself certain objects in which he seeks self-satisfaction, and that he does not allow himself to be drawn aside from these by the suggestions of chance desires' (PE, § 105): or, for the matter of that, by threats and blandishments. Thus, on the narrow construction a person has a particular structure of desire on which he not simply habitually acts but is concerned to act; and this structure of desire, which informs his actions, defines him socially as a centre of coherent activity.

Green's 'narrow' construction of character has four main elements. Character involves: (1) a self-conception; (2) categorical desires; (3) subscribed values; and (4) emotional engagement. The first two elements neatly combine in Green's reference to actions which 'result from a character which the conception of self has rendered possible, or express an interest in objects of which this conception is the condition' (Works I, 317). We have sorted out an early snag in understanding Green's notion of 'object' (3.7). Here we can say that 'objects' clearly include such projects as 'the acquisition of an estate, election to parliament, the execution of some design in literature or art' (PE, § 128). Subscribed values are automatically present through the consideration that character determines motive: motive embodies a conception of personal good. On the score of emotional engagement Green's theory of character has been criticized by H. D. Lewis for taking 'no particular account of emotions'.[14] But in PE, § 140 Green considers the case of an

---

[13] F. Nietzsche, *Beyond Good and Evil*, tr. M. Cowan, Chicago, 1955, 74.

[14] H. D. Lewis, ' "Self-Satisfaction" and the "True Good" ', *Proceedings of the Aristotelian Society*, 42 (1941–2), 173.

agent divided between the 'conflicting passions' engendered by his commitment to 'incompatible objects'. The case described is admittedly one of imperfection of character in the narrow sense: a clear self-conception does not inform the agent's desires. But it is the conflict of passions which is incidental to an imperfect state of character. Remove that imperfection, and still 'hatred of his rival stirs him'. Green certainly finds a place for the emotions in his theory of character. If he does not stress the emotions this is because his angle of interest in character does not require it.

We should not, however, fail to realize the suggestiveness of Green's moral psychology for a correct view of the emotions, and for an ethical theory apparently quite unrelated to his own. Emotivism, the theory to which I refer, has had a bad press not least because the nature of emotion has been widely misunderstood. If the emotions are construed 'irruptively' as, like Humean desires, passively undergone by the agent (4.3), then to analyse moral and aesthetic judgements in terms of such occurrences is implausible for all the textbook reasons. But given Brentano's thesis of the intentionality of the emotions, i.e. their sensitive dependence on beliefs about the objects on which they are directed, and given further Green's prime fact of self-intervention with respect to desires on which the emotions also depend, emotivism begins to shed its more obvious implausibility. I return, however, to our main theme.

5.9 CHARACTER AND ACTION

In 4.10 I described a young journalist under the fourth aspect of the multi-perspectival model. Such a person's commitment to a lifeplan produces just the kind of character which Green has in mind on the narrow construction. Suppose, then, we develop the 4.10 example, taking matters a few years on, to see how character relates to action. I shall keep the detail light, to let the essential points emerge.

David is now a Fleet Street journalist; his special interest is the culture and welfare of the Indian community in Britain. To organize the example I shall use the purely provisional terminology of self-conception, objective, strategy, goal, and project. Explanation and example are as follows. David sees himself as an Indian affairs journalist; this is his self-image, his self-conception. His categorical desire, the main desire relevant to this example at least, is to continue pursuing his special interest. David's current objective is to launch, edit, and run a non-loss-making, quarterly, bi-lingual (English-Punjabi) magazine. He has specified this objective to the stated level of detail. To achieve this objective he needs a strategy: the magazine, he decides, must be of general interest and take advertising. This strategy sets a goal: to commission ten first-rate articles, and to attract five major advertisers, within the next six months. The goal in turn produces a project, an action plan, to make so many phone calls to sympathetic journalists of high standing, and to write so many letters to major advertisers, in the coming week. Accordingly on the following Monday he telephones his friend, the distinguished journalist Robert Crescens, asking him to write on any subject of broad interest for the new magazine. He explains that the magazine cannot afford to pay a fee.

Then how does a character explanation work for this type of example? Specifically, how does David's categorical desire, to continue pursuing his special interest, explain his action of telephoning his friend on the following Monday?

One idea is to try a covering law explanation. So we might say: given his self-conception, objective, strategy, goal, and project, David did what, in that situation, any rational agent would have done or what any such agent would have been most likely to do. Assuming then that David was a rational agent at the time of action, we need simply look for a descriptive generalization to cover the action of rational agents in such situations. The immediate problem with this idea is that it seems rarely possible to fillet out from the concept of rationality a unique action which, in a particular situation, described at this level, of detail, 'any rational agent' would do or would be most likely to do. Nor is the problem essentially reduced if we switch from a unique action to a disjunctive set of possible actions: defining that unique disjunction presents difficulties hardly less sharp.

A different idea is to require of a character explanation only that it exhibit the rationale of an action: that it present the action as having rational point for the agent, as a reasonable (but not the sole rational) thing for him to do, as something which in this example he judged likely to help his project and thus advance his goal and so on up to his objective. This type of explanation accommodates the viewpoints of both agent and spectator. For the rational point of an action is defined relative to the agent (as account is taken, for instance, of the circumstances in which he believed himself to be). By establishing that rational point (being told or conjecturing what it is) the spectator can ease his curiosity and explain why the agent acted as he did. No condition is written into this type of explanation that every action must pass the test of rationality: agents are not uniformly rational, even those with categorical desires. This is a workable type of character explanation. Is it Green's?

Green has two ways of talking about character explanations of action. The first uses the language of causality. He refers, for instance, to motives as 'determining causes', to 'this causality of motives' (PE § 87): and motives are 'definitely determined' by character (PE, § 95). As long as the formation of character is not construed in a way that defeats moral responsibility, then it is 'true enough' that 'a man's action is the joint result of his character and circumstances' (PE, § 106). The language is causal, explicitly or by implication. I shall give some notice of Green's views on causation in 5.11. What I want to develop here is another way Green has of talking about character explanations, one more clearly in line with the type of explanation outlined in the last paragraph. To fix on this second way of talking is not an arbitrary preference. Green himself plainly is uneasy about his causal language. 'That moral action'––i.e. 'distinctively human action' (5.2)—'is a joint result of character and circumstances is not altogether an appropriate statement of it' (PE, § 107). The language for which he settles is that of 'expression': 'action is the expression of a man's character, as it reacts upon and responds to given circumstances' (ibid.). Even earlier Green stresses that circumstances do not interact with character 'like forces converging on an inert body which does not itself modify the direction of the resulting motion' (PE, § 98).

Here Green's imagery and his language of 'expression', 'reaction', and 'response' consort ill with the notion that there is something which just any rational agent would do if he had certain goals, projects, objectives, in particular circumstances. But we need to set out Green's ideas carefully; several considerations apply. I think Green does regard action as 'the necessary result' of character connecting with circumstances (PE, § 109); and that this is his stable view. His causal misgivings have a twofold origin.

First he wants to deny that if character is a causal factor it is subject in turn to the determination by which cold causes ice or a spark causes an explosion. An agent is active in the formation and revision of his own character. Green's way of putting this is to say that an agent is a 'free cause', 'a self-distinguishing and self-seeking subject' (PE, § 106) whose character, as expressed in the desires on which he acts, is open to his own control across time. This pulls us straight back to the 'self-conscious principle' and to the third and fourth aspects of the multi-perspectival model.

Secondly, Green has a strong sense that a person's character is inaccessible to full knowledge. The complete explanation of any action would take us through 'the relation' which that action 'bears to . . . the universe of a character' (PE, § 316). And that relation, he says flatly, 'is not in any case ascertainable by us' (ibid.). It is not that the explanation of action by character is non-causal, but rather that talk of causal explanation may suggest a level of precise knowledge which is not available to us about a person's character, and perhaps not available to the person himself, on either the wide or the narrow construction. Character is a fold of opacity in Green's largely transparent world. The point is not metaphysical, about the nature of character and its agency, so much as epistemological, about the data available to us in our explanations.

This tentative approach to the data is clearly apparent in Green's reconstruction of the background to Esau's action (5.7), Green tries to exhibit the rationale of this action; he describes the circumstances as far as known, and aims to make intelligible 'the result which Esau's character yields under the pressure of animal want'. He attempts to show, or better said he indicates the process by which one might eventually show, the rational point of Esau's action.

5.10 FREE AGENCY

The narrow construction of character is the key to Green's idea of free agency (3.1). The idea is that one part of a person's freedom is his being self-determined or having self-mastery. Anybody who acts on desires which are inconsistent with those on which he feels committed to act, lacks a kind of freedom. His self-determination fails in a way which blocks the fulfilment of his most important desires just as effectually as if another person had interfered with them. But another person has not interfered, the objection might be put, and we should here talk of self-determination, if that is what we mean, not of freedom. In one mood Green allows the charge of 'metaphor' (Works II, 309). I should myself take a firmer line and regard freedom as, or as relevantly similar to, a natural kind concept of which the extension can spring surprises as pertinent phenomena are studied. Moreover, the main disquiet over the view of self-determination as freedom stems from its use in quite other contexts: as when a person is prevented by public authority from acting on certain desires, and the calm reassurance is forthcoming that he is thereby being 'forced to be free': the desires in question are desires on which he does not 'really' or, if fully informed, would not 'really' want to act. This is the argument of Rousseau and Bosanquet. But Green's ethical theory is exempt from such applications of the concept of freedom, as will be clear when we examine his political philosophy in Chapter 8.

The connection between free agency and free will is less direct but not difficult. All that the free-mind and ontological arguments of Chapter 3 show, in Green's view, is that decision-making can involve free choice: moral responsibility survives the impact of reductive materialism and one-way physicalism. But such choice is, in Green's words, a 'formal freedom, which becomes real in so far as the self-consciousness, instead of being simply passive and receptive in regard to motive (as when motive is sensual pleasure) originates it, as when it constitutes a law to itself in shape of idea of duty, or recognizes state-law as its own' (MS 10A, 4). The reference to 'state-law' edges ahead of the present discussion; this is a matter for Chapter 8. What was metaphorical freedom just previously is real freedom now.

Green's point is plain. Free will gives us nothing to choose; it is in this sense empty. Free agency means a structure of desire in terms of which we can make substantive ('real') choices. The 'real' freedom of free agency Green also calls 'inward' freedom, the 'power of presenting a general end to oneself and of being determined to action by this, as distinct from momentary want' (Aristotle B, 20). This is not, for our present discussion, to say anything about the nature of the 'general end': on the constraints that must be observed if the agent is actually to find 'an abiding satisfaction of an abiding self', or on the relation of that 'general good' to morality.

But the connection between free agency and free will, benign on Green's account, has appeared problematic to two critics: A. E. Taylor and, repeating and reinforcing Taylor, C. E. M. Joad.[15] The Taylor–Joad thesis is that Green's account of character defeats moral responsibility. Green, we know very well, does not regard free will as involving indeterminate possibilities of action. Character is no such fluid moral cement. The state of one's character fixes the options. Then the moral life, liberated by free will, is constrained by character. My desires are of a certain variety and strength; I cannot act in spite of them. That, after all, is just Green's point against Kant (5.6). To say, as we did in 3.16, that 'A could have done otherwise, if his character and desires had been different', is to acknowledge no freedom of A to act otherwise here and now; and if he cannot act otherwise than he does, how does he have free choice in any sense relevant to moral responsibility?

Green could reply, legitimately in my opinion, that the multi-perspectival model, gives an agent a degree of freedom in the formation and revision of his character. I have already remarked (2.1) on the tendency of contemporary moral philosophy to restrict its view of the agent virtually to the point of action; and from an earlier period the Taylor–Joad thesis suffers from that precise fault. The wide construction of character allows for greater conflict between desires, but Green sees this as no

---

[15] A. E. Taylor, 'The Freedom of Man', in J. H. Muirhead, ed., *Contemporary British Philosophy*, 2nd Ser., London, 1925, 277; C. E. M. Joad, *Matter, Life and Value*, Oxford 1929, 316. For a useful but little-known discussion of Taylor's paper, see Adrian Coates, *A Sceptical Examination of Contemporary British Philosophy*, London, 1929, 106–44.

source of free will or 'moral freedom': 'A certain appearance of moral freedom arises from conflict of desires in stage of imperfect habituation. Hence the young seem more "free" than the old.' But he insists: 'Really suspense of equal conflict between desires quite different from alternative of doing or not doing' (MS 10A, 'Other End', 11). The bottom line is that in any state of character, wide or narrow, if the agent's wants 'constitute an alien world' (MS 10A, 'Other End', 14), then 'there is no mechanical force that moves him' (Aristotle B, 38) permanently to act on them. No habit, with its predisposing desire, no 'equal conflict between desires', is so strong that its hold cannot be loosened under the third aspect of the multi-perspectival model. Time is an essential dimension of free will.

Before summarizing Green's theory of character and then proceeding to discuss some contrasts between Green's theory and the rival theory of J. S. Mill, I should like to draw attention to a feature of Green's theory which bears unexpectedly on recent work on personal identity. Derek Parfit has made familiar the claim that personal identity, with its dependence on memory and convention, is not all-or-nothing but a matter of degree.[16] This view, very different in idiom from the usual thread of British Idealist writing, none the less finds affinities in the work of Bernard Bosanquet and H. H. Joachim:[17] and we can see how Green himself could support Parfit's claim. For Green has no stake in ideas of mental substance or the Cartesian Ego which underpin the all-or-nothing view of personal identity which Parfit aims to refute (4.9). As on the narrow construction of character a person's self-conception and the structure of his desires change under the third and fourth aspects of the multi-perspectival model, so that sense in which he is 'the same person' must drastically be qualified. When Green speaks of 'an abiding satisfaction of an abiding self' this cuts across nothing here. Green presents such satisfaction as an ideal to which the person may aspire: the 'abiding self' is not an ineluctable fact of psychological continuity but is to be created, and here we recall Green's talk of 'self-realization' (4.13).

[16] D. Parfit, *Reasons and Persons*, Oxford, 1984.
[17] B. Bosanquet, *Logic*, i. Oxford, 1911, 51: 'Macaulay after his mind was gone was still Lord Macaulay and his father's son, but what else was he that he had been?' H. H. Joachim, 'Some Preliminary Considerations on Self-Identity', *Mind*, 23 (1914).

Ethically one point of difference between Green and Parfit is that Parfit downplays personal identity in order to undermine the rationality of self-interest. Green, by contrast, points up personal identity through self-realization and draws out the rationality of moral action from a theory of the unconditional human good. Another difference concerns Parfit's utilitarianism. But that is too complex a topic for a side-discussion.

5.11   REVIEW

Let us summarize Green's theory of character. This theory is concerned with intentional action; and to act on a desire is to adopt that desire as a motive. Motives are informed by a conception of personal good. Character signifies, across the range of a person's actions, 'the way in which a man seeks self-satisfaction'. Wide character includes all the inclinational and intentional desires which feature in the explanation of a person's actions. Everyone possesses character in the wide sense. Narrow character, by contrast, centres on the kind of systematic structure of desire outlined under the fourth aspect of the multi-perspectival model; these are two ends of the same chain. Narrow character informs Green's idea of free agency, the essence of which is self-determination. To have character on the narrow construction is to have desires on which one feels committed to act; and Green argues that anyone who acts on desires which are inconsistent with those on which he feels committed to act, lacks a kind of freedom.

Habit, which grounds character on both the wide and the narrow construction, imposes constraints on action (Green disagrees with Kant); and those constraints remove character from the category of merely summary or future-hypothetical dispositions mentioned in 5.1. At the same time, the possibility of self-intervention against desires on which we habitually act, defuses any threat to free will from the constraints of habit; no habit is unrevisable (Green disagrees with Aristotle).

Any person's character is a complicated phenomenon of which full knowledge is impossible. Character explanations of action rely, therefore, on our being able to work back from any action to the circumstances which gave that action some rational point for the agent.

5.12 CHARACTER: JOHN STUART MILL

The nineteenth century was an age of 'character' in British philosophy: a century in which the concept of character was perceptively and luminously discussed by a number of philosophers including John Stuart Mill, Shadworth Hodgson, and John Grote.[18] And this is to say nothing of the ideology of character presented by such writers as Samuel Smiles.[19] In Mill's account of character we possess a background against which Green's own account can be laid to set the context for his major critique of utilitarianism.

Mill is a determinist on the free will issue. 'Our will causes our bodily actions in the same sense, and in no other, in which cold causes ice, or a spark causes an explosion of gunpowder' (*A System of Logic*, 1843, III.5.2). But in what sense is this? Hume's treatment of causation had underlined regularities, 'constant conjunctions'. Mill is more alert to the need for a theory of causation to handle countervailing causes. He also recognizes more clearly the problem of the plurality and composition of causes: that there is more than one way in which the same effect may be produced, and that to the same effect more than one cause may actually contribute. The centre of Mill's own treatment of causation lies in what he calls the 'sum total of conditions': 'The cause then, philosophically speaking, is the sum total of conditions, positive and negative taken together' (III.5.3). Said another way, the cause is 'the antecedent, or concurrence of antecedents, on which it [a phenomenon] is invariably and unconditionally consequent' (III.5.6). In a nutshell we have 'the unconditional invariable antecedent, or cause' (III.102).

Action results from just such a sum total of conditions, the conditions being the agent's character and circumstances. 'No

---

[18] J. S. Mill, *A System of Logic*, London, 1843. Quotations have been taken from the 8th edn. 1872. S. Hodgson, *The Theory of Practice*, London, 1870; J. Grote, *A Treatise on the Moral Ideals*, Cambridge, 1876, *passim*.

[19] D. Becquemont, 'Travail social, argent et individualité(s) à l'époque victorienne', *La Pensée*, no 228 (1982).

one who believed that he knew thoroughly the circumstances of any case, and the characters of the different persons concerned, would hesitate to foretell how all of them would act. Whatever degree of doubt he may in fact feel, arises from the uncertainty whether he really knows the circumstances, or the character of some one or other of the persons, with the degree of accuracy required' (VI.1.2).

Thus Mill no less than Hume rejects liberty of indifference. We do not, he insists, equate the free with the unpredictable (either the unpredictable in principle or the unpredictable by us). Regular action from habit is to be distinguished from compulsion. Character yields predictability. In the absence of compulsion an action produced by character is a free action. But how is this position to be developed? Mill does not see eye to eye with Robert Owen in his view of the external determination of character (VI.2). Owen held that a person's character is made not by him but for him. Through the early influences of environment it is uniquely determined by circumstances for which the agent is not responsible.[20] Mill's opposite view is that a person's 'character is formed by his circumstances . . . , but his own desire to mould it in a particular way is one of those circumstances, and by no means the least influential' (VI.2.3). This possibility of 'self-culture', to revise our character, is quite unmysterious for Mill. We can change our character if we desire to do so, and that desire is a product of experience; 'experience of the painful consequences of the character we previously had, or . . . some strong feeling of admiration or aspiration accidentally aroused' (ibid.). No break in Mill's determinism opens here; nor, I suggest, does a significant break with Green. There are metaphysical boundaries to Green's and Mill's moral psychologies. Cross these, and we encounter disagreements. Green does not accept that character causes action in just the way in which cold causes ice or a spark causes an explosion. In the formation and revision of his own character a person is a 'free cause'; and Green constructs the elaborate metaphysics of self-consciousness outlined in Chapter 3 against which that view is to be taken. But Mill's basic concession remains: that a person

---

[20] See Robert Owen, *A New View of Society: or, Essays on the Principle of the Formation of the Human Character*, London, 1813. A useful secondary source is Crane Brinton, *English Political Thought in the Nineteenth Century*: ch. 2.3, 2nd edn. London, 1949.

can revise his own character if he becomes critical of it. That central fact is agreed between Green and Mill.

It may, however, be as well to add here, for completeness, that this metaphysical difference is not the only difference which separates Green and Mill in the treatment of causation. Green disagrees with Mill explicitly over the analysis of causation (Works II, 302; cf. PE, §§6, 17, 75). Green is right to claim a serious weakness in Mill's analysis. Quite in general, and apart from its role in the explanation of human action, Mill's 'sum total of conditions' is an unlikely candidate for an 'invariable antecedent'. Can in fact such a 'total' be repeated?

To return: if we asked why Green needs a concept of character we might pose the same question about Mill. Mill follows, if with a queasy sense of paradox (3.6), the general empiricist 'serial' model of the mind; and if his philosophy is not directly tied to the introspective psychology of Hume's 'impressions' and 'ideas', still he does not reject associationism. Why then does he not rely completely on the association of ideas in his philosphical psychology? And what work is open to the concept of character in ethics when, on the utilitarian view, the moral value of an action is determined purely by its consequences?

On the association of ideas we need to look at the Sixth Book of *A System of Logic*. Here Mill relies on associationism as a major tool in what he terms, quite simply, psychology. This is the most general study of the succession of mental states. Such states originate from sensation. Between them various laws of association hold. 'The subject, then, of Psychology, is the uniformities of succession, the laws, whether ultimate or derivative, according to which one mental state succeeds another; is caused by, or at least, is caused to follow, another' (VI.4.3). One law of association is that 'similar ideas tend to excite one another' (ibid.), but Mill's examples are slight and, for those who can sustain that marathon journey, the longer road of discussion lies through James Mill's *Analysis of the Phenomena of the Human Mind* (1829). The qualification, 'ultimate or derivative', is unpuzzling. It reflects Mill's explicit hesitation to accept what we have called one-way physicalism. He suggests that in the current condition of natural science psychology cannot be modelled on a physiological base: it should work independently until the relations between physical and mental states are better understood.

While psychology is a valid inquiry, however, it is inadequate to mental diversity in Mill's view. Psychology is occupied solely with what is 'universal or abstract', with the factors common to all mental states. Mill argues that psychology requires a complement, a 'concrete' inquiry into the different mental states which are produced when the same laws of association operate in different circumstances. The unmanageable complexity into which such an inquiry seems likely to run because of minute differences in personal circumstances can, he thinks, be avoided. There are, he claims, repetitions of circumstances which operate with broadly similar effect between individuals in any given state of society. The study of these effects is assigned by Mill to a new science of ethology, 'the Science of Character', of which he announces the groundwork (VI.5).

This distinction of abstract from concrete is one difference between psychology and ethology. Another difference is methodological. Psychology works empirically by a process of generalization. Ideally its laws of mind would be exceptionless generalizations, but even so, unless derived from physiology, it would essentially describe and not explain. Ethology, by contrast, explains the formation of character deductively from the laws of mind and descriptions of circumstances. Furthermore, psychology is concerned with all mental states. Ethology, with its accent on character, underlines agency and practice. Ethology is emphatically a practical inquiry. From its deductions we are to probe the social lessons to be learnt, from a utilitarian viewpoint, for the formation of desirable kinds of character. A full, critical account of the work and ideas of Mill's friend, William Ellis, in applying the new science to education, still remains to be written.[21]

Ethology is not complementary solely to psychology. On Mill's complete view there are three complementary and

---

[21] William Ellis (1800–81). See especially *Philo-Socrates*, 4 vols., London, 1861–4. A general account of Ellis's ideas is given in E. K. Blyth, *The Life of William Ellis*, London, 1889. See also F. W. Robinson, 'William Ellis and His Work for Education', University of London MA thesis, 1919. I am grateful to Keith Banks, who stimulated my original interest in William Ellis; and to Roger James, Headmaster of the William Ellis School, London, for granting me access to the school's archives.

interdependent parts of a single 'science of human nature' (VI.3).[22] The remaining part he calls social science. Its job is to explain systematically the development of social conditions in which the repetitions of circumstances of the kind covered by ethology arise.

This, then, is Mill's theory of character. But we need to look a little more at the relation of that theory to the underlying logic of utilitarianism.

5.13   MOTIVE AND ACTION

Utilitarianism is driven by states of affairs. This fact is more important than are the differences between utilitarians over the constituents or distribution of states of affairs. For Bentham the relevant states of affairs are experiences of pleasure; a latter-day utilitarian may stress the satisfaction of ordinal utility functions. For Sidgwick there is a requirement of equality between individuals in the distribution of utilitarianly desirable states of affairs; J. S. Mill makes no such requirement when he formulates the principle of utility in terms of the 'greatest amount of happiness altogether'.[23]

For nineteenth-century utilitarianism, Green's point of entry into the debate, actions are to be assessed morally by their production of states of affairs: and two conditions apply. Only by virtue of its production of a state of affairs can an action be assessed morally; just what assessment it receives, its complete moral value, is fixed by the state of affairs which it actually produces. The *moral value* of an action may be distinguished from the *morality* of the action, as consequence is distinguished from intention. The morality of an action is the moral value of the state of affairs which the agent intended to produce.

One way of expressing this view of action would be to say that actions themselves are agents as producing states of affairs. The human agent is instrumental in getting actions done. This is a highly public, or, in Alfred Barratt's broad sense, 'political' view

---

[22] See further M. Cowling, *Mill and Liberalism*: ch. 3, Cambridge, 1963; and P. Smart, 'Mill and Human Nature', *Politics and Human Nature*, ed. I. Forbes and S. Smith, London, 1983.

[23] *The Essential Works of John Stuart Mill*, ed. M. Lerner, New York, 1971, 199.

of the agent.[24] Actions figure in the public realm; the agent shrinks to a point on the circumference of action. We need inquire about him only enough to control his motivation; for the sole significance of 'motives' is that they produce actions which in turn produce states of affairs. A motive is, Bentham tells us, 'anything whatsoever, which, by influencing the will of a sensitive being, is supposed to serve as a means of determining him to act, or voluntarily to forbear to act' (Bentham, *Introduction to the Principles of Morals and Legislation*, chapter 10). The point, for ethics, is to get actions of a utilitarianly desirable sort done by working on the agent's motives; and Bentham, just to keep him in view, has various things to say (ibid., chapter 3) about the sanctions which enable us to control motives in the required way.

Then we can read Mill's projected science of ethology as an attempt to produce the regularity of motivation most likely to produce utilitarianly desirable actions. And here the definitive divide between Green and Mill is at once apparent. Mill sees character as simply one more agency for bringing about states of affairs. For Green, a person seeks to 'realize' himself in a certain state of character. Said another way, the narrow construction of character unfolds the implications of the fourth aspect of the multi-perspectival model; it gives a fuller picture of the person who is intent on achieving 'self-satisfaction' through a self-conception and a coherent structure of desire. Within this fundamental contrast between Green and Mill, more detailed disagreements emerge. To gauge these we need to look at the basic distinction between motive, action, and consequence. I shall say something about the concept of consequence shortly. On the relation of motive to action there is of course Mill's later claim in *Utilitarianism*, chapter 2, that 'utilitarian moralists have gone beyond almost all others in affirming that the motive has nothing to do with the morality of the action.' In detail:

The morality of the action depends entirely upon the intention—that is, upon what the agent wills to do. . . . But the motive, that is, the feeling which makes him will so to do, when it makes no difference in the act, makes none in the morality: though it makes a great difference in our moral estimation of the agent, especially if it indicates a good

---

[24] A. Barratt, 'Ethics and Politics', *Mind* 2 (1877), 453.

or bad habitual disposition—a bent of character from which useful or from which hurtful actions are liable to arise.[25]

Green takes great exception to this: 'That the motive should make no difference to an act, in its true or full nature, we should pronounce . . . to be an impossibility' (PE, § 292 n.). Green's objection would have more obvious point if Mill were excluding from the morality of an action both motive and intention. But the morality of an action, on Mill's account here, is a matter of the intention with which that action is done. Consider a shopkeeper's action in giving the right change to a confused tourist. We can assess the moral value of his action: the state of affairs that resulted was utilitarianly desirable, let us suppose. Let us further suppose that the shopkeeper intended to give the right change; he did not mean to cheat, giving the right change only by arithmetical incompetence. The shopkeeper stood, then, in a particular relation to a utilitarianly desirable state of affairs, the relation of intending to produce it; and in this relation the morality of his action consists.

Mill is not saying that motive is irrelevant to morality. The notion of motive is cardinal in the moral assessment of the agent. Independently of Mill and Green we can distinguish, at first look, what an agent intends to do from why he intends to do it, his intention from his motive. The description by which action is connected with intention can be more or less analytic: we can say, 'he dropped the book, but he didn't intend to do so', not 'he lied, but he didn't intend to do so'. The description of an action as a 'lie' already contains an ascription of intention, but not necessarily of motive. 'He lied, but only to help a friend'; 'he lied, purely for profit'; 'he lied, purely for fun.' In present-day language, Green wants to say that here we do not have the same (type of) action, namely lying, done from different motives, but three different action tokens, into the 'true or full', and separate, 'nature' of which the respective motives enter. The action type to which 'lying to help a friend' belongs may be e.g. that of 'protecting a friend's interests'. But we cannot assign it to this action type without knowing the agent's motive; if we do not know why he lied we can only say that he lied.

Green has a case. On Mill's account we can identify that action and then talk separately about the motive. Green insists that until we have identified the motive we do not know what action to talk about. The examples we have considered on Green's behalf have a fairly obvious intuitive appeal. But then, two points are to be noted. First, Mill can reply that if we use motive in this definitory way, the analysis merely reshapes itself and the motive emerges as the intention: when Philip lies he intends to protect a friend's interest, and a fresh question has now to be asked about the motive to this action. Is Philip's motive that of concealing e.g. his own complicity in a joint crime? Is that why he lies to protect his friend's interest? Secondly, we cannot resolve any of this with much point unless we return to the basic perspective that divides Green from the utilitarians: the central relevance of states of affairs.

A utilitarian wants certain states of affairs to be produced; and actions are instrumental to the production of states of affairs. To states of affairs there are three relations in which an agent may stand, and these relations we can identify interrogatively. What state of affairs does the agent in fact produce? What state of affairs does he intend to produce? Why does he intend to produce that particular state of affairs? Further refinements of course are possible: we can ask not simply regarding the state of affairs an agent intends to produce, but also regarding the reasonableness of the beliefs on which his intention is based. But essentially the three questions apply. They define the architecture of consequence, intention, and motive.

The passage from *Utilitarianism* in which we met the distinction between the morality of the action and the morality of the agent is merely one part of Mill's attempt to organize a coherent ethics around the three relations in which an agent can stand to states of affairs. And in a utilitarianly well-run society, ethology, to return to our point of departure, would control the formation of character so that certain motives predominate. Benevolent motives can never guarantee, but do at least favour, beneficent actions: actions of which the intention and the consequence are utilitarianly sound. Mill underlines in *Utilitarianism* the possibilities of moral education, and thus the guidance of conscience (which he sees as a social product); he moves away from Bentham's emphasis on physical sanctions and the criminal law. But a wide interval still separates Green's concern with persons and structures of desire from the utilitarian stress on states of affairs. It is utilitarian consequentialism which is the real stumbling-block.

5.14　UTILITARIAN CONSEQUENTIALISM

Nothing is as simple as it seems, but one matter which I do not want to stay long in considering is the 'floating point' between action and consequence. Take the following example. Making his anger clear to Adam, Paul burst into Adam's room, slammed the door violently, thus causing a vase to wobble briefly then fall from the table and break. That no fixed point separates action from consequence is plain from the possibility of (indefinitely many, but at least) two descriptions:

(1) Paul slammed the door violently, with the consequence that the vase wobbled briefly then fell from the table and broke.
(2) Paul broke Adam's vase.

The consequence in (1) disappears into the action in (2). But this is only to say—nothing new—that the line between action and consequence is description-relative. A more significant point is the following. One way of taking utilitarianism is to see it as dividing abruptly the viewpoints of past and future, of agent and spectator. From the viewpoint of the spectator, assessing what an agent has done, the central fact for ethics is that the consequences of an action can diverge from the motive and intention with which it was done. In giving money to the mendicant drunk, Tad meant the unlucky individual to buy food. In the event he bought alcohol and died. Tad's motive was benevolent; his intention was utilitarianly good, but the actual consequences of his action split sharply from those he intended. And as utilitarian spectators, we feel free to determine the moral value of his action in terms of its consequences. If we take the agent's viewpoint at the time of action, however, this unforseseen split is plainly irrelevant, logically askew to the question of what to do. (I assume that the split is not due to carelessness, to lack of deliberation.) If Mill's aim is to organize a coherent ethics around the architecture of motive, intention, and consequence, one problem at least is how the two viewpoints, of past and future, of agent and spectator, are to combine?

The problem is not to be solved by greater precision about the notion of consequence. For a utilitarian, it will be recalled, the morality of an action is its assessment in terms of what the agent intended to bring about; its moral value is determined by the state of affairs actually produced. Tad's action had the harmful consequence that a man died. But Tad intended the mendicant drunk to go off and buy food. This intention is subject to separate assessment, as is the motive of benevolence (assuming, for example, that Tad was not simply trying to impress his girlfriend). The utilitarian has enough distinctions at work here to pick out all the relevant elements of the moral situation. Our problem is not one of deciding the limits of moral responsibility; that is a topic on which no one need lack ideas. One thought on the line of responsibility to be drawn between action and consequence would be this: deduct from what happened the insufficient but necessary condition contributed by Tad. The deduction defines his action; the rest is consequence. In these terms, Tad's action is his giving money to the mendicant drunk. If Tad had not given him the money then (other things equal) he could not have bought alcohol and would not have died. But Tad could have given him money without the man's death resulting; say nobody was selling alcohol that day. Tad's giving money to the drunk was thus a necessary but insufficient condition of what happened. None of this however resolves the discrepancy of past and future viewpoints by which agent and spectator are divided.

An agent is poor in imagination; his action is rich in consequences. However carefully he makes his decisions, by faultlessly utilitarian criteria, every action he does may be morally valueless. This is an extreme case to make a point: that the moral value of his action is a backward-looking dimension of assessment over which the agent, forward-looking in deciding what to do, has no control. For just this kind of reason Kant denied that an action has any moral value in respect of its consequences. What Green suggests, midway between Kant and the utilitarians, is that motive and consequence are not capable of the sheer separation which both sides assume to be possible.

5.15 MOTIVE AND CONSEQUENCE

We have already taken Green's claim (5.13) that motive is definitory of action, that the 'motive . . . *is* the act on its inner side' (PE, § 105) as Green also expresses the point. The present claim for examination is that the consequences of an action are a precise criterion of its motive, since 'There is no real reason to doubt that the good or evil in the motive of an action is exactly measured by the good or evil in its consequences' (PE, § 295). This claim looks problematic, not least in respect to certain considerations which Green himself advances. Green allows that an action may have the same 'outward form' whether done 'instinctively' (i.e. non-motivationally) or from different motives (PE, § 93). 'It may have the same effect on the senses of an onlooker, the same nervous and muscular motions may be involved in it, the same physical results may follow from it' (ibid.). But if this is so, then how are consequences criterial of motive, if the same consequences may follow from, e.g. just and unjust motives? As well, if the motives are different, as just or unjust, in what sense is the same action done from just or from unjust motives when 'the motive is the act on its inner side'?

Green's reply to this line of criticism would be, I think, that the standpoint from which we talk of the same motive and different consequences, of the same consequences and different motives, is the purely practical one of 'ordinary judgments' (PE, § 294). We talk in this way because practically, under constraints of urgency and ignorance, we cannot make finer discriminations. (Green has a slight tendency, without any consistency of usage, to reserve 'act', as distinct from 'action', for that of which we can talk without reference to the motive from which it is done, e.g. your returning something which you have borrowed (8.3).) But what enables Green's philosophical discrimination that consequences are criterial of motive? How is that claim to be made good?

Two ideas might be taken to support Green's claim. The first is a view which he takes about the concatenation of motives: 'motives do not admit of isolation' (PE, § 252). When an action has a selfish motive but beneficial consequences to other people, then the selfish motive may have been accompanied by other, unselfish motives. (This reinforces the problem of the inaccessibility of character noted in 5.9) In clearing my house of unwanted furniture I consult the purely personal convenience of an uncluttered home: but in disposing of this furniture to a local charity, with beneficial consequences to other people, I am at least not so anti-social that I would rather burn the stuff than let anyone have it free. On the lines of this kind of example the clear division between selfish motivation and socially beneficial consequences begins to blur; and the process continues if we take Green's second, closely related idea, which is simply that more than one person's motives contribute to the consequences of an action. After all, in the case of the mendicant drunk, if the wine-sellers had been less anxious to make money and more concerned to help the human wreck in front of them, Tad's action might not have had its harmful consequence. Green elaborates this idea in his political philosophy, especially in the famous lecture entitled 'Will, not Force, is the Basis of the State' (Works II, 427–47; HM, 89–106). Green's point is obvious; it does not need to be laboured.

These ideas make a neat argument, one which shows that consequences may measure motives. But they do not immediately answer the claim from which we started. That claim was that the consequence of an action are a precise criterion of its motive. Green's argument shows how, if we take into account all relevant motives of all relevant agents, motives and consequences diverge less than we might suppose if we fail to realize the concatenation of an agent's motives and, taking one 'motive' in unreal isolation, measure the consequences of his action against that. But this does not resolve the discrepancy of past and future viewpoints by which agent and spectator are divided. For the consequences of any one agent's action are contingent on the motives of other agents, perhaps in a situation which they have contrived. About those motives the agent does not have full knowledge; over them he has incomplete control.

In fact, however, to bring these considerations against Green is only to introduce a fresh facet of his moral philosophy. The detailed topic does not belong to this chapter; but a major point of interest in Chapter 7 will be Green's ideas on a morality of social roles in a coherent form of social organization. In that perspective the agent is insulated from just the discrepancy of viewpoints which has occupied us here (see in particular 7.9.3.).

5.16 GREEN AND MILL ON THE HUMAN GOOD

There is a closing remark to be made about Mill. To much of his writing the straightforwardly utilitarian idea that actions are to be assessed morally by their production of states of affairs is an adequate guide. We all know the modifications which Mill made in *Utilitarianism*, chapter 2, to Bentham's quantitative hedonism; and we know that Mill breached psychological hedonism in his discussion of habitual action (1.7). This and much else would occupy a full discussion of Mill's relationship to Benthamite utilitarianism. But the central utilitarian emphasis on states of affairs is reasonably uncomplicated in Mill's writings up to the celebrated essay *On Liberty*.

Although I cannot argue the point here, I do not believe that in *On Liberty* Mill is plagued by contradictions between his defence of individuality and his utilitarian base. That is a familiar picture; I do not endorse it. What is clear, I think, is that Mill widens his interest in agency. The individual agent had previously had a poor time of it from Mill. Given the central moral relevance of states of affairs, actions were significant as producing states of affairs, and agents were instrumental in getting actions done. This gave agency a subordinate significance which was not even compensated when the agent reappeared at the start of the chain as a beneficiary of states of affairs. Mill wanted to maximize happiness; we have seen that he did not require equality of distribution, and so the agent as beneficiary might find his benefits withheld for the sake of the greatest total happiness.

On Liberty marks a change of view. Mill begins to consider how the agent's 'experiments in living' can suggest certain states of affairs as desirable which otherwise we might not have imagined. Instead of starting from a list of utilitarianly desirable states of affairs which we work on the agent's motivation to get him to produce (the picture of 5.11), Mill now looks to the agent to enlarge our perception of what states of affairs might be desirable. This puts a radical stress on 'individuality'.

The trouble with this part of Mill's ethics is that his account of individuality is uninformed by any systematic theory of the human good. 'I regard utility as the ultimate appeal on all ethical questions; but it must be utility in the largest sense, grounded on the permanent interests of man as a progressive being' (*On Liberty*, ch. 1). Mill fails to develop any comprehensive and coherent account of what those permanent interests might be. The individual's 'experiments in living' are to be conducted with scarcely any guidance on the kinds of self-development to undertake; and this forms a real contrast to Green's moral philosophy. Green attempts, as we shall see in the next chapter, to define a high-level set of conditions on the quest for self-satisfaction—conditions which he believes to be rooted in a valid conception of human nature.

That conception also grounds a final contrast which we may note between Green and utilitarianism: but this time, contemporary utilitarianism. Such utilitarianism, certainly when it features in welfare economics, standardly takes the satisfaction of antecedent desires as its criterion of value (2.10). The notion of antecedent desire informs the concept, e.g. of a utility function. But plainly, if Green offers a theory of the human good, then desires can be assessed in terms of it: and if the theory is sound then the satisfaction of antecedent desire, just as such, is not of central moral relevance. Nor is the bare notion of an antecedent desire adequate to the complexities brought in by our having desires about our desires, the kind of possibility explored under the third aspect of the multi-perspectival model. Nor again, to conclude, is the desire to form a coherent structure of desire, to be a particular kind of person under the fourth aspect of the model, the kind of desire which could simply be satisfied by a state of affairs in the standard utilitarian sense of a logically complex entity in the external world. What is required here is not a state of the world in which desires are satisfied, but a state of the person in which he is satisfied with his desires.

5.17 CHARACTER AND THE WILL

So far I have omitted to cite a concept to which Green certainly refers in his discussion of character, motive, and action: the concept of the will. This omission reflects my view that 'the will' is, and is recognized by Green as being, a redundant term of explanation.

Two main factors have combined to cast opprobrium on the concept of the will. On the one hand the faculty view of the will is rejected, the view of the will as a kind of dubious antecedent or ghostly trigger to action. This view involves a causal theory of action stated in terms of what has to take place in the agent before he can act. Its answer to the Wittgensteinian question of 5.2 is that the extra condition needed to take us from 'My arm went up' to 'I raised my arm' is an act of will. This faculty view of willing, criticized for example by Melden, is now widely regarded as indefensible.[26] On the other hand, and this is the second factor, idealists in particular are thought to have entangled themselves unhelpfully in the notion of the will. We may note, disparately, Bradley's long and extremely obscure treatment of the will in *Collected Essays* and the dark grandiloquence of Bosanquet's political ethics in which the agent's 'actual will' stands over against his 'real will' as embodied in the laws, institutions, and conventions of a state-organized society.

Bosanquet deserves further mention. A fundamental contrast is hardly served by terms so close as 'real' and 'actual'. As often with idealists, the mystery is in the language, not in the ideas. Bosanquet means roughly this: on a spot check we have any number of beliefs, desires, and dispositions to emotion and behaviour. Call this a person's 'actual will'. Those beliefs and the rest would alter on fuller and more accurate information, a clearer understanding of consequences, and a greater range of imagination. Such alteration is a kind of logical implicate of a person's actual will; and Bosanquet gives the name 'real will' to the actual will as thus ideally transformed. He adds the crucial claim, hedged with qualifications but still predominant, that a person's real will is embodied in the laws, institutions, and

---

[26] A. I. Melden, 'Willing', *The Philosophy of Action*, ed. A. R. White, Oxford, 1968.

conventions of a state-organized society. Green shares Bosanquet's emphasis on beliefs, desires, and dispositions to emotion and behaviour; he is with Bosanquet against Prichard's faculty view. But he does not share Bosanquet's 'idealization' of state-organized society or the organicist implications of Bosanquet's full political philosophy (6.7).[27]

The essential point about Green's account of the will is that everything of importance which he has to say about action can be stated in terms of the other concepts which this chapter has been concerned to explore. Although PE, Book II exercises itself nominally on questions about the relationship between desire and the will and between the will and the intellect, the redundancy of the will emerges sharply in such a remark as that 'The will is simply the man' (PE, § 153), or in the reference to 'character or habit of will' (PE, § 246). Or, beyond PE, in the interpretation of will in terms of 'a constant principle' by which an agent 'seeks to give reality to' a 'conception of . . . well-being' (Works II, 523; HM, 168). Certainly Green derides by anticipation the kind of faculty account which Prichard offers. There are of course deep philosophical differences here between Prichard and Green. Prichard's account has an ultimate affinity with Descartes's theory of the two substances, a thinking, non-extended mental substance and a non-thinking, extended material substance, which supports this basic picture of the mind acting on the body. We have already noted Green's rejection of the relevant notion of a thinking substance (4.9). In less historically involved terms Green maintains that a faculty is simply a possibility (PE, § 6). A billiard ball has a faculty of motion, that is, subject to conditions it is able to move. Any attempt is quite vacuous to explain the ball's movement by its faculty of motion. Similarly for the will. If someone is able to distance himself from his desires and to decide to satisfy a particular desire, it is idle to try to explain this ability by reference to a faculty of will. Talk of the will simply re-describes this ability.

Such talk occurs in Green as a mere *façon de parler*, without (in our own terms) ontological commitment. It occurs perhaps more readily in a nineteenth-century context than today. The

---

[27] B. Bosanquet, *The Philosophical Theory of the State*, London, 1899, 4th edn. 1923, ch. 5, 'The Conception of a "Real" Will'.

concept of the will plays no independent part in Green's moral psychology and may be eliminated from its discussion.

5.18 CHARACTER: THE EXISTENTIALIST CRITIQUE

The final issue centres on the need for a concept of character in ethics. The challenge from existentialist ethics should not be refused. This challenge applies to character even on its wide construction. Part of that construction, it will be remembered, is the idea that actions of a particular type become easier to do and their non-performance becomes more difficult the more often that type of action is done (5.7).

Integral to Sartre's notion of authentic, radically free choice, however, is the recognition of freedom in every situation of action.[28] In Sartrean terms the attack on the concept of character, on its wide construction, is twofold.

First, to think of a person as constrained by habit is quite false; and certainly if anyone thinks of himself in that way then he has taken up an attitude of *en-soi* towards himself. He has given a particular aspect of himself, namely, his character, an object-like quality. To do this is to be in a state of inauthentic existence, of *mauvaise foi*. Fully symptomatic of this attitude of *en-soi* would be Green's view, cited previously, that given the state of his character, 'A man's possibilities of doing and becoming at any moment of his life are as thoroughly conditioned as those of an animal or plant.' For Sartre, on the contrary, no such limitation of possibilities is real. Character fixes nothing and represents nothing fixed. Action is free, its possibilities indefinite.

Secondly, if Green were right and habits really set constraints on action, the result would be an existentialist tragedy. A person could destroy his own authenticity by destroying, through the formation of habits, his power of unlimited choice.

We may follow Sartre where we can. No one can follow him

---

[28] Fr Magin Borrajo's lucid, scholarly, and critical 'Moral Perspectives in the Existentialism of Jean-Paul Sartre', one of the best things written on Sartre's ethics, is available only in a remote and obscure journal, *Philippiniana Sacra* 3 (1968). My Sartrean quotations are taken from *Existentialism and Humanism*, tr. P. Mairet, London, 1948.

everywhere. His views on radical choice are underpinned by a metaphysical scheme as elaborate as anything contained in PE, Book I. That scheme cannot be investigated here. I introduce the existentialist angle in order to exhibit an approach to character quite different from Green's: and different from it not simply as a rival theory like J. S. Mill's, but as antagonistic to the very concept of character. It is illuminating to see how Green could defend himself in face of this kind of attack.

In the first place, Green has an answer to the charge of undermining free choice. The real issue is not the fact of freedom but, in J. S. Mill's phrase, 'the venue' of freedom. Sartre locates this at the point of action. But Green can reply that freedom is to be located centrally in the formation and revision of character. This location is exactly right to secure that 'abiding satisfaction of an abiding self' which is the ideal human condition. But even at the point of action the agent is free to make a novel interpretation of his circumstances; this freedom we examined in drawing out the connection between character and imagination.

Secondly, the kind of 'self-realization' which informs character formation under the third and fourth aspects of the multi-perspectival model exactly fulfils Sartre's formula that for human beings 'existence precedes essence'. A human being has no pre-established nature, in contrast to an artefact which is defined by its function. Rather, 'man first of all exists, encounters himself, surges up on the world—and defines himself afterwards'. If someone has not 'defined himself' who has self-consciously moulded his character in the light of the kind of person he wants to be, then the phrase is hard to construe.

Finally, Green supposes no more than Sartre that man has a pre-set function. But he diverges from Sartre in holding that a human being has a nature such that certain forms of conduct and conditions of the agent can, while others cannot, yield 'an abiding satisfaction of an abiding self'. The aim is 'to create and appropriate that which will satisfy a subject, that can only be satisfied with itself' (MS 10A, 'Other End', 11). Human nature is such that there is an unconditional good which links self-satisfaction with a condition of moral virtue. Green produces his arguments; these are to be considered in the next chapter. In

Sartre's agonized condition of bare 'authenticity', radical choice is ultimate. If a person chooses to act cruelly, deceptively, or however, there is nothing we can say to him. Existentialist ethics, since morality contains an essential dimension of concern how one's actions affect others (2.2), remains problematic. We must now see how Green accomplishes his own transition to morality.

6

The Transition to Morality (1): 'The True Good'

6.1 INTRODUCTION

We have scanned a significant range of topics in Green's moral psychology. I want now to look briefly back; first in order to review what has unavoidably been a complex discussion, secondly to mark the end of one phase of our examination of Green's philosophy. The topics introduced in this and in the following chapters belong to Green's ethical theory rather than to his moral psychology. The distinction emerges as follows.

Self-consciousness, we saw in Chapter 3, is the key to knowledge. Isolated sensations do not yield knowledge; for knowledge sensations must be united by the mind. This process of unification, taken to be the condition of the possibility of knowing a world where things change, withdraws the mind from the threat of physical determination, the main threat to free will. In his complete epistemology and metaphysics Green argues that he can not merely withdraw the mind from the threat of physical determination, but, through an analysis of relations in our knowledge of a world of objects, show the physical world to be dependent on the mind. Admittedly this takes him beyond the human mind to the eternal consciousness; and it replaces the traditional distinction between appearance and reality with that between partial and complete knowledge. For our purposes the chief point is that Green applies his 'self-conscious principle', by which the mind unites sensations, also to the phenomena of impulse and desire. A person is able (the burden of Chapter 4) to detach himself from his own desires, to revise them, and to form a systematic structure of desire, so as to achieve 'an abiding satisfaction of an abiding self', by means of self-intervention. This process we traced in outlining the multi-perspectival model of deliberation. A systematic structure of desire, when a person has a self-conception and categorical desires under the fourth aspect of the model, yields Green's 'narrow' construction of character, the construction in which he is specially interested; and in Chapter 5 we drew out some of the practical implications of that construction in a theory of action.

This is complex, but not a beginningless knot. It is a pattern and direction of argument. What it is not is ethics in the sense of an argument for the rationality of moral action. It is the foundation of nearly everything Green wants to say as a moral philosopher. But consider: we have brought in some ethical topics prelusively, have even referred illustratively to moral progress, but we have not said at all why morality should inform the deliberations of Green's agent, intent on 'self-satisfaction', on 'an abiding satisfaction of an abiding self'. From self-satisfaction what road leads, then, into the moral life?

To answer that question is the main task of the next two chapters. This part of Green's philosophy has been dismissed as moralistic, as internally inconsistent, as incoherent with other parts of *Prolegomena to Ethics*, and as vacuous. While A. J. Ayer neatly characterizes the career of Oxford idealism in terms of 'the uplift coming primarily from Balliol and the subtleties from Merton',[1] C. D. Broad astringently laments how 'Even a thoroughly second-rate thinker like T. H. Green, by diffusing a grateful and comforting aroma of ethical "uplift", has probably made far more undergraduates into prigs than Sidgwick will ever make into philosophers'.[2] The charge of internal inconsistency comes from Sidgwick himself, who argues that Green's concept of the good will founders on wider and narrower notions of the true good between which Green is inextricably confused.[3] The stricture of incoherence is most prominent in Prichard, who argues that Green's theory of the common good and his account of motivation are discordant elements which cannot be aligned.[4] Vacuousness is the complaint of H. D. Lewis, who pursues vigorously one of Green's own worries and concludes that the notion of the good

---

[1] A. J. Ayer, 'The Making of a Logical Positivist', *The Listener*, 74 (1965), 699. Cf. R. H. S. Crossman, 'Political Realities', the *Times Literary Supplement*, 28 Sept. 1962, 453. Ayer's reference to Merton is to F. H. Bradley (1846–1924) and H. H. Joachim (1868–1938).

[2] C. D. Broad, *Five Types of Ethical Theory*, London, 1930, 144.

[3] H. Sidgwick, *Lectures on the Ethics of T. H. Green, Mr. Herbert Spencer, and J. Martineau*, London, 1902, 61–71.

[4] H. A. Prichard, *Moral Obligation*, Oxford, 1949, 71.

will, central to Green's ethics, circles upon itself and defines its own content.[5]

Through the remarks of Ayer and Broad are *obiter dicta* of philosophers not themselves deeply versed in Green's ideas, the whole tribe of exegetists cannot be thus dismissed. Some of Sidgwick's limitations as a commentator have been noticed already; and Prichard was in general an unimaginatively austere critic. But Sidgwick's and Prichard's familiarity with Green's text is not in doubt; and H. D. Lewis is a recognized authority. To their negative reaction the views of older commentators such as Bosanquet, who observed that Book III of the *Prolegomena*, unlike the metaphysics and philosophical psychology of Books I and II, 'has been generally studied and admired', forms an abrupt contrast.[6] In what follows I shall mainly expound Green on my own account, setting out how I think he tries to make the transition to morality and with what success. The above criticisms will be taken up, at appropriate points, incidentally to that independent exposition and so far as their substance merits.

Green's transition to morality comprises two stages. The first stage involves the idea of constraints on what can actually produce 'an abiding satisfaction of an abiding self'. This is to say that on Green's account there is a true or unconditional human good, namely an abiding satisfaction of an abiding self, on the achievement of which there are certain conditions and about which mistakes can be made. In the second stage a view of morality is defined on which morality uniquely fulfils the conditions of the true good. The first stage of the transition will be examined in the present chapter; the second will be taken up in Chapter 7.

The organization of the present chapter is this. I shall begin by setting Green's theory of the 'true' or unconditional human good in the general context of the philosophy of value. I shall then define the five criteria which Green lays down for the true good: that whatever form or structure of life yields an abiding satisfaction of an abiding self (i) is achievable only as an object of pursuit, (ii) contains a constructive element, (iii) is imperatival, (iv) is non-exclusive and non-competitive, and (v) is social or

---

[5] H. D. Lewis, 'Does the Good Will Define its Own Content? A Study of Green's Prolegomena', *Ethics*, 57 (1948).

[6] B. Bosanquet, *Science and Philosophy*, London, 1927, 150.

common. I shall disambiguate the notion of a common good and examine some of Green's ideas on the social nature of human beings. I shall close by noting one thing which Green is quite sure cannot yield abiding satisfaction, namely pleasure; by answering an argument from John Dewey that, on Green's moral psychology, nothing can abidingly satisfy; by resisting Prichard's attempt to draw, also from Green's moral psychology, consequences damaging to his account of the common good; and by straightening out a misinterpretation (first identified by Bosanquet) of the relation between the true good and states of consciousness.

6.2 THE PHILOSOPHY OF VALUE

The philosophy of value has four main tasks. Of these the first is to enumerate and define the different types of value (aesthetic, economic, moral, and so on). The second is to specify the bearers of value, the kinds of thing which in principle can have these values. The third task is to interrelate the different types of value, examining the logical relationships between them and the possibility of a hierarchy of values. The fourth task is to investigate the objectivity of value. Full investigation of any one of these tasks, subdividing into separate, precise inquiries, would make a Chinese maze between ourselves and the philosophy of Green; the work of expounding Green would be postponed indefinitely for that of finding an exit from this way of introducing it. Since there is no safety in philosophy, hence no wisdom in caution, I shall make certain assumptions.

On the objectivity of value it is best, I think, not to confront Green directly with the question 'can value judgements be true?' Philosophers divide, notoriously, over the fact–value distinction: and not only in ethics. Is it a claim capable of truth or falsity that Morten Harket is handsome, that Brooke Shields is a beautiful woman, that the Parthenon is sublime? Or are such matters, as Hume would say in aesthetics no less than in ethics, 'more properly felt than judg'd of' (T 470)? Aesthetics aside, the central worry for ethics is not truth but rationality. Of course the notions of truth and rationality interlock. One part of rationality is to reason from premisses taken to be true. But the question for ethics is not whether there are moral facts, moral truths; it is whether we can give the agent good, i.e. rationally compelling, reasons for acting morally, for acting contrary to self-interest or inclination in the promotion of other agents' interests (2.2). I can certainly give you good reasons for wearing a raincoat on a wet day; can I give you equally good reasons to consider other interests besides your own? If such reasons are available it will be time enough, when we have them, to see if they offer moral 'facts' or 'truths' of any of the diverse kinds that we find in mathematics, science, or history. And without such reasons the practical relevance of moral 'facts' or 'truths' would be still to seek; there are indefinitely many facts of which I take no account in deciding what to do. Green's aim is to determine on what conditions 'an abiding satisfaction of an abiding self' is possible and (as we shall see in the next chapter) to draw out the rationality of moral action from those conditions.

Then, working backwards through the list of tasks for the philosophy of value, we may note a significant feature of Green's ethics: that in an important respect Green leaves the agent free to decide his own hierarchy of values. In 2.9 we had the case of the 'aesthetic man' who fixes a scale of values running from the aesthetic down through the cognitive, the social, the political, and the economic to the religious. Green's account of an agent's contribution to the 'common good' spans a whole diversity of such hierarchies of values. In a homely example which is entirely apt: a lifeplan which would suit an actor, D. F. Niente, might not suit me. Green's ethics is no Procrustean bed; it sets no rule that 'all persons must be developed in the same way' (PE, § 191). As to the logical relationships between values, we shall see that this is just the area to which Sidgwick's charge of inextricable confusion belongs; and in answering Sidgwick (7.14) we shall discover how Green relates moral to other values. The primary bearers of value, to continue the list, are human beings in the sense at least of the following passsage. 'Our ultimate standard of worth is an ideal of *personal* worth. All other values are relative to values for, of, or in a person' (PE, § 184; HM, 256). This can mislead, as Bosanquet warns us, if it is read in the sense that 'Nothing has value except the conscious states of conscious beings' (6.12). But persons are at least Green's prime focus; and his theory of the true of unconditional human good is at least an account of the sole conditions on which a person can maximize the value of his life. On the enumeration and definition of the different types of value, we can regard Green's ethics as itself, largely taken, a definition of the moral; and his political philosophy defines a particular understanding of the nature of politics. One finds, however, only isolated and fragmentary indications of Green's views on other types of value. It is for the reader to judge the material for reflection contained in such remarks as: 'Our habitual language about art involves just the conception of nature being beautiful in itself and yet made so by us. We make nature what it is, in itself, sc. beautiful. . . . (N)ature has beauty or ugliness, only so far as we take ourselves into it' (MS 10A, 'Other End', 14, 16). To myself, these remarks are thin hands to encompass the world of art and beauty.

6.3 CRITERIA OF THE TRUE GOOD

Green plainly thinks of the true good as the unconditionally good or intrinsically valuable: 'true' has the force at once of genuine as opposed to false or spurious, and of ultimate as opposed to derivative or conditional (PE, §§ 171, 191; cf. relatedly 'untrue, in <the> sense of being inadequate', MS 15). The time at which Green wrote was one which saw a florescence of work on the philosophy of value in both Germany and Austria; and it is curious that in spite of his obvious interest in German philosophy, and the fact that he contributed to the translation of Lotze who first enshrined the fact-value distinction, Green proceeds in total independence not only of Lotze but of Wieser, of Gossen, Menger, Meinong, of any in fact of the contemporary Middle European philosophers whose subtle, penetrating work might have exercised an influence on his axiology.[7]

The notion of an unconditional human good needs careful handling. There are at least two salient points. First, it matters that we are concerned with the unconditional *human* good.

_____

[7] Green's theory of the 'true good' is excellently summarized, but somewhat differently treated, in I. M. Greengarten, *Thomas Hill Green and the Development of Liberal-Democratic Thought*, Toronto, 1981, 32–49. I am in Greengarten's debt.

Something might be unconditionally good, i.e. necessarily and non-instrumentally good, good in all possible worlds in which it existed, without being the unconditional human good. Such would be the case, the point is obvious, if all possible worlds in which that good existed were worlds in which there were no human beings. Secondly, if an unconditional human good is to emerge from Green's philosophy, the signpost to it is already clearly marked. '[T]he generic definition of the good is . . . that it satisfies some desire' (PE, § 171). The true or unconditional human good is that which fulfils the agent's desire for 'a satisfaction on the whole', 'an abiding satisfaction of an abiding self'. The problem confronted by the present chapter is to see how that unconditional good can be realized in forms or structures of human life; to ascertain the conditions, in other words, which such forms or structures must fulfil in order to yield abiding satisfaction.

Here a slight awkwardness presents itself. For, it might seem, if the true or unconditional human good fulfils the agent's desire for abiding satisfaction, its value is plainly conditional on that fulfilment: that is, it is merely an instrumental good, not an unconditional good at all. But this skews the logical relationship. A form or structure of life cannot embody the agent's true good unless it yields an abiding satisfaction of an abiding self; that much conditionality must be conceded. Equally, however, there can be no abiding satisfaction without a form or structure of life; and the self is not 'a mysterious abstract entity' over and above the feelings, desires, thoughts, and habits (4.9, 5.7) which a form or structure of life embodies. Self and form or structure of life are two sides of the same thing. There can, of course, be a form or structure of life without abiding satisfaction. To close that gap is exactly the point of defining the conditions of the true good.

Both these points separate Green from Kant. On the one hand, at least as a moral philosopher, Kant is not greatly concerned about the specifically human good. The moral good, exemplified in the good will, is free from the contingent conditions of humanity in this sense: that the moral agent fulfils principles which apply universally to all rational beings. On the other hand, Kant accepts a distinction between the unconditional good and the complete good. Only a good will is unconditionally good, but it is not the complete good; other things such as health and prosperity are necessary to complete the human good.[8] Green's aim is to define a true good which is at once unconditionally good and the complete human good.

Although Green nowhere sets forth a tidily succinct account of the conditions of the true good, he does at different places define five characteristics in the sense of criteria which, if a form or structure of life is to yield abiding satisfaction, it must fulfil. Two cautions before we proceed.

One, the reference to 'desire' as the 'generic definition of the good' needs to be firmly boxed off from a cluster of subjective views on the relation of value to desire. We advance nowhere in the understanding of Green if we think, for example, of the Hobbesian view that 'whatsoever is the object of any man's appetite or desire, that is it which he for his part calleth good' (*Leviathan*, ch. VI). It is no part of Green's view that value judgements are expressive of desire; or, from a different angle, that there can be no argument with or within a man about the desires we should have. Green approaches value through the idea of what can satisfy the desire for abiding satisfaction.

The other caution about Green's theory of the true good is that the five criteria operate as, and are meant to be, serious constraints on the transition to morality. Green does not fix on the rationality of moral action and simply use the five criteria contingently and *ad hoc*, so that if the moral life should turn out not to satisfy them, others might be forthcoming. The five criteria are critical success factors. Nothing, Green thinks, which fails to meet the five criteria can produce 'an abiding satisfaction of an abiding self'. We are not to regard Green as a philosopher who is straightway offering to disclose the true good substantively as Bentham equated the good with pleasure. An appropriate image under which to think of the true good in Green's philosophy is that of a pentagon of which the sides are the five criteria. That this pentagon encloses the moral life is a separate claim; and the case for it is separately argued.

On Green's criteria, then, to repeat from 6.1, the true good (i) is achievable only as an object of pursuit; (ii) contains a constructive element: (iii) is imperatival; (iv) is non-exclusive

[8] H. J. Paton, *The Moral Law*, London, 1966, 62.

and non-competitive; and (v) is a social or common good. But the list is abstract; these characteristics must now be explained.

6.4 THE CRITERIA DEFINED

The true good, first then , is achievable only as an object of pursuit. G. E. Moore in his final chapter, on 'The Ideal', in *Principia Ethica*, holds that 'by far the most valuable things which we know or can imagine are certain states of consciousness'— the enjoyment of friendship and the contemplation of beauty. (The contemplation of beautiful friends may appear an obvious economy; but friendship is interactive, contemplation is detached from practice. There is, however, no positive requirement to seek ugliness in our friends.) These states of consciousness which are, for Moore, genuine, underivative, and unconditional goods, are in effect his candidates for the true good. Such states of consciousness may be open to a person accidentally, simply in virtue of the situation in which he finds himself. This is certainly true of the contemplation of beauty. Green's version of the true good, by contrast, is based crucially on a view of agents as self-determining and self-conscious. (I shall refer to states of consciousness again in 6.12, to disclose a further division between Green and Moore.)

We should not see Green as denying that Moore's contemplation of beauty can be an element of human good, but rather as stressing the importance of an active element. The agent, traversing the series of his wants, as Green expresses it (PE, § 85), forms an idea of himself as not merely obtaining the fulfilment of these wants, one by one or connectedly, but of achieving some state of himself which will bring what some philosophers have called happiness and what Green himself generally calls 'self-satisfaction'. A double activity of self-consciousness is at work: (*a*) the fact of desire secures the notion of practice—'It is this consciousness (sc. of wanted objects) which yields, in the most elementary form, the conception of something that *should be* as distinct from that which *is*, of a world of practice as distinct from that world of experience of which the conception arises from the determination by the Ego of the receptive senses' (PE, § 86). However, (*b*) this 'elementary . . .

conception' is played back upon the agent himself; he forms the idea not simply of the world as different from what, from the viewpoint of his desires, it should be, but of his desires (his own appetitive condition) as different from what they in turn should be if 'a satisfaction on the whole' is to be achieved. The agent, *qua* self-conscious, 'has the impulse to make himself what he has the possibility of becoming but actually is not, and hence not merely, like the plant or animal, undergoes a process of development, but seeks to, and does, develop himself' (PE, § 175). Activity, if only that of self-reformation, to achieve the true good is inseparable from its attainment.

The constructive element in the true good emerges when Green says that the human 'end' must be seen 'as a character not a good fortune, as a fulfilment of human capabilities from within not an accesssion of good things from without, as a function not a possession' (PE, § 246). The rejection here of a passive 'accession of good things from without' makes a close link with the active aspect of the first criterion, but suggests also, in its gnomic formula of 'a fulfilment . . . from within', that the true good is created or constructed in some way by the agent himself. This constructive aspect is specifically developed in the 'Lectures on Kant', where Green refers to the self-conscious agent's endeavour to find an end' adequate to himself, an end which he 'can in truth only find by making it'. He continues:

The 'good,' the 'desirable' (as distinct from the desired), the 'should be,' the 'moral law,' are different ways of expressing the relation of the self-conscious subject to such an end. So long as reason seeks it in what does not depend on itself, in what it finds but does not make . . . it is seeking it in what relatively to it is accidental.—(Works II, 153).

There is, however, a fine balance to be struck. If the true good is something which human beings in some sense create or construct, none the less there are defeasibility conditions fixed by the other criteria of the true good. Only within the confines set by human nature, by the agent's nature as a self-conscious being, can the true good be constructed. There can be no self-satisfaction which ignores 'the "law of his being" which . . . prevents him finding his satisfaction in the objects in which he ordinarily seeks it, or anywhere but in the realisation in himself of an ideal of perfection' (Works II, 327).

One way of pulling the first two criteria together is to suggest that the state of himself in which the agent's true good consists is not something 'given'. Rather, it has gradually to be brought about (hence the constructive element) by some form of self-endeavour (hence the active element).

This opens readily on to the next criterion of the true good, its imperatival nature. For if the self-conscious agent 'ordinarily seeks' 'a satisfaction on the whole' in objects which are incapable of yielding it, then 'in relation to a nature such as ours, having other impulses than those which draw to the ideal, this ideal becomes . . . an imperative' (PE, § 196). In the phrase, 'ordinarily seeks', Green is referring to the tendency to seek one's good in pleasures and material goods, but as we shall see when we examine the true good under its social aspect, there are perfectly common desires and involvements drawing the agent to seek his true good in social relationships which really can produce self-satisfaction.

The non-exclusive and non-competitive aspect of the true good is something for which Green offers no explicit arguments. He says straight out that 'there can be no competition for its attainment between man and man' (PE, § 281; HM, 285). Green's supposition is, I think, that anything which could be endangered or frustrated by competition between agents, anything of which one agent's possession would exclude its possession by another, would be an imperfect candidate for the true good. It is a somewhat puzzling condition in some ways. Even Moore's nominations for the role of sole intrinsic goods, the enjoyment of friendship and the contemplation of beauty, do not meet the requirements of non-exclusivity and non-competitiveness. There plainly can be competition in the contemplation of beauty, and friendships are elective affinities. At least part of Green's reason for imposing this criterion is, I think, that he holds a monistic theory of human nature and makes a particular assumption.

There is, Green supposes, a single human nature which is common to all self-conscious agents. In terms of this nature Green is fully prepared to talk of 'the law which determines where . . . self-satisfaction is to be found' (Works II, 308; HM, 228: and his chief point in analysing the true good is precisely to determine this locus. That alone would not secure the non-exclusivity and non-competitiveness of the true good, but on an extra assumption the rationale of these criteria begins to emerge. For Green assumes that if he can secure, through his theory of the true good, the possibility of an abiding satisfaction of an abiding self, then he can pluralize and specify the conditions for an abiding satisfaction of abiding selves. The true good, that is to say, has to be compossible for a plurality of agents. Perhaps Green would want to argue that if individual enjoyments of the true good were exclusive and competitive, this would introduce an incoherence into that eternal consciousness of which individual human beings are partial reproductions. The point is not one I shall pursue.

On an end note, one of the matters involved in this criterion may be a point from the last chapter. For a possible connection holds between the criterion of non-competitiveness and the concatenation of interpersonal motives which we examined in 5.14. There we saw that the consequences of one agent's actions are always to be explained by reference to motives other than those of the agent himself. 'Competition necessary as long as you retain principle that every man is to be rewarded according to his works, for how otherwise is proper reward to be determined?' Green asks (Platonis de Republica, 138). But this kind of competitive allocation depends on an apportionment of contribution which is practically arbitrary and inexact. ('Proper' need not have the sense of 'morally proper'; at this stage it may be taken simply to convey that the matter cannot be settled by rational argument.)

The final criterion of the true good is that it is a common or a social good. Probably nothing in Green's ethics has been more severely handled by his commentators than his account of this notion in PE, Book III, ch. 3 and PPO, §§ 17–36. So problematic has the notion been found that I shall take it separately.

6.5 THE COMMON GOOD

Two problems are connected with Green's notion of a 'common good'. The first is the tendency of commentators to assume that the phrase has an independent life: that one can determine various shades of meaning of which the phrase is capable, check their logical coherence, and then measure what Green has to say against each possibility. The second problem is that there is a logically harmless but expositionally awkward ambiguity in Green's use of 'common good' and related expressions.

One sense in which the true good is a 'common good' is that indicated briefly above. Individual realizations of the true good must be compossible. Multiplication is part of the arithmetic of the true good. A form or structure of life which cannot multiply out into what H. W. B. Joseph (in a very sound exposition of Green) called 'a form of common life' cannot embody the true good.[9] What creates an ambiguity is that Green is also apt to refer to that form of common life, a network of social roles, as itself a 'common good'.

Partly we can read compossibility from a view which Green takes of the social nature of human beings. We shall shortly consider this area of his thought more fully. For now, we may note that, for Green, human agents tend to see their own interests as involving those of other people. This may be only limitedly so, extending not far beyond the family. But such *de facto* social identification does occur. The phenomenon is one on which, diversely, the ethics of Hume and Mrs Foot rely (2.4. 1–2). Its analytical significance is clear. Green says of this type of occurrence: 'The man cannot contemplate himself as in a better state, or on the way to the best, without contemplating others, not merely as a means to that better state, but as sharing it with him' (PE, § 199; HM, 263): and such sharing may take the form of one person's advancing the welfare of other persons 'on account of his interest' in them (PE, § 92). If a theory of the true good is to respect this human tendency, as a datum on which to proceed, then one person's welfare must be seen as compossible with that of others. For if one person identifies with another (I want to you to have X, which you want, and I want this because X is what you want), then their welfares are not separately satisfiable. To this extent, in this sort of case, the true good is to be regarded as a common good.

Partly also, however, Green assumes that beyond the range of such *de facto* social identification, the lifeplans of individual

⁹ H. W. B. Joseph, *Some Problems in Ethics*, Oxford, 1931, 116–8.

agents to achieve abiding satisfaction are capable of coherence. A form of social organization is possible in which individual lifeplans of the kind we considered under the fourth aspect of the multi-perspectival model converge harmoniously. This is the kind of perspective from which his remark is to be assessed that 'the state is an institution for the promotion of a common good' (Works II, 437; HM, 97). A form of social organization, when Green talks in this way, is itself a common good, one which the state promotes. The ambiguity of these different uses of the phrase, a 'common good', between the present and the previous paragraph, creates no confusion in Green's argument. Another point is more important.

Not merely may the state need to reorganize society in order to enable this kind of harmony; but further, individuals may need to revise their lifeplans relative to the criteria of the true good. If we give the phrase, a 'common good', an independent life and think in terms of, e.g. a general social welfare function which maximizes the sum of the welfare of individual agents as choosers, we add nothing to the understanding of Green. K. J. Arrow has shown that such a welfare function involves conditions which no social decision function can jointly satisfy nondictatorially.[10] W. G. Runciman wades in heavily at this point with the observation that any useful theory of a 'common good' must take account of Arrow's conclusions.[11] But Arrow's 'paradox' explicitly takes individual choices, 'individual orderings', as it finds them: Green wants to construct lifeplans, hence choices and 'orderings', and to reform society, in the light of a theory of the true good. Arrow's conclusions and Green's premises simply fail to meet. In sum, Green's notion of a 'common good' is a nested notion within his own theory of the true good. It is to be insulated from the resonances which, in other contexts, the bare phrase, a 'common good', may have.

6.6 THE SOCIAL SELF: (1) ATOMISM

There is no single, compact text in which Green's views on the

---

[10] K. J. Arrow, *Social Choice and Individual Values*, 2nd edn. Yale, 1963.
[11] W. G. Runciman, 'Sociological Evidence and Political Theory', in P. Laslett and W. G. Runciman, eds., *Philosophy, Politics and Society*, 2nd Ser., Oxford, 1962, 43.

social self, the social nature of man, are systematically presented. If we cull points at random we are unlikely to retrieve more than an endorsement of G. H. Lewes's reference to 'the social medium' (Works I, 471 ff.), and such isolatedly opaque dicta as Green's own reference to 'the human spirit, according to the law of its being, which is a law of development in society' (PE, § 176; HM, 251). One point on which we are already clear is that a person's understanding of his own good may include essential reference to another's welfare (if only in an *égoïsme à deux*). His true good has, so taken, a social object. A further point is equally clear: that for Green the true good of different persons is jointly realizable. Individual 'true goods' are socially compossible to realize. Beyond these points the best step is to heed the fruitfulness of the negative and to consider two views of the relation of persons to society which Green definitely rejects. The two views are social atomism and social organicism.

Social atomism is a view of the individual as essentially pre-social, as determined only marginally by his or her membership of society. To a first approximation, anything that holds good of an individual in society would equally hold good if individuals have never entered society or if society were to be dissolved. Exactly how these social atoms, these individuals in their essential natures, are understood is a matter of variation between different theories. To Hobbes, their essential nature is to be self-interested; and forms of social interdependence are simply means, if necessary means, by which the individual seeks to realize his or her particular ends. J. S. Mill finds much the same view in Bentham:

Bentham's idea of the world is that of a collection of persons pursuing each his separate interest or pleasure, and the prevention of whom from jostling one another more than is avoidable, may be attempted by hopes and fears derived from three sources—the law, religion, and public opinion.[12]

For Bentham this pursuit of self-interest is benign. Social arrangements are possible by which the individual, acting to maximize his 'separate interest', also promotes the 'greatest happiness of the greatest number'. Politically, although

[12] J. S. Mill, 'Bentham', in F. R. Leavis, ed., *Mill on Bentham and Coleridge*, London, 1962, 70.

Bentham sets, and can set, no formal limits to state activity to promote the greatest happiness, his position is also perfectly consistent with the conception of a minimal state, especially in the economic sphere: with the idea, inbuilt in Smithian classical economics, of an untrammelled free market which efficiently secures the greatest public good.[13]

On a different view, such as Locke's in the *Second Treatise of Civil Government*, no assumption of self-interest applies. Man is naturally a moral being, capable of concern for the effects of his actions on other people. A state-regulated society, born of a social contract, is needed, however, for the impartial settlement of disputes and the enforcement of principles of justice. Man has natural rights; and these are brought forward from the state of nature into civil society. The social contract is, from this standpoint, simply a device for the maintenance of natural rights. Such rights lapse in civil society only when a man disregards the natural rights of others.

Here is not a mere miscellany of views drawn from the history of ethics and political philosophy. Green repudiates social atomism. From this centre his criticisms stretch in radial arms to all these views. We have already seen how Green will not allow self-interest to be written into the definition of desire (4.12); and in the next chapter we shall examine his account of *de facto* social identification (7.4). In Chapter 8, which draws out connections between ethics and politics, we shall observe Green's dissatisfaction with certain economic forms of the minimal state. Also in Chapter 8 we shall consider his rejection of natural rights.

The heart of Green's quarrel with social atomism is really the claim which we cited briefly above in the dictum that 'the human spirit' is subject to 'a law of development in society'. Green believes that, in an elementary way, the conditions of the true good are realized when one person identifies himself with the interests of another, typically in the socially limited form of friendship and family life. In a more advanced way the true good is realized when a person absorbs himself or herself in the requirements of a social role which structures his desires and

---

[13] On Adam Smith's construction of the relation of economics to politics, see F. Petrella, 'Individual, Group or Government? Smith, Mill, and Sidgwick', *History of Political Economy*, 9 (1977). For some pitfalls in this topic, see 1.7

defines his self-conception. The kind of development which a person undergoes, through such forms of social identification, are completely specific to society; they are in principle unavailable to the pre-social individual. Green also believes that the very conceptions on which social atomism relies are themselves the products of social reflection. (As his own idea of 'an abiding satisfaction of an abiding self' is another such product.) Pre-social individuals of the sort presupposed to social atomism are 'imaginary individuals in that detachment from social relations in which they would not be men at all' (PE, § 288). Or as he more tersely puts it: 'Without society, no persons' (PE, § 190; HM, 258). But it is the developmental point, the idea that only by social identification can 'abiding satisfaction' be attained, which is fundamental to Green's ethics. For, as the argument will go in Chapter 7, this social identification is itself the core of morality.

Green rejects, it will be recalled, another view of the relation of persons to society: social organicism. No more than social atomism is this view to be regarded as a single idea.

6.7 THE SOCIAL SELF: (2) ORGANICISM

The last thing which is true of social organicism is that it is a vague notion. If it were vague, one could make it precise. The trouble is rather that quite distinct and sometimes incompatible ideas are drawn together under one label as though they were identical or interdependent. We are not to look for the phrase, 'social organicism', in Green himself. Under that label we can, however, distinguish certain ideas which he rejects.

Green does not believe that a state-regulated society is a person or an individual. *A fortiori* he does not believe, an additional point, that such a society is a person or an individual on a higher level of reality and value than the self-conscious human beings we call persons or individuals. *A fortiori* he does not believe, an additional point, that the latter derive whatever reality and value they possess solely by contribution to the functioning of an ontologically and axiologically higher individual. There is no doubt that when Green says, to repeat from 6.2, 'Our ultimate standard of worth is an ideal of *personal* worth. All other values are relative to value for, of, or in a person', the persons to whom this statement refers are self-conscious human beings. And if it be added that we have not yet done with the logic of organicism, for a person or an individual, supposing a state-regulated society to be such, is not, or is not necessarily, an organism, and that an organ may have a higher value in detachment from the organism of which it is a part, those points are well-taken. As stated above, quite distinct ideas need to be, and are apt not to be, kept apart.

It would be an interesting project in a separate study to draw out the connections between seventeenth-century science and Hobbes's philosophically celebrated anti-organicist picture of a state-regulated society as an artefact or machine, and nineteenth-century science and the spread of social organicist views. However that may be, Spencer in 'The Social Organism' (1860) took the lead in our period with an explicit, minutely detailed analogy between societies and living bodies:[14] 'a very able and ingenious essay' which T. H. Huxley devastated in 'Administrative Nihilism',[15] and which Spencer, quite undaunted, reapplied in *Principles of Sociology* (1876–96). It is worth emphasizing that Spencer is unusual among organic theorists. His social organicism is primarily a theory not of the relation of the individual to society but of society to the state.[16] Society is organic in the sense that 'industrialized societies', advancing 'from an indefinite incoherent homogeneity to a definite coherent heterogeneity', are open to a degree of self-regulation which serves progressively to deprive the state of the ground on which its regulative work is needed.

Idealist attitudes to social organicism fell into three broad divisions: first an attitude, such as that of Henry Jones in 'The Social Organism' (1883), that at least organicist views avoid the errors of social atomism.[17] Secondly an attitude, for example that of Bosanquet in the 1918 Aristotelian Sociaty volume, *Life and Finite Individuality*, that a state-regulated society really does occupy a higher level of reality and value than the self-conscious

[14] H. Spencer, 'The Social Organism, in D. Macrae, ed., *Spencer: The Man Versus the State*, Harmondsworth, 1969.
[15] T. H. Huxley, 'Administrative Nihilism', *Fortnightly Review*, 10 (1871).
[16] Some years ago at LSE David Thurston helped me to see this point.
[17] H. Jones, 'The Social organism', in A. Seth and R. B. Haldane, eds. Essays in Philosophical Criticism, London, 1883.

human beings whom I call persons and Bosanquet called 'finite individuals'. You and I are social adjectives in the grammar of Bosanquet's idealism: finite individuals have an 'adjectival', not a 'substantive' mode of being.[18] Thirdly an attitude of analytical rigour, such as McTaggart applied in separating out the conflation of ideas he thought to be embodied in statements of social organicist views.[19]

Green's own attitude to social organicism is not explicit in such ways. But we have seen what he rejects.

6.8 REVIEW

Green's central concern is the person who aims to achieve 'an abiding satisfaction of an abiding self'; and in outline we explored the notion of such satisfaction under the fourth aspect of the multi-perspectival model in Chapter 4. In Chapter 5 we saw in fuller detail, on the narrow construction of character, how that same notion expands into an account of a person's self-conception, categorical desires, subscribed values, and emotional engagements. The theory of the true good, with which the present chapter is taken up, sets out to determine the conditions on which alone 'abiding satisfaction' can be had: and so we are presented with five criteria of the true good. These we have defined. The most problematic of these criteria, that the true or unconditional good must be a social or common good, leads to a double reference or harmless ambiguity of the phrase, a 'common good', in Green's writings. Green sometimes speaks of a form of social organization which realizes the true good jointly for different persons as itself a common good; at other times he speaks of the true good's having this social aspect of joint realizability as its being a common good. The joint realizability of the true good obtains in virtue of two features of human beings: the tendency of one person to identify his or her

---

[18] B. Bosanquet, 'Do Finite Individuals Possess a Substantive or an Adjectival Mode of being?' *Life and Finite Individuality*, London, 1918, 75–102, 179–94. Cf. B. Bosanquet, 'Hegel's Theory of the Political Organism', *Mind*, 7 (1898). On Bosanquet's organicism see R. E. Dowling, 'Bosanquet's Political Philosophy', thesis: University of London, 1955.

[19] J. M. E. McTaggart, 'The Conception of Society as an Organism', *Studies in Hegelian Cosmology*, Cambridge, 1901.

interests with those of another, and the need on a larger scale for human beings to encapsulate their lifeplans in social roles. Such roles provide the fullest conditions for 'abiding satisfaction'. We separated this perspective on the social nature of man from two views which Green rejects: social atomism and social organicism.

With the five criteria now defined and clarified, two questions remain: are the criteria really distinct, incapable of reduction? And if they are distinct, why are the criteria of the true good heterogeneous in just this way? Otherwise put: why are there five criteria and precisely these five?

As to reduction one concession is easy: that the criteria of non-competitiveness and non-exclusivity on the one hand, and, on the other, the requirement that the true good be a social or common good, do overlap. For it follows, if the true good is a common good, with the examples Green has in mind, that it is non-competitive and non-exclusive: as applies for instance when one person identifies himself or herself with another's interests. But a logical separation has still to be observed. The true good could be non-competitive and non-exclusive even if we withheld the extra facts which Green assumes about the social nature of human beings.

It is not possible, within the small compass of this chapter, to validate completely Green's theory of the true good. This is to move to the second question. I will suggest, however, three tests that may be considered. In the first place, a test of non-contradiction can be applied. If there is a true or conditional human good for which criteria can be defined, those criteria cannot be contradictory. To all appearance Green's criteria clear this hurdle. That is of course a fairly minimal condition. Secondly and more substantially, a theory of the true good must pass a test of universality. It must vindicate its claim that all human beings, or all 'normal' or all 'rational' human beings, are such that this is the true good for them. For Green the claim would cover all agents to whom the conditions of moral responsibility apply (2.2, 3.16). We need, however, to be careful in the matter of universality. Take the person, a business shark, who totally repudiates the requirement of non-competitiveness and non-exclusivity. For him the good life is one of strenuous competition, and 'the devil take the hindmost'. Moral philosophy should not take too short a way with such a person; but a point may come at which we let the devil take the business shark as well. As we have all learned to say, explanation is relative to an interest. Green's criteria of the true good do not presuppose a moral point of view; but they do presuppose an interest in how the rationality of moral action might emerge from such criteria. Perhaps Green can best be taken as saying, in language very different from his own: 'if you grant me this account of the human good, an account which does not itself presuppose a moral point of view, I can vindicate the rationality of moral action'. That possibility strikes me as significant. But I do not know how Green or any other moral philosopher can produce an account of the rationality of moral action unless we allow into our understanding of the human good assumptions which at least are consistent with morality, as those of the business shark are not.

The third test is empirical. It means a psychological assessment of human beings in conditions in which the five criteria are fulfilled or frustrated. The snag with this test is obvious: that an idea of human flourishing would presumably need to inform the assessment, and just such an idea is what the theory of the true good itself aims to supply.

Then I shall work mainly with the second test, as interpreted. In the remainder of this chapter I shall take Green's rejection of one candidate for the true good, i.e. pleasure; consider Dewey's claim that abiding satisfaction is inherently unachievable even on Green's own account; disentangle Green from a *reductio ad absurdum* carefully engineered by Prichard; and note how 'states of consciousness' can wrongly be taken to generate paradoxes for Green's theory of the true good.

6.9 PLEASURE

Green's critique of pleasure has a certain peculiarity in terms of the above exposition. Since he denies that pleasure is the true good, one might expect its claims to be measured adversely against some or all of the criteria we have defined. Yet this is not how Green proceeds; he uses against pleasure two perfectly general arguments of which the plausibility does not at all depend on our accepting the five criteria of the true good. The explanation is, I think, twofold. To begin with, it must be borne in mind that the criteria as here set forth represent a recovery of dispersed ideas. We find a 'theory' of the true good in Green only by organizing data; and so we are not to expect Green to make the sort of ready appeal to his criteria which would be quite natural if he had presented them systematically. Besides that, Green does not dismiss pleasure as simply an inferior candidate for the role of the true good; he believes that pleasure is radically not the kind of thing which could possibly be the true good. Detailed measurement against the five criteria would take us the long way round in rejecting a candidate whose claims, he is sure, can be more briskly dismissed.

This dismissal involves the two arguments outlined in 1.7 and there called the logical object argument and the no-summation argument. The first argument goes as follows. (Its manner is strongly reminiscent of Butler's critique, against Hobbes, of 'the seflish theory of human nature': *vide* PE, §§ 161, 225.) Pleasure supervenes on the satisfaction of desire. We can aim at pleasure only through the satisfaction of desires. Absent those desires, which are not themselves for pleasure, and pleasure cannot itself be aimed at: a supervenient phenomenon has nothing on which to supervene. Green allows that, in a sense, a person can desire pleasure: 'there is really a desire for it which co-operates with his various interests; but it could not take the place of the objects of these various interests without destroying the interests and with them its own possibility' (PE, § 224).

The argument has its strength. Pleasure can be the supervenient phenomenon Green says it is. I want to tidy the garden; passers-by have after all been complaining. So I work frantically all day, see the results and take pleasure in what I have done. In retrospect: I certainly did not aim at that pleasure. Equally, I could not have taken that pleasure if I had not had an independent desire to tidy the garden. Green's argument fits this type of example very well. But suppose I set myself a different task, 'how can I get some pleasure today?' and go to a friend who slips me an amazing potion which fills me with pleasure for the rest of the day. The lightness of this example should not conceal its logic: no desire independent of the desire for pleasure itself is here at work. On a further point, however, Green is not vulnerable. Imagine this objection: why should it matter, in a comparative assessment, that pleasure has a supervenient aspect? 'An abiding satisfaction of an abiding self' has a similar aspect: that also supervenes on the satisfaction of desires. To this the correct reply is that abiding satisfaction identifies the true good; and we are examining one candidate for the true good, i.e. pleasure, with a view to its yielding abiding satisfaction. The objection confuses logical levels. This is not, of course, the end of the matter.

For if we are examining pleasure as a candidate for the true good, why should it not yield 'an abiding satisfaction of an abiding self'? This introduces Green's second, no-summation argument. Here the summation of pleasures is not the topic ingeniously explored by Dorothy Wrinch in her 1918 paper.[20] Wrinch is concerned with the kind of 'influence' which occurs between pleasures when, for example, Matthew's pleasure in seeing a Robert Fuller film in the company of Verity is greater than would have been the pleasure of seeing the film on his own; and when, correspondingly, his pleasure in Verity's company is greater in the presence of the film than would have been the pleasure of Verity's company without it. Green's continually reiterated polemic is the argument which Bradley deployed and made famous in *Ethical Studies* against an infinite, perishing series'.[21] It would be disingenuous to suppose that it was Green who took the argument from Bradley. But whatever the niceties of historical indebtedness, Green's argument is to the effect that pleasures, occurring serially, produce no sum. 'For the feeling of a pleased person, or in relation to his sense of enjoyment, pleasures cannot form a sum. However numerous the sources of a state of pleasant feeling, it is one, and is over before another can be enjoyed' (PE, § 221). The pleasure of drinking wine last week occurred and has gone. It is no more a present pleasure than if it had never occurred. Green does not deny that the current recollection of drinking wine last week may itself be pleasant. But such recollection yields in turn a purely occurrent pleasure which is incapable of contributing to a sum of pleasures.

[20] D. Wrinch, 'The Summation of Pleasures', *Proceedings of the Aristotelian Society*, 18 (1917–18).   [21] F. H. Bradley, *Ethical Studies*, 2nd edn. Oxford, 1927,95.

The obvious question that needs to be asked is: why does Green use the notion of summation? If somebody were defending the claims of pleasure to be the true good he would be more likely, or better advised, to employ the notion of a whole: to argue that a life of pleasure is a temporal whole of which the (not necessarily continuous) parts are pleasant experiences. Why should it matter to the 'argumentative Hedonist' of PE, § 228 that 'A man who is enjoying a pleasure for the thousandth time *has* no more pleasure, however much more an enumerator might reckon him to have *had* . . . than the man who is enjoying it for the first time' (PE. § 227)? The hedonist could appeal to Sidgwick's idea of a 'continually renascent satisfaction'. We have seen the resources available to Green to answer that appeal (4.16). The exact point of the no-summation argument is still to seek.

That point is to be found, I think, in the idea that for the 'pleasure-seeker' (PE, §, 237), life is only as good as his latest pleasure, or the latest pleasure he can remember or look forward to. Last week's water will not cure my present thirst; if a person's pleasures stop, he has nothing. Even the recollection of past pleasures may serve only to sharpen the absence of pleasure now. For the person with a lifeplan, by contrast, success is additive. If I mean to learn Latin, and last week mastered the declension of nouns and this week have sorted out the declension of adjectives, these achievements are additive. They combine in such a way that I am closer to my goal this week than I was last. My achievements are not 'over' as the pleasure of drinking last week's wine is now 'over'. This is the familiar ground of 4.12.

Yet given all this, H. D. Lewis still posed the question, 'Was Green a Hedonist?'[22] For Lewis this is a real question; for me there is a real answer, no. But Lewis noticed a point previously overlooked by Green's commentators. As Sir David Ross says in just this connection, self-satisfaction 'is a particular form of pleasure';[23] and Green, the polemicist against pleasure, uses self-satisfaction as a central notion in his moral psychology. The paradox can, I think, be punctured as follows. It is not that Green's agent has, hedonistically, a purely general idea of self-

[22] H. D. Lewis, 'Was Green a Hedonist?', *Mind*, 45 (1936).
[23] W. D. Ross, *Foundations of Ethics*, Oxford, 1939, 297.

satisfaction which he cultivates and fulfils particular desires as a means of achieving. He already has particular desires, which may owe nothing to the idea of self-satisfaction; and he systematizes those desires, constrains or develops them, in a 'plan of life' on the fulfilment of which self-satisfaction supervenes. That those particular desires are not themselves desires for pleasure is the burden of the logical object argument above.

Pleasure is not what it was. By this I mean that the concept has slid into the background of contemporary ethics; and Green's views on pleasure have a greater significance in the context of nineteenth-century British moral philosophy than for the present day. They will not be explored further here.

6.10 DEWEY'S CRITIQUE

John Dewey in his early writings was an extensive critic of Green. Here I shall note a line of criticism according to which Green's notion of 'an abiding satisfaction of an abiding self' is self-defeating. In his 1892 paper, 'Green's Theory of the Moral Motive', Dewey cites Green's remark at PE, § 85:

At the same time as the reflecting subject traverses the series of wants, which it distinguishes from itself while it presents their filling as its object, there arises the idea of a satisfaction on the whole—an idea never realisable, but for ever striving to realise itself in the attainment of a greater command over means to the satisfaction of particular wants.[24]

Dewey presses the point that there seems a curious self-defeatingness about emphasizing 'the idea of a satisfaction on the whole' if such an idea is 'never realizable'. The right reply is, I think, that the unrealizability which Green has here in mind is that of complete and perfect achievement. He certainly accepts that the 'true good' which is the basis of such 'satisfaction on the whole' as we can obtain is subject to a continual refinement in our clarity about it and in the social institutions in which it is embodied. An asymptotic approach to such satisfaction is

---

[24] J. Dewey, 'Green's Theory of the Moral Motive', *The Early Works of John Dewey*, 3, 1889–1892, ed. J. A. Boydiston *et al.*, Carbondale and Edwardsville, 1969, 162.

definitely possible as such refinement proceeds. Dewey takes unrealizability in the too drastic sense of total non-achievement.

But he has not yet finished with Green's 'satisfaction on the whole'. According to Dewey, 'Green shows that the process of our active experience demands that the self, in becoming conscious of a want, set that want before itself as an object, thus distinguishing itself from the want; but he shows us no road back from the object thus objectified to the self.'[25] Divested of its awkward language Dewey's point is, I think, that if the agent is able to distance himself from, or to identify himself with, the fulfilment of particular desires, then he has available to him merely serial satisfactions of the kind which Green's no-summation argument against pleasure itself relies on. But the answer to Dewey on this point is to be found in the distinctions which we drew in 4.12. Green's agent can have whole series of simple desires, yielding 'serial' satisfactions. But his 'satisfaction on the whole' depends on the realization of a 'plan of life' which does not pull him up and down, from happiness to discontent, as each simple desire is fulfilled or frustrated. Dewey in effect limits his view of Green to the third aspect of the multi-perspectival model, that aspect specially concerned with 'distance' and 'identification' between the agent and his desires. He misses the full picture.

6.11 GREEN AND PRICHARD

I turn now to consider a criticism from H. A. Prichard. In 'Green: Political Obligation',[26] Prichard attempts to draw consequences damaging to Green's account of the common good from Green's own moral psychology. Prichard had a passion for criticism; he saw inconsistency, paradox, ambiguity, *ignoratio elenchi*, the whole catalogue of philosophical faults, everywhere. In Prichard's hands the smoothest surface of philosophical argument soon crinkled in folds of paradox. Prichard ascribes two views to Green: the view that all motivation embodies a conception of personal good, and the

---

[25] J. Dewey, 162.
[26] H. A. Prichard, *Moral Obligation*, Oxford, 1949.

view that all desire is for a state of the agent. A motive, of course, is a desire on which the agent decides to act.

These views, Prichard argues, reduce Green to a dilemma with respect to the comon good. If in deciding to act I unavoidably consult my personal good, and if any desire on which I might decide to act is for a state of myself, then either (i) no common good is possible between any two persons, since states of different persons are numerically distinct (i.e. the states cannot be shared in such a way as to constitute a common good), or (ii) 'the two so-called different persons are really one and the same person, and so not different persons'.[27] Prichard next claims that this second position 'is exactly what Green does maintain':[28] and since this is patently unacceptable, Prichard considers that he has accomplished a *reductio ad absurdum* of Green's account of the common good.

In reply I cannot see that Green textually commits himself to this explicit position. Nor does he seem committed to it by logical implication from anything that he does say. The point clears itself up as follows. Prichard is right: Green does hold the view that all motivation embodies a conception of personal good (5.3). But he does not hold the other view which Prichard ascribes to him, that all desire is for a state of the agent. Desire relates to some activity or passivity of the agent (4.12). That is a different matter. If I want to help the old lady to cross the street, a certain activity on my part is built into this desire: I want to do something. But I really do desire a state of the old lady, that state which results from her safe transfer to the far side; and Prichard fails to reduce Green to logical embarrassment on this score.

6.12   A FALSE INTERPRETATION

It is easy, by a slippage of interpretation, to see Green's theory of the true good as plagued by contradictions. We have just resisted an interpretation of Prichard's; there is another interpretation to guard against. Bosanquet and Ann Cacoullos

[27] H. A. Prichard, 71.
[28] H. A. Prichard, ibid.

are exactly right to resist a 'states of consciousness' interpretation which makes havoc of Green's theory. That interpretation is the final main topic of this chapter.

Moore's account of the unconditional human good emphasizes 'states of consciousness', as we have seen (6.4); and this emphasis has seemed to some commentators to give the right point of view from which certain of Green's own remarks should be approached. Thus when Green says that 'all other values are relative to values for, of, or in a person', this can readily be taken in the sense, as Bosanquet points out, that 'nothing has value except the conscious states of conscious beings'.[29] Just in this sense Plamenatz takes Green's true good to be realized in 'states of mind';[30] and for this he is very properly taken to task by Cacoullos.[31]

If we adopt the states of mind or states of consciousness approach, the resulting damage to Green's philosophy is clear. For there is great difficulty in applying Green's criteria to states of mind or consciousness. Perhaps such states can be objects of pursuit, but do we 'construct' them? That question will suffice; we do not need to labour the obvious. The correct response to this approach starts really with Green's account of motivation in 5.3. We know that the human agent acts on a conception of personal good. This conception controls, and is expressed in, the sorts of desires on which he decides to act. On what sorts of desires, then, should he act if he wants to achieve 'a satisfaction on the whole', 'an abiding satisfaction of an abiding self'? The theory of the true good spells out certain constraints on desire; it tells me that unless what I want, in any desire on which I decide to act, can meet certain requirements, i.e. those specified by the criteria of the true good, then that desire and its fulfilment will not contribute to my 'satisfaction on the whole'. My personal good is, minimally, what will satisfy my desire; and my true good is what will satisfy me. '[T]he generic definition of the good' is that it fulfils some desire. But if I want to cook a meal tonight, that desire will not be satisfied by a state of mind and nor shall I.

---

[29] B. Bosanquet, *The Principle of Individuality and Value*, London, 1912, 302 ff.

[30] J. P. Plamenatz, *Consent, Freedom and Political Obligation*, 2nd edn. Oxford, 1968, 62–81.

[31] A. Cacoullos, *Thomas Hill Green: Philosopher of Rights*, New York, 1974, 127–9.

6.13 HISTORICAL SPECIFICITY

This completes the first part of Green's transition to morality. A word, however, before we leave Chapter 6. The present chapter does not simply mark a particular division of the discussion. It also terminates one level of Green's philosophy. Chapters 4–6 occupy the same level of generality. Chapter 4 gives essentially a view of how the self may be organized to achieve self-satisfaction. Chapter 5 presents a theory of action for the self so organized. Chapter 6, just ending, defines the conditions for self-satisfaction: it sets out certain constraints on self-satisfaction, however the self is organized. Throughout Chapters 6–6 the level of discussion has been abstract and ahistorical. It is not that Green has defined properties and capacities which must belong to anything that could count as a self, flex our imaginations as we may to the farthest conceptual horizons; he has drawn out possibilities within easily recognizable human limits. The point is rather that although Green realizes the social nature of human beings (6.5 ff.), we have encountered no focused, precise recognition of the historical encapsulation of human beings in particular forms of society. Chapters 7 and 8 bring a change of perspective. In Chapter 7 one element of Green's ethical theory is a morality of social roles. Clearly these are historically specific; and in Chapter 8 one element of Green's political philosophy is historically specific also in the tasks assigned to the state with regard to the social conditions for self-realization.

This ends my discussion of the unconditional human good: and I now pass to the second part of Green's transition to morality.

7

The Transition to Morality: (2) 'The Moral Good'

7.1 INTRODUCTION

The main task of this chapter follows directly from the last. Green's transition to morality, his account of the rationality of moral action, involves two stages. In Chapter 6 we completed the first stage, Green's theory of the unconditional good. The second stage defines our current task, to examine Green's claim that the moral life fulfils the conditions of the unconditional good.

That task subdivides and falls in with other tasks as follows. I begin by laying out the distinctions, as Green understands them, between moral, non-moral, and immoral action: the conceptual machinery for discussing the rationality of moral action. (For ease of reference 'moral' action will signify 'morally good' action.) Sharp questions encircle any attempt to demonstrate the rationality of moral action by philosophical argument; and the view that philosophy can accomplish no such result is essentially the charge from Ayer and Broad (6.1) that Green's transition to morality is moralism, no proper work for moral philosophy. That charge answered, I next examine Green's two main arguments for the rationality of moral action: a minimal argument based on *de facto* social identification, and a more ambitious argument which involves a morality of social roles. I align Green's morality of social roles with Rousseau's general will and Kant's kingdom of ends rather than with Hegel's ethical life (Sittlichkeit). The cogency of Green's transition to morality is assessed, and that assessment completes the main task of the chapter. As Chapters 4 and 5 introduced Green's ethical theory through his moral psychology, so the rest of the chapter largely expounds fresh connections between those two areas of Green's moral philosophy. I set out Green's account of the moral virtues and his notion of the good will. In regard to the good will, I answer H. D. Lewis's criticism of vacuity and Sidgwick's charge of inextricable confusion (6.1) between wider and narrower notions of the true good. On the coherence of moral experience as a candidate for the true or unconditional human good, I reply on Green's behalf to two lines of thought in the subsequent tradition of British Idealism. Finally I explain Green's moral epistemology and the dual model of moral reasoning to which it appeals.

7.2 THE DEFINITION OF THE MORAL

The sphere of non-moral action is that for which moral responsibility fails. Recall the necessary conditions of moral responsibility outlined in 3.16:

    (1) A was able to do X.
    (2) A did X knowingly.
    (3) A could have done otherwise, if his character and desires had been different.

Moral responsibility is always responsibility for an action under a description. Of course in the limiting case if an agent did not do an action then he is not responsible for that action under any description. Equally he is not responsible if he acted, not knowing what he was doing. Jess broke Rod's arm. The action was his: in seizing Rod's arm Jess broke it, but he was unaware, and he had no reason to believe, that Rod had lately undergone surgery. Again, the agent is not responsible if his own choice was irrelevant to what he did. Rupert reproduced Damien's signature on a blackmail letter, but Rupert's hand was gripped, vice-like, by villains who controlled its every movement. Such examples, and of course others which distinguish far subtler nuances of responsibility, are the staple of current discussion. In PE, Green follows similar lines.

He tells us that 'the world of practice—the world composed of moral or distinctively human actions, with their results—is one in which the determining causes are motives; a motive again being an idea of an end, which a self-conscious subject presents to itself, and which it strives and tends to realise' (PE, § 87; cf. 5.3). This clearly excludes such actions as we should normally regard as failing the above conditions for moral responsibility: actions which are instinctive (i.e. reflex), done in sleep, performed strictly under compulsion, or done by accident (PE, § 96; cf. Works II, 133).

Then is that all? Why does Green not discuss the sphere of non-moral action in any detail beyond these brief characterizations? I think because, in contrast to nineteenth-century utilitarianism, he is only slightly preoccupied with the extenuating conditions of moral judgement. For the utilitarians, moral responsibility follows moral judgement. To put the point in somewhat modern terms: as in moral judgement an action is assessed adversely or favourably under a description, so the question naturally arises whether the agent is morally responsible for that action under that description. In the utilitarian scheme, moral judgement is part and parcel of a process of social control by which praise and blame, rewards and sanctions, contribute to the greatest public happiness. In the context of such a process, extenuating conditions are important. I cannot be deterred by blame from repeating an action which occurred by unforeseeable accident. But Green does not have this kind of strong 'juristic' interest in moral judgement. Realize the inaccessibility of motives (5.9), and moral judgement is precarious. That aside, Green's primary interest is in self-realization and in the accompanying 'abiding satisfaction of an abiding self'. He aims to develop a coherent ethical theory relative to that interest.

If we shift the discussion from the moral/non-moral distinction to that of moral/immoral, we find that Green's ethical theory bends on another hinge of emphasis. Just as his primary interest in responsibility for actions is not excusatory and juristic but positive, with a view to self-realization, so his primary interest in moral goodness is not action-centred but person-based. The focal point of Green's ethical theory is the morally good person; and the chief problem for that theory is to establish the rationality of moral action relative to a 'plan of life' (4.12). Specifically: why should Green's agent, in quest of 'an abiding satisfaction of an abiding self', consider other interests besides his own?

That question is the centre to which every discussion returns.

The answer to it may best begin with a short account of how one agent's actions can affect other agents from a moral viewpoint. Very briefly we can, in acting, regard or disregard (*a*) the needs or (*b*) the rights of others. Benevolence is a regard for the needs of others; justice a regard for their rights. Both benevolence and justice are 'social' virtues; they necessarily regard the interests of other agents. The contrast here is with the 'personal' or 'self-regarding' virtues of which the exercise may, but does not necessarily, serve or recognize the interests of others (2.4.2). On the social virtues Green reads Plato adversely and criticizes him for collapsing the interpersonal depth out of the concept of justice. For now, to prepare the ground for Green's minimal argument for the rationality of moral action, I shall confine attention to benevolence. Benevolence can be specified slightly more exactly if we note four kinds of relation between an agent and others' needs. In terms of those needs the agent can (i) promote the interests of others; (ii) remove or prevent whatever harms the interests of others; (iii) refrain from undermining whatever serves the interests of others; (iv) refrain from working actively against and positively harming the interests of others.

These are the four imperatives of benevolence. In referring to them as 'imperatives' I am not endorsing any view to the effect that the moral agent has an indiscriminate obligation to promote and maximize the need-based interests of other people. My point is simply that an agent is benevolent to the extent to which his actions fulfil the four imperatives. The connection between benevolence and morality is that, pre-reflectively at least, one would be hard pressed to see somebody as a morally good agent or person if his actions never fulfilled any of the four imperatives: if he never promoted anyone's interests but his own, never prevented harm to the interests of anyone but himself, and so on. Of course I concede that the four imperatives, as listed, lack logical elegance. The list includes requirements of both action and abstention, and this suggests a higher-level regrouping under two headings. My aim is merely to cover the elementary grounds of benevolence. A blind man loses his way; I redirect him (requirement (i)). A child is about to fall from a river bank; I pull him back (requirement (ii)). A sick neighbour is peacefully sleeping; I refrain from playing my loudest tapes (requirement (iii)). Another neighbour is a luckier man than I, successful in whatever he sets his hand to. Though envious, I do not actively seek his discomfiture (requirement (iv)).

To the extent to which an agent respects these requirements I shall also say that he has, to establish a first hold on the notion, a 'good will'. The notion of the good will is fundamental in Green's ethical theory. His language is clear: the distinction between the good will and the bad will 'forms the true basis of ethics' (PE, § 115). The good will encompasses the whole of moral virtue; but that is not true of benevolence as above and standardly understood. Since benevolence stands separately from justice, therefore in handling benevolence we are not fully encompassing the good will. We shall anatomize the good will later (7.14). Note for now Green's sensitivity to a certain line of criticism. He feels that any distinction between a good and bad will may appear hard to justify on his theory of motivation. That theory, we recall from 5.3, rests on the view that personal good is the aim of all 'distinctively human' action. Green is emphatic: 'in all conduct to which moral predicates are applicable a man is an object to himself; . . . such conduct, equally whether virtuous or vicious, expresses a motive consisting in an idea of personal good, which the man seeks to realise by action' (PE, § 115). But, the difficulty supposedly is, if the virtuous and the vicious agent equally aim at a personal good, 'The first impression of any one reading this statement may probably be that . . . we have adopted a view which, if significant and true, would take away the only intelligible foundation of ethics by reducing virtuous and vicious action to the same motive' (ibid.).

Surely this is a factitious difficulty. Green has already used the key phrase, 'an idea of personal good', which clearly opens the possibility that it is not the same idea of personal good which motivates the virtuous and the vicious agent and which is reflected in virtuous and vicious conduct. If the distinction between the good and the bad will 'forms the true basis of ethics', this distinction may turn on divergent ideas of personal good held respectively by virtuous and vicious agents. We know of course from Green's theory of mind in Chapter 4 that such an 'idea' will be a coalescence of 'reason' and 'desire'.

Two further points will complete our introduction to Green's definition of the moral at this introductory stage. One, unlike a philosopher such as Spinoza, Green does not believe that it falls to him to create or adumbrate a new morality. Green aims to dissect and interpret the moral life, perhaps to examine it from certain angles which otherwise we would miss. But essentially he sees the moral life as a phenomenon for analysis, something already in being. Green's ethics is not the revelation of a new moral order.

Two, on Green's account it is not necessary, if an agent or his actions are to count as morally good, that he should self-consciously think morally. I can do what is morally good and be a morally good agent, in Green's view, without seeing myself or what I do in explicitly moral terms. (Cf. Hume: '*no action can be virtuous, or morally good, unless there be in human nature some motive to produce it, distinct from the sense of its morality*' (T479). As Green expresses the point: 'the idea is at work before it is reflected on' (PE, § 73). The process of reflection is captured by Green's reference to 'the supervention upon those moral interests that are unconscious of their morality, of an interest in moral qualities as such' (PE, § 243).

Before we examine 'those moral interests that are unconscious of their morality', however, I want to consider a basic objection to Green's 'transition to morality', an objection which, thrown across that transition, threatens to stop the way. It is just this. Even if Green does not regard himself as a moral innovator on the Spinozistic model, his whole endeavour to justify the rationality of moral action is, so the objection runs, an aberration from the proper path of moral philosophy. In seeking to establish the rationality of moral action, Green is recommending a way of life; the taint of moralism lies over his work. By way of historical contrast Green's fellow Oxford idealist, F. H. Bradley, concedes that 'ethics has not to make the world moral, but to reduce to theory the morality current in the world'.[1] The present objection takes us straight back to the criticisms of Ayer and Broad cited in 6.1.

7.3   MORAL PHILOSOPHY AND MORALISM

The charge of moralism from Ayer and Broad is not, I think, the same criticism from both writers. Ayer rejects any possibility of

[1] F. H. Bradley, *Ethical Studies*, 2nd edn. Oxford, 1927, 193.

showing the rationality of moral action; Broad does not. Broad displays no awareness of the detailed arguments which Green presents for the rationality of moral action. In face of those arguments, shortly to be set out, he might have rescinded his harsh judgement. Ayer's perspective on Green is more radical. Few moral philosophers would think that Green's commentator should be deterred in going about his business by the ethical views of Ayer in *Language, Truth and Logic* and 'The Analysis of Moral Judgements'. But we should not take too short a way with Ayer; he is not alone in thinking that Green is trying to do something which is no proper part of moral philosophy.

But then, one's understanding of the proper task of moral philosophy is dependent on one's understanding of the kind of thing morality is; and certain activities in which a moral philosopher might engage look very different as one understands morality in one way or another.

Two central portions of moral philosophy are clearly identifiable across the history of the subject. The first is presuppositional: for a philosopher to take the moral life as he understands it and to examine its conditions. To see, in other words, what assumptions it participants make (perhaps unselfconsciously) about man, society, and nature; and, more deeply as in Kant, to see what in turn is presupposed to the possibility of such assumptions. In such ways moral philosophy defines what J. A. Smith called the 'meta-ethical environment' of the moral life;[2] and, in contrast to this, instead of looking outwards to the assumptions on which morality depends, the other central portion of moral philosophy looks inwards to define the main terms of moral discourse, the main concepts of the moral life. For Greek morality this describes a large area of Aristotle's ethics.

If a philosopher engages in this presuppositional or conceptual work, he is doing moral philosophy on practically any account. Beyond that, nothing is safe; the frontiers of moral philosophy shift with one's understanding of morality. One might see the moral life as the sport of subjective preferences, with moral judgements expressing the spectator's feelings (early Ayer), or with moral principles embodying some surd, inexplicable personal commitment (Sartre) or non-rational decision (some varieties of prescriptivism). On such views of the

² J. A. Smith, 'Morals and Religion', *The Hibbert Journal*, 19 (1920–1), 622.

moral life any attempt to ground the rationality of moral action is personal by-play on the part of the philosopher, who, if he chooses to enter this area, can only preach, recommend, or give moral advice. There is no fact of the matter by which the rationality of moral action could conceivably be shown.

But to argue in this way is not to make a neutral claim about the nature of moral philosophy; it is to make a controversial claim about the moral life. Green believes that there is a fact of the matter about the rationality of moral action. We shall draw out that 'fact' in tracing the transition to morality from Green's theory of the unconditional human good. And of course we must see whether the transition works. As to the adequacy of its execution we cannot yet say; we have not considered Green's arguments. But the transition cannot be excluded from moral philosophy on the grounds that no such transition could be valid. To ignore something in philosophy is one thing; time presses, and not everything looks promising. To exclude Green's arguments from the very status of philosophy is a different matter.

Green's moral philosophy has a practical goal: to establish the rationality of moral action to anyone engaged in practical thinking with a view to 'self-satisfaction'. But three misconceptions must be guarded against. First, on Green's account moral philosophy can explain why a person rationally should act morally, why moral considerations are relevant to decision-making. It cannot say how those considerations apply to particular circumstances. Moral philosophy cannot tell Pam to return Jim's engagement ring any more than aesthetics can tell Jim to revise his poem. Green handles this problem separately by developing a dual model of moral reasoning, but the burden of such reasoning falls squarely on the self-reliant, critical thought of the individual. Secondly, moral philosophy's practical goal is not its sole object. Green himself does presuppositional and conceptual work. We have already seen the presuppositional work in Chapter 3. Thirdly, Green is not open to the charge of ignoring the conditional nature of practical rationality. One might say: the rationality of any action is conditional on the ends or interests one has. Green assumes an interest in self-satisfaction, in 'an abiding satisfaction of an abiding self'. That assumption grounds his account of the rationality of moral action. It is an open assumption; nothing is being surreptitiously slipped into the argument.

7.4 THE RATIONALITY OF MORAL ACTION: THE MINIMAL ARGUMENT

Then to return to 'those moral interests that are unconscious of their morality', recognition of which is the first step in Green's transition to morality. Green adopts a position akin to Mrs Foot's view of *de facto* social identification (2.4.2). Human agents are capable of taking an interest in others for their own sakes. Typically, and in a rudimentary way, this interest will mean providing for the maintenance of a family. This is the sphere of J. L. Mackie's 'self-referential altruism', a 'concern for others, but for others who have some special connection with oneself'.[3] One passage from PE will lead us conveniently into Green's ideas:

... such an end as provision for the maintenance of a family, if pursued not instinctively but with consciousness of the end pursued, implies in the person pursuing it a motive quite different from desire either for an imagined pleasure or for relief from want. It implies the thought of a possibly permanent satisfaction, and an effort to attain that satisfaction in the satisfaction of others. Here is already a moral and spiritual, as distinct from an animal or merely natural, interest—an interest in an object which only thought constitutes, an interest in bringing about something that should be, as distinct from desire to feel again a pleasure already felt. But to be actuated by such an interest does not necessarily imply any reflection on its nature; and hence in men under its influence there need not be any conception of a moral as other than a material good. Food and drink, warmth and clothing, may still seem to them to be the only good things which they desire for themselves or for others.—(PE, § 242.)

On this view the germ of morality is present in the most elementary social phenomena. It is a view which brings Green closer to Hume than to Kant. Green's 'interests that are unconscious of their morality' supply the same kind of motivation that defines the 'natural virtues' in Hume. Kant would exclude any such motivation from morality. In ethics the

[3] J. L. Mackie, *Ethics: Inventing Right and Wrong*, Harmondsworth, 1977, 132.

contingent never looms into frame. The kind of motivation which Green and Hume have here in mind varies in intensity between different people and different occasions; and it is plainly inadequate to the full scope of morality. We have no need further to repeat this familiar Kantian criticism. The fact is that Green differs from Kant in two ways. Kant acknowledges two sources of motivation, moral and non-moral, but only one source of morality, namely reason. Green acknowledges only one source of motivation, 'an idea of personal good', but two sources of morality. For Green one part of morality is simply a form of human sociability. This is the source of morality which he has in view in his minimal argument. Another source of morality, to be considered under Green's more ambitious argument, emerges from the requirements of social roles.

To return: Green next imagines a process of reflection supervening on the *de facto* social identification of PE, § 242. The agent at this stage realizes that in providing for the long-term benefit of a family he has an extended goal over time, one which (so long as his identification with the family continues) offers the prospect of 'an abiding satisfaction of an abiding self'. A lifeplan is formed which links him with the interests of other people (his family, his friends). So far, so banal; but beyond this point a degree of subtlety pervades the picture. For it is open to the agent to realize that what secures his satisfaction is precisely an interest, his social identification. Thinking as he does of the permanent welfare of his family he must now, in consistency, view their sharing of a similar interest as a part of their own welfare, as something which will secure their own satisfaction. As Green introduces the point:

. . . *if* that interest [i.e. the agent's interest in the permanent welfare of his family: GLT], even in the form of an interest in the mere provision for the material support of a family, were duly reflected upon, those who were influenced by it must have become aware that they had objects independent of the gratification of their animal nature; and, having become aware of this, they could not fail with more or less distinctness to conceive that permanent welfare of the family, which it was their great object to promote, as consisting, at any rate among other things, in the continuance in others of an interest like their own; in other words, as consisting in the propagation of virtue.— (PE, § 242.)

The entire situation described in our two quotations from PE, § 242 may now be reviewed and developed. In this type of situation we already encounter one virtue, that of benevolence; towards his family and friends Green's agent as here characterized has exactly the attitude to act in line with the four imperatives of benevolence. Given that attitude, morever, other virtues come into play or become appropriate: the virtues of integrity, courage, and self-control or 'temperance'. A person, X, who so identifies with the interests of his family, will not readily break with them when a third party, Y, makes some easy appeal to X's self-interest; here we talk of integrity. Nor will X forsake his family lightly under threat; here we talk of courage. Nor again will he readily disregard his family's interests under the distractions of pleasure or amusement; here we talk of temperance. This is not the portrait of a saint; it is the recognizable likeness of a family man.

Such social identification expands easily into an integrated wide-interest system of the kind described in 4.10; and so we move into the area of self-satisfaction, of 'an abiding satisfaction of an abiding self'. In this way Green criticizes Plato: the *Republic* has 'no recognition of inarticulate reason or of reason in movement [operative] in family affections' (Platonis de Republica, 48). The connection between self-satisfaction and morality becomes more cogent still when the agent realizes that since this amalgam of benevolence, integrity, courage, and temperance is the condition of his self-satisfaction, therefore he may reinterpret the interests of his family to reflect that realization. Morality, at least towards his family, is the condition of his serving their interests; it is therefore the condition of his self-satisfaction. So the idea may gradually form that morality, the morality of identification, is itself among the interests of his family. If they reciprocate and identify with the interests of others, morality and self-satisfaction will interlock for them as for him. The decision, if he reaches it, to foster and inculcate morality in his family, the morality of identification and benevolence, marks a fresh construction of his family's interests.

Now obviously this style of moral argument hits the same limits as we met in Hume's account of the natural virtues (2.4.1). Whether it works as far as it goes, it does not go the full length of the moral life. Essentially it fails to embrace the virtue of justice. So I want now to look at Green's more ambitious argument, which extends the rationality of moral action beyond the scope of the kind of social identification on which the minimal argument relies.

7.5   THE RATIONALITY OF MORAL ACTION: THE MORE AMBITIOUS ARGUMENT

Though the two arguments, minimal and more ambitious, are not explicitly distinguished by Green, the latter argument can I think be traced in PE, Book III and PPO, §§ 117–36. But its most suggestive statement occurs in MS 10A, 'Other End', 20. We can set out the broad contrast between the arguments as follows. While the minimal argument relies on human sociability, it requires in principle only the cellular units of individual, friends, and family. On the more ambitious argument ('MAA' for convenience of reference), the moral life is a dimension of the entire network of social institutions.

The MS 10A passage reads thus:

Reason, to be free, demands a law (1) *universal*, not merely valid *for me* from time to time (however regularly the times be repeated); (2) which it gives, not receives.

How can any law satisfy condition (1) which is other than merely negative; or (2), unless obedience to it excludes pleasure, i.e. all satisfaction of desire, all personal sentiment?

This *theoretical* difficulty of reason <is> overcome by recognition of its own work in the objective social world, which de facto determines our desire and sentiment [particularizes our 'Duties']: recognition not of acquiescence but of cooperation and continual evolution.

The relation of <the> individual to society subjects him to a law which is at once universal, as result of unity of 'Ego' giving freely to itself in 'manifold of desire', and at same time articulated into specific duties as various 'positions in life' (and thus *pleases*).

This law at the same time interests the individual personally, because it is the organization of his personal desires; yet so organizes them, as to convert them into activities. These activities so absorbed in their objects, that the subject has no separate consciousness of their relation, to him, as pleasant. He has no time to consider whether he is pleased or not, and thus practically delivered from 'false abstraction of passivity from activity'.

A 'position in society' is, in more modern language, a social role. If we consider the actions done by individuals in a social system, then patterns of activity, regularities of behaviour, emerge. In terms of such patterns, individuals have a social status: they occupy a social role, that of parent, doctor, artist, teacher, businessman, or whatever. As social roles emerge from patterns of activity, so social institutions emerge from clusters of social roles: thus and minimally the institution of the family emerges from the social roles of mother, father, and child. Social roles support logically different transactions between individuals. I am a painter; I produce a canvas because I want to preserve the details of a dream. You buy a canvas because, though quite without aesthetic sensibility, you calculate that it will make a good investment. Our intentions, mine in producing the painting and yours in buying it, may be, and are in this example, altogether unrelated. Nor is there anything inherent in the role of a painter which leads to such transactions; social conditions are imaginable in which painters never sell their work. If, however, I am a sales assistant this is inherently a transactional role, and if this role connects us then our transactional intentions must exactly interrelate. I want to sell books, you want to buy one. So far as concerns our social roles, mine as sales assistant, yours as customer, this transaction exhausts our relationship. Nothing else connects us. But there is a further case. If I am an employer then my giving an instruction to you as a member of my staff presupposes a framework of relations between us. In that framework alone can my issuing an instruction and your responding to it be explained.

That is only a brief typology of social roles, very evidently not a full classification. For Green the special interest of social roles lies in the association between a social role and a practice. Roughly a practice is a rule-governed pattern of activity; a social role and a practice may readily appear, therefore, to be two perspectives on the same pattern of activity. More precisely a practice has the following logical structure. It is specifiable in terms of rules which are individually consistent and jointly coherent. The prescriptions contained in the rules must, for any 'practicable practice', match descriptions of the world; otherwise the practice is inapplicable. Finally the requirements of a practice must not exceed the conditions of moral responsibility outlined in 3.16. A 'practice' which paid no attention to what is possible for agents would be a contradiction. There could be no such rule-governed pattern of activity. So much, then, for the internal structure of a practice; the agent's relation to it plainly admits of two levels of competence at least: (i) when (say) as a house-decorator he is familiar enough with his practice to know some way or other in which to paint a room; and (ii) when, by contrast, he knows the correct way and can observe the most precise standards and procedures expected of a decorator. Finally, mastery of a practice does not necessarily involve the ability to formulate its rules and avow them explicitly.

From this modern language, back to Green. The MS 10A passage quoted above is not without its difficulties, even obscurities. No current philosopher is likely to accommodate lightly Green's talk of the ' "Ego" giving freely to itself in "manifold of desire" '. Previous discussions yield the necessary background, however. The broad picture is this. We have seen, from our account of reason, desire, and self-consciousness in Chapter 4, that the individual is able to propose to himself a 'plan of life' in which his desires are so organized over time as to produce 'an abiding satisfaction of an abiding self'. For present-day interest, suppose we take Green's suggestion to be that for 'the objective social world' of (say) late twentieth-century industrial society, social institutions are capable of patterning the individual's desires in just such a lifeplan. A career, a social role, 'is the organization of his personal desires; yet (it) so organizes them, as to convert them into activities'.

If these suggestions secure the possibility of a link between social roles and self-realization, how does morality enter the scene? How can there be a morality of social roles which respects that link? Before we left Green's minimal argument I said that its morality of identification and benevolence is inadequate to the full scope of the moral life; I added that MAA aims to encompass the virtue of justice. It is on the connections between social roles, morality, and justice that I want now to concentrate.

7.6 SOCIAL ROLES, MORALITY AND JUSTICE

Justice, we said in 7.2, is a regard for the rights of others. It has traditionally two, but arguably three, aspects. Hence we may speak, with Aristotle, of distributive and rectificatory (corrective) justice (NE V.2) and, with Bergson, of absolute justice.[4] Distributive justice is the allocation of benefits and burdens according to a rule of proportionate equality: a rule not to treat all cases in the same way but to treat like cases equally, and to treat them according to their rights (rights deriving from merit, need, or whatever). Corrective or rectificatory justice aims to remedy some damage done to a person, some violation or disregard of a person's rights: as when a public figure is awarded 'damages' in court for defamation of character. Like damage requires equal correction; again justice is a matter of treating like cases equally. Absolute justice obtains when our dealings with a person respect the rights which belong to him simply as a human being. Bergsonian absolute justice proscribes slavery, for instance. It will recur briefly in 8.4.

Justice always observes a rule; and if we return to 7.5 we recall the association between a social role and a practice, where a practice is a rule-governed pattern of activity. On what conditions do the rules of a practice coincide with the requirements of justice? The main coincidence arises through something which we already know about justice, namely that whatever rule(s) we apply must be applied equally to similar cases. Justice, to repeat from above, is a matter of treating like cases equally. This is exactly, at first glance, what the rules of a practice require. John is a university administrator; one of his responsibilities is to sift graduate school applications. The conditions to be observed are these: applicants must have a first degree of a certain standard, must indicate clearly their prospective field of research, and must be willing to undertake undergraduate teaching. Or whatever: the immediate point is not what the conditions are, but how John observes them. If he sorts the applications impartially and puts forward all and only those which meet the conditions, then he does his job, he fulfils (this part of) the practice of a university administrator, and he

---

[4] H. Bergson, *The Two Sources of Morality and Religion*, tr. R. A. Audra and C. Brereton, London, 1935, 54–65.

fulfils the requirements of justice. He treats like cases equally; and we can start to generalize. If my neighbour and I see a solicitor about a shared nuisance, the solicitor invokes the same legislation, points out the same means of legal remedy, for both of us. If the same blood vessel supplying the brain becomes blocked in two patients, a doctor does not recommend surgery for one and coloured water for the other. There is no need to multiply examples. The essence of Green's argument is that a range of social roles are associated with practices which require equal treatment of like cases. A morality of justice is the outer casing of a social role.

Here, then, is a major link between social roles, morality, and justice; and a further connection can be drawn out as follows. Self-realization as Green understands it, with its requirement of a 'plan of life', presupposes a social background. The point is quite uncomplicated at this level. In the first place, the individual needs to call positively on the services of others to suggest or supply means of fulfilling his lifeplan. Secondly, he needs to be free from certain kind of interference; I cannot fulfil my lifeplan without protection from burglars, murderers, muggers, or even noisy neighbours. In so far as my lifeplan is informed by a morality of benevolence, on the minimal argument, or by a morality of justice, on MAA, the social roles on which I call as the indispensable background to my activities have this extra dimension of securing to me the possibility of a stable moral life. And so we have a social background which separates into the distinct roles of doctors, policemen, teachers, and the rest; a network of social roles which embodies a common good.

MAA is plainly reminiscent of Hegel's account of ethical life as fulfilled by the responsibilities of a role in the social life of a community. But the *ne plus ultra* of any parallelism here is that for Hegel the social system which organizes the lifeplan of the individual has a higher value, through its greater comprehensiveness and coherence, than the individuals whose lifeplans it organizes. For Green the human person is primary; and the Hegelian transcendence of the individual person as the ultimate unit of value is a point on which we know already that Green cannot follow Hegel (1.13). This point, rather than the comparatively minor disagreement specified by Sir Ernest

Barker on absolute monarchy and the possibility of an international morality,[5] separates Green impassably from Hegelian ethics.

7.7 GREEN, KANT, AND ROUSSEAU

If we are to set Green's MAA in an intellectual context, I think we should look not to Hegel but to Kant and Rousseau. The antecedents of Green's argument are traceable in Kant's idea of the kingdom of ends and in Rousseau's idea of the general will.[6] Integral to both ideas are the requirements of harmony and autonomy, of a non-conflictive social organization in which each person is a free decision-maker. Just so, Green's argument envisages a structure of human organization in which individual agents freely pursue social roles which fit their desires into coherent patterns and in which the lifeplans which thus emerge are non-conflictive between different persons. How far the manifold activities of a modern industrial society actually achieve the systematic coherence which this picture presents is another question. But it is plainly in so far as that ideal structure is approached that Green's argument, as an exercise in the sociology of morals, acquires plausibility.

Clearly this reliance on the coherence of actual social institutions separates Green from Kant and Rousseau. For Kant the kingdom of ends is 'admittedly only an Ideal', and we know from the *Contrat Social* that the general will operates solely under conditions of ideal direct democracy. Green's way of translating the general will from the ideal to the real world through the systematic coherence of actual social institutions does not, we recognize at once, ensnare him in the bizarre social psychology of a 'group mind'. Attempts have been made to analyse the notion of a general will, a will actually operative in society, not in terms (as in Rousseau) of a common object, namely 'the common interest . . . of individual desires' (*Contrat Social*, II.3: 'l'intérêt commun . . . volontés particulières), but in terms of a

---

⁵ E. Barker, *Political Thought in England*, London, 1915, 29.

⁶ On the cross connection of Kant's relation to Rousseau see E. Cassirer, *Rousseau, Kant and Goethe*, Princeton, 1963, esp. 1–25. Some of the less obvious implications of Kant's political image are unfolded in C. C. J. Webb, *Divine Personality and Human Life*, London, 1920, 127–8.

super-individual subject of desires, a social or group mind. This approach, represented by the work of Espinas, Durkheim, Wundt, and McDougall,[7] is a form of social organicism (6.7). No continuity holds between this and Green's own approach.

To cite the influence of Kant and Rousseau is not to deny that here as elsewhere Green takes what he will and isolates the ideas involved from the entanglements of surrounding doctrines. Thus in connection with the general will he is quite unsympathetic to that part of Rousseau's theory which concerns the legislator, or to Rousseau's proscription of partial associations within society; and he does not require that civic affairs be the principal concern of citizens. Equally, when Green speaks of persons as 'agents who are ends to themselves' (PE, § 190), he is not mistranslating Kant but underlining his own view of rational self-conscious agency. He is not invoking that specific network of Kantian ideas in which persons are ends in themselves through their dignity as universal moral legislators, but is rather stressing his own view that the rational self-conscious agent can conceive 'an ideal, unattained condition of himself, as an absolute end' (Works II, 350). He is addressing the fact, familiar enough by now, that such an agent can contemplate an altered state of himself, envisage changed patterns of desire, as an 'end' to be achieved.

7.8   CRITIQUE: (I)   THE UNCONDITIONAL GOOD

If the minimal argument and MAA represent Green's transition to morality, how adequately is that transition executed? Does Green really ground the moral life objectively? We face, I think, two tasks: we have first to measure Green's account of morality against the criteria of the true or unconditional human good. That must be done in order to check the internal consistency of his ethical theory. But we have secondly to satisfy ourselves that his account of morality itself survives criticism. Is Green's 'morality' of benevolence and justice adequate to the moral life? Said another way: if Green's account of 'morality' is objectively grounded, is what is thus grounded actually the moral life?

---

[7] See M. Ginsberg, 'The Theory of a Social or Group Mind', *Psychology of Society*, London, 1921, 46–69.

It is not to be expected that Green, who presents a dispersed account of the true or unconditional good, should organize a collected statement of how the moral life fulfils the criteria of the unconditional good. But from the minimal argument we can check the performance of the moral life against the five characteristics or criteria. I shall keep for now to the minimal argument, because I think the full resources of MAA will not emerge until we have considered, in 7.9–7.9.2, some criticisms of its adequacy to the moral life. The reader may then decide.

The first criterion of the unconditional good is, we saw, that it is an object of active pursuit; and Green exactly offers an account of the moral agent as pursuing 'such an end as provision for the maintenance of a family' (PE, § 242). The constructive element in the unconditional good, our second criterion, is closely linked. The end pursued by Green's rudimentary moral agent derives from a motive, something freely adopted. It represents 'an interest in an object which only thought constitutes, an interest in bringing about something that should be' (ibid.). I shall say something more about the constructive element in 7.16. The third criterion, by which we refer to the imperatival nature of the unconditional good, is easily embraced when we note that the moral agent may have 'the idea of what is good for him' (PE, § 179), in our example 'provision for the maintenance of a family', yet on any particular occasion 'the idea which he in fact seeks to realise in action' may not 'correspond to his conviction of what is truly good', since his 'desires and habits' are not fully attuned to it (PE, § 179). Hence the moral end of provision for a family is imperatival in face of contrary 'desires and habits'.

The non-exclusive, non-competitive aspect of the un-conditional good is equally unproblematic. For the agent's virtue, his elementary form of the good will, consists in his interest in seeking the permanent welfare of his family; he comes to see that welfare, it will be remembered, as including his family's reciprocation of that very interest. Precisely in this way the process, because reciprocal, is not exclusive or competitive. That my promotion of my family's interests may conflict with your promotion of your family's interests, as when we both seek to acquire the same new house, is purely contingent. There is nothing in this kind of *de facto* social identification which automatically and necessarily sets different agents at odds. The criteria of non-exclusivity and non-competitiveness are capable, moreover, of a certain development. The good will particularizes itself in the moral virtues. These virtues are non-exclusive, since whether or not the virtues compose a unity in such a way that I cannot have one without having all the rest (7.13), they are at least compossible. My having the virtue of courage does not present my having the virtue of justice in the way in which my having tough hands for weight-lifting prevents my having supple fingers for piano-playing. Equally and obviously, the virtues are non-competitive between different agents. My having the virtue of courage does not prevent anyone else from acquiring it. Fulfilment of the fifth criterion of the unconditional good follows automatically from the type of example we have considered: to identify with the interests of others is to recognize a common good.

7.9   CRITIQUE: (2) THE MORAL LIFE

Green's account of a structure of human organization, which rationally patterns the individual's desires through his social role and controls his activities through the requirements of a prac-tice, has a dual moral application. In the first place, social roles specify what is required of individuals in definite capacities; and, in turn, fulfilment of those requirements is just what is required of the individual as a moral agent in his social role. But secondly, if the individual's performance of his social role meets the requirements of morality, it also sustains, at least in part, the 'system of rights' (Works II, 335) necessary if other individuals are to pattern their desires rationally through the performance of their own social roles. The system of rights provides the conditions which 'render it possible for a man to be freely determined by the idea of a possible satisfaction of himself instead of being driven this way and that by external forces' (Works II, 338). Fundamental rights, by this criterion, are the rights of life, liberty, and property (Works II, 46–62). Green's contention is that, for each individual, the system of rights is respected if all other individuals fulfil the requirements of their social roles. (More will be said about rights in 7.9.2 and 8.9.) I can rationally organize my own life in terms of a lifeplan and a social role because other agents provide, at least in part, the conditions which enable me to do so.

This view of 'the institutions of civil life' (Works II, 338) as yielding 'positions in life' which define 'specific duties' and sustain 'a system of rights' supplies the clue, I think, to Green's initially baffling 'web of human action' passage in MS 15:

What is to be done?   question of art.
What is done?   question of science.

The two questions co-incide in morals, for that which ought to be done is that which *is* done . . . , though not consciously to those who do it. If one could place oneself outside the web of human action, its threads would be seen combining to one end and there would be no question of what ought to be. Being inside the web, this combination is invisible, and the end is to us not *being* realized, but what *ought to be* realized.

Green's point here, I suggest, is that if we view matters from the side of 'specific duties' and the 'system of rights', then we have a 'system of rights and obligations' (Works II, 335) which specifies 'that which ought to be done'; while from another angle, 'positions in life' specify 'that which is done', in so far as individuals actually do what is required of them (as moral agents) in their social roles. This switching of angles, so that apparently disconnected phenomena turn out to be different perspectives on the same thing, is a broad feature of Green's ethical theory and moral psychology. A social role is also a practice; a practice involves the equal treatment of like cases, and this is justice; and consider Green's agent under the fourth aspect of the multi-perspectival model. Recall Green's dictum (4.6) that 'the desires as organized by reason are (no) different from reason as organizing the desires'. This is offered from a neutral, analytical standpoint. But one way of interpreting the dictum would be to suggest a double viewpoint on the agent. As 'active', from a first-person viewpoint of deciding what to do, the agent desires to be a particular kind of person. As 'passive', from a third-person viewpoint in the explanation of action, the agent's specific objectives are intelligible only on condition of his having a certain conception, namely a self-conception relative to which he sees certain forms of activity as desirable.

Proper criticism of MAA, Green's morality of social roles (of my 'station' and its 'duties', PE, § 313), needs to recognize two points on which he is certainly not open to attack. First, Green's account involves no notion of an appointed station in life. *Prolegomena to Ethics* does not interleave with the Tudor *Book of Common Prayer*. The individual agent chooses his social role on Green's account; or more precisely, he chooses his role-set. Green is well aware of the different social roles which an individual may occupy concurrently. He sees a dimension of freedom in the double process of selection and combination. The second and related point is that, as Green is equally well aware, different values and priorities appeal to different agents. Green is quite free from the sort of bias which for example Aristotle has for a particular form of life. Aristotle is clear (NE X.7) that, though we need politicians and businessmen, the highest life is the theoretical. Green reserves no such supreme place for intellectual pursuits. His morality of social roles embodies different hierarchies, and (not the same thing) different realizations, of values (cf. 2.9).

*

7.9.1 The Morality of Social Roles: Three Criticisms

A morality of social roles may readily expect three criticisms. These I shall consider in 7.9.1; 7.9.2–3 will open up some larger issues and wider possibilities.

Then in this preliminary run the first criticism is that there is no à priori guarantee of coherence between social institutions, and every reason for thinking, a posteriori, that the coherence of actual social institutions is incomplete. To the extent to which social institutions fail to cohere, the prospects recede for realizing a coherent lifeplan through the fulfilment of social roles. The point is obvious and is implicitly admitted by Green himself when he invokes the state (8.9) to scrutinize the requirements of social roles. In Green's philosophy the morality of social roles occupies an intermediate level in a tripartite theory: (i) the individual seeks to organize his desires into the coherent structure of a lifeplan; (ii) this personal organization of desires is assisted by the system of social roles; and (iii) the state adjusts incoherencies in the system of social roles. Not that the potential incoherence of social institutions should be overplayed. Since the individual's 'position in society' on Green's account is not an appointed station, his role set is something which (within limits) he can select, and an internally coherent role set might still be possible even though the total set of social institutions is incoherent.

Problems remain, however. There is still a problem for the individual when he recognizes a discrepancy between 'the standard of social expectation' (PE, § 98) and his own understanding of the requirements of his social role. Equally, even if the individual agent's role set is internally coherent, performance by one agent of a social role may be impeded by the particular way in which (not his own role set but) related social roles are practised: as a social worker's concern for the elderly may be frustrated, e.g. by the low status of geriatric medicine. There is no blinking this last problem for a morality of social roles. On the previous problem Green might reply that the individual's moral freedom properly extends to his inter-pretation of his role: he must arrive at his own understanding of what his role requires in situations of social incoherence. For such situations, however, Green's bland assurance precisely fails: 'In fulfilling the duties which would be recognised as belonging to his station in life by any one who considered the matter dispassionately, . . . we can seldom go wrong; and when we have done this fully, there will seldom be much more that we can do' (PE, § 313).

The second likely criticism of a morality of social roles is that it relies on a view of social institutions as practices which define activities and standards—conventional modes of behaviour. We considered medical, legal, and some other examples in 7.6. There is a practice of medicine which defines (*inter alia*) the activity of being a doctor and specifies a standard of conduct ('medical ethics'). But is the practice of medicine quite clear-cut? Does it require a doctor to tell a patient that her headache has a 0.01 per cent chance of being brain cancer? If a doctor prescribes the contraceptive pill for an under-age girl, should he tell her parents? On such questions the practice of medicine turns misty. Nor when there is a firm social practice is there necessarily morality. That the simple following of rules does not make the relevant activity just is clear from the example of the aesthetic housebreaker: a burglar who selected only men with black hair and yellow eyes might be an interesting character, but he could scarcely be said to act justly and to respect the rights of others.

But the further consideration must be urged that not all social institutions embody practices in the way that MAA requires. Some social institutions are not practices but merely, in G. A. Cohen's phrase, 'the locus of practices'.[8] A business, or the private enterprise zone, is a social institution in this sense, but there is no specific mode of behaviour which is associated with a business career, and the expression 'business ethics' is usually ironic. And, for the matter of that, what standards unite the profession of journalism? By itself this is not decisive against the morality of social roles when we remember that Green operates with the notion of a role set: with no specific mode of behaviour associated with a particular role, the ranges of options defined by the different roles which the agent occupies may yet overlap. If role 1 defines options A, B, and C, role 2 options C, E, and F, and role 3 options C, G, and H, then the problem of a specific mode of behaviour is solved.[9] But the 'if' here is problematic and contingent. Green's argument remains of distinctly precarious application to social institutions which are not themselves practices.

The final criticism which I wish to consider stresses two types of moral risk associated with a morality of social roles. The first risk concerns the abnegation of responsibility which the performance of a social role may involve. This is the area of what John Benson has called 'the My Lai syndrome'. I am a soldier under orders and '(the) officer says "Shoot anything which moves", so it must be OK'.[10] This is a familiar problem in ethics, one which arises beyond the context purely of a morality of social roles. The most likely line of response on behalf of a position such as Green's is the following. The requirements of a social role are to be interpreted in the total context of, e.g.

---

[8] G. A. Cohen, review of J. P. Plamenatz, *Philosophical Quarterly*, 23 (1973), 93.

[9] M. Hollis, 'My Role and its Duties', *Nature and Conduct*, ed. R. S. Peters, London, 1975.

[10] J. Benson, 'Who is the Autonomous Man?', *Philosophy* 58 (1983), 11. See also Thomas Nagel's brilliant essay, 'Ruthlessness in Public Life', *Public and Private Morality*, ed. S. Hampshire, Cambridge, 1978.

military standards. So that, in our example, the disobedience of
orders is, in suitable circumstances, something which is
accommodated by military standards themselves. In other
words my social role as a soldier is *not* to obey orders in all
circumstances. Inbuilt into the role is a recognition that orders
are not always to be obeyed. From this point of view the My Lai
syndrome precisely identifies a case of not fulfilling the
requirements of a social role. Green would probably regard this
line of response as indicating a significant area of personal
responsibility, as emphasizing the 'conscientiousness' (PE,
§§ 297–309) which is necessary if we are to meet the
requirements of our social role 'fully' (PE, § 313). But it
appears, ethically, rather a case of the agent supporting his social
role than of the social role supporting the agent.

The second moral risk which is connected with a morality of
social roles concerns, not the moral sensitivity of the agent in
carrying out his social role, but that of others towards him in
virtue of his social role. This line of criticism is advanced by
Gabriel Marcel when he deplores the modern functionalization
of life in which the individual appears to others 'as an
agglomeration of functions'.[11] We think of the agent in terms of
his social role, say that of a bank clerk, a draughtsman, a
computer programmer. We categorize him in this way,
disregarding his individuality. Either everything he does is
'typical' of (say) a bank clerk; or if he acts untypically, voicing
opinions on religion or the arts, then such opinions may be
safely discounted since he is (only) a bank clerk. Equally, Jim
Morrison cannot have been a serious poet since he was (only) a
rock star. Marcel plainly feels keenly this harmful situation in
which individuality is disregarded: and his views are set partly
against F. H. Bradley, whose morality of 'my station and its
duties' is not wholly discrepant from Green's. Yet in fairness to
Green, this would seem rather to represent a particular way in
which the functionalization of life might go. If it were an
inseparable consequence of functionalization, this would clearly
be significant for Green's ethical theory. But I cannot see that
Marcel does more (at best) than to apostrophize a contingent
tendency of contemporary life.

---

[11] G. Marcel, *The Philosophy of Existence*, tr. M. Harari, London, 1948, 1.

7.9.2 *Facing the Good Society*

In major part the above criticisms rely on a contingent feature of Green's morality of social roles, his commitment to a sociology of morals. He believes that the existing organization of society supports such a morality; and this connection between ethics and sociology is not without its strengths, one of which is that Green's emphasis on social roles falls in very well with a distinct recent interest in just how far such roles extend. What are assumed to be natural categories can turn out to be social categories, social roles which are cast on us. Broadly speaking I sympathize with that view and with the sociology of gender to which it belongs: and in this connection Green's stress on roles is a useful analytical or heuristic device. What I want to suggest here, however, is that we should make a particular departure from the sociology of morals. For that sociology may well be regarded as an excess content in Green's ethical theory. More specifically, and without any serious departure from his views elsewhere, there is no reason why Green's morality of social roles has to be taken as an inaccurate description rather than as a normative ideal: no reason why it cannot be inverted to serve as a basis for criticizing the social order. From Green's standpoint, as we shall see in 8.4, nineteenth-century England hardly represented the ideal social condition. And in the meantime why forget his passion for radical ideas (1.4)? Green chose, in that portion of his ethical theory which we have just examined, to underline the moral potential of the existing social organization. Elsewhere he was an unsparing social critic. Both the morality of existing social roles and the moral criticism of existing society derive support from Green.

If we abandon our commitment to a particular sociology of morals, this works both ways of course. If on the one hand we abandon the moral endorsement of the existing network of social roles, we cannot on the other hand say a priori how far Green's ethical theory will impeach the existing social organization. For that we must simply look and see: so far there are no grounds for preference between Marx's 'revolutionary reconstitution of society at large' and Oakeshott's 'pursuit of intimations'. Green certainly does believe that we have a tolerably exact idea of 'the moral ideal', of the good will and its particularization in the moral virtues. The scope afforded to that ideal by existing social institutions is another matter entirely.

The main thrust of MAA is at those social roles for which, regardless of my personal involvements, all persons brought into contact with me are entitled to equal treatment. It is concerned, in Michael Ignatieff's phrase, with 'the needs of strangers'.[12] For, as Green himself says, 'With most men, as strangers, one can only deal on <a> footing of *right* (MS 15).

From the viewpoint of MAA, then, the ethical merit of social institutions is justice; a good society would at least be one in which every social role was associated with a single practice, and every practice respected the rights of those affected by it. (For any social role just one, and one just, practice.) What then is a 'right'? I cannot embrace this vast subject under all its facets; but I suggest the following view.[13] Central to the notion of a right is that of an interest; at the very least the rationale of a right is that it secures an individual's interest. Clearly, however, if rights depend on interests, they are not uniquely determined by them. It is certainly in my interest to enjoy absolute priority of advanced medical treatment whenever my health fails; that I have a right to this is by no means evident. What cuts any simple connection between rights and interests is, of course, that interests conflict. If I have absolute priority of advanced medical treatment then others' interests are postponed to mine. So we need a decision procedure to weigh the interests of individuals when interests conflict. As the different weights are determined, so rights emerge. We already have the requirement of justice that like cases are to be treated equally. Beyond this requirement, the good society would be one which secured the fundamental interests of individuals (hence their fundamental rights, already mentioned in 7.9), or which, under failure of social resources, never put the satisfaction of one individual's lesser interests before the satisfaction of another's fundamental interests.

One way of regarding an individual's fundamental interests, on Green's account, would be precisely in terms of a 'plan of life' with associated social roles which yield 'an abiding satisfaction of an abiding self'. The good society would

---

[12] Michael Ignatieff, *The Needs of Strangers*, London, 1984.
[13] This view is based primarily upon Margaret Holmgren, 'Raz on Rights', *Mind*, 94 (1985).

accordingly be one in which, to the extent of social resources, those fundamental interests were secured to each individual and in which no individual's lifeplan and associated social roles interfered with the like fundamental interests of others. Such a form of social organization would clearly represent a common good; and on this picture those respects in which 'provision for the maintenance of a family' satisfies the full criteria of the unconditional good (7.8) are readily translatable to the other, more 'public' social roles which an individual occupies. The good society bears of course only a problematic relation to present society. So has Green established the actual rationality of moral action or only (in respect to justice) its conditional rationality, given this form of social organization which we have sketched? At this point some compromise must be made with Green's sociology of morals. For that sociology does largely capture at least a cluster of existing social roles and practices: the practice of law, of medicine, of public administration. Green secures a real but limited rationality of moral action; and the limits of that rationality are not rigidly confined but capable of extension along the lines of the good society.

But what if someone should still decide, even in the good society, to 'ride the system', to maximize his individual best interest at the expense of others? The conceptual arm-lock is never far from the minds of moral philosophers, the move that will force the individual, on pain of total irrationality, to act morally. To any such individual as the immoral rider Green has a response, which I give in my own words: As a rational agent you should be moved by considerations, of the kind set out in Chapter 4, of 'self-satisfaction', of 'an abiding satisfaction of an abiding self'. This in fact represents your individual best interest. My ethical theory explains how you can achieve that satisfaction, the *summum bonum* for a rational human agent in all likely conditions for the future, through a social role which also respects the right of others. Anything missing from the morality of social roles or from the more limited morality of benevolence associated with it can be discounted as irrelevant to self-satisfaction. Go for it if you will, practise any variety of injustice, but none of this is necessary. Immorality is surplus to requirements. If my interpretation of Green is right, this is as good a response as any I know in ethics.

7.9.3 *Social Roles, Relativism, and Objective Duty*

Is a morality of social roles a version of relativism? Relativism here would be a view such as the following: that if one meets the requirements of one's social role(s), one necessarily fulfils the requirements of morality. As a representation of Green's view, that formulation is ambiguous. Morality does not shape itself to the contours of social roles. The boot is firmly on the other foot: social roles impose a requirement of morality, and the practices with which they are associated serve the interests of others. That at least is the ideal picture. But the match is not automatically exact. Practices can be more or less determinate; they are only more or less appropriate to follow even when they are determinate. The individual has a permanent obligation to adjust his personal practice to the exact circumstances of action, to see what his social role requires here and now and not to settle for the rough approximation of past practice to present needs. In other words, if one meets the requirements of one's social role, then one necessarily fulfils the requirements of morality, but those requirements embody the sharpest insight and fullest consideration of which the individual is capable: they are not, or not necessarily, the conventional directions of action which a practice is generally understood to involve. We shall return to this point in our examination of moral reasoning (7.16). Requirements are real demands, perhaps unobvious, possibly troublesome, not conventional expectations.

In so far, however, as the individual meets the requirements of his social role(s), an ethical theory such as Green's prevents the rifts of perspective from which distinctions between objective and subjective duty arise: rifts of the kind which we encountered in the discussion of utilitarianism (5.13). The concepts of a practice (7.5) is one which is capable in principle of binding motive and consequence so as to prevent the relevant discrepancy of viewpoints between agent and spectator. If an agent's practice secures the interests of those it is meant to serve, it also organizes the agent's desires and thus controls the motive on which he acts: a good practice is one which produces reliably good consequences, a good agent is one whose motive is set by a good practice. In directly ethical terms, rifts between objective and subjective duty,[14] discrepancies of viewpoint between spectator and agent, create questions such as the following.

An individual acts or fails to act. How then are we to judge him? By what his circumstances actually require or permit, given the real state of the world? Albert has angina pectoris. He suffers an acute heart attack and falls to the ground in great pain. What this situation 'objectively' requires (I guess) is that Bill should place Albert in a comfortable position and loosen his clothing. Given that he wants to help, this is the best thing that Bill could do for Albert. Unfortunately Bill is not medically knowledgeable; he shakes Albert violently and covers him with blankets. This really is what, 'subjectively', he believes Albert's situation to require. We might stretch subjectivity further: and so distinguish between what Bill's circumstances would require or permit, were they as he supposes them to be, and what he believes his circumstances to require or permit, given what he supposes them to be. (Anyone who has read *Moral Obligation* will know that Prichard was a master of these tricky paths.) Part of the attraction of a morality of social roles is that, through the requirements of a practice which the individual learns, it presses the subjective and objective sides of a situation together. Typically, for example, the above distinctions are redundant in assessing what a doctor does in the situation described. He knows what Albert's situation 'objectively' requires, and acts accordingly. Not everyone can have a doctor's knowledge: but can Bill even carry out his social role of father or friend if he treats a casualty in this disastrous way? Albert might be his son. The morality of social roles lets no one off lightly.

7.10 REVIEW (1)

It will be convenient to take stock of the topics and arguments examined so far.

Analytically this chapter divides into three parts, two of which are now complete. The first part defines the conceptual machinery for Green's transition to morality: (i) the double

---

[14] On this distinction see D. A. Rees, 'The Idea of Objective Duty', *Proceedings of the Aristotelian Society*, 52 (1951–2).

distinction of moral from non-moral and immoral action; (ii) the goal of self-satisfaction; and (iii) the criteria of the unconditional good on which self-satisfaction depends. Elements (i) and (ii), briefly indicated at starting, have been brought forward from Chapters 4 and 6 respectively. Green's distinction of moral from immoral action has been shown to be closely in line with current discussions of moral responsibility. Pivotal to the moral/immoral distinction is Green's notion of the good will. Pending full specification (7.14), this notion has at least been shown to be free from a 'logical embarrassment' to which Green is sensitive: that his theory of motivation (5.3) puts all motivation, moral or immoral, on a level. Given this conceptual machinery, the second part has taken us through Green's transition to morality.

In the second part, just completed, we have examined two arguments by which Green seeks to establish the rationality of moral action, given the conceptual machinery defined above. Of these the minimal argument takes its origin from *de facto* social identification very much in line with Hume's account of the natural virtues: from the involvement of a person with his family and friends. This has been shown to embody a rudimentary form of the moral life. It sets the key to a morality of benevolence. Clearly such social identification can structure a person's desires in an interest system of the kind which Chapter 4 described as a precondition of self-satisfaction and which Chapter 5 built into a 'narrow' conception of character. Green's more ambitious argument (MAA) envisages a network of social roles. A social role (or role set) also structures a person's desires and, by the requirements of a 'practice' with which it is associated, serves the interests of others. Respecting their rights, it sets the key to a morality of justice.

The third part, with which the remainder of the chapter will be taken up, is largely concerned with issues of moral psychology. Essentially Green's ethical theory comprises the theory of the unconditional good and two arguments for the rationality of moral action. In Chapters 4 and 5 we prepared the ground for that theory in Green's moral psychology. Now that we have the ethical theory, fresh aspects of Green's moral psychology emerge: his view of the ethical ultimacy of character (mentioned without explanation in 5.4), his account of the moral virtues, the full specification of the notion of the good will, and

Green's moral epistemology with its dual model of moral reasoning.

Green's morality of social roles suggests the idea of a coherent form of social organization in which each role is associated with a practice that respects the rights and serves the interests of individuals. The complete network of social roles provides the conditions in which the individual, all individuals, can achieve self-satisfaction through self-realization. Each individual's role organizes his own desires in a 'plan of life' and helps others to conceive and fulfil their own lifeplans, without any conscious reference necessarily on the part of the individual to serving a common good. The question naturally arises of how far this describes, or is meant to describe, present forms of social organization, how far it promotes an ideal form of social organization to which present forms approximate—at best. We have noted an ambiguity in Green's attitude here. The 'web of human action' passage in MS 15 is offset by Green's insistence elsewhere on the need for social reform. I have suggested that we can embrace both sides of the ambiguity. Green's morality of social roles describes those roles which are tightly defined by practices (e.g. legal roles); for the rest it can be held up as an ideal to be realized. To idealize the real or to realize an ideal: the elements for both interpretations are easily assembled. My own view is that the first interpretation is strongest when Green wants to stress that something is currently available to the individual who is deliberating in the way outlined in Chapter 4. The second interpretation looks best when Green is hunting the argument of a morality of social roles dispassionately and looking critically at present forms of social organization in the light of it.

One point before we move into the third part of the chapter. We have talked of a morality of benevolence and a morality of justice. It is easy to see the relationship between these moralities as benign and unproblematic. In those social roles to which my personal involvements (family ties and friendships) are irrelevant, all persons with whom I am brought into contact are entitled to equal treatment. That is their right; this is the sphere of justice. Beyond such roles lie other roles to which, by contrast, my personal involvements are acutely relevant. In these roles I consult, not people's rights but their total interests. My friend and I are both achingly hungry; justice indicates an equal division of the available food. But if I so identify with my friend's interests that I pass all the food to him, that is my business in a morality of benevolence. Aristotle, after all, goes so far as to hold that friends have no need of justice (NE VIII.I). Such examples do not fully illuminate the relation of justice to benevolence. For there definitely are circumstances in which, without justice, benevolence is simply an inadequate guide to conduct; also in which the promptings of benevolence simply conflict with the requirements of justice. On a historical note I surmise that these considerations, rather than the limited scope of benevolence, inform Butler's denial in the *Dissertation* that benevolence is 'the whole of virtue'.[15]

Suppose that a mother, a single parent in straitened circumstances, loves her two children equally. Problems might still arise which only recourse to considerations of distributive justice will solve. One child might greatly want to learn to sing, the other to learn to play the piano. If income will not stretch to cover instruction for both, then some way must be found of assessing the children's interests on a common scale. Benevolence lacks the complete resources to handle this type of problem; considerations of justice must be brought to bear. In a different example considerations of justice and benevolence pull apart. What if the university administrator of 7.6 comes upon an application from somebody with whom he is personally involved, somebody whose interests he is anxious to promote? By slipping a sub-standard application into the list of candidates accepted for interview he may act benevolently towards the person concerned. He hardly acts justly towards rejected, equally sub-standard candidates.

This point, that considerations of benevolence and justice can both intermingle and conflict, aims to remove any idea that they belong to sheerly separate moralities: that as we have examined two arguments, the minimal argument and MAA, so the morality of benevolence and the morality of justice revolve in totally distinct orbits. Green is committed to no such view; and I

[15] *Butler's Sermons and Dissertation on Virtue*, ed. W. R. Matthews, London, 1967, 253-5.

have been concerned here merely to erase any contrary impression created by my talking separately of the morality of benevolence and the morality of justice.

7.11   ETHICS AND CHARACTER

Just above I listed the ethical ultimacy of character as the first topic for the third part of the chapter. That topic may be introduced as follows. 7.9.3 ended with the point that the morality of social roles lets no one off lightly from what their situation 'objectively' requires. But what if, through unavoidable failure of knowledge, the objective and subjective sides of a situation come apart and the above distinctions apply? How then are we to judge the individual? Clearly in this connection there is only one thing of which moral judgement can take account, the individual's deciding to do what he believes his circumstances to require or permit, given what he supposes those circumstances to be. If we omit wilful ignorance of fact and carelessness of deliberation, how else can we ask or expect the individual to act? *Ex hypothesi* no other considerations are available to him to produce a different decision. This is not to say that if he decides to do what he believes his circumstances to require or permit, given what he supposes them to be, we have simply to go along with the outcome of that decision: that I ought never to inter- fere with someone's acting as (in the sense defined) he believes he may or ought. I cannot morally criticize his deciding to act as he does; but I can morally regret his decision. I can morally reject the state of affairs which his proposed action would bring about or support, because it would violate the rights of others. I can intervene decisively, with a clear conscience, to prevent his action.

Then the ethical ultimacy of character emerges in this way. Take any action: an individual is morally answerable only for his decision to do that action, or to refrain from doing it, under the conditions of moral responsibility. To decide to do an action is to adopt a certain desire, inclinational or intentional (4.8), as a motive (5.3); and motives, as we know, are a function of character. An agent acts from a motive; taken more deeply his action is the 'expression' of his character as it reacts upon and responds to particular circumstances (5.9). Since the motives available to an agent at any given time are fixed by the state of his character, and character is amenable to revision through self-intervention under the fourth aspect of the multi-perspectival model, so character is the final point of reference in the moral assessment of an individual. Moreover, the closer we bring together the objective and subjective sides of action in a morality of social roles, the less the moral assessment of the individual will diverge from the (objective) assessment of his actions. The door forced open by utilitarianism slowly closes: the gap disappears between motive and intention on the one hand, action and consequences on the other. None of this overrides the moral epistemology of 5.9, which implies the practical inaccessibility of character to moral judgement.

7.12 GREEN AND ARISTOTLE: THE PRACTICAL SYLLOGISM

Green's theory of character also brings him into collision with the Aristotelian model of practical reason as represented by the practical syllogism of NE VII.3. Very roughly this is a tripartite model involving (i) general principles relating to happiness or the good life (major premisses); (ii) particular descriptions of the world which are relevant to action under those general principles (minor premisses); (iii) decisions or intentions to act, or judgements that it would be appropriate to act, as major and minor premisses combine to suggest.[16] I have carefully skirted round one danger zone of Aristotelian interpretation, the issue whether minor premisses simply establish external means to ends, or whether the means they specify are capable of a more constitutive status. But if we immerse ourselves in Aristotelian exegesis we may never resurface; this issue is not relevant to Green's disagreement with Aristotle. Closer to the point is to see how the practical syllogism basically works:

> Major premiss: I need a job.
> Minor premiss: Here is a suitable vacancy.
> Conclusion: Decision or intention to apply for the job, or judgement that this would be a good thing to do.

[16] No commentary on one philosopher is to be trusted when it discusses another. See therefore W. F. R. Hardie, *Aristotle's Ethical Theory*, chs. 12–13, 2nd edn. Oxford, 1980; and D. J. Allan, *The Philosophy of Aristotle*, ch. 13, 2nd edn. Oxford, 1970.

Aristotle refers to three categories of case in which this kind of practical syllogism is available to the agent, but in which appropriate action fails to result: there is an information-based failure when the agent lacks some conscious realization of the situation he is in; there is compulsion or constraint which means that his action is not the outcome of his own decision, intention, or judgement; and there is *akrasia* in which the agent acts contrary to his better judgement. How is *akrasia* possible? Aristotle's chief suggestion is the idea of competing syllogisms. A person, say, is sick and knows that, in order to recover, he must not eat sweets. A sweet is placed before him. One syllogism runs as follows:

> Major premiss: I ought not to eat sweets.
> Minor premiss: X is a sweet.

The other syllogism accepts the minor premiss, but differs in its major:

> Major premiss: Sweets are pleasant.
> Minor premiss: X is a sweet.

Aristotle represents the *akrates* as overcome by his desire to eat something pleasant; that desire is so strong, the fact that sweets are pleasant occupies his imagination so vividly, that he follows the second syllogism, not the first. Green has a rather indecorous response to this explanation of *akrasia*. It is, he says, a 'dodge' (Platonis de Republica, 90).

The reason for Green's response takes us back to 5.4 and to the distinction between wide and narrow character. If *akrasia* is to be explained by reference to competing syllogisms, Green regards this as simply inviting the question how those syllogisms come to compete in this way, with that result, on the occasion of action. If the agent has a 'better judgement', if he holds some idea (in Green's language) of the requirements of 'abiding satisfaction', this opens up the narrow conception of character. But he stifles that judgement on the occasion of action, and it is his total character, his character on the wide conception, which really explains that result. The total state of his character is such that his 'better judgement' is not entrenched in a sufficiently dominant narrow character. That syllogisms compete, with a particular result, is the outcome to be elucidated; it explains nothing without character as the fundamental point of reference.

7.13 THE MORAL VIRTUES

Green's classification of the moral virtues is essentially that of Plato in *Republic* IV. In the classification of the virtues, though not in their full analysis, the achievement of Greek ethics 'was in fact final' (PE, § 252). No mention is made in PE of the full range of Aristotelian virtues in NE III–IV. The four virtues of *Republic* IV are: wisdom, courage, temperance, and justice. The virtue of benevolence, which plays a role in Green's minimal argument for the rationality of moral action, is seldom explicitly invoked by him. Two reasons can be offered for this apparently puzzling omission. First, Green does I think regard benevolence as a highly limited virtue operating only in rudimentary forms of the moral life: in the family, among friends, in Good Samaritan situations of obvious need. At one stage he was even disinclined to accept this kind of 'natural' involvement with others as 'moral'. MS 15 has a passage which contrasts 'moral' and 'natural' in exactly this way: 'relation of father to child . . . not moral. Moral opposite of natural.' The point here was the stress on the rights of others, which justice respects, as the 'basis of <a> moral relation' between persons. Typically a father does not feed his child because the child has a right to be fed; the child is fed because his father loves him. The second reason for Green's relative disregard of benevolence lies, I think, in the chequered and, in Green's view, confused debates of eighteenth-century British moral philosophy in which 'benevolence' was contrasted with 'self-love', and various problematic relations were explored between them (PE, §§ 225–7). The thrust of Green's account of morality in both the minimal and the more ambitious arguments is away from this contrastive idea of individual interests versus the interests of others. The term 'benevolence' is caught up, in Green's mind, with the unhappy associations of past ethical debates.

Exclude for now the virtue of wisdom. Green's dissatisfaction with the Greek analysis of the moral virtues, and his main notion of subsequent moral progress, concerns two points: the range of persons included in its application, and the requirements of behaviour included within its scope (PE, §§ 206, 218). Green argues, for instance, that the Greeks confined the application of morality to members of the *polis*, allowing its application to members of other *poleis* than one's own, but not to barbarians. To say this is not simply to make an easy point against the moral imagination of the Greeks. For in Greek terms virtue was related to function, a man's function as citizen, father, soldier, and function was defined by the social life of the *polis*. In the absence of a shared social life between Greeks and barbarians the practice of virtue was incoherent. Green's account of Greek ethics appeared wrong to the Cambridge philosopher, E. E. C. Jones, particularly with regard to the analysis of courage. Issue was joined with A. E. Taylor, who on this occasion (cf. 3.14) defended Green.[17] Green was essentially correct in holding that, as to range of persons, the moral life for the Greeks encompassed solely the Greek community. Also the virtue of courage was seen as having primarily if not purely military application (PE, § 259); and in our more expanded idea of courage we are surely right in seeing the objects of courage in broader than military terms. Yet Jones's criticisms should not be entirely disregarded. *Laches* and NE seem to confirm totally the primarily military connotation of the virtue of courage, but with respect to the *Republic* the picture is not so clear. While *andreia* has initially the usual military context, Plato's analysis tends distinctly towards the 'interiorization' of courage as a factor in moral development of the psyche which reinforces the rational element against the appetitive; it is thus increasingly detached from a predominantly military connotation. The relevance of this is the more acute since, as indicated above, it is on Plato that Green's account of Greek ethics principally relies.

Green further adopts the Greek conception of 'the essential unity between one form of virtue and another' (PE, § 252)—the familiar idea of the unity of the virtues. He offers little clarification of precisely how this idea is to be taken over (PE, §§ 253 ff.). My own view is that the unity of the virtues is a highly ambiguous matter which Green's examples do not really resolve. I am not clear, for instance, that Green would accept the provisional account which I gave of courage in 2.4.2 where I said that courage is the ability to pursue projects in the face of unpleasant obstacles. This account means that courage can be used to promote any projects that we happen to have. On the

---

[17] E. E. C. Jones, 'Green's Account of Aristotle's Ethics', *Hibbert Journal*, 1 (1903); and A. E. Taylor, Review of Sidgwick, The Ethics of T. H. Green, *Hibbert Journal*, ibid.

Aristotelian view, by contrast, my approach simply makes courage a variety of *enkratia*, of strength of will. To make it a virtue Aristotle requires us to build into it a notion of the right sort of project. So one might take a modern example and say that your terrorist cannot, but my freedom fighter can, display courage. The problem is that Green's examples of courage are designed merely to show up, against Aristotle (here his chief stalking-horse), the inadequacy of confining courage to the activities of the 'citizen-soldier' (PE, § 259). 'The Quaker philanthropist', he insists, can equally display courage, or 'fortitude' as he actually calls it, if we 'trace the identity of principle' (ibid.) through different cases. Green does not supply an example of courage used for ends of which he would disapprove; and the problem is to know whether he is influenced in this by the kind of Aristotelian thinking just explained.[18]

Minimally the unity of the virtues must mean that the effective exercise of one virtue can always be defeated if we lack another. This even applies to courage: if I lack temperance or self-control then in particular circumstances my susceptibility to pleasure may undermine my ability to pursue projects in the face of unpleasant obstacles. The same holds good for the other-regarding virtues of justice and benevolence. I cannot satisfy the requirements of those virtues if I am deterred by the least frown of opposition, let alone active interference, from other agents. In those circumstances, without courage my justice or benevolence is nugatory. Green at least accepts this. He is not preoccupied with the above problem of the mutual detachability of the virtues; his aim is not to see how far the virtues can be separated but to consolidate them in a 'plan of life'. To such a plan, on the minimal and more ambitious arguments, no virtue is irrelevant. Morality is the absolute framework on which a social role is built.

The Platonic virtues of courage, temperance, and justice fit readily into Green's ethical theory, but what of the virtue of wisdom? Has the bleakly cognitive any proper place in ethics? The most illuminating approach to this question is through the fourth aspect of Green's multi-perspectival model of deliberation. Under that aspect Green's agent has high-level knowledge, a broad-brush view, of what he is doing. He has a

---

[18] This paragraph responds to some comments put to me by Michael Inwood.

self-conception in the light of which he has fashioned and continues to evolve particular structures of desire. The model is underpinned by Green's theory of the unconditional human good which defines the constraints on what can actually produce 'an abiding satisfaction of an abiding self'. The moralities of benevolence and justice are corollaries, in Green's view, of precisely those constraints. This conception of morality embodies the 'wisdom', here to call it so, of adjustment 'to the law which determines where ... self-satisfaction is to be found' (Works II, 308; HM, 228).

7.14 THE GOOD WILL

Green's account of the good will is *prima facie* brief and troubled. Part of the trouble is of Green's own making. When he refers to 'the logical embarrassment *attending the definition of a moral ideal*' (PE, § 194), i.e. the definition of the good will, we appear to be caught in a hopeless interlock between the good will and the unconditional good. Only the good will is unconditionally good and, the logical circle from which H. D. Lewis will not let Green escape, the only unconditional good is the good will.[19] Green appears to have cornered himself in a vacuous ethical paradox; and this is no light matter since the notion of the good will is supposedly central to ethics (7.2). Green, who is so sharp to dispel the errors of other philosophers, seems himself to have ultimately nothing to say. Or so the critical suggestion runs. It is easy to refute.

For the quick answer is surely that the good will encompasses the whole of moral virtue; and the moral virtues are the outer casing of social roles. The good will is as specific as the requirements of such roles. Under a morality of benevolence, if I provide for the maintenance of a family, this is how the good will manifests itself in my relations with them. Under a morality of justice, if I sort applications impartially as an administrator, this is how the good will manifests itself in my relations with applicants. What we cannot do is to specify in detail what my social roles will require: no ethical theory can halt the free flow

[19] H. D. Lewis, 'Does the Good Will Define its Own Content? A Study of Green's Prolegomena', *Ethics*, 57 (1948).

of the imprevisible. It can require only that we be prepared for what we cannot foresee.[20]

To do justice to Green, however, we have no cause to endorse his own criticism of Kant. On Green's account the good will is quite empty on its Kantian construction. This interpretation of Kant is neither unfamiliar nor cogent; it was not even new in Green's day. Green subscribes to a standard misinterpretation of the categorical imperative. In Kant's ethics the good will and the categorical imperative are closely linked notions. The categorical imperative supplies a formal test of the good will, since the good will wills only what can be, on the prescription of the categorical imperative, universal law for all rational beings. But of course indefinitely many things, if not quite everything, could be universal law for all rational beings. So the categorical imperative, in this formulation at least, is dismissed as empty, alternatively as a blank cheque. As a practical rule of conduct it prescribes nothing in particular that we should do and so renders vacuous the related notion of the good will. Hence Green's comment on Kant's 'leaving the idea of duty a mere empty abstraction, an idea of nothing in particular to be done' (Works II, 154). The correct reply to this is that the categorical imperative derives its content from maxims already presupposed. 'Act on that maxim etc.', as Kant continually insists. Kant assumes that the agent will already have various inclinations and susceptibilities, those subjective principles of action which the term 'maxim' identifies, to which the test of universalizability may then be applied. The problem of vacuity cannot arise if we attend carefully to the role of maxims inbuilt into Kant's account of the categorical imperative.

7.15 ETHICS AND PERFECTION

But Green's notion of the good will is not yet free from attack. At this point I take up Sidgwick's criticism from 6.1. Sidgwick

[20] Since this distinction is apt to encounter resistance, a non-ethical example may help. Lucien, a dedicated office worker, is impeccably efficient; his correspondence is filed in exact chronological order. He does not know, cannot foresee, that the office manager will ask next Tuesday at 17.00 hours for copies of every letter which Lucien received on 27 March 1987. But Lucien is prepared for this request, so organized that he can easily deal with it.

aims to drive a wedge, to force a discrepancy, between a wider and a narrower conception of the true or unconditional human good in Green. In Sidgwick's view the wider conception emerges when Green stresses the link between the true good and self-satisfaction. The corresponding state of the person is that of what Sidgwick calls 'Culture', complete self-realization or, a term which Green sometimes bravely uses, 'perfection'. But, Sidgwick continues, when Green stresses the non-competitive nature of the unconditional good, then the narrower conception comes into play on which the unconditional good is restricted to virtue or the good will.[21] Ann Cacoullos credits Sidgwick with being 'the first critic to note' this discrepancy;[22] I should be glad to be the last to handle it.

There is no discrepancy in Green. There is simply the slow roll of argument between Chapters 4 and 7 of the present book. The upper limit of self-realization (Chapter 4) is 'perfection', a structure of desire which defines a 'narrow' conception of character (Chapter 5), fulfils the criteria of the unconditional human good (Chapter 6), and is encapsulated in a person's social roles (Chapter 7). To meet the requirements of one's social roles is to practise a morality of benevolence (minimal argument) and a morality of justice (MAA). To talk of a person's morality is, on Green's account, to illuminate the outline of his social roles where his actions affect the interests of other people. As a direction of argument this is perfectly clear and consistent; its adequacy of execution is a separate matter on which different views will be taken. In brief there is nothing of philosophical substance to support Sidgwick's criticism.

Sidgwick was a far clearer and more exact writer than Green; and he applied his own standards of exposition to Green's work. In some respects Green resembles Locke; a coarse veil of presentation obscures a rich suggestiveness of view. Sidgwick, transparently honest intellectually but ever inclined to read real differences of view in slight variations of language, was the last person to do proper justice to Green.

Along the lines of 'perfection' one might, however, have a different worry about Green's ethics. How, the objection might be urged, can the moral life sustain self-realization at the upper

---

[21] H. Sidgwick, *The Ethics of T. H. Green*, 61–71.
[22] A. Cacoullos, *Thomas Hill Green*, 63.

limit of 'perfection' when moral experience is inherently defective? History first, then analysis.

Green's insistence on the coherence of moral experience is a point of separation between his philosophy and the subsequent tradition of British Idealism as represented by Bradley, Bosanquet, de Burgh, Collingwood, and Oakeshott. Green alone, among the British Idealists, attempted to construct a fully developed ethical theory on a metaphysical basis. Bradley's *Ethical Studies* (1876) is of comparable scope to PE in its treatment of the principal topics of moral philosophy. But Bradley explicitly declines in *Ethical Studies* to examine the metaphysical basis of ethics; and when in *Appearance and Reality* (1893) he undertakes a systematic metaphysical investigation, the result is a wholesale rejection of the conceptual scheme on which the moral life and every other department of common experience rests. Moreover, even in *Ethical Studies* Bradley is finally sceptical of the coherence of moral experience, suggesting in his 'Concluding Remarks' that 'Morality is an endless process, and therefore a self-contradiction.'[23]

Two lines of thought about morality are discernible in British Idealism. In the first place, writers such as de Burgh and Oakeshott hold that moral experience is paradoxical, inconsistent.[24] Thus de Burgh says of the moral agent:

If he rests satisfied with his code, doing 'the best he can' within its limits, oblivious of the claims of the standard of perfection, he falls into a complacent formalism, and his morality is revealed as immorality. If, on the other hand, he realizes the implication of perfection, he is shattered by the crushing burden of the contrast between the demand of the moral law and his utter inability to accomplish it .[25]

But secondly, a different line of thought, represented for example by Bosanquet, holds that the moral life is a defective form of experience because other forms of experience can cancel the need for it.[26] The idea is scarcely novel. Think back to Aristotle's view in 7.10 that friends have no need of justice,

[23] F. H. Bradley, *Ethical Studies*, 2nd edn. Oxford, 1927, 313.
[24] M. J. Oakeshott, *Experience and its Modes*: vi. 3, Cambridge, 1933. For de Burgh, see below.
[25] W. G. de Burgh, 'Right and Good: The Contradiction of Morality', *Journal of Philosophical Studies*, 5 (1930), 584.
[26] B. Bosanquet, *The Value and Destiny of the Individual*, London, 1913, *passim*.

though in Aristotle the idea has no religious background. The view which Bosanquet stresses is that morality is applicable only where human life is impoverished: love, friendship, and religious experience may 'transcend' morality since moral experience is confined to 'the world of claims and counter-claims', the world of sharply sundered individuals each keenly conscious of his rights against others.

I cannot see that Green's account of morality creases along these lines of thought. De Burgh's criticism of moral experience seems to rely on an ethics of merit: on the idea that however well a person acts he might have done better, and however well he has acted in the past there may be demerit in his next action. The moral life fractures across individual actions, separately assessed. But Green's is an ethics of virtue in which what de Burgh calls 'the demand of the moral law' is carried by the requirements of a person's 'plan of life' in social roles which there can be real satisfaction across time in fulfilling. On the other hand, when we look at Green's dual model of moral reasoning we shall see that it allows no place for 'a complacent formalism'. Against Bosanquet the point should be clear that Green accommodates love and friendship within morality; these are exactly the phenomena on which his minimal argument turns. Bosanquet's critique of morality may have some weight against Kant, whose ethical theory expressly excludes such phenomena, but not against Green. In sum, just as Chapter 3 freed Green's ethical theory from theological dependence (3.14), so the present argument preserves it from religious transcendence.

7.16 MORAL EPISTEMOLOGY

We have now descended a long slide of concepts: *de facto* social identification, social roles, practices, the moral virtues, the good will. Practical reason faces the question 'what should I do?' Any moral philosophy owes us an account of how the agent is to know or decide the answer to this question. And so we are led into Green's moral epistemology and into his account of moral reasoning.

Two aspects of Green's moral epistemology need to be considered, negative and positive. Negatively, what does Green reject? Certainly he rejects Plato's approach which grounds moral knowledge and decision-making on the philosopher's apprehension of transcendent Forms. (There is more to Plato than this, of course: particularly his use of the concepts of *harmonia* and *metron*, harmony and measure (Rep. I and IV), to bring the philosopher's vision into contact with the requirements of particular circumstances of action.) Green's relation to Aristotle is more complex, but we have noted Green's reservations about the practical syllogism, the central concept of Aristotle's theory of practical reason. In British moral philosophy Green cannot accept Butler's view of conscience as the voice of God (Sermon 2), infallible in its guidance on particular decisions except when its light is obstructed by 'superstition' (religious error, Sermon 3). For Green this view depends on a crude division of the mind into faculties; we have seen in Chapter 4 the resistance of his own moral psychology to the faculty approach.[27] Hume, of course, believed that 'Morality . . . is more properly felt than judg'd of' (T470). A particular 'moral sentiment' arises through 'sympathy' in particular types of situation. Any concept of moral reasoning is invalid because the root concept of practical reason itself is false. In Chapter 4 we heard Green's appeal against Hume's denial that reason can be practical. Bentham is completely beyond the pale. He bases moral decision-making on the calculation of pleasure and pain. We already have Green's exclusion of pleasure from the true or unconditional human good (6.9). J. S. Mill is more interesting to Green.

In *Utilitarianism*, Chapter 1, Mill introduces a broad distinction between two types of moral philosophy: intuitive and inductive. He associates himself, and the utilitarian school generally, with inductive ethics, and seeks to ground moral obligation on 'observation and experience'. For intuitionist ethics, 'the principles of morals are evident à priori' in the intellectual apprehension of moral truths. Mill takes a supposedly universal desire for happiness as the inductive basis for the utilitarian 'principle of utility'. This principle is applied

---

[27]   For Green's main discussion of Butler, see Works III, 98 ff.

to particular cases by recourse to 'corollaries from the principle of utility', secondary principles which embody common experience of 'the tendencies of actions' (Chapter 2).

Green denies this dissociation of utilitarianism from intuitionism. His attack comes in MS 15:

> False antithesis between Intuitionism and Utilitarianism, as if Utilitarianism judged of action by reasoning of its results, Intuitionism by immediate feeling. Judge action by results—all agree question is as to source of that general conception of an end with reference to which we judge of results. According to every possible school, the ultimate ground of this idea must be intuitive, in sense of not being deduced or inferred. Question is whether it is *feeling of pleasure*, or whether a *formative universal idea*. According to Utilitarianism proper, it is former: and hence they are the people who make morality depend on feeling in opposition to *rationalists*.

Green's point is clearly that utilitarianism assumes the ultimate desirability of happiness, construed in terms of pleasure (taken crudely by Bentham as introspectible, discrete items of feeling, more sophisticatedly by Mill). Since that assumption cannot be deduced or inferred from anything else, the ultimate desirability of happiness figures as an intuitive element in utilitarianism. For Green himself the ultimate desirability of 'an abiding satisfaction of an abiding self' is equally non-deducible, although Green would claim that it is encased in a more adequate moral psychology (Chapters 4 and 5) and philosophy of value (Chapter 6) than anything to be found in utilitarianism.[28]

---

[28] For idealism there are, of course, larger issues in the distinction between intuitive and discursive thought. Strictly taken, intuition involves self-evidence or simple apprehension distinct from any process of analysis or synthesis of the kind on which discursive thought relies; but the possibility of simple apprehension as owing nothing to 'the workmanship of the mind' (3.9) is problematic on any idealist theory of mind. Further discussion of these issues would take us too far afield. See G. R. G. Mure, *Idealist Epilogue*, Oxford, 1978, 3–13; and E. I. Watkin, *A Philosophy of Form*, London, 1935, 140. As far as concerns the present difference between Green and Mill, a looser sense of 'intuition' is applicable: one in which intuition involves the acceptance of something which is (taken to be) incapable of proof. For the later history of nineteenth-century ethics Mill's separation of utilitarianism from 'intuitionism' (in this looser sense) fails to hold good for Sidgwick: *Methods of Ethics* relies on an intuition of pleasure as the sole good, an intuition of rightness in the promotion of that good, and the intuition of a principle of fairness in the distribution of pleasure. On Sidgwick, see G. E. Moore, *Principia Ethica*, Cambridge, 1903, 59.

Lastly in this negative historical conspectus we may turn to Kant, whose moral epistemology hardly fits into Mill's intuitionist/inductivist distinction. Moral judgement is imperatival from the requirements of practical reason. Practical reason imposes a constraint of universalizability on decision-making; very roughly if we observe the principle of universalizability we act morally. Kant appears to think that moral decision-making under the principle of universalizability is perfectly straightforward and uncomplicated. He says in the *Critique of Practical Reason*: 'What is required in accordance with the principle of autonomy of choice is easily and without hesitation seen by the commonest intelligence. . . . That is to say, what duty is, is plain of itself to everyone.'[29] Choice is autonomous when it follows reason; to follow reason in ethics we have simply to apply the principle of universalizability. The application of this principle to any proposed action is an easy matter which removes distractions of moral view, as one might deftly pull down a blind over a window. In our earlier language the principle of universalizability applies a dominant description (2.10).

Green's response to this part of Kant's moral epistemology is already available to us; the principle of universalizability yields categorical imperatives, and the categorical imperative is 'a mere empty abstraction' (7.14). That response is, I think, completely wrong. If we cut deeper, however, we can open up some of the complexities that are involved in Green's own moral epistemology. For Kant's is an ethics of formulas; that action is morally permissible which fulfils a certain description supplied by the principle of universalizability. It is, as such matters are crudely expressed, a rule morality. We need to look closer at the notion of a moral rule. Positively, the text for Green's moral epistemology is this: 'To question, what is Duty, man does not discover, but constructs answer. A Problem, not a Theorem. A Problem of which <the> construction is never complete' (MS 15). The remainder of the chapter may be seen as a commentary on that view.

---

[29] *Critique of Practical Reason*, tr. L. W. Beck, Indianapolis, 1956, 38. See Walter McDonald's discussion, 'Ethics-Made-Easy', in *The Principles of Moral Science*, Dublin, 1903, 38–41.

7.17 MORAL RULES

One way of classifying ethical theories is in terms of their attitude to moral rules: claims are made for or against the idea that 'morality is a matter of rules'. But quite different, and interestingly deep, views about the nature of morality are crudely clustered if we argue at this level of generality. In the rejection of rule morality, for instance, is the claim (*a*) that rules have no part in morality, in moral action, or are we dealing with the lesser claim (*b*) that morality cannot be wholly a matter of following rules? In the defence of rule morality, is the claim (*c*) that morality is wholly a matter of following rules, or are we to deal with the lesser claim (*d*) that it is primarily a matter of following rules? Claims (*a*) and (*b*) are not the same; nor are claims (*c*) and (*d*); and nor, across the divide of rejection and defence, are claims (*b*) and (*d*) necessarily inconsistent. Nor, finally, is the debate on rule morality greatly marked by referential convergence; it is far from the case that all discussants intend the same thing by 'moral rules'.

There is, however, a more consensual logic of rules; a wider agreement, aside from their role specifically in morality, on certain features of rules as such. A rule is (at least understood or intended to be) something which can be followed. Said another way, part of the concept of a rule is that a rule can function as a guide to action. Connectedly, acceptance of a rule can provide a reason for action. Again, a rule has generality. If it applies to one situation then it applies to any other situation relevantly similar; if a rule gives me a reason for acting in a particular way in one situation then it gives me an equal reason for acting in the same way in a relevantly similar situation. Besides that, part of the concept of a rule is that it must be a determinate matter, at least in a range of cases, whether the rule has been fulfilled or broken. Lastly, in this preliminary look, a rule must be formulable in principle. Even if the rule which somebody follows is too complicated, in relying for instance on perceptual discrimination, for him actually to formulate, a formula is possible by which that rule can be captured. These are not the only conceptual truths about rules; I do not claim that just anybody must accept them as conceptual truths; I do not claim that they introduce matters in more than an approximative way. But they offer a first picture to serve as a background to the discussion of moral rules.

In the light of that background we can see already that some of the standard complaints against rule morality are unfounded or rest on assumptions which, as such, a rule conception of morality need not make. Consider Robert Nozick's view that 'There is no reason to assume that all the modulations of responsiveness can be captured by stable moral principles of a complexity we can manage.'[30] If this is taken to be a criticism of rule morality, the response is clear. Rule morality does not require us actually to manage the statement, the formulation, of a moral rule: only that there be a moral rule which we can follow. Or consider the view that moral rules prescribe or forbid definite detailed actions: always to give up one's seat to an elderly person on a train, never to kiss on a first date unless one intends a serious relationship. A rule morality may descend to this level of detailed surveillance of the moral life. But there is no conceptual necessity for it to do so. A moral rule may be defined at the level of saying, for example, that promises should be kept. Consider finally the view that, in descending to the level of definite detail of the train and first-date sort, a rule morality seeks to determine every action. For sheer stylish mordancy this view has never been better stated than by Bradley in *Principles of Logic*:

But I would not grudge Casuistry a Christian burial . . . And, if I am to say what I think, I must express my conviction that it is not only the Catholic priest, but it also is our Utilitarian moralist, who embraces the delusion which has borne such a progeny. If you believe, as our Utilitarian believes, that the philosopher should know the reason why each action is to be judged moral or immoral; if you believe that he at least should guide his action reflectively by an ethical code, which provides an universal rule and canon for every possible case, and should enlighten his more uninitiated fellows, then it seems to me you have wedded the mistake from which this offensive offspring has issued.[31]

But only on condition, and on a certain reading of the condition, that 'each action is to be judged moral or immoral' does this onslaught succeed. A rule moralist does not necessarily

---

[30] R. Nozick, *Philosophical Explanations*, Oxford, 1981, 471.

[31] F. H. Bradley, *The Principles of Logic*, ii, 2nd edn. Oxford, 1922, 269.

believe, even if he descends to the level of definite detail of the train and first-date examples, that every possible action is either morally required or morally forbidden: that each such action is 'moral or immoral' in the sense which excludes a category of neutral actions which are merely permissible. The rule moralist must have 'an universal rule' to determine 'every possible case' only if every possible action is to be determined as morally required or morally forbidden. I think Bradley makes a fair reading, in this respect at least, of nineteenth-century act utilitarianism. But to anathematize casuistry is not to excommunicate the rule moralist as such.

For the present discussion I shall take 'moral rule' in a special way. I shall regard as a moral rule any unconditional requirement on the action of a moral agent: not in the sense in which the good will is such a requirement, but in the sense which requires a particular action to be done (or omitted). The function of a moral rule is to determine conduct; it displaces other considerations and applies without exception. 'Tell the truth', 'pay your debts', 'keep your promises'. If one rule, as formulated, conflicts with another, then either (*a*) both rules require supplementation by a third and 'higher' rule which fixes their relative priority, or (*b*) one or other rule must be reformulated to limit its application so as to avoid the conflict. By using 'moral rule' in this comprehensive way, I shall neglect such distinctions of level as were illustratively sketched in 3.13 under 'moral principle', 'moral rule', 'moral precept'. Taking moral rule thus widely I shall argue that Green rejects a rule morality, but that normative statements such as, and especially, 'tell the truth', the requirement of veracity, figure extremely strongly as moral presumptions.

7.18   ACTION, VIRTUE, AND CHARACTER

We can, however, easily mistake the exact import of certain passages in which Green reduces the place of rules in the moral life. He holds, for instance, that 'there are no intellectual formulae of which the adoption will serve as a substitute for discipline of character' (PE, § 208). But I take his point here to be that there is more reliability in action from habit than in action from mere intellectual assent to an explicitly formulated rule. In this sense character grounds the moral virtues. Take a contrast: virtue is not merit. Merit is acquired by a person through the actions he does; it is a person's moral curriculum vitae. But regularity of performance is no sure evidence of habit (5.4) and no guarantee for the future. Virtue, on the contrary, is a habit of acting morally well; and habit is an element of character. Here I understand Green to be making this point: not to be saying, even if he believes, that character is situationally more flexible and responsive than such rules, which may prove inadequate to situations radically different from those in which they were formulated. He does recognize the latter problem, first when he remarks on 'the relativity of . . . general rules of conduct' which, as formulated, 'admit of exceptions according to circumstances' (PE, § 314), and secondly when he observes that 'New circumstances do arise which no given rule will fit' (MS 15).

But this problem is less significant than it might appear. On Green's account, rules such as 'tell the truth' are fundamental to morality, but not as rules: rather as moral presumptions. That it may be morally right to lie to an unstable patient about the condition of his health is nothing against such presumptions. It is a complete mistake, from Green's viewpoint, to see the formulation of moral rules as a process of perpetual incremental refinement. Only refine, the idea might be, keep changing the formulation of a rule, and we can sensitize it to the requirements of a greater range of circumstances. No, says Green: to regard an unqualified 'tell the truth', for example, as inadequate to the real complexities of action is to miss the force of a moral presumption. The matter can be approached as follows.

Take Green's agent as he moves cognitively about the world. He has a 'plan of life' which he is carrying out. He identifies with the interests of at least some other people, his family and friends, whose interests he aims to advance. He occupies a social role; he wishes to increase his mastery of the associated practice. Like the rest of us he needs to organize his time and resources; to estimate the future and to make risk decisions; to influence and convince; to understand other people; to realize his own strengths and weaknesses; to generate ideas that have some change of relevance to the problems they address. These preoccupations define his interests. None of these interests is typically served, Green argues, if we are unveracious to him.

Veracity has two aspects: a positive telling of the truth, and a negative forbearance from lying. Crudely, if the agent is planning to act in the world he needs to know how the world is. Typically, either sort of unveracity towards him so far impedes his effectiveness if he is taken in by it. If we lie to an agent or (say, by equivocation) withhold from him materially relevant portions of the truth, Green's view is that this is typically harmful to the agent's interests and is typically meant to be so. 'Typically', 'normally', or as Green says 'ordinarily' (PE, § 315), these are the keywords here. There is a moral presumption against unveracity; and the rationale of that presumption is quite secure from the urge to write in qualifications to 'truth-telling' as a guide to action. It may be right, Green allows, to lie on a particular occasion. We shall see shortly how a decision to lie might be validly derived. (But in a quick example, perhaps an agent is caught in a paradox of achievement: he can only achieve one result if he falsely believes, and is encouraged in the belief, that he can achieve another. Guy would write nothing if he did not believe that he would write a great novel. His talents do not stretch so far; he actually produces an extremely competent piece of work. His friends may well be right to lie to him about his abilities so that he does at least do justice to the talents he has.) But unveracity is presumptively immoral; and a decision to lie requires the utmost caution in the making of it. Green believes, moreover, that a similar rationale supports such requirements as 'pay your debts', 'keep your promises'. Remember from 7.2 that Green does not see himself as a moral innovator on the Spinozistic model.

Allied to this is a further point. Without such markers as 'tell the truth' and so on, the various moral virtues are completely unspecific. Consider the following passage in which Green examines a problem in the relation of character to action:

... action expression of character. 'Morally good', designation of *character*, but this character does not exist at all unless it shows itself in corresponding acts. Through these alone can any man know even of himself whether his character is morally good or not. It follows that there must be some test of action<s>, other than their relation to character. If we can only say good character is there when it issues in corresponding actions, and can say no more of these actions than that they *do* correspond to morally good character, then we are none the forwarder.—(MS 12, Lectures on the Moral Philosophy of Hume and Kant.)

I interpret the passage as follows. 'Tell the truth', 'pay your debts', 'keep your promises', and the rest—these presumptive requirements relate to actions. Suppose we set presumptions and actions aside and concentrate instead on character. Then take any morally relevant character-trait: suppose we say that a person is just. Justice is a matter at least of treating like cases equally. But to say this is to identify the character trait in terms of some presumption of what just action involves: unless we can talk of treating like cases equally, we have no purchase on the relevant character trait. We literally do not know what it is to be a just person: 'we are none the forwarder', in Green's succinct phrase.

7.19 MORAL REASONING: THE DUAL MODEL

It is clear, then, that Green rejects a rule morality where rules are unconditional requirements on the action of a moral agent. He uses the term 'rule' without embarrassment, but only to mark what I have called a moral presumption. Such presumptions are ineliminable from morality. How, though, do they operate? If they are always present, exactly how are they to be taken into account?

Green is an intransigent enemy of the dominant description (2.10, 7.16). Every student of ethics is early made familiar with the view that moral considerations 'silence' or displace other considerations, eliminate certain options. A dominant description can be applied in this way; but it has another aspect by which it displaces other moral considerations. So the fact that something would be an act of lying is sufficient from a Kantian viewpoint to block any other moral consideration of it; the fact that placing a bomb on an aeroplane comes under a moral description of political liberation is enough to discount totally, a 'terrorist' will say, the death of innocent people. Green might allow the moral validity of a person's deciding in either way here: to tell the truth, to place the bomb. What he will not allow is that a dominant description can be applied automatically to halt moral reasoning *in limine*. 'To question, what is Duty, man does not discover, but constructs answer.' Green says very little about regular decision-making which is a matter of fulfilling or coping with ordinary abrasions to a lifeplan or carrying out the everyday requirements of a practice: how a lawyer goes about advising a client in a perfectly standard litigation, how David will decide what to do next if his magazine fails (5.9). That area was explored in Chapter 5 (ibid.). Ethically Green is interested in two main types of situation that call for moral reasoning: (1) the situation in which presumptions clash, and (2) the situation in which there is uncertainty and a need to examine what a presumption actually involves. To cope with these situations we can draw from Green the materials for a dual model of moral reasoning.

Moral presumptions can clash in a variety of situations which there is no need exhaustively to classify: no need, because for Green the salient feature of these situations is simply that presumptions do clash. Their resolution proceeds in the same way. One practice can conflict with another, for the same agent or between different agents. The desire to save a sister who has been charged with a crime of which one is convinced that she is innocent, may conflict with the presumptive requirement of truth-telling. This last is an example which Green himself considers when he cites the case of Jeannie Deans in Scott's *Heart of Midlothian* (PE, §§ 315–16). The discussion of Esau is also relevant (PE, §§ 95–8) to what we are now examining, the first part of Green's model of moral reasoning.

Moral presumptions clash, so how is the conflict to be resolved? Should Jeannie Deans tell the truth, or save her sister? Green rephrases this question in terms of motives: 'whether the motive which suggests adherence to the rule of veracity, or that which suggests departure from it, is the worthier of the two?' (PE, § 315). It is vital to realize that for Green no general answer is possible. The agent must make a decision of which the morality cannot 'be detached from the relation which it [the decision: GLT] bears to the whole history of a life, to the universe of a character' (PE, § 316). She, Jeannie Deans, must make a decision, all things considered, in the light of her personal commitments and her 'plan of life'.

Take an example which frees us from fidelity to Scott. Rita is an advertising executive. She is married to Bob, who is also an advertising executive. But Bob works for a rival company. Bob's career has been shaky of late, his sensitivity to market trends is duller than it once was. Not to put too fine a point on it, Bob has got to secure the Blue Butter contract or start looking for another job: easier said than done at the age of 49. Muttering in his sleep Bob reveals his company's plans for landing the contract. As ill luck would have it, Rita is under pressure to secure the same contract. Only for her it is a case of proving her worth for a job which is hugely important to her career, a place on the board of management. Moreover, the extra money which would result from promotion would help fund a medical research project in which Rita greatly believes. And in any case if Bob clears this hurdle, he will probably fall at the next; the man is most likely on the way out. What Bob has revealed in his sleep puts an entirely new light on the way that Rita's company would be best advised to approach Blue Butter. What is Rita to do? All that Green can tell Rita to do is to consult 'the whole history of a life, ... the universe of a character'. If the instruction is short, the detail is immense.

It may seem that an easy way here is simply to point back to Green's theory of character; the question is not what Rita should do but what she can do. The state of one's character fixes the options (5.10). But this is to miss the point; Rita's problem may be that she does not know what the relevant state of her character is until she has dissected her dilemma, to which her 'ultimate guide' is 'self-reflection' (PE, § 95). If she decides that her overriding commitments are to her company, her career, to promotion, to the medical project, this perhaps follows a recognition of her priorities which is as surprising to her as it is unfortunate for her husband. In the light of that recognition she may even try to alter those priorities under the fourth aspect of the multi-perspectival model of deliberation (4.10). Again she may be later uncertain of the precise motivation for her decision, or unclear whether that decision was for the best, two kinds of 'practical perplexity' which Green recognizes (PE, § 314). But her decision might go a different way. She may find herself so committed to her husband that she feels justified in lying to her company about her knowledge of the opposition's plans: not in order positively to mislead her company, but in order to withhold information of which the disclosure would violate the trust between her husband and herself. Something like this account of moral decision-making, Green could argue, must be true: for even to halt moral reasoning at the outset by the application of a dominant description must itself be an expression of character. On this point it is simply a matter of whether one is clear-sighted enough to perceive the real nature of moral decision-making. We are far removed from the deductive model of 3.14.

The second part of Green's model of moral reasoning traces to the possibility of analogic responsiveness cited in 5.7. To recap: this part of the model is concerned with situations in which there is uncertainty and a need to examine what a moral presumption actually involves. Luke has, let us suppose, a particular commitment to the welfare of animals. He opposes animal circuses as degrading. He is not at all happy about aquaria in which whales are induced to perform for public amusement. You perhaps share his views, attitudes, and anxieties; perhaps not. But he sees things that way. His relevant moral presumption is something of this order: that the animal creation should be respected, not simply used for our amusement. Now he begins to worry further, for he keeps a dog. Is there really a respect for animals expressed in the way he treats his dog—organizing its life, walking it on a lead at times convenient to himself, isolating it in a suburban house away from the rest of the animal world? This development of a particular kind of worry is just the illustration we need for the idea of analogic responsiveness in morality. Note that this worry is not to be settled by any recourse to extra evidence. Luke knows how he treats his dog: the question, and his moral problem is whether that treatment is analogous to the treatment which he condemns of animals in circuses and aquaria. The example is not without its irony. Green was personally insensitive to the welfare of animals.

This process of reflection exactly captures Green's notion, introduced earlier, of tracing 'the identity of principle' through different cases (7.13). The 'principle' here is that of respect for the animal creation. Question: is that principle violated as effectively by Luke's treatment of his dog as by the circus treatment of animals? This question seeks similarities and resemblances, in a word 'analogies'. There are two obvious ways in which analogies can be drawn out. The formal nature of analogy is simply this: that as A is to B, so C is to D (A : B = C : D). Argument by analogy can yield perfectly tight, deductively valid conclusions: since 100 : 50 = 71.28 : 35.64, and 100 is twice 50, therefore 71.28 is twice 35.64. Patently, however, most applications of analogy in ethics do not start from given identities of proportion, but seek to establish them. This, then, is the second way in which analogies can be drawn out: when we pick out a number of analogous relations between two things and try for a probable or 'reasonable' overall result. Luke might argue out his problem as follows: 'Quite a lot of the relations between a circus and its animals carry across to my relations with my dog. Certainly the way a circus treats its animals is morally wrong; it looks likely, then, that my treatment of my dog is morally wrong.' This is, of course, a simplification; Luke's argument would need to include disanalogies, points in which his relations with his dog are dissimilar from the relations between a circus and its animals. But the result is scarcely going to be a deductively valid conclusion, rather an idea of what is likely from a broad variety of considerations. At most we can ask Luke to produce the considerations, the resemblances and dissimilarities, from which he decided one way or the other about the overall morality of his treatment of his dog.

Such responsiveness to analogies is, I think, how Green understands the main direction of moral progress. So, for instance, his disagreement with Aristotle in the analysis of courage is that Aristotle sees the objects of courage exclusively in military terms: but Green argues, as we have seen (7.13), that courage can be displayed in other than purely military contexts. As a soldier stands to his stronger enemy, so the office worker stands to his vulgar, domineering boss. We have simply to analogize, to 'trace the identity of principle' through different cases.

7.20 THE DUAL MODEL: REVIEW

The two models of moral reasoning connect, of course, since, for example, Luke's relation to his dog may be taken in the context of 'the whole history of a life, ... the universe of a character'. But three points of greater interest emerge.

First, although the decision for example to tell a lie might be validly derived on a particular occasion by either model, Green presses the utmost caution in overriding the moral presumption of veracity. His discussion of the example of Jeannie Deans stresses the self-deception which can be involved in deciding to override such a presumption. We think that we are acting morally in telling a lie, when really the explanation is that veracity would cause us 'trouble' or would conflict 'with some passion' which we wish to indulge (PE, § 316). The point is that Green is almost Kantianly rigid about veracity; the descriptive moral psychology of self-deception fits somewhat awkwardly, however, with the second point. This is that in fastening moral decision-making to the agent's character, Green effectively precludes the possibility of external judgement—and this for reasons relating to the concatenation of motives which we examined in 5.14. The 'whole history of a life' passage reads in full:

For purposes of moral valuation neither the desire to save the life of the beloved person, nor the determination at any cost to adhere to the rule of strict veracity, can be detached from the relation which it bears to the whole history of a life, to the universe of a character; and this relation is not in any case ascertainable by us.—(PE, § 316)

This opens a further similarity between Green and Kant. Take the Kantian claim that because an action is morally good simply by reason of its intention, independently of any results which the action may have, and because intentions are 'invisible', internal to the agent and imperfectly accessible to the agent himself, therefore we cannot be sure of any action, our own or another person's, that it really was morally good. Kant goes so far as to express his complete uncertainty whether a morally good action has ever been done. Green would, I think, regard such scepticism as exaggerated. But he is closer here to Kant than to Hegel, who would consign both viewpoints to the sphere of *die Moralität*.

Both Kant and Green are separated, not merely historically, from that phase of recently past philosophy, the robust externalization of the mental life, which we find, e.g. in Ryle's

The Concept of Mind and Anscombe's *Intention*. The keener practical grasp belongs to Kant and Green. A judge who suspects a witness of playing a deep game, a social worker nonplussed by seeming inconsistencies of behaviour in his client, a detective trying to unravel a complicated domestic relationship, such practical inquirers are more likely, I think, to recognize the uncertainties of Kant and Green than the mental transparencies of Ryle and Anscombe. This essential point should not be lost if moral psychology has moved on from some of the points where Kant and Green left it.

The third point is that the dual model of moral reasoning has implications for a morality of social roles. For this type of reasoning may precisely concern the adequacy of past practice to present needs; and there is no guarantee that, even granted good will, two agents will see their separate but related roles consistently.

Let us give a fresh direction to the example from 5.9 of David the journalist whose special interest is the culture and welfare of the Indian community in Britain. Suppose a totally imaginary situation. Five years ago, this fictitious example goes, a computer program was written to sort applications for jobs in the public sector. Through an error in the program, applications from candidates of Punjabi descent received a code which weighted their applications unfavourably. The error was detected last year and corrected; the program now sorts all applications fairly by the prescribed criteria. But the question arises of what to do about the intervening years of computer-aided injustice. Edward Fleuret is a politician whose ministry will have to decide this question. Fleuret is aggrieved at the past injustice, but is sure that 'the best way forward' is to prevent any public release of information. Old suspicions will be reawakened, new fears will grow, if hard information about real unfairness is released. 'All things considered', silence is the best policy. Fleuret's lips are very consciously sealed about the whole affair.

David, however, gets to hear of it. He takes a different view. He is equally aggrieved, and is quite clear that his duty as a journalist requires him to make the facts public. Fresh fears are only too right if this kind of thing can happen, no matter how 'innocent' the programming error may have been. Morever, injustice has been done to failed Punjabi applicants;

compensation is due to them. Social roles, the roles of politician and journalist, twist in a tangle of dissonance. Each person understands his role as requiring him to prevent the very outcome which the other person seeks.

7.21   REVIEW (2)

This completes the third part of the present chapter, that part concerned with aspects of Green's moral psychology which have emerged from the full statement of his ethical theory. In this connection we have discussed the ethical ultimacy of character, Green's account of the moral virtues, his notion of the good will, and finally his incorporation of a dual model of moral reasoning in a moral epistemology. Instead of merely skimming the details of these discussions I shall suggest a perspective that encompasses the entire span of the chapter.

Practical reason poses the question, 'what should I do?' Morality fixes one constraint on the answer to that question when it requires us to consider other interests besides our own. In our own terms, if the conditions of moral responsibility cited in 3.16 are not met, then an action is non-moral. To make a morally good action we need to add to those conditions a requirement to consider others' interests. For brevity, and to connect this requirement with the conditions of moral responsibility, we might try this: a morally good action involves an unforced concern for others' interests. But to say this is only to set a constraint on action; it is not to return a full answer to the question, 'what should I do?' Green has taken us through his account of practical rationality, which has broadened the question 'what should I do?' roughly into the question 'what should I be?', and more precisely into an inquiry concerning the kind of person to become if I want to achieve 'self-satisfaction', 'an abiding satisfaction of an abiding self'. One part of the response to that inquiry is that I need to organize my desires into systematic interests, integrated wide-interest systems, 'cases of concentrated purpose' (PE, § 128). The other part of Green's response is to define the constraints on what can actually produce 'an abiding satisfaction of an abiding self', since not just any systematic interests can organize our desires to produce this result. And so we have Green's theory of the true or unconditional human good. His transition to morality is a matter of showing that particular structures or organizations of desire equally serve the requirements of morality and the requirements of self-satisfaction.

If morality involves consideration of others' interests, there are presumptively better and worse ways of serving those interests. This is the rationale of moral 'rules' such as 'tell the truth', 'pay your debts', 'keep your promises'. These are not absolute requirements on action. But there is always a presumption in their favour; a person's interests are not typically served, for example, by unveracity towards him. For clarity, and with some departure from Green's own usage, I have spoken here of moral presumptions rather than of moral rules. Such presumptions also define the moral virtues. We do not typically serve a person's interests, e.g. by discriminating against him, nor do we typically serve a plurality's interests by discriminating in favour of one of their number: the just man treats like cases equally. The good will encompasses the whole of the moral virtues, where the classification of the latter is essentially the Platonic list of Rep. IV: wisdom, courage, temperance, and justice, with benevolence added. The unity of the virtues does not mean that the requirements of (say) justice and benevolence are compatible in every situation. In any particular situation a person must resolve the claims of competing moral presumptions in the total context of his life and character. (To take a parallel: in chess all a player's pieces can be moved in a connected strategy to win the game, but the position of one piece can occasionally block the movement of another.) The virtues are simply a catalogue of sensitivities to others' (and one's own) interests, more or less applicable and combinative as circumstances dictate. What actions particular circumstances do dictate is down to the agent to decide. Only the dual model of moral reasoning can help if someone is uncertain which moral presumption to follow in the event of a clash or exactly what a particular moral presumption involves.

A final point will lead us to the next chapter. Kant insisted, no one more strongly, on the autonomy of morals: on the idea that the requirements of morality are not answerable to non-moral considerations of any kind. Morality, the practical observance of universal law, is a function of our rational nature. Morality is an independent expression of reason; it does not use reason to serve human welfare, say, or to fulfil divine commands. Kant allows a certain play of welfare within morality; but welfare is not the rationale of the total institution of morality. (On Kant, cf. Green, Works II, 129.) Now, whatever we think of Kant's principle of the autonomy of morals, I cannot see that Green's moral philosophy violates it. Admittedly if we shift from Kant to Green, moral autonomy looks different; there is the perspective of a different moral psychology. Kant links morality to reason, as clearly distinct from desire. Green links morality to that fusion of reason and desire which is embodied in a 'plan of life'. Self-satisfaction under the conditions of the true good requires certain structures of desire, organized in family life, friendship, and social roles. Those structures are defined by a concern for the interests of others which, whether or not the agent sees it as such, is typically moral. This is plainly not a matter of subordinating morality as a means to some further end. The same autonomy cannot be claimed for Green's politics. For Green the role of the state is to pluralize, to provide conditions for the moral life in which every citizen can achieve self-satisfaction. Politics derives from ethics.

8

The Transition To Politics

This chapter aims neither at a full discussion nor at a condensed statement of Green's political philosophy. Its point is to consider the political implications of Green's ethics—the implications which he actually drew or, if there is a difference, the implications which he should consistently have drawn. I said in 1.4 that in his philosophical work Green has only a slight sense of the autonomy of politics. Green sees politics as inseparably connected to ethics, as deriving its rationale from it. From the side of ethics this means that the moral life requires a level of political support. But we must be careful not to put into Green's mouth a position which he would reject.

The autonomy of politics might be denied on two grounds. In the first place the claim might be made that political statements and concepts can be translated into more primitive or basic non-political statements and concepts. This is a form of reductionism: and one idea here might be that statements about the public interest can be translated without remainder into statements about the interests of individual persons. Or that statements such as that 'Germany invaded France' can be translated without remainder into statements about the actions of individual persons. If the claim is that this process can be carried out for all political statements and concepts, this amounts to a denial of the autonomy of politics. A different claim, equally inimical to the autonomy of politics, would be that political activity is not what it appears to be: that it can be explained away in terms of some more fundamental determinant of human conduct. So although political agents might make distinctive statements and use distinctive concepts, political activity is a mere epiphenomenon determined by (say) economic activity, fate, or divine providence.

These claims, the reductionist and the epiphenomenalist,

cannot be fully discussed in the space I have available here: nor is a full discussion necessary. For Green certainly does not endorse either claim about politics. He does not argue that political activity is uniquely determined by some other form of activity, but only that it should be determined by ethics. Nor does he try to translate political discourse, with its concepts of 'state', 'law', 'punishment', and the rest, into more primitive or basic statements and concepts. Green denies the autonomy of politics on a third ground: that politics should support the moral life and that it has no other proper function.

But even this moral teleology of politics can be misunder stood. The view that politics should support the moral life and that it has no other proper function appears to separate Green from a range of political philosophies, of which perhaps that of Michael Oakeshott is typical, for which politics is not itself an enterprise, directed to an end.[1] For such philosophies, the role of political activity is merely to regulate the conditions in which different individuals can pursue separate and possibly divergent ends. But no easy antithesis snaps into place. Green's frequent references to the 'common good' should not lead us to mistake form for substance. Formally, and in the absence of certain obvious defects, in a morality of social roles whatever I do will serve a common good: my role is one element in the structure of a moral life of joint self-realization in which I participate along with others. Substantively, what you do may be something separate and divergent from my activities. Your tennis-playing may take people away from my lectures. Green does not deny the autonomy of politics in the interests of floating some vast, integrated, single-plan social enterprise.

The central concept of Green's political philosophy is that of the state. This should not be an obvious remark.[2] The centrality of the state is not an inseparable feature of political philosophy

[1] M. J. Oakeshott, 'On the Civil Condition', *On Human Conduct*, Oxford, 1975, 108– 84. For a discussion, see J. Liddington, 'Oakeshott: Freedom in a Modern European State', *Conceptions of Liberty in Political Philosophy*, ed. Z. Pelczynski and J. Gray, London, 1984, 289–320. In my view *On Human Conduct*, a late work, has a meditative depth far outreaching the eager polemics of *Rationalism in Politics* and the Cambridge essays. *On Human Conduct* is not an epilogue; it is Oakeshott's central and permanent philosophical contribution.

[2] See B. de Jouvenal, *Sovereignty*, Cambridge, 1957, 16–17; and A. Skillen, *Ruling Illusions*, Hassocks, 1977, 12–44.

as such. For one thing, the concept of the state (to be precise about it) belongs to modern politics. Aristotle propounds a political philosophy which centres on the *polis*; the *polis* is not the state. For another thing, constructions of politics are available on which disputes and competition in social decision-making count as political without the machinery of law and ultimate coercion which we associate with the state. But if matters could stand differently, they do not. Green's understanding of politics is dominated by the concept of the state; and our task in this chapter is to connect the state with the moral life, to see what function the state can fulfil in relation to the moral life as described in the previous chapter.

The present chapter proceeds as follows. I first distinguish between state and society, following Green's own recognition of this distinction. I describe the restrictions which Green sets against the state in relation to the moral life, the kind of support which politics cannot render to ethics. This idea of the moral limitations of politics is a distinct feature of Green's political philosophy. I next set out Green's view of how social conditions can impede the moral life. Against the background of that view, the function of the state is to provide conditions for the moral life in which every citizen can achieve self-realization. I consider two criticisms of Green's view of politics: that Green's state violates the moral life by excessive activity (the 'conservative' view) and by insufficient activity (the 'socialist' view). I next dispose of an objection, traceable to Mark Pattison, that this view of the state's function is incompatible with his metaphysics. I then represent the state's function of providing conditions for the moral life in terms on its maintenance of rights. I remove the appearance of paradox from Green's claim that rights depend on recognition. Green's view of political obligation is defined, a view which links obligation, disobedience, and rebellion to the state's performance in relation to the moral life. This completes the two main parts of the chapter: having indicated what, in Green's view, politics cannot do for ethics, and also what it should do for ethics, I close by examining some tensions between moral and political viewpoints which Green does not, I think, wholly succeed in neutralizing.

8.2 SOCIETY AND STATE

To fix ideas consider two notions with which a political philosophy may be concerned, the notion of a good society and that of a good state.[3] The latter notion is capable of a twofold construction: one wide, the other more constricted. The wide notion of a good state is that of a state whose function is to create and maintain the conditions for a good society; the more constricted notion is, to a first approximation, that of a state in which the laws are justly administered and in which there are no unjust differences of political status between individuals.

Green has something, but not much, to say with regard to the more constricted notion of a good state. Some of this we have already noted in 1.4 in respect to proportional representation and women's suffrage. Political participation receives a definite endorsement: 'citizenship only'—i.e. citizenship alone—'makes the moral man; ... citizenship only gives that self-respect, which is the true basis of respect for others, and without which there is no lasting social order or real morality' (Works III, cxii). One extreme of injustice in the political status of individuals, through inequality of political participation, is represented by nineteenth-century Russia. It is only, Green says, 'by a sort of courtesy' that Russia, where the supreme autocratic power belongs to the Czar, is counted a state (Works II, 443; HM, 103). On the other hand, Green does not share Aristotle's view of the moral superiority of the political life. For Aristotle in NE 1.3 it is a finer thing to promote the *eudaimonia* of the whole *polis* than to confine one's activities to a smaller social group. For Green the good will and the moral virtues can be fully displayed in any social role; the scope of a role is less important than the attitude with which an agent approaches it.

On the wide construction of a good state, on which the state creates and maintains the conditions for a good society, Green plainly recognizes a distinction between state and society. 'A state presupposes other forms of community, with the rights that arise out of them, and only exists as sustaining, securing, and completing them' (Works II, 445; HM, 104). I shall consider

---

[3] In writing this paragraph I have had the benefit of seeing some unpublished notes by David Rees.

shortly how the state can promote the good society. First we should be clear, in examining the relation of ethics to politics, that one way in which the state cannot support the moral life is through the enforcement of morality.

8.3 MORALITY AND THE STATE: THE NEGATIVE THESIS

What are the bounds on what politics can do? The moral value of an action depends on its motive, which in turn depends on the agent's character. It is to character that moral responsibility ultimately relates (3.16, 5.4). Moreover, on the deepest analysis of action, action is an 'expression' of character (5.9, 7.11). Furthermore, a morality of social roles prevents that rift between motive and consequence by virtue of which action and agent might be judged differently (7.9.3). Since motives cannot be compelled, morality cannot be enforced. I can make you return my favourite Rick Nelson album. I cannot, in any sense relevant to morality, make you want to do so. I cannot, the contradiction is patent, compel you to display that unforced concern for my interests which morality here involves. (With this point in mind Green sometimes refers to 'free morality', see, e.g. Works II, 524; HM, 169.) 'The question sometimes put, whether moral duties *should be* enforced by law, is really an unmeaning one; for they simply *cannot* be enforced. They are duties to act, it is true, and an act can be enforced: but duties to act *from certain dispositions and with certain motives*, and these cannot be enforced' (Works II, 340; HM, 17). There is valid scope for the political enforcement of action, but 'Those acts[4] should be matter of legal injunction or prohibition of which the performance or omission, irrespectively of the motive from which it proceeds, is so necessary to the existence of a society in which the moral end . . . can be realised that it is better for them to be done or omitted from that unworthy motive which consists in fear or hope of legal consequences than not to be done at all' (Works II, 344; HM, 20).

---

[4] Quite correctly to Green's meaning, if falsely to his text, the wording of Works II, 344 diverges from that of Harris and Morrow: Nettleship's edition reads 'Those acts only should . . .'. Nettleship also puts a comma after 'realised'.

If this negative thesis holds good, and the moral value of an action depends on its unenforceable motive, social conditions might appear equally irrelevant to the moral life. If the state cannot enforce action from a particular motive, how can social conditions prevent action from that same motive? How can 'the social order' foster or impede the play of moral motivation? It seems that I can be unforcedly concerned about the interests of others in virtually any social context, from a concentration camp to a California beach.

The problem with this line of questioning is that it assumes the full-fledged moral agent. Green's account of practical rationality centres on an inquiry into the kind of person I might become in order to achieve 'self-satisfaction'. Moral agency emerges from the consequent organization of my desires into systematic interests; and social conditions can evidently play a major part in determining the imaginative possibilities open to me and the practical possibility of forming systematic interests. We glimpsed some of this territory when we observed Green's political and social views in 1.4.

8.4 THE SOCIAL ORDER AND THE MORAL LIFE

In his political philosophy Green is not a social revolutionary. The 'system of social relations, with laws, customs, and institutions corresponding' embodies the insight of generations into the unconditional human good (Works II, 312; HM, 232). Green has no sense, of the kind which strikes us in Plato's *Republic*, of the need for a complete erasure and renovation of the social structure in the interests of morality. Equally, however, he offers no easy endorsement of the status quo. His practical philosophy points to a 'free career in life', a full chance for the individual to realize his 'possibilities' and work 'towards perfection' (Works III, 374, HM, 201; Works II, 308, HM, 228). This can be seen as Green's embodiment of Bergsonian 'absolute' justice (7.6). Green does not minimize the gap between what such a 'free career' demands, the chance to achieve 'an abiding satisfaction of an abiding self', and what 'the social order' actually provides.

❧

With the condition of nineteenth-century England in mind, Green cites four aspects of that gap. The first concerns education. 'Without a command of certain elementary arts and knowledge, the individual in modern society is as effectually crippled as by the loss of a limb or by a broken constitution. He is not free to develop his faculties' (Works III, 373–4 ; HM, 201). Writing in 1880, Green might regard the case for compulsory education as convincingly made out; but here was one respect in which, till recently, 'the social order' had failed an appreciable segment of the community. Only with the Education Act of 1870 did elementary education become compulsory and free. Green was equally concerned about the detailed content of education. His 'General Report' and 'Report on King Edward's School, Birmingham', written when he was an assistant commissioner for the Schools Inquiry, are packed with reflections on the mental constriction of a 'commercial', business-orientated education and on the need to inculcate a broad culture.

Secondly, Green sees relations of disadvantage between social roles. So, for example, a labour force without capital, a 'proletariate' dependent on employers for work, is in a weak position to resist low pay, secure sanitary working conditions, reasonable hours of work, and other economic rights. Classical economics had tended to depoliticize such issues—to assign them to individual responsibility (the worker should look for a better employer) or to ineluctable economic laws (if wages are low this reflects the relation of the stock of circulating capital to the number of workers, the so-called wages-fund theory). Green is unconvinced. No worker's 'progress towards perfection' is helped by this sort of economic adversity. And the dire result is a commonplace of Victorian social history. 'For the sake of that general freedom of its members to make the best of themselves, which it is the object of civil society to secure, a prohibition should be put by law, which is the deliberate voice of society, on all such contracts of service as in a general way yield such a result' (Works III, 373; HM, 201). Accordingly Green supported legislation to impose the necessary controls, to assist the formation and strengthen the effectiveness of trade unions and so forth.

In the third place, Green dismisses some social roles as morally invalid. He was a decided partisan of measures against the drink trade. Here he did not simply aim to reform, to impose stricter conditions of sale. The drink trade, manufacturing and retail, was to be helped out of existence, I have already described Green's 'temperance' attitudes in fair detail (1.4); there is no need to repeat the discussion here.

Fourthly, the social order is at fault where it permits an engrossment of social assets by a particular class. In this connection Green was specially exercised by the accumulation of landed property through primogeniture. This accumulation, the unintended social consequence of innumerable individual actions, worked against 'the sale of agricultural land in small quantities, and thus hinders the formation of that mainstay of social order and contentment, a class of small proprietors tilling their own land' (Works III, 378; HM, 205). Green held that the situation was even worse in Ireland which, broadly speaking, 'has no industry but agriculture out of which a living can be made' (Works III, 381; HM, 208).

In all four respects the actual social order is a kind of adversary of the moral life; and to interpose an opinion before we continue, Green's lecture on 'Liberal Legislation and Freedom of Contract', from which most of the quotations in this section have been taken, is in my view a model for the integration of philosophy with public affairs: if political philosophy has 'practical relevance' it lies in just this kind of interplay between conceptual analysis, moral judgement and empirical observation (cf. 9.3). I state the opinion; I will not press it. The general significance of Green's social critique is this. If we do not educate a person, he is disadvantaged in the lifeplans he can imagine; if we do not protect him from weak economic bargaining, he is equally disadvantaged in the lifeplans he can fulfil. If we let the economic system go unregulated, the consequences may work drastically against the opportunities of one social class in favour of another. If we allow scope to some social roles, they may injure far more interests than they help. We return in fact to the characterization of the good society given in 7.9.2: the good society is one which (i) secures the fundamental interests of individuals, (ii) under failure of social resources, never puts the satisfaction of one individual's lesser interests before the satisfaction of another's fundamental interests, and (iii) does not suffer the interference of one individual's lifeplan and associated social roles with the like fundamental interests of others.

8.5 POLITICS AND MORAL REASONING

But if the actual social order is a moral adversary and the objective is the good society and the abiding satisfaction of abiding selves, what is Green's political strategy? If we look into this part of Green's political philosophy we quickly discover the dual model of moral reasoning (7.19). Take the issue of land reform. Here Green observes that political activity cannot proceed 'on any absolute principle' (Works II, 534; HM, 178). He accepts, and this is his main complaint, that the accumulation of land in a few hands, through primogeniture, has produced 'a proletariate, neither holding nor seeking property', and thus deprived of 'the conditions of a free life' (Works ibid.; HM, 177). But this is only one—major—element in a complex situation. Should primogeniture be ended or curtailed? Should we reduce a parent's power of bequest? The implications of this kind of intervention in private property represent a further major element to be taken into account. At this level of general statement Green retreats into a cloud of qualifications: in the end, as for what we should do, 'It depends on circumstances' (Works II, 534; HM, 178). Here at least is the historical specificity of 6.12. Green is actually far more definite than this in his own ideas about what should be done. But here the general model of reasoning follows the lines of the first part of Green's model of moral reasoning.

Analogic responsiveness also finds its place. In economic bargaining, if someone has the 'choice' of accepting risky, ill-paid, and insanitary work or going hungry, Green can bring this choice analogically into the category of unfreedom. Only in a superficial sense am I free to walk away if you seriously brandish a gun and demand my wallet; but only in the same sense, Green would argue, am I free to turn down undesirable work if I lack all other means or prospect of support. To insist that economic contracts are free, since anyone can offer or withhold his labour, is a clear case of failing to trace the identity of a principle, that of freedom, through different cases (Works III, 373; HM, 201).

This, then, in broad outline is Green's view of the relevance of political activity to the moral life: the function of the state is to provide conditions for the moral life in which every citizen can achieve self-realization. The point looks obvious that there is less inequality now than there was in Green's day: the social order is different. But I want now to consider two criticisms of Green's politics which are not directly touched by this social difference: first a 'conservative' view that Green's state violates the moral life; and secondly a 'socialist' view that Green restricts the moral scope of political activity through unnecessary economic assumptions. I then consider a metaphysical claim, Mark Pattison's objection that even the limited degree of social intervention which Green's political philosophy sanctions is inconsistent with his general philosophy.

8.6   CONSERVATISM AND ETHICS

The 'conservative' view I want to examine is that of Robert Nozick in *Anarchy, State, and Utopia*. Not only is Nozick's view of the function of the state sharply at variance with Green's, but some examples which the two philosophers use closely overlap. Nozick's special significance is that in his view Green's political objective is wrong, the very kinds of political activity by which Green seeks to promote the moral life amount, for Nozick, to a violation of morality. Nozick does not consider Green's political philosophy; their disagreement is implicit.

In Nozick's terms Green defines an 'end state' or 'patterned' conception of the social order; Green has a vision of the good society, and the function of the state is to realize that vision. Nozick need not dissent from Green's vision; their disagreement centres on the proper role of political activity in relation to it. Nozick's 'minimal state' is not Green's state; and Green's state is morally objectionable on Nozick's understanding of the relation of ethics to politics.

That understanding is this. The moral requirement which is central to politics is expressed in Kant's second formulation of the categorical imperative: that we should always treat persons as ends, never as mere means.[5] This requirement sets 'side constraints' on any kind of political activity such that the only functions allowable to the state are to protect the individual against force, fraud, non-performance of contracts, and so forth. A state thus restricted in its functions is a 'minimal state'; only the minimal state respects the categorical imperative. This briefly outlines one portion of Nozick's political philosophy; it sets the essential background to Nozick's disagreement with Green. Take the issue of land reform. On Nozick's account, 'historical principles' are the key to this issue. How was the land appropriated or acquired? Locke's view was, very roughly, that a person's legitimate property is that with which he has 'mixed his labour' (*Second Treatise*, § 27). How this 'mixing' can transform what originally belonged to nobody into private property is perhaps not quite so clear as Locke supposes.[6] But the immediate point is that whereas Locke's labour theory of property confines the legitimate appropriation of land to con-ditions in which 'there [is] enough and as good left; and more than the yet unprovided could use' (*Second Treatise*, § 33), Nozick lets those requirements lapse. His consideration is 'whether appropriation of an unowned object worsens the situation of others'.[7] If it does worsen that situation, all that is due is compensation. If anyone's freedom has been reduced, the appropriator must compensate for the net disadvantage he has caused. Provided these conditions of just appropriation are met, a person's property holdings (in respect of land) are just; and what has been justly appropriated can be justly acquired by voluntary transfer. Anyone has the right to do what he will with whatever property he justly holds; historical principles close any political argument. No proper function of the state allows us to redistribute justly held property for the sake of some more

---

[5] R. Nozick, *Anarchy, State, and Utopia*, Oxford: Blackwell, 1974, 32. On this supposed link between Kantian ethics and conservative political philosophy, cf. R. Scruton, *The Meaning of Conservatism*, Harmondsworth, 1980, 23 *et passim*.

[6] At the very least my labour cannot transform what belongs to nobody into private property unless, in some sense, I 'own' my labour. Locke suggests in § 27 that I own my labour because I own my body ('every man has a property in his own person'). But the claim seems tenuous that I own my body in the same sense in which I own, e.g. the soil with which I have 'mixed' my labour.

[7] R. Nozick, 175.

'desirable' end state, e.g. Green's social order in which every body has the resources to achieve self-realization. To redistribute on this basis is to treat the property owner as a 'means' whose rights can be disregarded for the benefit of others.

We need to approach rather carefully the disagreement between Green and Nozick on this issue. For first appearances might suggest that Green requires only the compensation for which Nozick also looks in cases of net disadvantage. Thus Green ponders arrangements by which land, remaining under concentrated private ownership, might be long-term leased to smallholders. But this is not at all what Nozick's political philosophy will sanction; Green is talking of argument, persuasion, but ultimately of compulsion to use landed property in particular, socially desirable ways. Nor can the disagreement be removed by the idea that Nozick has in mind conditions of just appropriation, while Green denies that the historical appropriation of land was, in many cases, anything but theft. Green might hesitate to intervene in the use of private property, but he will sanction intervention if the conditions of a good society require it. This is a difference of philosophical principle. How is it to be resolved?

It is to be resolved, I think, in Green's favour. For any moral position such as Nozick's, which seeks to mark out precisely what is due to an individual to appropriate, runs into a point that can be developed from the 'concatenation of motives' which we examined in 5.14: the claim that more than one person's motives contribute to the consequences of an action. We can generalize from motives to resources: the knowledge, skills, and instruments which the individual applies to produce a particular result depend on a social contribution. Others have supplied him with knowledge, taught him skills, produced the instruments he uses. In an ethical theory closely related to Green's, just this line of argument is, of course, the extensive burden of Bradley's *Ethical Studies*, Essay V. Only by lines which are uncertain and more or less artificial can we determine, mark out, what a person's 'works' entitle him to appropriate (6.4; and cf. 6.6).

A more apt 'conservative' case would, I think, centre on a tension which Green's view of the function of the state creates for another view which he holds, that of the distinction between state and society. For, as the activity of the state extends to secure the fundamental interests of individuals, so the distinction between state and society blurs. In the first place and obviously the state forms certain social roles through its own activity; and secondly the fundamental interests which the state aims to secure are crucially subject to interpretation through the . expectations which any given level of state activity itself engenders. The problems which an individual sees himself as confronting in his 'plan of life', for example, will be defined partly by the level of support which he expects from the state. None of this disturbs Green's moral teleology of politics, his view of the proper function of the state, but it does mean that state and society lose something of their mutual distinctness, and that the instrumental role of the state is more ambiguous than at first appears.

8.7 SOCIALISM AND ETHICS

Green would not, however, regard Nozick's inquiry as the deepest question about property. Nozick aims to determine the conditions of just appropriation and acquisition. Green accepts this as a valid inquiry, but treats it as secondary to an elucidation of the rationale of property. We need first to establish what property is and to see how the concept of property has any place in a coherent ethical theory (Works II, 517 ; HM, 163). If no one should be executed it is otiose to examine the conditions on which a particular person should be hanged; similarly, if there is no morally legitimate institution of property, it is otiose to examine the conditions of just appropriation and acquisition. In a socialist perspective Green himself fails to inquire sufficiently deeply about property. The explicit institutional setting for Green's ethical theory is a regime of private property; and the critical suggestion is that from arguments which might justify at least an institution of property and perhaps even certain forms of private property, Green draws unwarranted conclusions for a complete regime of private property: and so the criticism is not, as with Nozick, that Green's political objective is wrong, but that his strategy is superficial. On this view Green does not understand the need to supersede an economic system which is driven by a logic of profit that will always produce exploitation and alienation. In this respect, now or a hundred years ago, nothing is essentially different. So runs the criticism.

Green's chief philosophical discussion of property occurs at PPO, §§ 211–32 (Works II, 517–35; HM, 163–78). For purposes of the present discussion, the scope of 'property' is fixed by two of the economist's 'factors of production': land, along with natural resources generally, and capital (fixed capital such as plant and equipment, and working capital such as raw materials and finished goods). In Green's view the rationale of property is that a person needs a 'constant apparatus through which he gives reality to his ideas and wishes' (Works II, 520; HM, 165). Property is such an apparatus: 'a permanent apparatus for carrying out a plan of life' (Works II, 525; HM, 170). To write this book I need paper, pens, the use of a word-processor or a typewriter, a desk, a quiet room: much more, of course, but at least 'a certain permanent apparatus beyond the bodily organs' (Works II, 522; HM, 167). In these short quotations Green's whole theory of property is implicit.

Where there is property there is a form of control over factors of production, over land and capital. Private property is that form of control by which, absolutely or within wide limits, I can dispose of property as I wish. I have a moral right of private property when my control is warranted. For Nozick, control is warranted by just appropriation or just acquisition. For Green it is warranted by a moral agent's need to realize 'a plan of life'. A regime of private property is one in which all or most property is private. Suppose such a regime is associated with a market economy in which the transfer of land and capital is determined by economic bargaining. It seems that a market economy can offer no guarantee that, through bargaining, a particular moral agent will receive the resources, the 'permanent apparatus', he needs to realize a lifeplan. Green wants to retain the market economy and to guarantee 'a permanent apparatus for carrying out a plan of life'. In Phillip Hansen's expressive phrase the issue is one of 'T. H. Green and the Moralization of the Market'.[8] Is Green trying for an impossible reconciliation?

From a socialist viewpoint Green's attitude to a regime of

---

[8] P. Hansen, 'T. H. Green and the Moralization of the Market', *Canadian Journal of Political and Social Theory*, 1 (1977): an informed and thoughtful article which should be read by anyone interested in this aspect of Green's political philosophy.

private property and a market economy is apt to look mildly perverse. For consider how a socialist might argue from premisses supplied by Green himself. Land and capital are social assets; and in no clear-cut way of desert can those assets be apportioned in terms of a person's effort or 'works'. That point derives from 8.6. There are, however, fairly clear lines between those social assets and the 'permanent apparatus' a person needs 'for carrying out a plan of life'. Then we may proceed by straight distributive justice: social assets are to be apportioned by a rule which secures the fundamental interests of individuals and, under failure of social resources, never puts the satisfaction of one individual's lesser interests before the satisfaction of another's fundamental interests (8.4).

I think there are fairly deep reasons for Green's commitment to a market economy. One reason is, I surmise, an assumption of practical incommensurability. Take the Niente point from 6.2. Green's theory of the unconditional human good imposes no requirement that 'all persons mut be developed in the same way' (PE, § 191). This sensitivity to individual differences means, however, that any attempt by the state to allocate resources centrally runs into the problem of trying to evaluate the widely disparate needs set by different lifeplans. Should a racing-driver be given a new vehicle or should the university library be given the books for my next research project? Green's political prognosis along these lines is 'a complete regulation of life' (Works II, 528 ; HM, 172) which, under scarce resources, could never sensitize itself to the exact assessment and comparative evaluation of different individuals' needs. The market economy supports a regime of private property which enables the individual to assess his own needs, on something like (presumably) Bentham's assumption that in this matter the individual is likely to be the best judge. Provided that the market can be so 'moralized' that it does not defeat particular individuals' chances of self-realization, it has a clear advantage, in Green's view, in matching social assets to individual needs.

A second reason is, I think, as follows. Green appears to require of the economic system that it should provide one sort of equality of opportunity. He does not use that expression, but I think he has the relevant conception. An opportunity is, to a first approximation, a useful choice; a person has the opportunity to do something if, under some description, it is a desirable thing to do and he can do it if he chooses. What equality of opportunity amounts to is far from clear. Three possibilities are: (i) Identical opportunities (we have equality of opportunity if, seeking careers in broadcasting, we are both offered the job of a television announcer); (ii) exactly equivalent opportunities (the job which is offered to you in broadcasting is as good as my job opportunity in journalism); and (iii) fundamentally equivalent opportunities (you have better opportunities than I have overall, but our fundamental opportunities, those that really matter, are equivalent).[9]

Green appears to incline towards the third construction of equality of opportunity. The individual should have the resources for self-realization, for a 'free career in life' by which 'abiding satisfaction' can be achieved. Green cannot support identity of opportunity in view of the Niente point. He seems not to be greatly concerned about inequalities of opportunity as such; he accepts a kind of endemic human acquisitiveness by which, granted a market economy and a regime of private property, individuals will in varying degrees outvie one another in the accumulation of resources to meet future wants (PE, § 85 and Works II, 526–8; HM, 170–2). Such inequalities can be tolerated so long as the market does not withhold property altogether from certain individuals. If the necessary resources for a 'free career in life' are guaranteed, this fundamental equivalence (equality) of opportunity is all that vitally matters.

But how is that guarantee forthcoming? That question introduces Green's third reason for commitment to a market economy: the idea that the market can be tamed. With Victorian capitalism in mind Green might regret 'the manner in which property is possessed among us' (Works II, 526; HM, 171), but such inequalities of property as are harmful to self-realization are not an essential feature of a market economy and a regime of private property; they are detachable accidents. Green places a heavy burden of responsibility here on the historical origins of the European land system (Works II, 533–4; HM, 177–8). He has a broad variety of ideas on how the market might be moralized: he considers the ending of primogeniture, the spread

---

[9] See D. A. Lloyd Thomas, 'Competitive Equality of Opportunity', *Mind*, 86 (1977).

of trade unions to strengthen the bargaining power of labour, the fostering of benevolent societies and of private insurance schemes. How impressive one finds such ideas will depend on factors far beyond the reach of this book: on a complete cluster of political and economic beliefs, hypotheses, and attitudes. Green will not persuade everyone that 'a permanent apparatus for carrying out a plan of life' requires a complete regime of private property covering not only my word processor but all land and natural resources, raw materials, plant, and equipment. That aside, no close reader of PPO, §§ 211–32 and 'Liberal Legislation and Freedom of Contract' can mistake an intense meditative commentary on the workings of a market economy in relation to the moral life.

We have now considered two criticisms of Green's view of politics: that Green's state violates the moral life by excessive activity (the conservative view) and by insufficient activity (the socialist view). Next an objection which is due to Mark Pattison: the claim that social intervention even of the limited kind that Green envisages to provide conditions for the moral life in which every citizen can achieve self-realization, to correct the tensions between the social order and the moral life examined in 8.4, is inconsistent with his general philosophy.

8.8 METAPHYSICS, ETHICS, AND POLITICS: THE PATTISON THESIS

I argued in 3.13 that Green's metaphysics stands in a 'transcendental' or presuppositional relation to his ethics. Green does not deduce ethical conclusions from metaphysical premises as one might deduce step-by-step practical instructions from the nature of the eternal consciousness. Metaphysics does not enable detailed ethical conclusions; it grounds the very possibility of ethical premises by answering the challenge of reductive materialism and one-way physicalism. I have also argued, however, that Green's politics derives from his ethics. Now Mark Pattison enters the picture; for Pattison argues that Green's politics is inconsistent with his metaphysics. If Green's politics is deducible from his ethics, but his ethics presupposes a metaphysics which is inconsistent with his politics, one deduction at least is safe: that Green has a problem. What then of the Pattison thesis that Green's metaphysics is inconsistent with his politics?

In his *Memoirs* (1885), Pattison glances rapidly at Kantian metaphysics, and adds:

What is curious is that this new à priori metaphysic, whoever gave it shape in Germany, was imported into Oxford by a staunch Liberal, the late Professor Green. This anomaly can only be accounted for by a certain puzzle-headedness on the part of the Professor, who was removed from the scene before he had time to see how eagerly the Tories began to carry off his honey to their hive.[10]

D. G. Ritchie is right.[11] What Pattison is doing here is to follow, in different language, the distinction which J. S. Mill introduced in his *Autobiography* between 'two schools of philosophy, that of Intuition, and that of Experience and Association'.[12] Mill thought this distinction no 'mere matter of abstract speculation'. On the contrary the distinction is 'full of practical consequences'. 'Intuitionism', for Mill, is the view that the mind is vouchsafed a power of discovering truths independently of sense-experience or analysis. Not only did such a view set all Mill's critical faculties on edge; he was also clear that the 'truths' so discovered were of a specially repellent type, inconsistent with 'the rational treatment of great social questions' and well-matched 'to conservative interests generally'. Thus he saw intuitionism as a disagreeable element in 'Germano-Coleridgean Philosophy'; and the high severity of his *Examination of Hamilton* comes chiefly from Hamilton's involvement, on Mill's interpretation, with the errors of intuitionism: an involvement only exacerbated by Sir William's great philosophical reputation.

Such intuitionism cannot, however, be correctly equated with Kantian metaphysics. For Kant expressly rules out the sort of claim which intuitionism makes to 'transcendent' knowledge (3.11, 5.6). Nor, it is almost unnecessary to say, is Green's

---

[10] M. Pattison, *Memoirs*, London, 1885, 167. I am grateful to David Rees for reminding me of the relevance of Pattison's criticism.

[11] D. G. Ritchie, *The Principles of State Interference*, London, 1891, 132 ff.

[12] For quotations from Mill in this paragraph, see *The Essential Works of John Stuart Mill*, ed. M. Lerner, New York, 1971, 160; cf. R. P. Anschutz, *The Philosophy of J. S. Mill*, Oxford, 1953, ch. 4.

relation to Kantian metaphysics one of straight endorsement. Green's philosophy embodies the self as unifying experience, but abandons 'things-in-themselves', the two-world Kantian scheme of phenomena and noumena. How any of this is inconsistent with Green's politics, either his political philosophy or his practical political commitments, is a question that dissolves when we realize the multiple misunderstandings on which Pattison's thesis is based.[13]

8.9 RIGHTS AND RECOGNITION

The state, on Green's account, provides conditions for the moral life in which every citizen can achieve self-realization; this at least is its proper function. He has another way of putting this, which is to say that the state maintains 'the rights of its members as a whole or a system' (Works II, 444; HM, 103).

Green holds—the view is notorious in the secondary literature—that moral rights depend on 'recognition' (e.g. Works II, 350; HM, 25–6). Two responses typically follow. The sympathies of many commentators snap resolutely shut at the first sight of Green's claim. Did Jewish rights depend on their explicit legal endorsement by the Third Reich? Do the rights of animals depend on explicit consensus that factory farming is wrong? And if factory farming is not wrong, how has the fact or absence of explicit consensus anything to do with the matter? Such awkward questions really need the word 'explicit': and that is my quarrel with this first response. We have to probe quite carefully what Green means by 'recognition'. Such a word is a turntable of ambiguity from which the argument might proceed in many directions. The second response is to start from a notion of explicit recognition and to see the full set of Green's remarks about rights as a series of more or less embarrassed and confused manœuvres and retreats by which he tries to meet such awkward questions as those above. Most of the relevant texts belong to Green's Lectures on the Principles

---

[13] The best general introduction to these issues, without specific reference to Green, is J. W. N. Watkins, 'Epistemology and Politics', *Proceedings of the Aristotelian Society*, 58 (1957–8). See also H. H. Price, 'The Permanent Significance of Hume's Philosophy', *Philosophy* 15 (1940), 8.

of Political Obligation; and these were not prepared for publication by Green himself. There is no reason, à priori, why the drafts of these lectures should yield a coherent theory of rights. Anyone who has written lectures or even an article knows that first, second, and later drafts can be badly organized, that one can easily repeat oneself in slightly different language, change one's mind, contradict oneself, in strikingly short periods of time. So I am not determined to extract coherence from Green on rights. I do not believe that such determination is necessary; the point is to locate Green's theory of rights in a total pattern of argument about the moral life and the function of the state. In that context a coherent theory readily discloses itself. It is analysis that is needed, however, not impressionistic reaction.

Analytically our task easily subdivides: first, what is a right? Or what does Green mean by a right? Secondly, what does Green mean by 'recognition'? Thirdly, in what sense does a right depend on recognition? How does Green believe this is so? Whatever we say about rights must return to these questions.

If moral rights depend on recognition, let us try a strong construction of 'dependence': recognition is a necessary and sufficient condition of the existence of moral rights. For any putative right: if that right is not recognized there is no moral right; if that right is recognized, then there is a moral right. This looks similar to a loosely Berkeleian argument about objects: existence depends on perception. If X is not perceived it does not exist; if it is perceived then it does exist. For both arguments it is the necessary condition which seems problematic. If an object is perceived it does exist; if a moral right is recognized there is such a right. But why should the existence of an object depend on its being perceived, the existence of a moral right depend on its being recognized? How, one might puzzle, except on stretched 'idealist' assumptions, can the existence of any thing depend on its being recognized? As Prichard might have said, 'the thing is the other way on'. Recognition itself depends on the prior existence of what is recognized.

We need to understand, I think, that for Green what I shall call the basis of a moral right, its 'foundation' (Works II, 462;

HM, 118), does not depend on recognition. The moral ontology of the matter is that what grounds a right is not dependent on recognition as its necessary condition; it is the moral epistemology of rights to which recognition is central.

The ground of a moral right is what is necessary for or appropriate to the individual's 'progress towards perfection'. In a lifeplan Green's agent conceives 'an ideal, unattained condition of himself, as an absolute end' (Works II, 350; HM, 25): and the ground of a moral right is that it enables the agent to fulfil the requirements of a lifeplan. Green is speaking essentially from a morality of social roles, where such roles embody the lifeplans of individual agents. Clearly in relation to such a morality he wants to impose three requirements: (i) that a person has the resources to conceive of a lifeplan, and moreover to take stock of a sufficient plurality of lifeplans and associated social roles; (ii) that a person has the resources to fulfil a lifeplan, to carry out the requirement of a social role; and (iii) that social roles really do secure the interests of those they are meant to serve. For simplicity I shall concentrate on requirement (ii).

These requirements can be read in an 'ideal' way: what they demand may involve powers, for 'A right is a power' (Works II, 419; HM, 82), which would be granted to the agent, and modifications of practice which would be seen to be appropriate were certain considerations available to us. Those considerations might fall beyond present conception or imagination. Green says that these powers are rights 'potentially' (Works II, 462; HM, 118). They are powers which agents ideally should have, but which have no practical bearing on moral or political discourse. We can call them 'rights' if we wish; Green does so on occasion. But to cite such ideal powers is to assign no tasks to a state whose function is to maintain rights. We cannot decide to grant such powers or to withhold them either; at this level of absolutely ideal desirability we simply do not know what they are. And so the conditions of moral epistemology are not met. Crudely: the state cannot maintain (or, more strictly here, call into existence) that for which it cannot recognize the need.

What the state can maintain are, in Hohfeld's classification, claim-rights.[14] We are talking of agents with lifeplans in social roles. Green's agent, X, has a right to A (some action or forbearance from action) on the part of another agent, Y, by reason of R (X's social role). Claim-rights are central to anything which we can ask of the state: a power which a person lacks can be supplied to him only through the medium of such rights. The relation of claim-rights to recognition is far less problematic than that of 'ideal power'-rights: less problematic but by no means unsubtle. A right is explicitly recognized when the 'laws, customs, and institutions' of 8.4 acknowledge it. Thus in present British society there is an acknowledgement that within limits a doctor has a right of confidentiality in his relationship with a patient. Then if a women seeks medical advice and does not wish her condition to be divulged to her husband, the doctor has, by virtue of his social role, a right not to be pressured by the husband for information on the woman's medical condition; and the state, in the form of the nearest policeman, will enforce that right. Here is (*a*) legal enforcement of (*b*) what is widely acknowledged to be (*c*) a fair claim of confidentiality made by the practitioners of a certain social role. For a morality of social roles this example may be taken to contain the full elements of explicit recognition. But this is only one kind of recognition; and Green's moral epistemology of rights does not rest on any idea that the individual has only such rights as fulfil the conditions of explicit recognition. If a practice has an ascertainable requirement, the requirement identifies a moral right. This is the irreducible component of 'recognition' in Green's theory of rights. If one cannot ascertain a requirement, what action can A claim, what action can the state enforce, against X? No rights can be specified.

What a practice ascertainably requires may be a long way from what is widely acknowledged, let alone legally enforced. Does the practice of medicine require confidentiality in the relationship between a doctor and an under 16 year-old who asks to go on the pill (7.9.1)? Remember Green's point from 7.16: 'To question, what is Duty, man does not discover, but constructs answer. A Problem, not a Theorem.' An 'implicit' right may have to be teased from the anomalies and contradictions of what

[14] W. N. Hohfeld, *Fundamental Legal Conceptions as Applied to Judicial Reasoning*, New Haven and London, 1964.

is explictly acknowledged (Works II, 450–1; HM, 108–9). We have only the resources of the dual model of moral reasoning to help us in constructing our 'answer'.

Three sets of questions were defined in 8.9 as the touchstone of our analysis. First, what is a right? Or what does Green mean by a 'right'? A right is a power which enables the agent to fulfil the requirements of a lifeplan. For moral ontology what thus grounds a right is not dependent on recognition as its necessary condition: and in this connection Green is prepared to talk of 'natural' rights in the sense of rights which are 'necessary to the end which it is the vocation of human society to realise' (Works II, 340; HM, 17). But in the context of a morality of social roles, only such powers as can be ascertained as necessary or appropriate to a practice have any relevance to moral or political discourse. Moral epistemology enjoys thereby a degree of separation from moral ontology. Ascertainability is the key to Green's notion of recognition, which takes us back to the second question: what does Green mean by 'recognition'? One might try: a right is recognized when a power which is necessary or appropriate to a practice is claimed by a practitioner himself, when it is acknowledged as necessary or appropriate by the 'laws, customs, and institutions' of a society (separately or in combination), or when it would be so acknowledged if anomalies and contradictions within those laws, customs, and institutions were removed. Then to the third set of questions: in what sense does a right depend on recognition? How does Green believe this is so? At its most general level a right identifies a relation between persons which has implications for their conduct. Unless a power which is necessary or appropriate to a practice can be ascertained, it cannot regulate conduct: without recognition in this sense there is no moral right, nothing by reference to which conduct can be regulated. If such power has been ascertained, then there is a moral right. For a moral right is just such a power.

The following quotation is perhaps the most famous of Green's pronouncements on rights: that the individual has rights only '(1) as a member of a society, and (2) of a society in which some common good is recognized by the members of the society as their own ideal good, as that which *should be* for each of them' (Works II, 350; HM, 25). At the very least, rights are social as depending on interpersonal relations. If there is no person on whose conduct I have a claim, the concept of a right has no purchase. In this admittedly slightly stretched sense, my rights are dependent on my membership of a society, 'society' in the sense of social relations. As to Green's second claim, we need to recall that he is speaking from a morality of social roles in the context of a theory of the unconditional human good. Self-realization must observe the social nature of man (6.6–7). If a right is a power which enables the agent to fulfil the requirements of a lifeplan, which involves a social role and an associated practice, this is a fair reading of Green's second claim.

No one could suppose that Green's theory of rights as here set out is quite free from difficulty. For one thing, my references on Green's behalf, to 'what is widely acknowledged' are more easily made than exactly construed beyond a select range of examples. For another, the dual model of moral reasoning is open to variation between the 'answers' constructed by different individuals (7.20). In a full discussion of Green's political philosophy we should need to press far more closely the political implications of these points. In this discussion I have simply aimed to say briefly what is involved in the state's maintenance of rights, and to show how Green's moral philosophy does not carry a theory of rights which is vitiated by paradoxical requirements of political and social 'recognition'.

8.10   POLITICAL OBLIGATION

In the history of political philosophy, answers to the question, 'why should I obey the state?', typically cite the state's goal or its origin. So we should obey the state because it serves the common interest, or because it is leading us to the ideal society, or for whatever goal-directed reason. Alternatively we should obey the state because 'the powers that be are ordained of God', or because we promised to do so, where such reasons claim a rightness of obedience connected with the origin of the state. The details and cross-connections matter less for present purposes than the broad division. Given that division, Green clearly falls on the goal-directed side. It is not that Green supposes a general answer will actually say why, all states being as they are, we should always obey them. Disobedience may be justified. But he does believe, as we have seen, that the state should provide conditions for the moral life in which every citizen can achieve self-realization; said another way, that it should maintain a system of rights. If the state fulfils those requirements, this is the basis of political obligation; and there is no other general reason why we should obey the state.

At the limit a state which is completely oppressive, which imposes 'no-choice', so that what I do has, by external intervention, no connection with my own motives and intentions, so far stifles the moral life. To the extent to which, short of oppression, the state employs coercion, it also works against the moral life: the state cannot enforce morality, and so far as it compels or induces the individual to act or to refrain from acting it deprives his actions of moral value. But, as we have seen, such coercion may be necessary to protect the conditions of the moral life for other individuals (8.3). To the extent to which the state excludes political participation, so that its citizens have decisions concerning their own interests imposed on them, it blocks an essential dimension of individual moral development (8.2).

But the state's performance in relation to the moral life is the key to its political evaluation. Representation is one thing; an exact responsiveness to public demands and to shifts of public opinion is quite another. Green is largely uninterested in reforming the electoral system, say by the introduction of proportional representation, to increase that responsiveness (1.4). That the state is to be judged by its moral performance is simply to repeat, of course, that Green entertains predominantly the wide notion of the state distinguished in 8.2.

If the state's promotion of the moral life gives the key to political obligation, it gives the key equally to political disobedience or rebellion: it grounds the proper function of the state, and justifies disobedience and rebellion (revolution) on certain conditions when the state fails to carry out that function. To give an impression of Green's views: he envisages three circumstances in which political obligation is problematic. The first arises when 'the state' is ambiguous through a conflict of *de jure* authorities or of *de jure* authority with *de facto* authority (Works II, 417–21; HM, 81–84). Green's advice here is simply to divaricate good from evil or, less dramatically, better from worse 'by reference to the end . . . in which we conceive the good of man to consist' (Works II, 420; HM, 83).

The second circumstance applies when the state is bad in the sense of ruling in the interest of a section of the citizens only: 'for the benefit of a few against the many' (Works II, 416; HM, 80). What is at issue here is rebellion, armed action on the part of citizens against the state. When is rebellion morally justified? Green enumerates four conditions: (1) the state must be 'systematically' bad, i.e. consistently bad in matters of deep substance affecting the fundamental interests of its citizens (it is 'systematically' 'hostile to the public' (Works II, 416, 417; HM, 80, 81); (2) its harmful political activities must be incapable of remedy by lawful means, 'there is no means of obtaining a repeal of the law by legal means' (Works II, 422; HM, 85); (3) there must be a reasonable likelihood that rebellion will succeed; the ethics of revolution turns on a probability of $\geqslant 0.5$. 'What prospect is there', Green asks, 'of resistance to the sovereign power leading to a modification of its character?' (Works II, 424; HM, 86). The final condition is that (4) the sense of the state's badness must be widely felt, 'the attitude of the mass of the people in regard to a contemplated resistance to established government must always be most important in determining the question whether the resistance should be made' (Works II, 423; HM, 85–6).

The third circumstance obtains when an individual law of the state, 'a law', 'some command' (Works II, 416–17; HM, 80) is bad, but the state itself is not bad in the sense just defined. The vital consideration here is whether the means of lawful remedy are available. If they are, even a bad law should be obeyed; obedience should continue until the law has been repealed under pressure (Works II, 417; HM, 80).

An adequate discussion of Green's views on disobedience and rebellion would require a political treatise; and I have taken only the principal points from a complex and high qualified discussion (Works II, 416–26; HM, 80–9). But in sum, Green thinks of political obligation, disobedience, and rebellion as all grounded on considerations relating to the moral life. Essentially: how is that life best served? This is what the state must decide; this is what we must decide, if necessary against the

state. The end of the state, its proper function, is more significant for Green than its origin or form. But there is one point on
which I feel inclined to put myself between Green and the
reader. The above conditions which justify disobedience or
rebellion are Green's interpretation of how one might think
morally about this part of politics. In broad terms they represent
his own moral reflection under the dual model of moral
reasoning. Green's agent should not be held back by Green's
own thinking here. If the state is such that a bad law can be
repealed, then the law should be obeyed until it has been
repealed. It is hard to see, however, why this should be so when
what the law requires violates 'the universe of character' (PE, §
316; see 7.19) and when, since one makes no attempt to resist
the penalty, disobedience of the law is 'easily separable from that
on which the general maintenance of social order and the fabric
of settled rights depends, that it can be resisted without serious
detriment to this order and fabric' (Works II, 417; HM, 81). But
perhaps Green concedes as much when he says that in all cases
the citizens, as moral agent, 'judges for himself' (Works II, 416;
HM, 80).

8.11 ETHICS AND POLITICAL REASONING

I want finally to examine some tensions between moral and
political viewpoints, between moral and political reasoning,
which Green does not, I think, quite manage to reconcile. There
are four points to consider.

The first is that the state must take a broad view of the moral
life and of the kind of support which political activity can render
to it. We require results of the state; and an element of
consequentialism is inseparable from the evaluation of political
activity. 'What is the kind of thing we must stop?' This is a
typical political question; see how it might be applied. Suppose
there were a run of cases in which children in public care were
found to have been abused by persons with a legal record of
offences against children. A law might be enacted (a regulation
brought into force, etc.) by which no one with such a record
should have public care of children. This might be inappropriate
to a particular person, inasmuch as his record is a long way

behind him and (in all probability) he is someone with whom children would be safe. In my view the public policy would be right: the children come first. This is to concede, however, that the occasional individual may suffer. There are more extreme examples. The individual, on an ethical theory such as Green's, has a right to work 'towards perfection'; and the basic end of the state is to maintain a 'system of rights' of which this individual right is one. From internationl aggression, however, or any of an indefinite number of political contingencies, that right may be abridged, and conscientiously abridged through political activity to preserve the very existence of the social order. The necessity, through political activity, to take or to sacrifice an individual's life, belongs to a common understanding of politics, however narrow the range of circumstances might be in which we allow it to be morally right. The point is not one to which I should attach preponderant weight; it does not invalidate Green's ethical theory or cut totally the relation of ethics to politics in his work. But it is an eloquent reminder of the moral limitations of politics for an ethical theory which sees politics as inseparably connected to ethics, as deriving its rationale from it.

Secondly, the autonomy of politics works its revenge. The state cannot simply consider the common good; as in contemplated rebellion so here, 'account must be taken of the state of mind of the majority in considering whether it is for the public good or no' (Works II, 423; HM, 86). In other words, in determining the requirements of particular social roles, the state cannot follow the bare logic of moral reasoning; an enforceable law is, practically, one that is not too far in advance of public opinion. In this commonplace of political reflection again we meet the moral limitations of politics.

Thirdly, in enforcing a law, the state punishes a criminal. A section of PPO is concerned with the philosophy of punishment (Works II, 486–511; HM, 138–59). But a moral tension is inbuilt in any institution of public punishment; that the state must look both to what is due to the criminal and to what is required to serve the 'public good', to maintain 'the rights of its members as a whole or a system'. What is due to the criminal is in no case precisely ascertainable, through the inaccessibility of character (5.9, 7.20). There is no clear light between the legal prohibition of certain actions as 'necessary to the existence of a society in which the moral end . . . can be realised' (8.3), and the relation which those actions bear, from person to person and occasion to occasion, to 'the universe of a character'.

Fourthly, law (as Aristotle recognized) has a certain inflexible generality. It applies universal formulas rigidly. Of course no lawmaker can foresee all possible cases, or take into account the full range of nuances of those cases which he does foresee; and so any advanced legal system assigns a role to 'equity', which reinforces the law and fills its lacunae with a sensitivity to the particular case (NE V. 10). But there are limits to this sensitivity. Justice is the distinctive merit of public institutions. Like cases must be treated equally. There is a constant, politically proper need not to allow particular features of a case to be considered beyond a consensus that acknowledges their relevance. The requirement of uniformity of treatment tends inherently to keep the administration of the law, and public policy generally, within the limits of that consensus. Once more, and finally, we encounter sharply the moral limitations of politics.

8.12 REVIEW

Traditionally political philosophy has covered at least three activities: the attempt to define and interrelate the main terms and concepts of political discourse; the attempt to justify or prescribe, broadly to recommend, certain forms of political action; and the attempt to discover laws of politics—patterns of political change, preconditions of political stability. Very little of the third activity, a prefiguration of political science, is to be found in Green.

Then to cut deeper, there are at least three ways in which Green's political philosophy, set out in PPO and in other political writings, might be taken. One might examine it, in the first place, simply as a political philosophy: as a cohesive, interlocking series of ideas, arguments, and recommendations involving major concepts of political thought. In this way one might consider the bearings of Green's political philosophy on such topics as political obligation, rights, punishment, freedom, law, and morals, some of the topics we have taken up, and carry across from Green's ethics just enough to illuminate the margins of what he is saying. So Green's role for the state is to provide conditions for the moral life in which every citizen can achieve self-realization, and we need some understanding of the relevant portion of Green's ethics in order to see what this political claim involves: but the political claim has a logic of its own and it must fit connectedly into Green's other political ideas, arguments, and recommendations if it is to form part of something as coherent as a philosophy of politics. No amount of reference back to ethics could, as such, give those ideas, arguments, and recommendations the degree of organization required of a political philosophy. Their measurement against that requirement is a proprietary task of political philosophy itself. To say this is to take one view of political philosophy as an autonomous inquiry.

Secondly, we might consider Green's political philosophy 'horizontally' as part of a large philosophical enterprise to integrate the fields of metaphysics, epistemology, ethics, and politics. The position of Green's political philosophy in his total view of human thought and activity is the vantage-point of this approach. And thirdly, Green's political philosophy might be taken 'vertically' in relation to the history of political philosophy. This approach involves comparisons between Green's political ideas, arguments, and recommendations and those of previous and later thinkers: between, for example, his conception of freedom and that of Locke, J. S. Mill, or Hayek. An extra level is built into this approach by Green's own historical survey of the political philosophies of Aristotle, Hobbes, Locke, Spinoza, Rousseau, and Hegel; and again by the historical medium through which, in the final quarter of the twentieth century, we look back at Green.

A full discussion of Green's political philosophy would take all three approaches. This chapter has followed firmly the second approach. Its point has been simply to articulate the implications of Green's ethics for his political philosophy; to see what implications Green himself draws, to test whether they follow, and to check the suggestions of critics that Green's political philosophy actually violates that moral life which it would serve. Where the discussion has skirted other approaches, it has done so incidentally to that point. Green's 'Lectures on the Principles of Political Obligation' are widely counted among the classics of political philosophy. Left to myself I would rather *Prolegomena to Ethics* were widely counted among the classics of moral philosophy, and the Lectures read as one attempt, not itself of privileged importance but rather partial and at times precarious, to draw out the political implications of an ethical theory.

9

Conclusion

9.1 INTRODUCTION

In this chapter I want to stand back from the detailed exposition, interpretation, and criticism of Green's moral philosophy and to look reflectively at its main features. Not to summarize: a rapid survey of the ground we have covered can be taken from the introductory and review sections of previous chapters. My intention is not to repeat that material but to catch in sharp outline the kind of enterprise that emerges from the ideas and arguments which make up Green's moral philosophy and my account of it in this book.

9.2 CONTEMPORARY RELEVANCE

There are philosophers whose main interest depends on their precise arguments being right. Berkeley's paradoxical conclusions are of slight importance unless his arguments carry them; I think the same applies to the Russell of 1905–19. Certain other philosophers are more than the sum of their arguments; their chief significance is fixed by the perspectives they open, the approaches they take. This holds good, I think, of Kant and of Locke. It would take a peculiar sort of philosophical blindness to dismiss Locke's discussion of personal identity simply because several of his arguments are actually bad. I introduce this classification, not to suggest a 'good ideas, bad arguments' appraisal of Green, but to emphasize that Green's relevance to contemporary ethics is largely a function of what he wants to do, of the kind of enterprise in which he is engaged. If we insist that every argument he uses has to work, we miss that relevance.

One part of Green's interest is simply that his moral philosophy sets a particular challenge to the philosophical imagination. His ethical theory and moral psychology span an ambitious range of ethical topics: the virtues, moral reasoning, the good will, moral rules, the rationality of moral action, the nature of the unconditional human good, moral rights, and the rest. This range of topics is included, moreover, in a general philosophy which runs in a sequence of consistencies from metaphysics, through epistemology, philosophy of mind, moral philosophy, to political philosophy. Green's ethics engages his metaphysics; his metaphysics engages his epistemology; and his epistemology engages a philosophy of mind of which the central concept is what Green calls the 'self-conscious principle': and moving in the opposite direction we can see Green's general philosophy as unfolding (sometimes uncertainly) the implications of the self-conscious principle in a diversity of contexts, from knowing that something is the case to deliberating on a 'plan of life' and providing politically the conditions for self-realization. None of this is the outcome of smooth system-building. It is genuine philosophy, hard work for Green and no short task for his reader.

There are of course more specific matters. In Chapter 2 I made three claims for Green's contemporary relevance: on the explanation of action, the rationality of moral action, and the nature of agency. These topics are closely cognate, but take first the rationality of moral action. By one of those ironies of philosophy, Green's approach has something in common with that of Spencer, who observes in *The Data of Ethics*, that 'Great mischief has been done by the repellent aspect habitually given to moral rule by its expositors',[1] as though the requirements of morality stood over against the individual as constraints which he must be induced painfully and with inconvenience to accept.

Green belongs to a different ethical tradition for which morality and practical reason are inseparably linked. Aristotle holds, for instance, that practical reason aims at *eudaimonia* or happiness, and that happiness, the human good, is 'activity of the soul in accordance with virtue'. Virtue may conflict with inclination but not, on such a theory, with the individual's interest. Green works, in the Aristotelian manner, with an ethical theory for which personal good and moral good interlock. Contrasts abound: in Kant's moral philosophy, for example,

---

[1] H. Spencer, *The Data of Ethics*, London, 1879, Preface, iv.

duty is perfectly capable of conflicting with interest. Through a conception of the social nature of human beings Green envisages, in his own approach to the rationality of moral action, a coherent form of social organization in which the individual achieves 'self-satisfaction', 'an abiding satisfaction of an abiding self', through carrying out a social role which both embodies a lifeplan and fulfils the requirements of morality. This is a bold vision, part description of present society and part programme for social change; and, to make a different but related point, there is no real line between moral philosophy and practical reason. Green's moral philosophy has a practical goal, to demonstrate irrevocably the rationality of moral action to anyone engaged in practical thinking with a view to 'self-satisfaction'. This is a long way from the moral preaching criticized by Ayer and Broad.

This account of the rationality of moral action takes a comprehensive view of the agent; it encompasses everything involved in the conception and fulfilment of a lifeplan. This introduces our next topic, the nature of agency. Green's attempt to establish the rationality of moral action could not so much as begin without this view of what I called in 2.1 the 'integral agent'. The embodiment of lifeplans in social roles within a coherent form of social organization respects, moreover, the autonomy of the agent's practical reason, the second aspect of the nature of agency cited in 2.1. The tension which utilitarianism acknowledges between the viewpoints of agent and spectator, between motive/intention and consequence, is lessened through the idea of practices associated with social roles. As a practice incorporates (in the good society at least) the best available conception of what a social role requires, and as the complete network of social roles provides the conditions in which the individual, all individuals, can achieve self-satisfaction through self-realization, so there is no sharp line between motive and consequence. If I am motivated and intend to do what the practice of my social role requires, the consequences of my actions are automatically controlled by the network of social roles. This is the social blueprint which, on Green's account, we should seek to realize. Or is it already real?

Some ambiguity affects Green's attitude here. On occasion he stresses what is socially available to the individual who is deliberating in the way outlined in Chapter 4; at other times he looks critically at present forms of social organization. But one strength of Green's morality of social roles is not directly touched by this ambiguity; and to explore it is to return to the rationality of moral action by a new route. If Green belongs to the Aristotelian ethical tradition he also belongs to the Hegelian tradition which stresses how, in work and activity, the individual transforms not only the world but himself (4.17); and how the social medium in which this transformation takes place has tendencies of development, a 'social logic' of unintended consequences as some have put it, which can operate to general disadvantage and (in Green's terms) defeat the conditions for self-realization of any number of individuals (8.4). Hegel did not point up the negative aspects of this social logic with Marx's biting severity and copious explanations; and the origin of this aspect of Green's thought is not exclusively Hegelian (1.13). But Green is sensitive to this social phenomenon, which informs the discussion, in his political writings, for example of the effects of primogeniture on the ownership of land. Thus we return to the rationality of moral action; for in trying to establish the rationality of moral action Green cannot disregard the social context. Such disregard of the social medium is easily recognizable in current discussions of the rationality of moral action. Neither Foot nor Nagel, for instance, appears to consider the implications for moral rationality, or even for the possibility of coherent action, of the particular form of society in which the individual finds himself. (Derek Parfit's work is a distinguished exception to the rule.) The question is heretical but not therefore unsound: why should the rationality of moral action not be conditional on a particular form of social organization? One decided emphasis of Green's moral philosophy is on the necessity of specific social conditions for the moral life.

We have now considered the nature of agency and the rationality of moral action, two of our three topics of contemporary relevance. As a social role embodies the individual's lifeplan, so his lifeplan embodies a conception of himself as a particular kind of person, and this carries across to the explanation of action, our third topic. If the Humean belief–desire theory may be aptly shadowed forth by the image of fusion between belief and desire to produce action, Green's multi-perspectival model of deliberation suggests the altered image of belief and desire as convex and concave aspects of a curve. Under the fourth aspect of the multi-perspectival model the agent forms a certain structure of desire; in action that structure and the agent's conception of himself are simply two sides of the same phenomenon—as Green would say, of the agent's character. Then against the cognitive model, Green escapes the Nagelian trivialization of desire. He avoids also the rigid separation of belief (reason) and desire which is integral to Kant's version of the cognitive model, on which the determination of action by reason is its determination by 'pure reason', reason which is 'pure of everything "empirical" or "sensuous"—of any sort of desire', as Green expresses Kant (10A, 15). What is now different in ethics is that there are three models of action explanation credibly in the field: the belief–desire theory, the cognitive model, and Green's multi-perspectival model.

In drawing out Green's contemporary relevance through these topics—the explanation of action, the rationality of moral action, the nature of agency—I have presented his ideas and arguments on issues in ethical theory, moral psychology, political philosophy, epistemology, metaphysics, philosophy of mind. Thereby I have conveyed some idea of Green's whole philosophy, and a fairly exact idea (I hope) of his ethics. A reminder, though, of what I said in 1.18: that in recovering Green's ideas and arguments, although I should be sensitive to his own concerns I should be more sensitive still to the needs of the present. The distributions of emphasis in PE, for example, do not coincide absolutely with my own notions of what is currently important; and so, to take one instance, I have but lightly touched on Green's anti-hedonist polemic. Again, there are parts of Green's general philosophy which I have passed over because their connection with ethics is tenuous or unapparent. Hardly anything has been said, for example, of Green's philosophical logic. If I have violated historical finesse, dismembered the integral whole, I see no philosophical harm in this: no other way in which to establish rapport between Green and a contemporary philosophical readership in the Anglo-American tradition.

9.3 PHILOSOPHICAL STATUS

Contemporary relevance was one claim which I made for Green in the Introduction. There were other claims, namely that (in works such as PE) Green is principally a philosopher, that his ethical theory and moral psychology yield a coherent body of moral philosophy, that he is an independent thinker.

At this stage the strictly philosophical nature of Green's ethics should not be open to doubt. That what is offered in PE is principally philosophy—argument, distinction-making, the detection of ambiguity, the tracking of presuppositions, the denial that certain conclusions follow from given premises, the interrelation of the most general concepts of moral thought— can this now be disputed and philosophical status withheld from Green's ethics? If the force of that question is for others to determine, my own answer is clear.

Let me run over the main parts of that answer. Green's philosophy divides into two distinct steps: a move from metaphysics to ethics, and a move from ethics to politics. Those who deny that Green is principally a philosopher argue that both moves skid on major errors. In brief, for these critics, the first move, from metaphysics to ethics, involves Green's attempt to derive evaluative (ethical) conclusions from descriptive (metaphysical) premises; and the second move, from ethics to politics, involves an equally invalid attempt to move from ethical conclusions to political recommendations.

Then consider the first move. For Green, metaphysics is a presuppositional inquiry (Works II, 158). Very roughly its questions are these: what must we assume about the human mind in order to explain how knowledge or belief are possible? How must the mind be, if there can be knowledge or belief? The point of these questions for Green stems from the issue of free will. Green aims to vindicate the possibility of intentional action. Morality presupposes freedom of action, the agent's ability to act otherwise if he chooses and to choose otherwise than he does. Green cannot grant this mere presuppposition; he wants to know whether action really can be free, whether (in this sense) moral action is possible.

His central worry, in the context of nineteenth-century physics, is that mental events (including, crucially, decisions to

370 CHAPTER 9 [9.3]

act) might be uniquely determined by physical events. Metaphysics enters in this way: Green argues that knowledge, and specifically our perceptual awareness of change, involves a 'self-conscious principle' which defeats the determination of mental by physical events. The details are given in Chapter 3; note here the direction of the argument. Green works backwards from an idea of free action which is part of the concept of morality, to a metaphysical guarantee that this idea is not empty, that free actions really occur. He does not work forwards from descriptive (metaphysical) premises to evaluative (ethical) conclusions. Said another way, the argument is not that because reality has such-and-such characteristics, therefore promises should be kept and, in particular, you should return my video recorder. Rather, given Green's metaphysical defence of free will, there is a moral question of whether you should return the recorder, because you have that freedom of action which gives moral questions their point. So much for criticism of the first move.

The second move, from ethics to politics, is taken to violate the separation between philosophy and practical politics. For one thing, the criticism runs, we expect a philosopher to keep to analytical and conceptual inquiries, not to tell us how we ought to think and act in politics, economics, or anything else; for another, the level of practical guidance on which Green operates (when he talks for instance about amending the law of contract) is one to which philosophy cannot possibly descend. Political recommendations entwine with empirical views, with matters of fact and probability, on which the philosopher, as such, has no competence to pronounce. Philosophy can fulfil no such normative role.

But then, if moral action is rational as Green argues, the morality of social roles plainly has empirical preconditions. How far social roles are internally consistent and jointly coherent, how well they serve interests within a society, how most effectively the shortcomings of particular social practices might be remedied, are empirical matters into which (it may be agreed) the philosopher, as such, has no special insight. But 'the philosopher' is an abstraction. When Green makes political recommendations (to revise the distribution of land, to change the law of contract), there is no sense of telling other people, solely on the authority of philosophy, how they should think and act politically. Green engages in analytical and conceptual inquiries as a philosopher, but thinks as a whole personality. He has his own empirical views as a close student of society, together with a set of practical commitments. This seems to me a paradigm of the practical relevance of philosophy; its normative role is not to 'help' other people to conduct their lives. There is no hint of magisterial suggestion; the aim is to clarify the conceptual basis of one's own commitments. As a practically committed thinker, concerned about the condition of his society, and equipped with empirical views, Green makes political recommendations. This is no arbitrary union, but a fusion of legitimate interests.[2]

To return now to the second claim, that of coherence. Two comments are due. First and negatively, I have deflected the criticisms of commentators who have seen severally in Green's moral philosophy a tangle of paradox (Prichard), an aggregation of inconsistent elements (Sidgwick), vacuity (H. D. Lewis), demonstrable error (Moore and Taylor). Positively of course the book must speak for itself—and be answered not only (as may be) by other commentators but by the reader himself or herself in reflecting on the original texts.

Secondly, however, there is another dimension of coherence. Aside from the hostility of Prichard, Sidgwick, and others, I mentioned, in 1.17, the sympathetic reservations of Caird and Nettleship: reservations of incompleteness. One kind of incompleteness is unavoidable and anodyne; any set of ideas and arguments contains more implications than any philosopher can recognize even in his own work. A more serious incompleteness occurs when a philosopher, in discussing a topic or in analysing an issue, fails to cover some part of it which we should expect any philosophical discussion or analysis to include. Is the coherence of Green's moral philosophy broken by this sort of 'gappiness'?

Points have emerged in passing; Green does not analyse the complete range of moral virtues, nor is he fully informative on the unity of those major virtues which he does consider. And, perhaps more significantly, what are we to say of his model of

---

[2] This topic is examined from a different angle in my 'Strange Days for Philosophers', *Radical Philosophy*, 44 (1986).

moral reasoning? Looking back we can see that this has not simply two parts, 'self-reflection' and analogic responsiveness, but two levels: (i) it defines moral presumptions of which it specifies the basis in terms of what typically serves others' interests, and (ii) it sets the agent to apply those presumptions in the particular circumstances of action. As to (i) we are left unclear on the complete list of moral presumptions; and as to (ii) Green merely indicates, in respect to 'self-reflection', that the agent is to consult 'the universe of a character'.

Green's probable response to (i) would be that we should start from 'the recognised social code' and, where necessary, extract its 'higher meaning . . . , giving reality to some requirements which it has hitherto only contained potentially' (PE, § 301). On (ii) we should recall that Green defines a morality of social roles in which normally the requirements of a practice will be a sufficient guide to action. Where that guide fails we may not care for the terseness of Green's language but we are faced by his problem, we can only look to 'the universe of a character'. In a dilemma, given the kind of person I am and the commitments I have, what am I to do? If I am a dedicated trade unionist but am totally convinced that, on a specific issue, the union leadership is dangerously wrong, what am I to do? Should I cross the picket line or not? If I cross the line and you, also a dedicated trade unionist, are my friend, what are you to do about our relationship if you support the union leadership? Sharp questions; but these are just the kinds of predicament to which Green is pointing. It is not a special defect of his moral philosophy in particular that he cannot illuminate the approach to such predicaments other than in general terms.

The final claim, that Green is an independent thinker, is the claim that his work does not rigidly imitate some historical philosophy, that of Kant, of Hegel, or of Aristotle, whose ideas he coldly repeats. No single set of ideas dominates Green's philosophy; nor again does he haphazardly associate diverse elements from different sources. But of course to be independent is not to escape all influence. I have traced the influence of Kant. Green embodies the sovereignty of the moral self, but rejects the kind of opposition between reason and desire on which this is based in Kant; and he emphasizes the self as unifying experience, but he abandons 'things-in-themselves', the two-world scheme of phenomena and noumena. I have traced the influence of Hegel. Green embodies the critical relation of a person to his own desires and those elements of the Hegelian tradition picked out in 9.2, but he does not endorse the account of the detailed levels of self-consciousness in Hegel's dialectic, and he separates vitally from Hegel over the primacy of persons. Here is no Oxford transposition of the philosophy of Hegel. I have traced the influence of Aristotle in Green's idea that we act only with a view to some good, but divergences have opened across a series of issues from the practical syllogism to the supremacy of the intellectual life and the range of persons and actions included in the scope of the moral virtues. Nothing here, Kantian, Hegelian, or Aristotelian, is the sole or master key to the page by page discussion of detailed issues and topics through which the exposition, interpretation, and criticism of Green's moral philosophy has taken us.

9.4   GREEN AND THE PERMANENT CRISIS OF ETHICS

One last point. Ethics is a subject permanently under siege. There are ethical nihilists for whom moral relationships are unreal, a kind of illusion; Thus Spake Zarathustra. There are those who see in moral judgement merely a primitive form of social technology, a mechanism of social control. There are others who deny free will, the possibility of blameworthiness, from the side of physical or psychological determinism. Others again press the claims of religion: moral relationships are real but there can be no moral obligation without a religious basis. 'Morally obligatory' means 'commanded by God', or without the fear of divine sanctions we cannot be relied on to act morally. And there are those who look to the disappearance of the moral life because a technology of abundance will remove the need for distributive justice (as though distributive justice were the whole of morality), or because a religion of love will transcend the need for moral categories. Green's moral philosophy is an emphatic repudiation of all such lines of thought. Beneath the security of philosophical status, beneath the contemporary relevance of topics, of issues, and of imaginative challenge, the interest of Green's moral philosophy extends through a theory of the unconditional human good to the deepest defence of the moral life.

BIBLIOGRAPHY

I SUGGESTIONS FOR FURTHER READING

FOR the reader whose interests are primarily philosophical the best short introduction to Green's writings is his 1868 paper, 'Popular Philosophy in its Relation to Life', reprinted in Works III. I suggest, among the longer texts, PE and PPO: in that order. The temptation to read PPO before PE, because of the former's easier availability, should be resisted.

W. H. Fairbrother's commentary, *The Philosophy of T. H. Green*, London, 1896, is a good general account: less deep than Henry Sidgwick's *Lectures on the Ethics of T. H. Green, Mr. Herbert Spencer, and J. Martineau*, London, 1902, but less controversial and confusing. Ch. 8 of Henry Sturt's *Idola Theatri*, London, 1906, pursues an unobvious, thought-provoking line of argument. Nettleship's *Memoir* in Works III is lucid, penetrating, and sympathetic; but a general introduction, not a critical exposition.

Detailed items in Green's Works should be followed up as interest directs; the contents of the Works are listed in IV below. A useful political bibliography is given in P. Harris and J. Morrow, *T. H. Green: Lectures on the Principles of Political Obligation and Other Writings*, Cambridge, 1986. An older political item which retains a good deal of value is Crane Brinton, *English Political Thought in the Nineteenth Century*: ch. 4.3, 2nd edn. London, 1949.

For the mainly historical reader the cardinal texts are J. Pucelle, *La Nature et l'esprit dans la philosophie de T. H. Green*, Louvain and Paris, 1961, 1965, and Melvin Richter's *The Politics of Conscience: T. H. Green and his Times*, London, 1964. W. H. Greenleaf's chapter on 'The Philosophical Tradition' in *Oakeshott's Philosophical Politics*, London, 1966, is brief but excellent. 'The Revolution in Philosophy', the background chapter of Anthony Manser's *Bradley's Logic*, Oxford, 1983, well repays study. (For my review of Manser, see *Mind*, 93 (1984).)

Idealist contrasts to Green can be found, for ethics, in Essay V of F. H. Bradley, *Ethical Studies*, Oxford, 1876, 2nd edn. 1927, and in Michael Oakeshott, *Experience and its Modes*: ch. 6.2, Cambridge, 1933; for politics, in Bernard Bosanquet, *The Philosophical Theory of the State*, London, 1899, 4th edn. 1923, and in Michael Oakeshott, *Rationalism in Politics*, London, 1962; for metaphysics in F. H. Bradley, *Appearance and Reality*, London, 1893, 2nd edn. 1897, in Bernard Bosanquet, *The*

Principle of Individuality and Value, London, 1912, and in Giovanni Gentile, *The Theory of Mind as Pure Act*, London, 1922; for philosophy of mind in J. A. Smith, *Knowing and Acting*, Oxford, 1910, probably the least-known item in the entire corpus of Oxford idealism.

II T. H. GREEN PAPERS: BALLIOL COLLEGE, OXFORD

The T. H. Green Papers fall naturally into four groups:

1. Biography
2. Philosophy
3. History
4. Religion

The following abbreviations are used:

CBG	Charlotte B. Green	ACB	Andrew C. Bradley
RLN	Richard Lewis Nettleship	JCW	John Cook Wilson

1. *Biography*

This heading includes (*a*) Green's correspondence, (*b*) recollections of Green sent to CBG and RLN, (*c*) documents connected with Green's social and political activities, and (*d*) biographical miscellanea.

(a) Green's Correspondence

Letters to ACB. Five letters:

20 September 1873	23 June 1881
6 December 1873	Undated ('16 Dec', no year)
Spring 1875	

Letters from ACB to Green. Four letters:

Spring 1875	15 July 1880
7 March 1880	Undated

Letters from C. D. Cave. Six letters on CBG's marriage settlement:

6 October 1871	18 April 1874
10 October 1872	3 August 1875
1 July 1873	4 December 1877

Letters from J. Conington. Six letters (1859–64) from the Latinist John Conington (1825–69), whose friendship covered Green's early years at Oxford:

27 September 1859	4 October 1861
10–11 January 1860	17 September 1863
24 September 1861	27 June 1864

Letter to D. Crawford (30 May 1863)

Letter to A. Fairbairn (1855)

Letters to CBG. Ten letters:

7 January 1871	8 March 1871
22 February 1871	15 March 1871
24 February 1871	10 April 1871
27 February 1871	25 April 1871
3 March 1871	25 June 1871

Letters to D. Hanbury. Eleven letters (1853–73) to Green's closest Rugby friend:

6 July 1853	Undated: probably 1855–7
November 1853	26 January 1863
December 1853	20 April 1865
March 1854	20 September 1871
Spring 1854	9 October 1871
24 September 1854	

Letter to Sir William Harcourt (9 January 1873?). Draft letter to Harcourt explaining Green's letter in the *Oxford Chronicle* of 4 January 1873. (See also Letters to Sir William Harcourt in T. H. Green Papers: Bodleian Library, Oxford (III below).)

Letters from Sir William Harcourt on the Licensing Bill (8 and 10 January 1873). The 8 January letter refers to Green's *Oxford Chronicle* letter; that of 10 January appears to refer to Green's reply (see above).

Correspondence with Longmans and Co. MS letter from Longmans (15 March 1882) and draft letter to the company about the publication of *Prolegomena to Ethics*.

Postcard from 'GCR' (George Croom Robertson, Editor of *Mind* 1876–91). Dated 2 March 1882 from 31 Kensington Park Gardens, London. Critical comment on a passage in the MS of Green's three-part article for *Mind*, 'Can there be a Natural Science of Man?'

Since only a few letters written by Green have survived in the original, we are mainly dependent on manuscript copies made by CBG. In addition to this source, quotations from Green's family correspondence occur in RLN's 'Notes for T. H. Green's Memoir' and 'Selections from Letters of THG (1871)'.

(b) Recollections of Green

Original MS recollections sent to CBG and RLN:

E. Caird	8 April 1882
A. V. Dicey	17 September 1882
C. Evans	10 October 1882

C. A. Fyffe	Undated
A. G. Liddell	6 July 1882
Henry Nettleship	Undated
W. L. Newman	27 November 1882
C. S. Parker	26 September 1888
J. Richardson	19 May 1888
H. Sidgwick	1 August 1882
E. Strachey	June 1886
J. A. Symonds	7 October 1882
A. R. Vardy	17 September 1887
C. E. Vaughan	Undated

Transcriptions of most of these recollections were made by CBG in two notebooks.

J. A. Symonds's recollections consist of undated notes for CBG on a 3 November 1866 conversation with Green, and a letter to CBG posted from Davros, Greece on 7 October 1882.

(c) Documents connected with Green's social and political activities

MS notebook containing information on secondary schools, written when Green was an Assistant Schools Inquiry Commissioner.

MS 'Evidence given before Commission'. Recommendations possibly made to, or intended for, the Select Committee on the Oxford and Cambridge Universities Education Bill. But the Committee's *Special Report*, published in 1867, does not appear to include any reference to Green's recommendations: see *Special Report*, 1867 (497) xiii. Whatever its target, Green's 'evidence' contains suggestions for reform of the Oxford professoriate.

MSS of two lectures delivered to the Central School, Oxford in February 1878 on 'The Elementary School System of England'. Printed in Works III.

MS of another speech on the same subject.

Two offprints of 'The Grading of Secondary Schools' from *Journal of Education*, 1877. Text of a lecture delivered to the Birmingham Teachers' Association in May 1877. Printed in Works III.

MS of lecture delivered to the Wesleyan Literary Society, 19 December 1881, on 'The Work to be Done by the Oxford High School for Boys'. Printed in Works III.

Two loose MS papers on the same subject.

Offprint of F. E. Kitchener, *Two Addresses to the Boys of Newcastle-under-Lyme School*. Privately printed, 1882.

Printed copy of the Rules of the Temperance Permanent Building Society (1872).

Tenancy agreement for house in St Clements, Oxford.

Letter from C. A. Pryce. MS letter, 13 April 1883, to RLN from C. A. Pryce (1852–1927, Mayor of Abingdon 1896–7) on Green's speech at the Liberal Hall, Abingdon in 1879 or 1880.

MS notes for undelivered political speeches in Abingdon, 7 March 1881 and Oxford, 15 March 1882; also copies of these by CBG.

MS of lecture on Liberal Legislation and the Freedom of Contract.

MS notes for a speech on church reform given at Merton College, Oxford, December 1881.

(d) Biographical Miscellanea

Vita prepared by CBG for the period 1850–70, along with an account of Green's health in his later years.

Notes on the Green–Vaughan family by one of Green's sisters. These notes appear to have been written after Green's death and sent to RLN for him to use in compiling his memoir. There is no indication which of Green's sisters wrote them. The Vaughan family was that of Green's mother.

Vaughan family tree by E. T. Green.

Photographs: (i) encased oval photograph of T. H. Green in middle age; (ii) a group photograph featuring Green and three others (unidentified); (iii) three copies of a photograph of Green as a young man.

Two MS copies by CBG of the 1858 minutes of the Old Mortality Society concerning Green's essay on 'Political Idealism'.

CBG's MS copy of Arnold Toynbee's preface to the *Lay Sermons*.

MS of Edward Caird's preface to *Essays in Philosophical Criticism* and CBG's copy.

Letters from Benjamin Jowett. Three MS letters of condolence to CBG:

26 March 1882
23 June 1883
2 April 1893

Jowett's 1893 letter does not concern T. H. Green.

Letter from CBG. MS letter from CBG to RLN on biographical details.

Letter from Henry Nettleship. MS letter to CBG on divinity lectures; letter dated 3 July, no year.

Letters from J. F. Bright and C. A. Fyffe. Two MS letters to CBG on the Lectures on the English Revolution. Bright's letter is undated; Fyffe's letter is dated 1 January 1883.

MS copy of extracts from two letters (4 and 10 March 1861) written to CBG by J. A. Symonds stating that Green helped to select the passages for *Statements of Christian Doctrine Extracted from the Writings of B. Jowett.* (See Religion, below.)

Notebooks. Two MS notebooks mainly on students' examination results and essays.

Diaries. Three pocket diaries, 1873–5. (Few entries; highly prosaic, of the order 'Temperance Conference 7.30' and 'Insurance to be paid'.)

Valuation of Green's property in Balliol College, 17 July 1877.

Share certificates for Girls' Public Day School Company, 3 June 1878.

Income tax demand, 17 December 1879.

Agreements with Longman's for the publication of Green's Works and with the Clarendon Press for the publication of *Prolegomena to Ethics.*

CBG's correspondence with publishers.

Sales figures for Green's published writings, 1883–1928.

Offprint of James Bryce, 'T. H. Green', *Contemporary Review*, 41 (1882).

Letter from Rudolph Hermann Lotze. JCW's MS copy of a letter from Lotze about the translation project which Green, JCW, ACB, and others were planning.

Scrapbooks. Two scrapbooks with obituaries from the local and national press and reviews of *Prolegomena to Ethics* collected by CBG.

RLN's 'Corrections in Green Works II in 2nd Edition'.

2. Philosophy

This section relates to (*a*) numbered MSS, (*b*) unnumbered MSS, and (*c*) annotated books.

(a) Numbered MSS

Most of Green's philosophical papers were listed by CBG, whose enumeration was revised by ACB, RLN, and JCW in their examination of Green's papers for publication. The enumeration, which duplicates MS 20, is neither philosophical nor chronological.

MS 1A   Lecture on Logic.

MS 1B   Logic: Greek.

MS 3   Analysis of *Republic*.

MS 4   Two sheets of an apparently early essay on Hegel together with other fragments on philosophy.

MS 5A   Fragments on Physiology, on the Logic of Aristotle and J. S. Mill, and on general philosophy.

MS 5B   Notes on Aristotle's Metaphysics.

MS 6A   Notes for Lectures on Locke, Hume, Kant.

MS 6B   Extracts from Hume and Lectures on Kant's *Kritik der reinen Vernunft*. Partly printed in Works II, 'Lectures on Kant'.

MS 7A   Notes for Lectures on Mill's Logic; Aristotelian Logic.

MS 7B   Mill's Logic; Kant.

MS 7C   Lectures on Logic and Project for Essay on Materialism.

MS 8   Extracts and Summaries from Locke.

MS 9   Four Loose Sheets on Moral Philosophy.

MS 10A   Notes of Lectures on Kant's Moral Philosophy (At Other End, Lecture on Moral Philosophy).

MS 10B   Kant [Moral Philosophy].
       1.   Analysis of *Grundlegung der Metaphysik der Sitten*
       2.   Part analysis of *Kritik der praktischen Vernunft*.

MS 11   Notes for Lectures on History of Greek Philosophy.

MS 12   Fragments of Lecture on Mill's Logic; lectures on the Moral Philosophy of Hume and Kant.

MS 14   Notes of Lectures on Kant's *Kritik der reinen Vernunft*.

MS 15   Notes on Moral Philosophy.

MS 16   Translation of Aristotle's *de Anima*. [Nearly complete but omitting the end of III.3 and the start of III. 7.]

MS 17   Four articles on G. H. Lewes and H. Spencer. [All reprinted in Works I.]

MS 18   Aristotle: Politics.

MS 19   Notes on Political Philosophy.

MS 20   Two notebooks on Aristotle: Ethics.

MS 22   Province of Moral Philosophy Determined. Professorial
& 22D   Lectures given in Trinity Term 1878. Partly printed in Works II, 'Lectures on Kant'.

MS 23   Professorial Lectures on Kant. Complete notes for Michaelmas Term 1878.

MS 24   Professorial Lectures. Hilary and Trinity Terms 1879.
& 20   Partly printed in Works II, 'On the Different Senses of 'Freedom' As Applied to Will and to the Moral Progress of Man'.

(b) Unnumbered MSS

Two MS notebooks marked 'T. H. Green', containing undergraduate essays:

Notebook I

The Character of Cicero
The Roman Idea of a National Religion
The Spirit of Poetry
The Duties of the University to the State
British Rule and Policy in India
On Eloquence
The General Difference between the Philosophers Before and After Socrates
The Political Influence of the Grecian Oracles.
Standing Armies
Conservatism
Legislative Interference in Moral Matters
The Relation of Language to Mythology
Stoicism
On Greek Humour with Special Reference to the Humour of Plato
How Far Moral Principles are Probable or Conventional
An Introduction to Greek History
On Definition
On the Platonic Doctrine of Ideas
On Authority or Private Judgement, or Reason and Faith
The Origin of Greek History
The Value of the Argument from Analogy
On the Origin of Ideas
Characteristics of the Mythic Period of Philosophy
Utility as a Principle in Art and Morality
The Comparative Influence of Plato and Aristotle on Subsequent Times
Compare and Contrast Greek and Roman Colonization
A Comparison between the Spartan Constitution and the Republic of Plato
The Nature and Use of Formal Logic
On Ostracism

Notebook 2

The Advantages and Disadvantages of Diffusive Reading
The Effect of Commerce on the Mind of a Nation
The Influence of Contact with Greece on the Language, Literature, Tastes and Opinions of the Romans
On the Nature and Use of Money

The Principle of Honour; Its History and Value in Ancient and Modern Times
The Comparative Value of Fact and Fiction in Education
The Utility of Classical Studies
Veracity
Loyalty
The Character and Opinions of Samuel Johnson
Can Interference with Foreign nations in any Cases be Justifiable?
 On Thackeray's Novels
'Quoniam etiam victis redit in praecordia virtus'. What is the Truth of This, as Viewed in the Light of History?
The English National Character as Compared with that of the Germans
The Character of Mahomet
Enthusiasm
The Influence of Civilization on Genius

The undergraduate essays also include Latin exercises. 'Quoniam etiam victis redit in praecordia virtus' is a quotation from Virgil: 'Sometimes courage returned even to the vanquished' (*Aeneid* ii, l. 367). Three of the essays, 'The Effect of Commerce on the Mind of a Nation', 'Loyalty', and 'Legislative Interference in Moral Matters', are printed in Harris and Morrow.

Untitled Notebook. This is a general philosophical notebook which looks at topics as diverse as utilitarianism, intellectual conception, and Aristotelian induction. It contains several loose-sheet insertions of the same character.

MS of article on 'The Philosophy of Aristotle' and offprint of the same article from the *North British Review*.

'Analysis of Hegel'. This is Green's translation of paragraphs 1–163 of Hegel's *Philosophische Propädeutik*, ed. K. Rosenkranz. Berlin, 1840.

Draft of paragraphs 78–80 of Hegel's *Philosophie der Religion*.

Notebook, 'Extracts from G. H. Lewes, H. Spencer and a few from W. B. Carpenter, H. C. Bastian and Fick'. (The last-named is Adolf Fick, whose *Die Naturkraft in ihrer Wechselbezichung*, Würzburg, 1869, was reviewed in M. Foster, 'Fick on the Transformation of Force', *Nature*, 1 (1869–70).)

Three offprints from the *Contemporary Review* (1877–81):
 'Mr Spencer on the Relation of Subject and Object'
 'Mr Lewes's Account of Experience'
 'Mr Hodgson's Article, "Professor Green as a Critic" '.

Printed copy of the philosophy paper in the Balliol Fellowship examination 1873.

Analysis of Politics of Arisotle. This also contains notes on A. C. Bradley's and H. H. Asquith's philosophical answers in the 1874 Balliol Fellowship examination.

MS of a part-translation of H. Ulrici, 'Das Naturrecht', *Gott und der Mensch*, Leipzig, 1873.

'Tutorial Lectures on Kant'. Printed in Works II.

'Lecture E. T. 78'. The MS, a critique of utilitarianism and hedonism, is severely incomplete.

'Mind and Matter'.

'Notes A–F':

 A Notes for Inaugural Lecture as White's Professor of Moral Philosophy
 B Pleasure
 C Rights
 D Pleasure
   Kant's Moral Philosophy
 E Practical Value of Moral Philosophy
 F Practical Value of Moral Philosophy.

Review of Edward Caird, *A Critical Introduction to the Philosophy of Kant*.

Review of John Caird, *An Introduction to the Philosophy of Religion*.

Lectures on The Principles of Political Obligation.

Incomplete MS and one offprint of 1882 *Mind* article, 'Can There Be A Natural Science of Man?'

Prolegomena to Ethics.

Miscellaneous: Undetermined. These notes, so entitled by RLN, are on general philosophy and ethics.

Three Miscellaneous Papers:

 1. Brief Notes on Claims and Duties.
 2. References to Hobbes, Locke, Shaftesbury, Butler, and Hume.
 3. [Non-philosophical] Notes, probably on paintings.

There is amongst the A. C. Bradley Papers in Balliol College Library an item, 'Passages Copied by ACB from 1872 Logic Notebook of THG's'. This short item starts from the problem for philosophical idealism that thinking is intermittent.

(c) Annotated Books

Two copies of Aristotle, *Nicomachean Ethics*:

 Copy A: interleaved with Green's remarks in English and Greek.

J. E. T. Rogers, *Aristotelis Ethica Nicomachea*, Oxford, 1852.

Copy B: later copy also interleaved with Green's comments. Unnamed editor, Oxford and London, 1861.

Aristotelis Politicorum Libri VIII Et Oeconomica, Leipzig, 1871. Greek text of Aristotle's Politics and Economics.

Platonis . . . Libros de Republica, ed. G. Stallbaum, Leipzig, 1823. Greek text of Plato's Republic interleaved with Green's annotations, chiefly in English.

3. *History*

(a) MSS

Four Lectures on the English Revolution.

(b) Annotated Books

An Analysis and Summary of Herodotus, Oxford, 1848. Green's annotations in English.

An Analysis and Summary of Thucydides, Oxford, 1850. Green's annotations in Greek and English.

4. *Religion*

(a) MSS

'Life and Immortality Brought to Life by the Gospel'. MS of Green's first essay for the Ellerton Theological Prize (1860).

MS copy of the above by CBG.

'The State of Religious Belief Among the Jews at the Time of the Coming of Christ'. MS of Green's second Ellerton essay.

MS copy of the above by CBG.

Notebook: notes for lectures on early Christianity.

'Essay on Dogma'. MS of essay read to the Old Mortality Society. Printed in Works III.

Notebooks for divinity lectures.

Notebook on divinity labelled by CBG.

Notebook on the Fourth Gospel.

Green's divinity lectures on:

The Fourth Gospel
Epistle to the Romans
Epistle to the Galatians

The text of these lectures is Henry Nettleship's compilation from both Green's notes and the notes of students. Copies by CBG and G. T. B. Ormerod.

'Extracts from Lectures on the New Testament'. A compilation from Green's notes and from the notes of students by Henry Nettleship and RLN. Printed in Works III.

First translation of F. C. Baur, *Geschichte der christlichen Kirche*, Tübingen, 1863.

Second translation of Baur, marked 'T. H. Green'.

(c) Books

Printed copy of *Statements of Christian Doctrine, Extracted from the Writings of B. Jowett*, Oxford, privately printed, 1861.

Das Neue Testament . . . stereotypirt nach der Hallischen Ausgabe, London: Samuel Bagster, n.d.

Novum Testamentum. Greek text of the New Testament. Dated Oxford, 1847, but possibly edited by Charles Lloyd, Bishop of Oxford, 1844.

III   T. H. GREEN PAPERS: BODLEIAN LIBRARY, OXFORD

A small amount of material is held in the Department of Western Manuscripts in the Bodleian Library, Oxford.

1. *Biography*

(a) Manuscript Sources

'Biographical Notes on Thomas Hill Green' (MS Top. Oxon. d.517, fo. 31).

(b) Photography

Photograph of Green as a member of the Old Mortality Club (MS Top. Oxon. d.242).

(c) Letters

Letter to Bosanquet (MS Autogr. d.41, fos. 85–6). N.d. but if the letter is to Bernard Bosanquet (1848–1923) it probably belongs to the period 1867–9. It pre-dates Conington's death in 1869, and presumably was written after Bosanquet had entered Balliol in 1867.

Letters to A. H. Clough. Two letters: 12 December 1869 and 8 March 1870 (MS Eng. Lett. e.76, fos. 105–8, 129–34, 137–8).

Letters to R. Payne Smith, Regius Professor of Divinity. Two letters, n.d., on behalf of students wishing to attend Smith's lectures (MS Eng. Lett. e.46, fo. 145).

Letters to Sir William Harcourt (MSS Harcourt dep. 8, fos. 28–9; 246, fos. 69–70). Two letters: one without date, the other dated 16 November [1880]. The undated letter is incomplete; it part-reproduces the Balliol draft letter. A likely date is 9 January 1873.

Letters to the Rev. James Legge, Professor of Chinese (MS Top. Oxon. c.528, fos. 123–5). Two letters: 17 March and 29 April, undated by year.

Letter to Ingram Bywater (MS Byw. 58, fo. 110). Letter dated 17 March [1882].

Letter to T. H. Ward (MS Eng. Lett. e.118, fos. 149–51). Letter dated 16 September 1881. (Postmarked 15 September 1881.)

Letter to T. D. Acland (MS Eng. Lett. d.81, fo. 55). Letter dated 29 March 1880.

IV T. H. GREEN: PUBLISHED WRITINGS

Books

1874–5   *The Philosophical Works of David Hume*, ed. with T. H. Grose, 4 vols., London, 1874–5.

1883   *Prolegomena to Ethics*, ed. A. C. Bradley, Oxford, 1883. 2nd edn. 1894; 3rd edn. 1890; 4th edn. 1899; 5th edn. 1906.

——   *The Witness of God, and Faith. Two Lay Sermons*, ed. A. Toynbee, London, 1883.

1884   'Ontology' and 'Of Time'. Tr. of H. Lotze, *Metaphysic*: Book I and Book II, ch. 3, ed. B. Bosanquet, Oxford, 1884.

1885–8   *The Works of Thomas Hill Green*, I–III, ed. R. L. Nettleship, London, 1885–8. Reprinted in various edns and imps down to 1917.

Volume I:

     Introductions to Hume's Treatise of Human Nature
     Mr Spencer on the Relation of Subject and Object
     Mr Spencer on the Independence of Matter
     Mr Lewes's Account of Experience
     Mr Lewes's Account of the 'Social Medium'
     An Answer to Mr Hodgson

Volume II:

Lectures on the Philosophy of Kant
I.   The 'Critique of Pure Reason'
II. The Metaphysic of Ethics

Lectures on Logic
I.   The Logic of the Formal Logicians
II. The Logic of J. S. Mill

On the Different Senses of 'Freedom' as Applied to Will
and to the Moral Progress of Man
Lectures on the Principles of Political Obligations

Volume III:

The Force of Circumstances
The Influence of Civilisation on Genius
The Value and Influence of Works of Fiction in Modern
Times
The Philosophy of Aristotle
Popular Philosophy in its Relation to Life
Review of E. Caird, *A Critical Introduction to the Philosophy
of Kant*
Review of J. Caird, *An Introduction to the Philosophy of
Religion*
Review of J. Watson, *Kant and his English Critics*
Fragment on Immortality
Essay on Christian Dogma
The Conversion of St Paul
Justification by Faith
The Incarnation
'The Word is Nigh Thee'
'The Witness of God'
'Faith'
Four Lectures on the English Revolution
Liberal Legislation and Freedom of Contract
The Grading of Secondary Schools
The Elementary School System of England
The Work to be Done by the New Oxford High School
for Boys

Vol. III is prefaced by Nettleship's Memoir of Green.
N. B. page headings in Vol. III refer to 'The English
Commonwealth' but the title is that of 'The English
Revolution'.

1895   *Lectures on the Principles of Political Obligation*, reprinted from Works II and containing also 'On the Different Senses of "Freedom" as Applied to Will and to the Moral Progress of Man', London, 1895.

1911 *An Estimate of the Value and Influence of Works of Fiction,* edited with introduction and notes by F. Newton Smith, Ann Arbor, 1911.

1912 *Four Lectures on the English Revolution,* reprinted from Works III, with introduction by K. Bell, London, 1912.

1964 *The Political Theory of T. H. Green,* ed. J. R. Rodman, New York, 1964. Contains selections from Green's political philosophy.

1968 *Thomas Hill Green's Hume and Locke.* The 'Introductions to Hume' reprinted from Works I, with introduction by R. M. Lemos, New York, 1968.

1969 *Prolegomena to Ethics,* reprint of 2nd edn. 1890, New York, 1969.

1986 *Lectures on the Principles of Political Obligation and Other Writings,* ed. P. Harris and J. Morrow, Cambridge, 1986.

Contains, besides the Principles:

    Liberal Legislation and Freedom of Contract
    Four Lectures on the English Revolution: selections
        On the Different Sense of 'Freedom' as Applied to Will and to the Moral Progress of Man
    Prolegomena to Ethics: selections
    The Effect of Commerce on the Mind of a Nation
    Loyalty
    Legislative Interference in Moral Matters
    Notes on Moral Philosophy
    Notes on Ancient and Modern Political Economy

(The last item is included in MS 19, Bibliography II.)

Articles, Reviews, and Pamphlets

1858 'The Force of Circumstances', Undergraduate Papers, Oxford, 1858.

1862 *An Estimate of the Value and Influence of Works of Fiction in Modern Times,* Oxford, 1862.

1866 'The Philosophy of Aristotle', *North British Review,* 45 (Sep. 1866).

1868 'Popular Philosophy in its Relation to Life', *North British Review,* 48 (Mar. 1868).

—— 'Report on King Edward's School, Birmingham' and 'General Report', *Reports from Commissioners:* 1867–1868. *Schools Inquiry*, viii, London, 1868.

1877   'Hedonism and Ultimate Good', *Mind*, 2 (1877).

—— 'Mr Spencer on the Relation of Subject and Object', *Contemporary Review*, 31 (Dec. 1877).

—— Review of E. Caird, *A Critical Introduction to The Philosophy of Kant, Academy*, 22 Sept. 1877.

—— 'The Grading of Secondary Schools', *Journal of Education* May 1877.

1878   'Mr Spencer on the Independence of Matter', *Contemporary Review*, 31 (Mar. 1878).

—— 'Mr Lewes's Account of Experience', *Contemporary Review*, 32 (July 1878).

1880   Review of John Caird, *An Introduction to the Philosophy of Religion, Academy* (10 July 1880).

1881   'Mr Hodgson's Article "Professor Green as a Critic"', *Contemporary Review*, 39 (Jan. 1881). This article is reprinted in Works I under the title 'An Answer to Mr Hodgson'.

—— *Liberal Legislation and Freedom of Contract*, Oxford, 1881.

—— Review of J. Watson, *Kant and his English Critics, Academy*, 17 and 24 Sept. 1881.

1882   'Can There be a Natural Science of Man?', three-part article, *Mind*, 7 (1882).

—— *The Work to be Done by the New Oxford School for Boys*, Oxford and London, 1882.

V SECONDARY SOURCES

Acton, H. B., Review of M. Richter (1964), *The Listener*, 72 (1964).

—— 'T. H. Green et L'Antinaturalisme', in D. Y. Beneval, ed., *Histoire de la Philosophie*, iii, Paris, 1964.

Addison, W. G., 'Academic Reform at Balliol 1854–1882—T. H. Green and Benjamin Jowett', *Church Quarterly Review*, Jan. 1952.

Alexander, S., Review of Works I, *Academy*, 10 Oct. 1885.

Ansley, C. F., 'Thomas Hill Green', *The Columbia Encyclopaedia*, ed. Clarke F. Ansley, New York, 1944.

Asquith, H. H., *Memories and Reflections*, i, ch. 3, London, 1928.

Balfour, A. J., 'Green's Metaphysics of Knowledge', *Mind*, 9 (1884).

Barbour, G. F., 'Green and Sidgwick on the Community of the Good', *Philosophical Review*, 17 (1908).

BIBLIOGRAPHY 391

Barker, E., *Political Thought in England from Herbert Spencer to the Present Day*: ch. 2, London, 1915.

Barker, H., Review of Lamont (1934), *Mind*, 44 (1935).

Barker, R., 'Citizens and People', *Politics*, 1981.

Benn, A. W., *The History of English Rationalism in the Nineteenth Century*: ch. 19, London, 1906.

—— *History of Modern Philosophy*: ch. 5, London, 1930.

Boccara, N., *Vittoriani e Radicali. Da Mill a Russell. Etica e Politica nella cultura inglese tra 1'800 et il '900*, Rome, 1981.

Bonar, J., 'Thomas Hill Green', *Spectator*, London, 15 Dec. 1906.

Bongioanni, F. M., ' "Prolegomena to Ethics" di T. H. Green', *Rivista di Filosofia*, 27 (1936).

Bosanquet, B., Critical Notice of Sidgwick (1902), *Mind*, 12 (1903).

—— 'Recent Criticism of Green's Ethics', *Proceedings of the Aristotelian Society*, 2 (1903). Reprinted in *Science and Philosophy*, London, 1927.

—— *The Philosophical Theory of the State*: ch. 8, London, 1899; 4th edn. 1923.

Bowle, J., *Politics and Opinion in the Nineteenth Century*, London, 1954.

Brett, G. S., 'T. H. Green', *Encyclopaedia of Religion and Ethics*, vi, ed. J. Hastings, London, 1913.

Brinton, C., *English Political Thought in the Nineteenth Century*, 2nd edn. London, 1949.

—— 'Thomas Hill Green', *Encyclopaedia of the Social Sciences*, vii, ed. E. R. A. Seligman, London, 1932.

Britton, K., *John Stuart Mill*: ch. 3.10, Harmondsworth, 1953.

Bruno, A., *Aspetti del problema politico moderno: Rousseau, Green, Dewey, Croce*, Catania, 1968.

Bryce, J., 'Professor T. H. Green', *Contemporary Review*, 41 (1882).

Cacoullos, A. R., *Thomas Hill Green: Philosopher of Rights*, New York, 1974.

Caird, E., Preface to *Essays in Philosophical Criticism*, ed. A. Seth and R. B. Haldane, London, 1883.

—— 'Professor Green's Last Work', *Mind*, 8 (1883).

Calderwood, H., 'Another View of Professor Green's Last Work', *Mind*, 10 (1885).

Calgero, G., 'Thomas Hill Green', *Enciclopedia Italiana*, xvii, ed. G. Gentile, Milan, 1933.

Carritt, E. F., *Morals and Politics*: ch. 10, Oxford, 1935.

Chapman, R. A., Review of Richter (1964), *Political Studies*, 13 (1965).

—— 'Thomas Hill Green (1836–1882)', *Review of Politics*, 27 (1965).

Chevalier, C., *Ethique et idéalisme*, Paris, 1963.

Chin, Y. L., 'The Political Theory of Thomas Hill Green', thesis: Columbia University, New York, 1920.

Chubb, P., 'The Significance of Thomas Hill Green's Philosophical and Religious Teaching', *Journal of Speculative Philosophy*, 22 (1893).

Cohen, M., Review of Richter (1964), *Victorian Studies*, 9 (1965–6).

Conybeare, F. C., 'On Professor Green's Political Philosophy' *National Review*, 13 (1889).

Coutan, E., 'L'Attitude religieuse de Thomas Hill Green', *Annales de Philosophie Chrétienne*, Paris, 1912.

Cowling, M., 'Problems of Orthodoxy' (review of Richter (1964)), *Spectator*, 25 Sept. 1964.

Creighton, J. E., 'Is the Transcendental Ego an Unmeaning Conception?', *Philosophical Review*, 6 (1897).

Cunningham, G. W., *The Idealist Argument in Recent British and American Philosophy*: ch. 2, New York and London, 1933.

Davies, J. P., 'The Relations Between Ethics and Metaphysics, With Special Reference to the Work of Spinoza, Kant and T. H. Green', thesis: University of Wales, 1922.

Dewey, J., 'Green's Theory of the Moral Motive', *The Early Works of John Dewey*, 3, 1889–1892, ed. J. A. Boydiston *et al.*, Carbondale and Edwardsville, 1969.

—— 'The Philosophy of T. H. Green', *The Early Works of John Dewey*, 3, 1889–1892, ed. J. A. Boydiston *et al.*, Carbondale and Edwardsville 1969.

—— 'Self-Realization as the Moral Ideal', *The Early Works of John Dewey*, 4, 1893–1894, ed. J. A. Boydiston *et al.*, Carbondale and Edwardsville, 1971.

Eastwood, A., 'On Thought Relations', *Mind*, 16 (1891).

Economist, 'Practical Idealism', anon. review of Richter (1964), *The Economist*, 215 (1965).

Edmond E., *Oxford Metaphysics and Ethics Adapted to a Natural System. [Text Followed Being ... T. H. Green's Prolegomena to Ethics.]*, Edinburgh, 1889.

Eisler, R., 'T. H. Green', *Philosophen-Lexikon*, Berlin, 1912.

Fairbrother, W. H., *The Philosophy of T. H. Green*, London, 1896.

Fishman, E. M., Review of Greengarten (1981), *American Political Science Review*, 76 (1982).

Forsyth, T. M., *English Philosophy*: ch. 7, London, 1910.

France, H., 'Thomas Hill Green', *La Grande Encyclopédie*, xix, Paris, 1947.

Fujiwara, Y., 'Thomas Hill Green and "Positive Liberty" ', *Waseda Political Studies*, 11 (1976).

Fussi, M., *Il penziere morale di T. H. Green*, Florence, 1943.

Golomb, L., 'The Relation of Morality to Self-Consciousness in the

Philosophy of T. H. Green', thesis: University of Sheffield, 1946.

Gordon, P., and White, J., *Philosophers as Educational Reformers: The Influence of Idealism on British Educational Thought and Practice*, London, 1979.

Goretti, C., 'La metafisica della conoscenza in Thomas H. Green', *Rivista di Filosofia*, 27 (1936).

Greengarten, I. M., *Thomas Hill Green and the Development of Liberal-Democratic Thought*, Toronto, 1981.

Grieve, A., *Das geistige Prinzip in der Philosophie Thomas Hill Greens*, Leipzig, 1896.

Griffin, C. M., 'The Political Theory of T. H. Green and Its Relation to Liberal, Utilitarian and So-Called "Idealist" Schools of Nineteenth Century British Philosophy', thesis: University of London, 1962.

Günther, F. O., *Das Verhältnis der Ethik Thomas Hill Greens zu derjenigen Kants*, Dresden, 1915.

Haldar, H., 'Green and his "Critics" ' *Philosophical Review*, 3 (1894).

—— *Neo-Hegelianism*: ch. 2, London, 1927.

Hampshire, S. N., 'Oxford, Virtue' (review of Richter (1964)), *New Statesman*, 68 (1964).

Hansen, P., 'T. H. Green and the Moralization of the Market', *Canadian Journal of Political and Social Theory*, 1 (1977).

Harris, F. P., *The Neo-idealist Political Theory: Its Continuity with the British Tradition*, New York, 1948.

Hobhouse, L. T., *The Theory of Knowledge*: ch. 1, London, 1896.

Hodgson, R., 'Professor Green as a Critic', *Contemporary Review*, 38 (1880).

Hodgson, S., Criticism of B. Bosanquet, 'Recent Criticism of Green's Ethics', *Proceedings of the Aristotelian Society*, 2 (1903).

Hoover, K. R., 'Liberalism and the Idealist Philosophy of Thomas Hill Green', *Western Political Quarterly*, 26 (1973).

Houang, F., *Le Néo-hégélianisme en Angleterre*: ch. 1, Paris, 1954.

James, G. F., *Green und der Utilitarismus*, Halle, 1894.

Jessop, T. E., 'Thomas Hill Green', *A Dictionary of Christian Ethics*, ed. J. Macquarrie, London, 1967.

Johnson, R. B. C., *The Metaphysics of Knowledge. Being an Examination of T. H. Green's Theory of Reality*, Princeton, 1900.

Jones, E. E. C., 'Green's Account of Aristotle's Ethics', *Hibbert Journal*, 1 (1903).

Jones, Sir H., and Muirhead, J. H., *The Life and Philosophy of Edward Caird*: ch. 1, Glasgow, 1921.

Kagey, R., 'Coleridge', *Columbia University: Studies in the History of Ideas*, iii, New York, 1935.

Kawai, E., *The Philosophical System of T. H. Green*, 2 vols., Tokyo, 1930 [in Japanese].

Kemp, J., 'T. H. Green and the Ethics of Self-Realisation', *Reason and Reality*, ed. G. N. A. Vesey, London, 1972.

Ketels, L. H., 'The Philosophy of T. H. Green', thesis: Drew University, New Jersey, 1926.

Knox, H. V., 'Green's Refutation of Empiricism', *Mind*, 9 (1900).

—— 'Has Green Answered Locke?', *Mind*, 23 (1914).

Knysh, G. D., 'An Inquiry into the Political Thought of Thomas Hill Green', thesis: University of Manitoba, Winnipeg, 1962.

Lamont, W. D., *Introduction to Green's Moral Philosophy*, London, 1934.

Laski, H. J., 'The Leaders of Collectivist Thought', *Ideas and Beliefs of the Victorians*, unnamed editor, London, 1949.

Laurie, S. S., 'The Metaphysics of T. H. Green', *Philosophical Review*, 6 (1897).

Leland, A. P., 'The Educational Theory and Practice of T. H. Green', thesis: Columbia University, New York, 1911.

Lewis, H. D., 'Does the Good Will Define its Own Content? A Study of Green's Prolegomena', *Ethics*, 57, (1948).

—— 'Individualism and Collectivism: A Study of T. H. Green', *Ethics*, 63 (1952–3).

—— ' "Self-Satisfaction" and the "True Good" ', *Proceedings of the Aristotelian Society*, 42 (1941–2).

—— 'The British Idealists', *Nineteenth Century Religious Thought in the West*, ii, ed. N. Smart, J. Clayton, S. T. Katz, and P. Sherry, Cambridge, 1985.

—— 'The Moral Philosophy of T. H. Green', thesis: University of Oxford, 1935.

—— 'Was Green a Hedonist?', *Mind*, 45 (1936).

Lindsay, A. D., 'T. H. Green and the Idealists', *Representative Figures of the Victorian Age*, ed. F. J. C. Hearnshaw, London, 1933.

Lindsay, T. M., 'Recent Hegelian Contributions to English Philosophy', *Mind*, 2 (1877).

Lofthouse, W. F., *F. H. Bradley*: ch. 1, London, 1949.

Lukes, S., 'Philosopher's Conscience' (review of Richter (1964)), *New Society*, 4 (1964).

Macan, R. W., *Religious Changes in Oxford, during the Last Fifty Years. A Paper read Before the Oxford Society For Historical Theology . . . June 14, 1917*, revised and reprinted, Oxford, 1918.

MacCunn, J., *Six Radical Thinkers*, London, 1907.

Mack, M. P., Review of Richter (1964), *American Historical Review*, 70 (1964–5).

Mackenzie, J. S., 'Le Mouvement philosophique contemporain en Angleterre', *Revue de Metaphysique et de Morale*, 16 (1908).
—— *Outlines of Social Philosophy*: Bk 11, ch. 4, London, 1918.
MacKillop, I., *The British Ethical Societies*, Cambridge, 1986.
Macmillan's Magazine, 'A Lost Leader. In memoriam T. H. Green', anon. poem, *Macmillan's Magazine*, 46 (1882).
Manser, A., *Bradley's Logic*: ch. 1, Oxford: Blackwell, 1983.
Matross, G. N., 'T. H. Green and the Concept of Rights', thesis: University of Kansas, 1972.
Maurer, A. A., 'Idealism', *Recent Philosophy: Hegel to the Present*, ed. E. Gilson, T. Langan, and A. A. Maurer, New York, 1962.
McGilvary, E. B., 'The Eternal Consciousness', *Mind*, 10 (1901).
Merz, J. T., *A History of European Thought in the Nineteenth Century*, iv, 3rd edn. Edinburgh and London, 1914.
Milne, A. J. M., *The Social Philosophy of English Idealism*, London, 1962.
Mind, Anon. review of T. H. Green, *Prolegomena to Ethics*, *Mind*, 8 (1883).
—— Anon. review of T. H. Green, Works I, *Mind*, 11 (1886).
—— Anon. review of T. H. Green, Works II, *Mind*, 11 (1886).
—— Anon. review of T. H. Green, Works III, *Mind*, 14 (1889).
Misra, H. N., *Moral Philosophy: Green and Gita*, Kanpur, 1965.
Monro, D. H., 'Green, Rousseau and the Culture Pattern', *Philosophy*, 26 (1951).
Monson, C. H., 'Prichard, Green, and Moral Obligation', *Philosophical Review*, 63 (1954).
Montagné, P., *Un Radical religieuse en Angleterre au XIXe siècle; ou la philosophie de Thomas Hill Green*, Toulouse, 1927.
Mossner, E. C., *Hume: A Treatise of Human Nature*: Introduction, Harmondsworth, 1969.
Muirhead, J. H., 'How Hegel Came to England', *Mind* 36 (1927).
—— Review of Lamont (1934), *Philosophy*, 9 (1934).
—— *The Service of the State: Four Lectures on the Political Teaching of T. H. Green*, London, 1908.
Mukhopadhyay, A. K., *The Ethics of Obedience: A Study of the Philosophy of T. H. Green*, Calcutta, 1967.
Mure, G. R. G., Review of Pucelle (1961), *Philosophy*, 37 (1962).
Murray, R. H., *Studies in the English Social and Political Thinkers of the Nineteenth Century*, ii, ch. 7, Cambridge, 1929.

Nédoncelle, M., *La Philosophie religieuse en Grande-Bretagne de 1850 à nos jours*, Paris, 1934.
Nettleship, R. L., *Memoir* of Thomas Hill Green in Works III, London, 1888. Separate edn, London, 1906.

—— 'Professor T. H. Green', *Contemporary Review*, 41 (1882).

Nicholls, D., 'Positive Liberty: 1880–1914', *American Political Science Review*, 56 (1962).

Oakeshott, M. J., *The Social and Political Doctrines of Contemporary Europe*: ch. 1 and Introduction, Cambridge, 1939.

O'Sullivan, N. K., 'The Problem of Political Obligation in the Writings of T. H. Green, B. Bosanquet and M. Oakeshott', thesis: University of London, 1969.

Parodi, D., 'L'Idealisme de T. H. Green', *Revue de Metaphysique et de Morale*, 4 (1896).

Passmore, J. A., *A Hundred Years of Philosophy*: ch. 3, 2nd edn. London, 1966.

Pattison, M., 'Philosophy at Oxford', *Mind* 1 (1876).

Perry, R. B., *Philosophy of the Recent Past*: Pt III. 17, New York, 1926.

Pfannenstill, B., *Bernard Bosanquet's Philosophy of the State*: ch. 2 Lund, 1936.

Plamenatz, J. P., *Consent, Freedom and Political Obligation*: ch. 3, 2nd edn. Oxford, 1968.

Pringle-Pattison, A. S., *J. Locke: An Essay Concerning Human Understanding*: Introduction, Oxford, 1924.

—— *The Idea of God in the Light of Recent Philosophy*: ch. 10, Oxford, 1920.

Prichard, H. A., *Moral Obligation*, Oxford, 1949.

Pucelle, J., *La Nature et l'esprit dans la philosophie de T. H. Green*, Louvain and Paris, 1961, 1965.

—— *L'Idealisme en Angleterre*, Neuchâtel, 1955.

Quinton, A. M., *Absolute Idealism*, Oxford, 1972.

—— 'T. H. Green', *International Encyclopaedia of the Social Sciences*, vi, ed. D. L. Sills, New York, 1968.

Randall, J. H., Review of Richter (1964), *Journal of Philosophy*, 63 (1966).

—— 'T. H. Green: The Development of English Thought from J. S. Mill to F. H. Bradley', *Journal of the History of Ideas*, 27 (1966).

Rashdall, H., *Ethics*: ch. 4, London, 1913.

—— *The Theory of Good and Evil*: I.ii.v; II.i.i; II.iii.vi; III.i.x., 2nd edn. Oxford, 1924.

Reardon, B. M. G., *From Coleridge to Gore: A Century of Religious Thought in Britain*: ch. 9, London, 1971.

Rees, Daniel, *Contemporary English Ethics*, Leipzig, 1892.

Richter, M., *The Politics of Conscience: T. H. Green and His Times*, London, 1964.

—— 'T. H. Green and His Audience: Liberalism as a Surrogate Faith', *Review of Politics*, 18 (1956).

Ritchie, D. G., *The Principles of State Interference*, London, 1891.

Robbins, P., *The British Hegelians*, 1875–1925, New York, 1982.

Roberts, J., 'T. H. Green', *Conceptions of Liberty in Political Philosophy*, ed. Z. Pelczynski and J. Gray, London, 1984.

Rockow, L., *Contemporary Political Thought in England*, London, 1925.

Rodman, J. R., *The Political Theory of T. H. Green*, New York, 1964.

—— 'What is Living and What is Dead in the Political Philosophy of T. H. Green?', *Western Political Quarterly*, 26 (1973).

Roelofs, H. M., 'The Applicability and Practical Implications of the Political Philosophy of T. H. Green', thesis: University of Oxford, 1950.

Rogers, A. K., *English and American Philosophy since 1900*: ch. 5.2, New York, 1922.

Ross, W. D., *The Right and the Good*: App 1, Oxford, 1930.

Ruggiero, G. de, *Modern Philosophy*: III, ch. 2.2, Eng. tr. A. H. Hannay and R. G. Collingwood, London, 1921.

Ryosen, T., *Ryosen Zenshu* [Works of Ryosen], vi, Tokyo, 1922.

Sabine, G. H., and Thorson, T. L., *A History of Political Theory*: ch. 33, 4th edn. Illinois, 1973.

Sahakian, W. S., *Ethics: An Introduction to Problems and Theories*: ch. 5, New York, 1974.

Sankhdher, M. M., 'Theory of the Welfare State', *Contemporary Political Theory*, ed. J. S. Bains and R. B. Jain, New Jersey, 1980.

Schneewind, J. B., *Sidgwick's Ethics and Victorian Moral Philosophy*: ch. 14.iii, Oxford, 1977.

Selby-Bigge, L. A., *D. Hume: Enquiries Concerning the Human Understanding and Concerning the Principles of Morals*: Introduction, 1st edn. Oxford, 1894.

Selsam, H., *T. H. Green: Critic of Empiricism*, New York, 1930.

Seth, A., Critical Notice of Works II, *Mind*, 12 (1887). (N. B. Andrew Seth later changed his name to Pringle-Pattison (q.v.).)

—— *Hegelianism and Personality*: ch. 1, Edinburgh and London, 2nd edn. 1893.

Sidgwick, H., 'Green's Ethics', *Mind*, 9 (1884).

—— 'Hedonism and the Ultimate Good', *Mind*, 2 (1877).

—— *Lectures on the Ethics of T. H. Green, Mr. Herbert Spencer, and J. Martineau*, London, 1902.

—— *Lectures on the Philosophy of Kant and Other Philosophical Lectures*, London, 1905.

—— 'The Philosophy of T. H. Green', *Mind*, 10 (1901).

Silverthorne, M. J., 'The Moral and Political Philosophy of T. H. Green', thesis: University of Oxford, 1966.

Sinclair, M., 'The Ethical and Religious Import of Idealism', *New*

World, 2 (1893).

Smith, C. A., 'A Critical Study of T. H. Green's Theory of Political Obligation', thesis: University of London, 1977.

—— 'T. H. Green's Philosophical Manuscripts: An Annotated Catalog', *Idealistic Studies*, 9 (1979) (N. B. Smith's classification of the T. H. Green Papers, which is analytical by judgement of content, does not always keep the traditional titles.)

Smith, J. A., 'The Influence of Hegel on the Philosophy of Great Britain', *Verhandlungen des ersten Herelkongresses von 22. bis 25. April 1930 im Haag*, ed. B. Wigersma, Tübingen and Haarlem, 1931.

Smith, N. K., 'The Naturalism of Hume (I) and (II)', *Mind*, 14 (1905). Reprinted in N. K. Smith, *The Credibility of Divine Existence*, London, 1967.

Smith T. V., and Debbins, W., *Constructive Ethics*: ch. 7, New Jersey, 1948.

Soper, A., *T. H. Green as Theologian; An Historical-Theological Study with Special reference to the Sermon on Faith*, Pontificium Athenaeum Anselmianum, London, 1972.

Soper, D. M., 'An English Liberal', *Downside Review*, 88 (1970).

Sorley, W., *Recent Tendencies in Ethics*, Cambridge, 1904.

—— 'The Method of a Metaphysic of Ethics', *Philosophical Review*, 14 (1905).

Spencer, H. 'Professor Green's Explanations', *Contemporary Review*, 39 (1881).

Steintrager, J., Review of Richter (1964), *American Political Science Review*, 59 (1965).

Stephen, L., 'Thomas Hill Green', *Dictionary of National Biography*, viii, Oxford, 1959–60 reprint.

Stewart, H. L., *Questions of the Day in Philosophy and Psychology*: ch. 8, London, 1912.

Stewart, J. A., 'Ethics', *Encyclopaedia Britannica*, iv, 10th edn. London, 1902.

Stout, G. F., 'Perception of Change and Duration', *Mind*, 9 (1900).

Sturt, H., *Idola Theatri*: ch. 8, London, 1906.

Symonds, J. A., *The Memoirs of John Addington Symonds*, ed. P. Grosskurth, London, 1984.

Taylor, A. E., Review of Sidgwick (1902), *The Hibbert Journal*, 1 (1903).

—— Criticism of B. Bosanquet, 'Recent Criticism of Green's Ethics', *Proceedings of the Aristotelian Society*, 2 (1903).

—— *The Problem of Conduct*: ch. 2, London, 1901.

Thomas, G. L., 'Thomas Hill Green', *Cogito* 1 (1987).

Tilgher, A., 'La Filosofia Religiosa di Th. Green', *Religio*, 12 (1936).

Times Literary Supplement, 'The Liberal Teacher', anon, review of Richter (1964), *Times Literary Supplement*, 15 Oct. 1964.

Townsend, H. G., 'The Principle of Individuality in the Philosophy of Thomas Hill Green', thesis: Cornell University, Lancaster, USA, 1914.

Ulam, A. B., *Philosophical Foundations of English Socialism*, Harvard: Camb. Mass., 1951.

Upton, C. B., 'Theological Aspects of the Philosophy of T. H. Green', *New World*, 1 (1892).

Vincent, A., *The Philosophy of Thomas Hill Green*, ed. A. Vincent, Aldershot, 1986.

—— and Plant, R., *Philosophy, Politics and Citizenship*, Oxford, 1984.

Waite, C. B., *Herbert Spencer and His Critics*: ch. 8, Chicago, 1900.

Wallace, W., 'Professor T. H. Green', *Academy*, 1 Apr. 1882.

Walsh, W. H., *Hegelian Ethics*: ch. 10, London, 1969.

—— 'Thomas Hill Green', *The Encyclopaedia of Philosophy*, iii, ed. P. Edwards, New York and London, 1967.

Ward, M. A., *Robert Elsmere*, Lonon, 1888.

Ward, S., *Ethics: An Historical Introduction*: ch. 17, London, 1924.

Ward, T. H., 'Thomas Hill Green', *Men of the Reign*, ed. T. H. Ward, London, 1885.

Webb, C. C. J., *A History of Philosophy*: ch. 10, Oxford, 1949.

—— *A Study of Religious Thought in England from 1850*: ch. 5, London, 1933.

Webb, R. K., Review of Richter (1964), *Journal of Modern History*, 37 (1965).

Weinstein, W. L., 'The Concept of Liberty in Nineteenth Century English Political Thought', *Political Studies*, 13 (1965).

Westminster Review, Anon. review of *The Philosophical Works of David Hume*, i and ii, *Westminster Review*, NS, 46 (1874).

Ytrelius, H., *Individets Rettigheter i Thomas Hill Greens Filosofi* [The Rights of the Individual in T. H. Green's Philosophy], Oslo, 1956.

Yukiyasu, S., 'T. H. Green and J. Dewey', *Bulletin of Okayama College of Science*, 9 (1973).

—— and Fujiwara, Y., *Thomas Hill Green Studies*, Tokyo, 1982.

VI GENERAL

This part of the bibliography contains items not cited in the notes which bear upon the issues discussed in this book.

Abbott, E., ed. *Hellenica*, London, 1880. Articles by A. C. Bradley and R. L. Nettleship.

Bond, E. J., *Reason and Value*, Cambridge, 1983.

Bosanquet, B., *Social and International Ideals*, London, 1917.

—— *Some Suggestions in Ethics*, London, 1918.

Browning, D., *Act and Agent*, Miami, 1964.

Bussell, F. W., 'The Future of Ethics: Effort or Abstention?', *Personal Idealism*, ed. H. Sturt, London, 1902.

Case, T., *Realism in Morals: An Essay*, Oxford and London, 1877.

Crombie, I. M., 'Moral Principles', *Christian Ethics and Contemporary Philosophy*, ed. I. T. Ramsey, London, 1966.

Dickinson, G. L., *The Meaning of Good: A Dialogue*, Glasgow, 1901.

Heath, A. G., *The Moral and Social Significance of the Conception of Personality*, Oxford, 1921.

Hobhouse, L. T., *The Rational Good: A Study of the Logic of Practice*, London, 1921.

McDowell, J., 'Are Moral Requirements Hypothetical Imperatives?' *Aristotelian Society Supplementary Volume*, 52 (1978).

—— 'Virtue and Reason', *Monist*, 62 (1979).

McKeon, R., 'Ethics and Politics', *Ethics and Bigness*, ed. H. Cleveland and H. D. Lasswell, New York, 1962.

Oakeshott, M. J., *Religion and the Moral Life*, Cambridge, 1927.

Pastin, M., 'The Reconstruction of Value', *Canadian Journal of Philosophy*, 5 (1975).

Quinton, A. M., Ch. 12 'Value', in *The Nature of Things*, London, 1973.

Rees, D. A., 'The Classification of Goods in Plato and Aristotle', *Islamic Philosophy and the Classical Tradition, Essays Presented to Richard Walzer*, ed. S. M. Stern, A. Hourani, and V. Brown, Oxford, 1972.

Roberts, M., *Responsibility and Practical Freedom*, Cambridge, 1965.

Sigwart, C., 'The Methodological Principles of Ethics', in *Logic*, ii, tr. Helen Dendy, London, 1895.

Smith, J. A., 'Progress in Philosophy', *Progress and History*, ed. F. S. Marvin, Oxford, 1921.

Wallace, W., *Lectures and Essays on Natural Theology and Ethics*, ed. E. Caird, Oxford, 1898.

Webb, T. E., *The Veil of Isis: A Series of Essays on Idealism*, Dublin and London, 1885.

Wiggins, D., *Truth, Invention, and the Meaning of Life*, Oxford, 1976.

Williams, B., *Ethics and the Limits of Philosophy*, London, 1985.

INDEX